AF725488

BRUNEI

OIL, GAS EXPLORATION LAWS AND REGULATIONS HANDBOOK

VOLUME 1

STRATEGIC INFORMATION AND BASIC REGULATIONS

International Business Publications, USA
Washington DC, USA - Bandar Seri Begawan

BRUNEI

OIL, GAS EXPLORATION LAWS AND REGULATIONS HANDBOOK
VOLUME 1 STRATEGIC INFORMATION AND BASIC REGULATIONS

UPDATED ANNUALLY

We express our sincere appreciation to all government agencies and international organizations which provided information and other materials for this handbook

Cover Design: **International Business Publications, USA**

International Business Publications, USA. ***has used its best efforts in collecting, analyzing and preparing data, information and materials for this unique handbook. Due to the dynamic nature and fast development of the economy and business environment, we cannot warrant that all information herein is complete and accurate. IBP does not assume and hereby disclaim any liability to any person for any loss or damage caused by possible errors or omissions in the handbook.***
This handbook is for individual use only. Use this handbook for any other purpose, included but not limited to reproducing and storing in a retrieval system by any means, electronic, photocopying or using the addresses or other information contained in this handbook for any commercial purposes requires a special written permission from the publisher.

2016 Updated Reprint International Business Publications, USA
ISBN

For customer service and information, please contact:
in the USA: **International Business Publications, USA**
P.O.Box 15343, Washington, DC 20043
Phone: (202) 546-2103, Fax: (202) 546-3275.
E-mail: rusric@erols.com

Printed in the USA

For additional analytical, marketing, investment and business opportunities information, please contact
Global Investment & Business Center, USA
(202) 546-2103. Fax: (202) 546-3275. E-mail: rusric@erols.com

BRUNEI

OIL, GAS EXPLORATION LAWS AND REGULATIONS HANDBOOK

VOLUME 1

STRATEGIC INFORMATION AND BASIC REGULATIONS

TABLE OF CONTENTS

For additional analytical, marketing, investment and business opportunities information, please contact
Global Investment & Business Center, USA
(202) 546-2103. Fax: (202) 546-3275. E-mail: rusric@erols.com

STRATEGIC AND BUSINESS PROFILE

BRUNEI DARUSSALAM

Capital and largest city	Bandar Seri Begawan 4°53.417′N 114°56.533′E4.890283°N 114.942217°E
Official languages	Malay
Recognised	English
Other languages	• Brunei Malay • Tutong • Kedayan • Belait • Murut • Dusun • Bisaya • Melanau • Iban • Penan
Ethnic groups (2004)	• 66.3% Malays • 11.2% Chinese • 3.4% Indigenous • 19.1% other
Demonym	Bruneian
Government	Unitary Islamic absolute monarchy
- Sultan	Hassanal Bolkiah
- Crown Prince	Al-Muhtadee Billah
Legislature	Legislative Council
	Formation
- Sultanate	14th century
- British protectorate	1888
- Independence from the United Kingdom	1 January 1984
	Area
- Total	5,765 km^2 (172nd) 2,226 sq mi
- Water (%)	8.6
	Population
- Jul 2013 estimate	415,717 (175th)
- Density	67.3/km^2 (134th) 174.4/sq mi
GDP (PPP)	2012 estimate
- Total	$21.907 billion
- Per capita	$50,440
GDP (nominal)	2012 estimate
- Total	$17.092 billion
- Per capita	$39,355
HDI (2013)	0.855 very high · 30th
Currency	Brunei dollar (BND)
Time zone	BDT (UTC+8)

Drives on the	left
Calling code	+673
ISO 3166 code	BN
Internet TLD	.bn

Brunei officially the **Nation of Brunei, the Abode of Peace** is a sovereign state located on the north coast of the island of Borneo in Southeast Asia. Apart from its coastline with the South China Sea, it is completely surrounded by the state of Sarawak, Malaysia; and it is separated into two parts by the Sarawak district of Limbang. It is the only sovereign state completely on the island of Borneo; the remainder of the island's territory is divided between the nations of Malaysia and Indonesia. Brunei's population was 408,786 in July 2012.

At the peak of Bruneian Empire, Sultan Bolkiah (reigned 1485–1528) is alleged to have had control over the northern regions of Borneo, including modern-day Sarawak and Sabah, as well as the Sulu archipelago off the northeast tip of Borneo, Seludong (modern-day Manila), and the islands off the northwest tip of Borneo. The maritime state was visited by Spain's Magellan Expedition in 1521 and fought against Spain in 1578's Castille War.

During the 19th century the Bruneian Empire began to decline. The Sultanate ceded Sarawak to James Brooke as a reward for his aid in putting down a rebellion and named him as rajah, and it ceded Sabah to the British North Borneo Chartered Company. In 1888 Brunei became a British protectorate and was assigned a British Resident as colonial manager in 1906. After the Japanese occupation during World War II, in 1959 a new constitution was written. In 1962 a small armed rebellion against the monarchy was ended with the help of the British.

Brunei regained its independence from the United Kingdom on 1 January 1984. Economic growth during the 1990s and 2000s, averaging 56% from 1999 to 2008, has transformed Brunei into a newly industrialised country. It has developed wealth from extensive petroleum and natural gas fields. Brunei has the second-highest Human Development Index among the South East Asia nations after Singapore, and is classified as a developed country. According to the International Monetary Fund (IMF), Brunei is ranked fifth in the world by gross domestic product per capita at purchasing power parity. The IMF estimated in 2011 that Brunei was one of two countries (the other being Libya) with a public debt at 0% of the national GDP. *Forbes* also ranks Brunei as the fifth-richest nation out of 182, based on its petroleum and natural gas fields

Brunei can trace its beginnings to the 7th century, when it was a subject state of the Srivijayan empire under the name Po-ni. It later became a vassal state of Majapahit before embracing Islam in the 15th century. At the peak of its empire, the sultanate had control that extended over the coastal regions of modern-day Sarawak and Sabah, the Sulu archipelago, and the islands off the northwest tip of Borneo. The thalassocracy was visited by Ferdinand Magellan in 1521 and fought the Castille War in 1578 against Spain. Its empire began to decline with the forced ceding of Sarawak to James Brooke and the ceding of Sabah to the British North Borneo Chartered Company. After the loss of Limbang, Brunei finally became a British protectorate in 1888, receiving a resident in 1906. In the post-occupation years, it formalised a constitution and fought an armed rebellion. Brunei regained its independence from the United Kingdom on 1 January 1984. Economic growth during the 1970s and 1990s, averaging 56% from 1999 to 2008, has transformed Brunei Darussalam into a newly industrialised country.

Brunei has the second highest Human Development Index among the South East Asia nations, after Singapore and is classified as a Developed Country. According to the International Monetary Fund (IMF), Brunei is ranked 4th in the world by gross domestic product per capita at purchasing power parity.

According to legend, Brunei was founded by Awang Alak Betatar. His move from Garang [location required] to the Brunei river estuary led to the discovery of Brunei. His first exclamation upon landing on the shore, as the legend goes, was “Baru nah!” (Which in English loosely-translates as "that's it!" or "there") and thus, the name “Brunei” was derived from his words.

It was renamed "Barunai" in the 14th Century, possibly influenced by the Sanskrit word varunai (वरुण), meaning "seafarers", later to become "Brunei". The word "Borneo" is of the same origin. In the country's full name "Negara Brunei Darussalam" "Darussalam" means "Abode of Peace" in Arabic, while "Negara" means "Country" in Malay. "Negara" derives from the Sanskrit Nagara , meaning "city".

Brunei Darussalam, the host of the 1995 BIMP-EAGA EXPO is a stable and prosperous country which offers not only a well-developed infrastructure but also a strategic location within the Asean region. The country is chugging full steam ahead to diversify its economy away from an over-dependence on oil and gas, and has put in place flexible and realistic policies to facilitate foreign and local investment. The cost of utilities are the lowest in the region, while political stability, extensive economic and natural resources and a business environment attuned to the requirements of foreign investors go towards making Brunei an excellent investment choice

At present the country's economy is dominated by the oil and liquefied natural gas industries and government expenditure patterns. Brunei exports crude oil, petroleum products and LNG mainly to Japan, the United States and the Asean countries. The second most important industry is construction, a direct result of the government's investment in development and infrastructure projects. Gearing up towards putting on the mantle of a developed country in January 1996, Brunei allocated in its 1991-95 Five Year Plan a hefty B$5 billion for national development, over a billion dollars more than in the previous budget. About B$510 million was allotted for 619 projects while B$550 million or 10 percent of the development budget went to industry and commerce. Some B$100 million alone was reserved for industrial promotion and development.

STABLE, CONDUCIVE ENVIRONMENT

The oil-rich country, lying on the north-western edge of the Borneo island, has never experienced typhoons, earthquakes or severe floods. Profitable investment can be had as the country levies no personal income tax, no sales tax, payroll, manufacturing or export tax.

Competitive investment incentives are available for investors throughout the business cycle marked by the start up, growth, maturity and expansion stages. The tax advantages at start up and the on-going incentives during growth and expansion are among the most competitive around. There is no difficulty in securing approval for foreign workers, from labourers to managers. With a small labour pool of 284,500 Brunei people and Bruneians showing a marked preference for the public sector as employer, the country has had to rely on foreign workers. These make up a third of its work force.

In line with moves to promote the private sector, it is encouraging to note the contribution from the non-oil and gas sector of the economy has risen, contributing about 25 percent to GDP compared to the oil and gas sector's 46 percent. In terms of infrastructure, Brunei is ready for vigorous economy activity. At its two main ports at Muara and Kuala Belait, goods can be shipped direct to Hong Kong, Singapore and other Asian destinations. Muara, a deep-water port 29 km away from the capital of Bandar Seri Begawan, has seen continual increase in container traffic over the past two decades.

The Brunei International Airport at Bandar offers expanded passenger and cargo facilities. Its new terminal can accommodate 1.5 million passengers and 50,000 tonnes of cargo a year, which is expected to suffice till the end of the decade. A 2,000-km road network serving the whole country undergoes continual expansion. A main highway runs the entire length of its coastline, linking Muara, the port entry point at one end, and Belait, the oil-production centre, at another end.

Telecommunications-wise, Brunei has one of the best systems in the region with plans for major upgrading. Telephone availability is about one to every three people.

Two earth satellite stations provide direct telephone, telex and facsimile links to most parts of the world. Operating systems include an analogue telephone exchange, fibreoptic cable links with Singapore and Manila, a packet switching exchange for access to high-speed computer bases overseas, cellular mobile telephone and paging systems. Direct phone links are also available in the more remote parts of the country via microwave and solar-powered telephones.

PIONEER INDUSTRY INCENTIVES

Companies granted pioneer status enjoy tax holidays of up to eight years. Brunei's regulations governing foreign participation in equity are the most flexible in the region, with 100 percent foreign ownership permitted. A pioneer company is also exempt from customs duty on items to be installed in the pioneer factory and from paying import duties on raw materials not available locally or produced in Brunei for the manufacture of pioneer products.

GEOGRAPHY

Location: Southeastern Asia, bordering the South China Sea and Malaysia
Geographic coordinates: 4 30 N, 114 40 E
Map references: Southeast Asia

Area:
total: 5,770 sq km
land: 5,270 sq km
water: 500 sq km

Area—comparative: slightly smaller than Delaware

Land boundaries:
total: 381 km
border countries: Malaysia 381 km

Coastline: 161 km
Land use:
arable land: 1%
other: 12%

permanent crops: 1%
permanent pastures: 1%
forests and woodland: 85%

For additional analytical, marketing, investment and business opportunities information, please contact
Global Investment & Business Center, USA
(202) 546-2103. Fax: (202) 546-3275. E-mail: rusric@erols.com

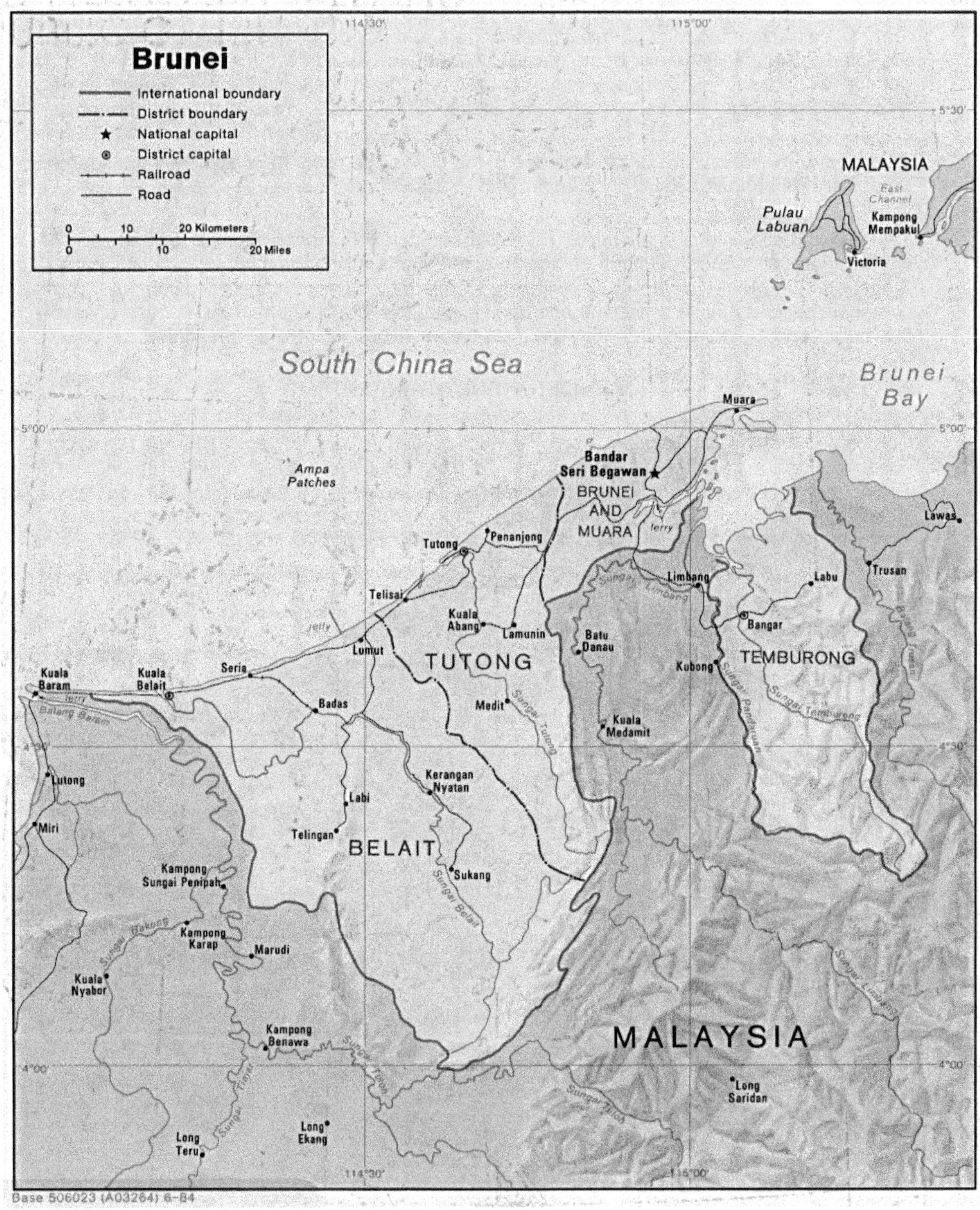
Brunei
International boundary
District boundary
National capital
District capital
Railroad
Road
0 10 20 Kilometers
0 10 20 Miles
MALAYSIA
Pulau Labuan
Kampong Mempakul
Victoria
South China Sea
Brunei Bay
Muara
Bandar Seri Begawan
BRUNEI AND MUARA
Ampa Patches
Tutong
Penanjong
Lawas
Trusan
Limbang
Labu
Bangar
Telisai
Kuala Abang
Lamunin
Batu Danau
Lumut
TUTONG
Kubong
TEMBURONG
Kuala Baram
Kuala Belait
Seria
Badas
Medit
Kuala Medamit
Lutong
Kerangan Nyatan
Labi
Miri
Telingan
BELAIT
Sukang
Kampong Sungai Penipah
Kampong Karap
Marudi
Kuala Nyabor
Kampong Benawa
MALAYSIA
Long Saridan
Long Ekang
Long Teru
Base 506023 (A03264) 6-84

Irrigated land: 10 sq km
Natural hazards: typhoons, earthquakes, and severe flooding are very rare
Environment—current issues: seasonal smoke/haze resulting from forest fires in Indonesia

Environment—international agreements:
party to: Endangered Species, Law of the Sea, Ozone Layer Protection, Ship Pollution
signed, but not ratified: none of the selected agreements

Geography—note: close to vital sea lanes through South China Sea linking Indian and Pacific Oceans; two parts physically separated by Malaysia; almost an enclave of Malaysia

PEOPLE

Population: 322,982

Age structure:
0-14 years: 33% (male 54,154; female 51,766)
15-64 years: 63% (male 106,492; female 95,921)
65 years and over: 4% (male 7,945; female 6,704)

Population growth rate: 2.38%
Birth rate: 24.69 births/1,000 population
Death rate: 5.21 deaths/1,000 population
Net migration rate: 4.35 migrant(s)/1,000 population

Sex ratio:
at birth: 1.06 male(s)/female
under 15 years: 1.05 male(s)/female
15-64 years: 1.11 male(s)/female
65 years and over: 1.19 male(s)/female
total population: 1.09 male(s)/female

Infant mortality rate: 22.83 deaths/1,000 live births

Life expectancy at birth:
total population: 71.84 years
male: 70.35 years
female: 73.42 years

Total fertility rate: 3.33 children born/woman

Nationality:
noun: Bruneian(s)
adjective: Bruneian

Ethnic groups: Malay 64%, Chinese 20%, other 16%
Religions: Muslim (official) 63%, Buddhism 14%, Christian 8%, indigenous beliefs and other 15% (1981)
Languages: Malay (official), English, Chinese

For additional analytical, marketing, investment and business opportunities information, please contact
Global Investment & Business Center, USA
(202) 546-2103. Fax: (202) 546-3275. E-mail: rusric@erols.com

Literacy:
definition: age 15 and over can read and write
total population: 88.2%
male: 92.6% *female:* 83.4%

GOVERNMENT

Country name:
conventional long form: Negara Brunei Darussalam
conventional short form: Brunei

Data code: BX
Government type: constitutional sultanate
Capital: Bandar Seri Begawan

Administrative divisions: 4 districts (daerah-daerah, singular—daerah); Belait, Brunei and Muara, Temburong, Tutong

Independence: 1 January 1984 (from UK)
National holiday: National Day, 23 February (1984)

Constitution: 29 September 1959 (some provisions suspended under a State of Emergency since December 1962, others since independence on 1 January 1984)

Legal system: based on English common law; for Muslims, Islamic Shari'a law supersedes civil law in a number of areas

Suffrage: none

Executive branch:
Brunei

Sultan	HASSANAL Bolkiah, Sir
Prime Minister	HASSANAL Bolkiah, Sir
Min. of Communications	Awang ABU BAKAR bin Apong
Min. of Culture, Youth, & Sports	MOHAMMAD bin Daud, Gen. (Ret.)
Min. of Defense	HASSANAL Bolkiah, Sir
Min. of Development	ABDULLAH bin Begawan
Min. of Education	Abdul RAHMAN bin Mohamed Taib
Min. of Energy	YAHYA bin Begawan
Min. of Finance	HASSANAL Bolkiah, Sir
Min. of Finance II	ABDUL RAHMAN bin Ibrahim
Min. of Foreign Affairs	MOHAMED Bolkiah, Prince
Min. of Foreign Affairs II	LIM Jock Seng
Min. of Health	SUYOI bin Osman
Min. of Home Affairs	ADANAN bin Begawan
Min. of Industry & Primary Resources	AHMAD bin Jumat, Dr.
Min. of Religious Affairs	MOHD ZAIN bin Serudin, Dr.
Senior Min. in the Prime Minister's Office	Al Muhtadee BILLAH, Crown Prince

Ambassador to the US	PUTEH ibni Mohammad Alam
Permanent Representative to the UN, New York	SHOFRY bin Abdul Ghafor

Legislative branch: unicameral Legislative Council or Majlis Masyuarat Megeri (a privy council that serves only in a consultative capacity; NA seats; members appointed by the monarch)
elections: last held in March 1962
note: in 1970 the Council was changed to an appointive body by decree of the monarch; an elected Legislative Council is being considered as part of constitutional reform, but elections are unlikely for several years

Judicial branch: Supreme Court, chief justice and judges are sworn in by the monarch for three-year terms

Political parties and leaders: Brunei Solidarity National Party or PPKB in Malay [Haji Mohd HATTA bin Haji Zainal Abidin, president]; the PPKB is the only legal political party in Brunei; it was registered in 1985, but became largely inactive after 1988; it has less than 200 registered party members; other parties include Brunei People's Party or PRB (banned in 1962) and Brunei National Democratic Party (registered in May 1985, deregistered by the Brunei Government in 1988)

International organization participation: APEC, ASEAN, C, CCC, ESCAP, G-77, IBRD, ICAO, ICRM, IDB, IFRCS, IMF, IMO, Inmarsat, Intelsat, Interpol, IOC, ISO (correspondent), ITU, NAM, OIC, OPCW, UN, UNCTAD, UPU, WHO, WIPO, WMO, WTrO

Diplomatic representation in the US:
chief of mission: Ambassador Pengiran Anak Dato Haji PUTEH Ibni Mohammad Alam
chancery: Watergate, Suite 300, 3rd floor, 2600 Virginia Avenue NW, Washington, DC 20037
telephone: (202) 342-0159
FAX: (202) 342-0158

Diplomatic representation from the US:
chief of mission: Ambassador Glen Robert RASE
embassy: Third Floor, Teck Guan Plaza, Jalan Sultan, Bandar Seri Begawan
mailing address: PSC 470 (BSB), FPO AP 96534-0001
telephone: [673] (2) 229670 *FAX:* [673] (2) 225293

Flag description: yellow with two diagonal bands of white (top, almost double width) and black starting from the upper hoist side; the national emblem in red is superimposed at the center; the emblem includes a swallow-tailed flag on top of a winged column within an upturned crescent above a scroll and flanked by two upraised hands

ECONOMY

Brunei has a small well-to-do economy that depends on revenue from natural resource extraction but encompasses a mixture of foreign and domestic entrepreneurship, government regulation, welfare measures, and village tradition. Crude oil and natural gas production account for 60% of GDP and more than 90% of exports. Per capita GDP is among the highest in Asia, and substantial income from overseas investment supplements income from domestic production. For Bruneian citizens the government provides for all medical services and free education through the university level. The government of Brunei has been emphasizing through policy and resource investments it strong desire to diversity its economy both within the oil and gas sector and to new

For additional analytical, marketing, investment and business opportunities information, please contact
Global Investment & Business Center, USA
(202) 546-2103. Fax: (202) 546-3275. E-mail: rusric@erols.com

sectors.

GDP (purchasing power parity):
$22.25 billion (2013 est.)
country comparison to the world: 128
$21.93 billion (2012 est.)
$21.73 billion (2011 est.)
note: data are in 2013 US dollars

GDP (official exchange rate):
$16.56 billion (2013 est.)

GDP - real growth rate:
1.4% (2013 est.)
country comparison to the world: 164
0.9% (2012 est.)
3.4% (2011 est.)

GDP - per capita (PPP):
$54,800 (2013 est.)
country comparison to the world: 12
$54,900 (2012 est.)
$55,200 (2011 est.)
note: data are in 2013 US dollars

GDP - composition, by end use:
household consumption: 22.1%
government consumption: 18.2%
investment in fixed capital: 14.6%
investment in inventories: 0%
exports of goods and services: 78.4%
imports of goods and services: -33.3%
(2013 est.)

GDP - composition, by sector of origin:
agriculture: 0.7%
industry: 70.9%
services: 28.4% (2013 est.)

Agriculture - products:
rice, vegetables, fruits; chickens, water buffalo, cattle, goats, eggs

Industries:
petroleum, petroleum refining, liquefied natural gas, construction, agriculture, transportation

Industrial production growth rate:
1.5% (2013 est.)
country comparison to the world: 135

Labor force:
205,800 (est.)
country comparison to the world: 169

Labor force - by occupation:
agriculture: 4.2%
industry: 62.8%
services: 33%

Unemployment rate:
2.6%
country comparison to the world: 21
2.7%

Budget:
revenues: $6.992 billion
expenditures: $5.366 billion (2013 est.)

Taxes and other revenues:
42.2% of GDP (2013 est.)
country comparison to the world: 29

Budget surplus (+) or deficit (-):
9.8% of GDP (2013 est.)
country comparison to the world: 5

Fiscal year:
1 April - 31 March

Inflation rate (consumer prices):
1% (2013 est.)
country comparison to the world: 24
0.5% (2012 est.)

Commercial bank prime lending rate:
5.5% (31 December 2013 est.)
country comparison to the world: 142
5.5% (31 December 2012 est.)

Stock of narrow money:
$3.472 billion (31 December 2013 est.)
country comparison to the world: 113
$3.509 billion (31 December 2012 est.)

Stock of broad money:
$11.92 billion (31 December 2013 est.)
country comparison to the world: 99
$11.41 billion (31 December 2012 est.)

For additional analytical, marketing, investment and business opportunities information, please contact
Global Investment & Business Center, USA
(202) 546-2103. Fax: (202) 546-3275. E-mail: rusric@erols.com

Stock of domestic credit:
$2.846 billion (31 December 2013 est.)
country comparison to the world: 127
$2.351 billion (31 December 2012 est.)

Current account balance:
$3.977 billion
country comparison to the world: 31

Exports:
$12.75 billion
country comparison to the world: 86
$9.88 billion

Exports - commodities:
crude oil, natural gas, garments

Exports - partners:
Japan 45.7%, South Korea 15.1%, Australia 9.1%, NZ 6.6%, India 5.8%, Vietnam 4.7% (2012)

Imports:
$3.02 billion (est.)
country comparison to the world: 147

Imports - commodities:
iron and steel, motor vehicles, machinery and transport equipment, manufactured goods, food, chemicals

Imports - partners:
Singapore 26.3%, China 21.3%, UK 21.3%, Malaysia 11.8%

Debt - external:
$0 (2005)
country comparison to the world: 202

Exchange rates:
Bruneian dollars (BND) per US dollar -
1.23 (2013 est.)
1.2496 (2012 est.)
1.3635 (2010 est.)
1.45 (2009)

ENERGY

Electricity - production:
3.723 billion kWh (est.)
country comparison to the world: 126

Electricity - consumption:

3.391 billion kWh (est.)
country comparison to the world: 127

Electricity - exports:
0 kWh (est.)
country comparison to the world: 111

Electricity - imports:
0 kWh (est.)
country comparison to the world: 123

Electricity - installed generating capacity:
759,000 kW (est.)
country comparison to the world: 129

Electricity - from fossil fuels:
100% of total installed capacity (est.)
country comparison to the world: 9

Electricity - from nuclear fuels:
0% of total installed capacity (est.)
country comparison to the world: 57

Electricity - from hydroelectric plants:
0% of total installed capacity (2010 est.)
country comparison to the world: 161

Electricity - from other renewable sources:
0% of total installed capacity (est.)
country comparison to the world: 162

Crude oil - production:
141,000 bbl/day (est.)
country comparison to the world: 45

Crude oil - exports:
147,900 bbl/day (est.)
country comparison to the world: 35

Crude oil - imports:
0 bbl/day (est.)
country comparison to the world: 166

Crude oil - proved reserves:
1.1 billion bbl (1 January 2013 est.)
country comparison to the world: 41

Refined petroleum products - production:
13,500 bbl/day (est.)

For additional analytical, marketing, investment and business opportunities information, please contact
Global Investment & Business Center, USA
(202) 546-2103. Fax: (202) 546-3275. E-mail: rusric@erols.com

country comparison to the world: 101

Refined petroleum products - consumption:
14,640 bbl/day (est.)
country comparison to the world: 144

Refined petroleum products - exports:
0 bbl/day (est.)
country comparison to the world: 159

Refined petroleum products - imports:
3,198 bbl/day (est.)
country comparison to the world: 169

Natural gas - production:
12.44 billion cu m (est.)
country comparison to the world: 38

Natural gas - consumption:
2.97 billion cu m (est.)
country comparison to the world: 73

Natural gas - exports:
9.42 billion cu m (est.)
country comparison to the world: 25

Natural gas - imports:
0 cu m (est.)
country comparison to the world: 167

Natural gas - proved reserves:
390.8 billion cu m (1 January 2013 est.)
country comparison to the world: 35

Carbon dioxide emissions from consumption of energy:
8.656 million Mt (2011 est.)

COMMUNICATION

Telephones - main lines in use:
70,933
country comparison to the world: 154

Telephones - mobile cellular:
469,700
country comparison to the world: 170

Telephone system:
general assessment: service throughout the country is good; international service is good

For additional analytical, marketing, investment and business opportunities information, please contact
Global Investment & Business Center, USA
(202) 546-2103. Fax: (202) 546-3275. E-mail: rusric@erols.com

to Southeast Asia, Middle East, Western Europe, and the US
domestic: every service available
international: country code - 673; landing point for the SEA-ME-WE-3 optical telecommunications submarine cable that provides links to Asia, the Middle East, and Europe; the Asia-America Gateway submarine cable network provides new links to Asia and the US; satellite earth stations - 2 Intelsat (1 Indian Ocean and 1 Pacific Ocean)

Broadcast media:
state-controlled Radio Television Brunei (RTB) operates 5 channels; 3 Malaysian TV stations are available; foreign TV broadcasts are available via satellite and cable systems; RTB operates 5 radio networks and broadcasts on multiple frequencies; British Forces Broadcast Service (BFBS) provides radio broadcasts on 2 FM stations; some radio broadcast stations from Malaysia are available via repeaters (2009)

Internet country code:
.bn

Internet hosts:
49,457
country comparison to the world: 96

Internet users:
314,900
country comparison to the world: 128

TRANSPORTATION

Railways:
total: 13 km (private line)
narrow gauge: 13 km 0.610-m gauge

Highways:
total: 1,150 km *paved:* 399 km *unpaved:* 751 km

Waterways: 209 km; navigable by craft drawing less than 1.2 m
Pipelines: crude oil 135 km; petroleum products 418 km; natural gas 920 km
Ports and harbors: Bandar Seri Begawan, Kuala Belait, Muara, Seria, Tutong
Merchant marine:
total: 7 liquefied gas tankers (1,000 GRT or over) totaling 348,476 GRT/340,635 DWT

Airports: 2

Airports—with paved runways:
total: 1
over 3,047 m: 1
Airports—with unpaved runways:
total: 1 *914 to 1,523 m:* 1 **Heliports:** 3

MILITARY

Military branches: Land Forces, Navy, Air Force, Royal Brunei Police

For additional analytical, marketing, investment and business opportunities information, please contact
Global Investment & Business Center, USA
(202) 546-2103. Fax: (202) 546-3275. E-mail: rusric@erols.com

Military manpower—military age: 18 years of age
Military manpower—availability:
males age 15-49: 88,628
Military manpower—fit for military service:
males age 15-49: 51,270
Military manpower—reaching military age annually:
males: 3,078
Military expenditures—dollar figure: $343 million
Military expenditures—percent of GDP: 6%

TRANSNATIONAL ISSUES

Disputes—international: possibly involved in a complex dispute over the Spratly Islands with China, Malaysia, Philippines, Taiwan, and Vietnam; in 1984, Brunei established an exclusive fishing zone that encompasses Louisa Reef in the southern Spratly Islands, but has not publicly claimed the island.

For additional analytical, marketing, investment and business opportunities information, please contact
Global Investment & Business Center, USA
(202) 546-2103. Fax: (202) 546-3275. E-mail: rusric@erols.com

IMPORTANT INFORMATION FOR UNDERSTANDING BRUNEI

PROFILE

OFFICIAL NAME: Negara Brunei Darussalam

Geography
Area: 5,765 sq. km. (2,226 sq. mi.), slightly larger than Delaware.
Cities: *Capital*--Bandar Seri Begawan.
Terrain: East--flat coastal plain rises to mountains; west--hilly lowland with a few mountain ridges.
Climate: Equatorial; high temperatures, humidity, and rainfall.

People
Nationality: *Noun and adjective*--Bruneian(s).
Population : 383,000.
Annual growth rate: 3.5%.
Ethnic groups: Malay, Chinese, other indigenous groups.
Religion: Islam.
Languages: Malay, English, Chinese; Iban and other indigenous dialects.
Education: *Years compulsory*--9. *Literacy* (2006)--94.7%.
Health: *Life expectancy (years)*--74.4 (men), 77.4 (women) yrs. *Infant mortality rate* --12.25/1,000.

Government
Type: Malay Islamic Monarchy.
Independence: January 1, 1984.
Constitution: 1959.
Branches: *Executive*--Sultan is both head of state and Prime Minister, presiding over a fourteen-member cabinet. *Legislative*--a Legislative Council has been reactivated after a 20-year suspension to play an advisory role for the Sultan. *Judicial* (based on Indian penal code and English common law)--magistrate's courts, High Court, Court of Appeals, Judicial Committee of the Privy Council (sits in London).
Subdivisions: *Four districts*--Brunei-Muara, Belait, Tutong, and Temburong.

Economy
Natural resources: Oil and natural gas.
Trade: *Exports*--oil, liquefied natural gas, petroleum products, garments. Major markets--Japan, Korea, ASEAN, U.S. *Imports*--machinery and transport equipment, manufactured goods. *Major suppliers*--ASEAN, Japan, U.S., EU.

PEOPLE

Many cultural and linguistic differences make Brunei Malays distinct from the larger Malay populations in nearby Malaysia and Indonesia, even though they are ethnically related and share the Muslim religion.
Brunei has hereditary nobility, carrying the title Pengiran. The Sultan can award to commoners the title Pehin, the equivalent of a life peerage awarded in the United Kingdom. The Sultan also can award his subjects the Dato, the equivalent of a knighthood in the United Kingdom, and Datin, the equivalent of damehood.

Bruneians adhere to the practice of using complete full names with all titles, including the title Haji (for men) or Hajah (for women) for those who have made the Haj pilgrimage to Mecca. Many

Brunei Malay women wear the tudong, a traditional head covering. Men wear the songkok, a traditional Malay cap. Men who have completed the Haj can wear a white songkok.
The requirements to attain Brunei citizenship include passing tests in Malay culture, customs, and language. Stateless permanent residents of Brunei are given International Certificates of Identity, which allow them to travel overseas. The majority of Brunei's Chinese are permanent residents, and many are stateless. An amendment to the National Registration and Immigration Act of 2002 allowed female Bruneian citizens for the first time to transfer their nationality to their children.

Oil wealth allows the Brunei Government to provide the population with one of Asia's finest health care systems. Malaria has been eradicated, and cholera is virtually nonexistent. There are five general hospitals--in Bandar Seri Begawan, Tutong, Kuala Belait, Bangar, and Seria--and there are numerous health clinics throughout the country.

Education starts with preschool, followed by 6 years of primary education and up to 7 years of secondary education. Nine years of education are mandatory. Most of Brunei's college students attend universities and other institutions abroad, but approximately 3,674 (2005) study at the University of Brunei Darussalam. Opened in 1985, the university has a faculty of more than 300 instructors and is located on a sprawling campus overlooking the South China Sea.
The official language is Malay, but English is widely understood and used in business. Other languages spoken are several Chinese dialects, Iban, and a number of native dialects. Islam is the official religion, but religious freedom is guaranteed under the constitution.

HISTORY

Historians believe there was a forerunner to the present Brunei Sultanate, which the Chinese called Po-ni. Chinese and Arabic records indicate that this ancient trading kingdom existed at the mouth of the Brunei River as early as the seventh or eighth century A.D. This early kingdom was apparently conquered by the Sumatran Hindu Empire of Srivijaya in the early ninth century, which later controlled northern Borneo and the Philippines. It was subjugated briefly by the Java-based Majapahit Empire but soon regained its independence and once again rose to prominence.

The Brunei Empire had its golden age from the 15th to the 17th centuries, when its control extended over the entire island of Borneo and north into the Philippines. Brunei was particularly powerful under the fifth sultan, Bolkiah (1473-1521), who was famed for his sea exploits and even briefly captured Manila; and under the ninth sultan, Hassan (1605-19), who fully developed an elaborate Royal Court structure, elements of which remain today.

After Sultan Hassan, Brunei entered a period of decline due to internal battles over royal succession as well as the rising influences of European colonial powers in the region that, among other things, disrupted traditional trading patterns, destroying the economic base of Brunei and many other Southeast Asian sultanates. In 1839, the English adventurer James Brooke arrived in Borneo and helped the Sultan put down a rebellion. As a reward, he became governor and later "Rajah" of Sarawak in northwest Borneo and gradually expanded the territory under his control.

Meanwhile, the British North Borneo Company was expanding its control over territory in northeast Borneo. In 1888, Brunei became a protectorate of the British Government, retaining internal independence but with British control over external affairs. In 1906, Brunei accepted a further measure of British control when executive power was transferred to a British resident, who advised the ruler on all matters except those concerning local custom and religion.

In 1959, a new constitution was written declaring Brunei a self-governing state, while its foreign affairs, security, and defense remained the responsibility of the United Kingdom. An attempt in 1962 to introduce a partially elected legislative body with limited powers was abandoned after the opposition political party, Parti Rakyat Brunei, launched an armed uprising, which the government put down with the help of British forces. In the late 1950s and early 1960s, the government also resisted pressures to join neighboring Sabah and Sarawak in the newly formed Malaysia. The Sultan eventually decided that Brunei would remain an independent state.

In 1967, Sultan Omar abdicated in favor of his eldest son, Hassanal Bolkiah, who became the 29th ruler. The former Sultan remained as Defense Minister and assumed the royal title Seri Begawan. In 1970, the national capital, Brunei Town, was renamed Bandar Seri Begawan in his honor. The Seri Begawan died in 1986.

On January 4, 1979, Brunei and the United Kingdom signed a new treaty of friendship and cooperation. On January 1, 1984, Brunei Darussalam became a fully independent state.

GOVERNMENT AND POLITICAL CONDITIONS

Under Brunei's 1959 constitution, the Sultan is the head of state with full executive authority, including emergency powers since 1962. The Sultan is assisted and advised by five councils, which he appoints. A Council of Ministers, or cabinet, which currently consists of 14 members (including the Sultan himself), assists in the administration of the government. The Sultan presides over the cabinet as Prime Minister and also holds the positions of Minister of Defense and Minister of Finance. His son, the Crown Prince, serves as Senior Minister. One of the Sultan's brothers, Prince Mohamed, serves as Minister of Foreign Affairs.

Brunei's legal system is based on English common law, with an independent judiciary, a body of written common law judgments and statutes, and legislation enacted by the sultan. The local magistrates' courts try most cases. More serious cases go before the High Court, which sits for about 2 weeks every few months. Brunei has an arrangement with the United Kingdom whereby United Kingdom judges are appointed as the judges for Brunei's High Court and Court of Appeal. Final appeal can be made to the Judicial Committee of the Privy Council in London in civil but not criminal cases. Brunei also has a separate system of Islamic courts that apply Sharia law in family and other matters involving Muslims.
The Government of Brunei assures continuing public support for the current form of government by providing economic benefits such as subsidized food, fuel, and housing; free education and medical care; and low-interest loans for government employees.

The Sultan said in a 1989 interview that he intended to proceed, with prudence, to establish more liberal institutions in the country and that he would reintroduce elections and a legislature when he "[could] see evidence of a genuine interest in politics on the part of a responsible majority of Bruneians." In 1994, a constitutional review committee submitted its findings to the Sultan, but these have not been made public. In 2004 the Sultan re-introduced an appointed Legislative Council with minimal powers. Five of the 31 seats on the Council are indirectly elected by village leaders.

Brunei's economy is almost totally supported by exports of crude oil and natural gas. The government uses its earnings in part to build up its foreign reserves, which at one time reportedly reached more than $30 billion. The country's wealth, coupled with its membership in the United Nations, Association of Southeast Asian Nations (ASEAN), the Asia Pacific Economic Cooperation (APEC) forum, and the Organization of the Islamic Conference give it an influence in the world disproportionate to its size.

Principal Government Officials
Sultan and Yang di-Pertuan, Prime Minister, Minister of Defense, and Minister of Finance--His Majesty Sultan Hassanal Bolkiah
Senior Minister--His Royal Highness Crown Prince Billah
Minister of Foreign Affairs--His Royal Highness Prince Mohamed Bolkiah

Ambassador to the United States--Pengiran Anak Dato Haji Puteh
Ambassador to the United Nations--Dr. Haji Emran bin Bahar
Brunei Darussalam maintains an embassy in the United States at 3520 International Court, NW, Washington, DC 20008; tel. 202-237-1838.

ECONOMY

Currency	Brunei dollar BND
Fixed exchange rates	1 Brunei dollar = 1 Singapore dollar
Fiscal year	1 April – 31 March (from April 2009)
Trade organisations	APEC, ASEAN, WTO. BIMP-EAGA
Statistics	
GDP	$20.38 billion PPP Rank: 123rd
GDP growth	2.8% Q1
GDP per capita	$51,600
GDP by sector	agriculture (0.7%), industry (73.3%), services (26%)
Inflation (CPI)	1.2%
Population below poverty line	1000 person
Labour force	188,800
Labour force by occupation	agriculture 4.5%, industry 63.1%, services 32.4%
Unemployment	3.7%
Main industries	petroleum, petroleum refining, liquefied natural gas, construction
Ease-of-doing-business rank	83rd
External	
Exports	$10.67 billion
Main export partners	Japan 46.5% South Korea 15.5% Australia 9.3% India 7.0% New Zealand 6.7% (est.)
Imports	$12.055 billion c.i.f.
Main import partners	Singapore 26.3% China 21.3% United Kingdom 21.3% Malaysia 11.8%
Public finances	
Public debt	$0
Revenues	$10.49 billion
Expenses	$5.427 billion
Credit rating	Not rated

Main data source: CIA World Fact Book *All values, unless otherwise stated, are in US dollars.*

Brunei is a country with a small, wealthy economy that is a mixture of foreign and domestic entrepreneurship, government regulation and welfare measures, and village tradition. It is almost totally supported by exports of crude oil and natural gas, with revenues from the petroleum sector accounting for over half of GDP. Per capita GDP is high, and substantial income from overseas investment supplements income from domestic production. The government provides for all medical services and subsidizes food and housing. The government has shown progress in its basic policy of diversifying the economy away from oil and gas. Brunei's leaders are concerned that steadily increased integration in the world economy will undermine internal social cohesion although it has taken steps to become a more prominent player by serving as chairman for the 2000 APEC (Asian Pacific Economic Cooperation) forum. Growth in 1999 was estimated at 2.5% due to higher oil prices in the second half.

Brunei is the third-largest oil producer in Southeast Asia, averaging about 180,000 barrels per day (29,000 m^3/d). It also is the fourth-largest producer of liquefied natural gas in the world.

Brunei is the fourth-largest oil producer in Southeast Asia, averaging about 219,000 barrels a day in 2006. It also is the ninth-largest exporter of liquefied natural gas in the world. Like many oil producing countries, Brunei's economy has followed the swings of the world oil market. Economic growth has averaged around 2.8% in the 2000s, heavily dependent on oil and gas production. Oil production has averaged around 200,000 barrels a day during the 2000s, while liquefied natural gas output has been slightly under or over 1,000 trillion btu/day over the same period. Brunei is estimated to have oil reserves expected to last 25 years, and enough natural gas reserves to last 40 years.

Brunei Shell Petroleum (BSP), a joint venture owned in equal shares by the Brunei Government and the Royal Dutch/Shell group of companies, is the chief oil and gas production company in Brunei. It also operates the country's only refinery. BSP and four sister companies--including the liquefied natural gas producing firm BLNG--constitute the largest employer in Brunei after the government. BSP's small refinery has a distillation capacity of 10,000 barrels per day. This satisfies domestic demand for most petroleum products.

The French oil company Total (then known as ELF Aquitaine) became active in petroleum exploration in Brunei in the 1980s. The joint venture Total E&P Borneo BV currently produces approximately 35,000 barrels per day and 13% of Brunei's natural gas.

In 2003, Malaysia disputed Brunei-awarded oil exploration concessions for offshore blocks J and K (Total and Shell respectively), which led to the Brunei licensees ceasing exploration activities. Negotiations between the two countries are continuing in order to resolve the conflict. In 2006, Brunei awarded two on-shore blocks--one to a Canadian-led and the other to a Chinese-led consortium. Australia, Indonesia, and Korea were the largest customers for Brunei's oil exports, taking over 67% of Brunei's total crude exports. Traditional customers Japan, the U.S., and China each took around 5% of total crude exports.
Almost all of Brunei's natural gas is liquefied at Brunei Shell's Liquefied Natural Gas (LNG) plant, which opened in 1972 and is one of the largest LNG plants in the world. Some 90% of Brunei's LNG produced is sold to Japan under a long-term agreement renewed in 1993.

The agreement calls for Brunei to provide over 5 million tons of LNG per year to three Japanese utilities, namely to TEPCo, Tokyo Electric Power Co. (J.TER or 5001), Tokyo Gas Co. (J.TYG or 9531) and Osaka Gas Co. (J.OSG or 9532). The Japanese company, Mitsubishi, is a joint venture partner with Shell and the Brunei Government in Brunei LNG, Brunei Coldgas, and Brunei Shell Tankers, which together produce the LNG and supply it to Japan. Since 1995, Brunei has supplied more than 700,000 tons of LNG to the Korea Gas Corporation (KOGAS) as well. In 1999, Brunei's natural gas production reached 90 cargoes per day. A small amount of natural gas is used for domestic power generation. Since 2001, Japan remains the dominant export market for natural gas. Brunei is the fourth-largest exporter of LNG in the Asia-Pacific region behind Indonesia, Malaysia, and Australia.

The government sought in the past decade to diversify the economy with limited success. Oil and gas and government spending still account for most of Brunei's economic activity. Brunei's non-petroleum industries include agriculture, forestry, fishing, aquaculture, and banking. The garment-for-export industry has been shrinking since the U.S. eliminated its garment quota system at the end of 2004. The Brunei Economic Development Board announced plans in 2003 to use proven gas reserves to establish downstream industrial projects. The government plans to build a power plant in the Sungai Liang region to power a proposed aluminum smelting plant that will depend on foreign investors. A second major project depending on foreign investment is in the planning stage: a giant container hub at the Muara Port facilities.

The government regulates the immigration of foreign labor out of concern it might disrupt Brunei's society. Work permits for foreigners are issued only for short periods and must be continually renewed. Despite these restrictions, the estimated 100,000 foreign temporary residents of Brunei make up a significant portion of the work force. The government reported a total work force of 180,400 in 2006, with a derived unemployment rate of 4.0%.

Oil and natural gas account for almost all exports. Since only a few products other than petroleum are produced locally, a wide variety of items must be imported. Nonetheless, Brunei has had a significant trade surplus in the 2000s. Official statistics show Singapore, Malaysia, Japan, the U.S., and the U.K. as the leading importers in 2005. The United States was the third-largest supplier of imports to Brunei in 2005.

Brunei's substantial foreign reserves are managed by the Brunei Investment Agency (BIA), an arm of the Ministry of Finance. BIA's guiding principle is to increase the real value of Brunei's foreign reserves while pursuing a diverse investment strategy, with holdings in the United States, Japan, Western Europe, and the Association of Southeast Asian Nations (ASEAN) countries.

The Brunei Government encourages more foreign investment. New enterprises that meet certain criteria can receive pioneer status, exempting profits from income tax for up to 5 years, depending on the amount of capital invested. The normal corporate income tax rate is 30%. There is no personal income tax or capital gains tax.

One of the government's priorities is to encourage the development of Brunei Malays as leaders of industry and commerce. There are no specific restrictions of foreign equity ownership, but local participation, both shared capital and management, is encouraged. Such participation helps when tendering for contracts with the government or Brunei Shell Petroleum.

Companies in Brunei must either be incorporated locally or registered as a branch of a foreign company and must be registered with the Registrar of Companies. Public companies must have a minimum of seven shareholders. Private companies must have a minimum of two but not more than 50 shareholders. At least half of the directors in a company must be residents of Brunei.

The government owns a cattle farm in Australia through which the country's beef supplies are processed. At 2,262 square miles, this ranch is larger than Brunei itself. Eggs and chickens are largely produced locally, but most of Brunei's other food needs must be imported. Agriculture, aquaculture, and fisheries are among the industrial sectors that the government has selected for highest priority in its efforts to diversify the economy.

Recently the government has announced plans for Brunei to become an international offshore financial center as well as a center for Islamic banking. Brunei is keen on the development of small and medium enterprises and also is investigating the possibility of establishing a "cyber park" to develop an information technology industry. Brunei has also promoted ecotourism to take advantage of the over 70% of Brunei's territory that remains primal tropical rainforest.

DEFENSE

The Sultan is both Minister of Defense and Supreme Commander of the Armed Forces (RBAF). All infantry, navy, and air combat units are made up of volunteers. There are two infantry battalions equipped with armored reconnaissance vehicles and armored personnel carriers and supported by Rapier air defense missiles and a flotilla of coastal patrol vessels armed with surface-to-surface missiles. Brunei has ordered, but not yet taken possession of, three offshore patrol vessels from the U.K.
Brunei has a defense agreement with the United Kingdom, under which a British Armed Forces Ghurka battalion (1,500 men) is permanently stationed in Seria, near the center of Brunei's oil industry. The RBAF has joint exercises, training programs, and other military cooperation with the United Kingdom and many other countries, including the United States. The U.S. and Brunei signed a memorandum of understanding (MOU) on defense cooperation in November 1994. The two countries conduct an annual military exercise called CARAT.

FOREIGN RELATIONS

Brunei joined ASEAN on January 7, 1984--one week after resuming full independence--and gives its ASEAN membership the highest priority in its foreign relations. Brunei joined the UN in September 1984. It also is a member of the Organization of the Islamic Conference (OIC) and of the Asia-Pacific Economic Cooperation (APEC) forum. Brunei hosted the APEC Economic Leaders' Meeting in November 2000 and the ASEAN Regional Forum (ARF) in July 2002.

U.S.-BRUNEI RELATIONS

Relations between the United States and Brunei date from the 1800s. On April 6, 1845, the U.S.S. Constitution visited Brunei. The two countries concluded a Treaty of Peace, Friendship, Commerce and Navigation in 1850, which remains in force today. The United States maintained a consulate in Brunei from 1865 to 1867.

The U.S. welcomed Brunei Darussalam's full independence from the United Kingdom on January 1, 1984, and opened an Embassy in Bandar Seri Begawan on that date. Brunei opened its embassy in Washington in March 1984. Brunei's armed forces engage in joint exercises, training programs, and other military cooperation with the U.S. A memorandum of understanding on defense cooperation was signed on November 29, 1994. The Sultan visited Washington in December 2002.

Principal U.S. Embassy Officials
Ambassador-- Craig Allen

Ambassador Craig Allen was sworn in as the United States ambassador to Brunei Darussalam on December 19, 2014.
Deputy Chief of Mission--John McIntyre
Management Officer--Michael Lampel

The U.S. Embassy in Bandar Seri Begawan is located on the third & fifth floors of the Teck Guan Plaza, at the corner of Jalan Sultan and Jalan MacArthur; tel: 673-2229670; fax: 673-2225293; e-mail: usembassy_bsb@state.gov

TRAVEL AND BUSINESS INFORMATION

The U.S. Department of State's Consular Information Program advises Americans traveling and residing abroad through Consular Information Sheets, Public Announcements, and Travel Warnings. **Consular Information Sheets** exist for all countries and include information on entry and exit requirements, currency regulations, health conditions, safety and security, crime, political disturbances, and the addresses of the U.S. embassies and consulates abroad. **Public**

Announcements are issued to disseminate information quickly about terrorist threats and other relatively short-term conditions overseas that pose significant risks to the security of American travelers. **Travel Warnings** are issued when the State Department recommends that Americans avoid travel to a certain country because the situation is dangerous or unstable.

For the latest security information, Americans living and traveling abroad should regularly monitor the Department's Bureau of Consular Affairs Internet web site at http://www.travel.state.gov, where the current Worldwide Caution, Public Announcements, and Travel Warnings can be found. Consular Affairs Publications, which contain information on obtaining passports and planning a safe trip abroad, are also available at http://www.travel.state.gov. For additional information on international travel, see http://www.usa.gov/Citizen/Topics/Travel/International.shtml.

The Department of State encourages all U.S citizens traveling or residing abroad to register via the State Department's travel registration website or at the nearest U.S. embassy or consulate abroad. Registration will make your presence and whereabouts known in case it is necessary to contact you in an emergency and will enable you to receive up-to-date information on security conditions.

Emergency information concerning Americans traveling abroad may be obtained by calling 1-888-407-4747 toll free in the U.S. and Canada or the regular toll line 1-202-501-4444 for callers outside the U.S. and Canada.

The National Passport Information Center (NPIC) is the U.S. Department of State's single, centralized public contact center for U.S. passport information. Telephone: 1-877-4USA-PPT (1-877-487-2778). Customer service representatives and operators for TDD/TTY are available Monday-Friday, 7:00 a.m. to 12:00 midnight, Eastern Time, excluding federal holidays.

Travelers can check the latest health information with the U.S. Centers for Disease Control and Prevention in Atlanta, Georgia. A hotline at 877-FYI-TRIP (877-394-8747) and a web site at http://www.cdc.gov/travel/index.htm give the most recent health advisories, immunization recommendations or requirements, and advice on food and drinking water safety for regions and countries. A booklet entitled "Health Information for International Travel" (HHS publication number CDC-95-8280) is available from the U.S. Government Printing Office, Washington, DC 20402, tel. (202) 512-1800.

EU-BRUNEI RELATIONS

Official Name	Negara Brunei Darussalam
Population	0.38 million
Area	6000 km²
Gross Domestic Product	5 bn euros
GDP Per Capita	14.173 €
Real GDP (% growth)	3.0 %
Exports GDP %	0.85
Imports GDP %	0.27
Exports to Brunei from EU (mn €, 2001)	108 EU imports from Brunei (mn €)
Imports to EU from Brunei (mn €, 2001)	72
Human Development Index (rank of 175°)	33
Head of State	HM Paduka Seri Baginda Sultan Haji Hassanal

	Bolkiah Mu'izzadddin Waddaulah (Sultan, prime minister, minister of finance and defence)

FRAMEWORK

The framework for co-operation dialogue with Brunei is the EC-ASEAN Agreement of 1980. There is no bilateral cooperation agreement.

POLITICAL CONTEXT

Brunei Darussalam became independent from the United Kingdom on 1 January 1984, and a week later joined the Association of South-East Asian Nations (ASEAN). Brunei is a constitutional monarchy with the Sultan Yang Di-Pertuan – Hassanal Bolkiah as the Head of State, Prime Minister, Defence Minister, as well as Minister for Finance. The Sultan presides over a 10-member cabinet which he appoints himself. Five councils advise the Sultan on policy matters: the Religious Council, the Privy Council, the Council of Succession, the Legislative Council and the Council of Ministers (the cabinet). Since 1962 the Sultan has ruled by decree. Thus, the system of government revolves around the Sultan as the source of executive power.

On 25 September 2004, the Legislative Council met for the first time in 20 years, with 21 members appointed by the Sultan. It passed constitutional amendments, calling for a 45-seat council with 15 elected members. In a move towards political reform an appointed parliament was revived in 2004. The constitution provides for an expanded house with up to 15 elected MPs. However, no date has been set for elections.

Brunei is a Muslim country, with a Ministry of Religious Affairs established to foster and promote Islam. Brunei continues to play a peacekeeping role in the Philippines, and is taking part in efforts to monitor peace in the Indonesian region of Aceh.

EUROPEAN COMMUNITY ASSISTANCE

By virtue of its advanced level of economic development Brunei does not benefit from bilateral development or economic projects.

EC co-operation with Brunei has for the greater part been limited to joint EC- ASEAN projects.

The EC has given financial support to the ASEAN-EC Management Centre (AEMC), located in Brunei, the contract for which has come to an end.

TRADE AND ECONOMIC

Since 1929, when oil was discovered in Brunei, the country has flourished. During 1998 and as a consequence of the Asia crisis, however, both exports and imports decreased in comparison with previous years.

- **Key role of oil and gas**: Brunei suffered little directly from the Asian financial crisis of 1997. But, in 1998, the Sultanate was hit by the sharp fall in oil sales and the bankruptcy of a locally-owned oil and gas company, resulting in a contraction in GDP of 4%. Subsequently, economic activity recovered in step with the resumption of oil and gas extraction and, in recent years, the sharp rise in the oil price. The latest available data for

For additional analytical, marketing, investment and business opportunities information, please contact
Global Investment & Business Center, USA
(202) 546-2103. Fax: (202) 546-3275. E-mail: rusric@erols.com

GDP shows real annual growth around 3%. Oil reserves are officially estimated at 25 years, but, great hopes are placed in two new drilling concessions.

Economic structure: Almost everything the country needs is imported. Even the industrial labour force comes from abroad, mainly from India, the Philippines, Indonesia and Bangladesh as most of Brunei's citizens are employed as civil servants (60% of the population) and prefer the status related to that occupation. This also explains the apparent contradiction between the necessity to employ foreign manpower and the rising unemployment rate (officially at 4.7% but estimated at 9%).

- At the beginning of 2000, the government of the Sultanate announced an ambitious programme of **economic reforms** in order to reduce the dependence on oil and gas. Two initiatives have been taken up till know– to develop tourism and to support the creation of an off-shore financial centre in developing Islamic banking business.

- The tourism industry is, however, handicapped by the shortage of quality infrastructure, and the geographical insulation of the Sultanate.

Brunei's trade surplus fell by an estimated 74% in US dollar terms in 1999 as the price of oil and gas collapsed. A strengthening oil price and long-term contracts for natural gas, paid in US dollars, should, however, ensure that Brunei's trade position remains healthy.

At present Brunei produces oil and gas almost to the exclusion of other products. The government is trying hard, however, to develop manufactured exports, in particular cement and roofing (tiles) which are both protected sectors. The garment industry is struggling after the abolition of global quotas on the textile trade. The Sultan has announced financial reforms.

Brunei has signed a free-trade pact with New Zealand, Singapore and Chile. A Brunei Tourism Board has been set up

The domestic economy: Brunei's economic growth remains fairly sluggish, at 2.6% year on year but a recovery is likely to have taken place in the second quarter of 2005. The non-oil and gas sector is expanding more rapidly than the energy sector. High global oil prices have lifted transport prices, but overall inflation remains low.

Foreign trade and payments: High oil prices lay behind an increase in the merchandises-trade surplus in the first quarter of 2005.The oil and gas sector continues to account for the bulk of exports; garments exports were much lower than in the year-earlier period.

The investment policy in Brunei is largely open to foreign investors, as indicated by a favourable legal environment and a policy allowing full foreign ownership in a majority of economic sectors. Foreign investments have been more particularly in the last years as they are considered by the government as a key element to contribute to the targeted diversification of the country's economy.

As part of this strategy to attract foreign investments, an Economic Development Board (EDB) was created in 2001. The main sectors and projects promoted by the EDB and susceptible to attract foreign investments include port infrastructure, industry, communication (aviation hub), eco-tourism, and financial services. In parallel with the creation of the EDB, major policy changes have been made in the last years to promote foreign investments. August 2000 saw the introduction of an offshore legislation in Brunei. New laws were drafted covering international banking, insurance, offshore companies, trusts, limited partnerships and registered agents.

Changes in the legislation are too recent analyze its effects. The volume of FDI has doubled between 2001 and 2002, while the figures available until mid 2003 include that the trend is positive and that investments do not only target natural resources but also services.

INVESTMENT AND BUSINESS CLIMATE

Brunei Darussalam is an energy-rich Sultanate on the northern coast of Borneo in Southeast Asia. Brunei boasts a well-educated, largely English-speaking population, excellent infrastructure, and a government intent on attracting foreign investment and projects. In parallel with Brunei's efforts to attract foreign investment, the country has improved its protections for Intellectual Property Rights (IPR).

Despite repeated calls for diversification, Brunei's economy remains dependent on the income derived from sales of oil and gas. Substantial revenue from overseas investment supplements income from domestic production. These two revenue streams provide a comfortable quality of life for Brunei's population. Citizens pay no taxes and receive free education through to the university level as well as free medical care and, frequently, subsidized housing.

Brunei's central location in Southeast Asia, with good telecommunications and airline connections; no personal income, sales or export taxes; and its stable political situation offer a welcoming climate for would-be investors, with tax relief programs in specified sectors. Brunei is a participant in the Trans-Pacific Partnership (TPP) trade negotiations.

Sectors offering U.S. business opportunities in Brunei include **Aerospace & Defense, Agribusiness, Construction, Petrochemicals, Energy & Mining, Environmental Technologies, Food Processing & Packaging, Franchising, Health Technologies, Information & Communication,** and **Services.**

In 2014 Brunei released an Energy White Paper outlining its vision of leveraging its oil wealth to diversify its economy, create local employment, increase foreign investment and sharply increase the use of renewable energy by 2035.

The Export-Import Bank of the United States (Ex-Im) and the Energy Department of Brunei's Prime Minister's Office signed a Memorandum of Understanding that calls for expanded information sharing regarding trade and energy business opportunities in the Asia-Pacific region as well as exploring options for utilizing up to US$1 billion Ex-IM Bank loans to finance U.S. exports in support of selected projects in the region. The MOU creates significant new opportunities for U.S. energy companies in Brunei and the Asia-Pacific region while advancing the goals set out by the United States-Asia Pacific Comprehensive Energy Partnership (USACEP).

In 2014 Brunei began implementing a penal code based on Islamic law (Sharia), in parallel with the existing Common Law-based criminal law system. The Sharia Penal Code is applicable to both Muslims and non-Muslims, including foreigners residing in Brunei. The first phase became effective on May 1, 2014. It expands restrictions in areas such as drinking alcohol, eating in public during fasting hours in the month of Ramadan, and indecent behavior. Two subsequent phases, the timing of which is not yet clear, are expected to introduce severe punishments such as stoning to death for certain sex-related offenses including anal sex and amputating the hands of thieves. Brunei officials say the most severe punishments will rarely if ever be implemented, given the very high standards for evidence and witnesses under the Sharia Penal Code. While the law does not specifically address business-related matters, potential investors should be aware that there is controversy surrounding the Sharia Penal Code issue.

1. OPENNESS TO, AND RESTRICTIONS UPON, FOREIGN INVESTMENT:

Attitude Toward FDI

Brunei has an open economy favorable to foreign trade and foreign direct investment (FDI) as it continues its economic diversification efforts away from its long reliance on oil and gas exports. FDI is important to Brunei as it plays a key role in economic and technological development. Brunei encourages FDI in the domestic economy through various investment incentives offered by the Brunei Economic Development Board (BEDB) and the Ministry of Industry and Primary Resources (MIPR) and through activities by the Ministry of Foreign Affairs and Trade (MOFAT), which offers favorable incentives for FDI and trade.

The 2014 World Bank and the International Finance Corporation report indicated that Brunei's ease of doing business ranking had improved by 20 points to rank 59th out of 189 countries. The report attributed the improvement to the establishment of the Public Credit Bureau under the Autoriti Monetari (Monetary Authority) Brunei Darussalam, which consolidated credit information within the country. The report also indicated improvements to indicators including protecting investors, paying taxes, and trading across borders. The rankings for five of the ten indicators slipped, including: starting a business; dealing with construction permits; registering property; enforcing contracts; and resolving insolvency.

Responding to the report, Brunei's Minister of Industry and Primary Resources called for more focused and comprehensive structural, operational and regulatory reforms to be undertaken by relevant ministries to ensure significant improvements in future reports. He urged the government to keep pace with the aggressive rate of reforms to remain a viable and competitive economy capable of adapting to the needs of a modern and vibrant business environment and to improve the efficiency and productivity of government services. Brunei has maintained its ranking as the number four country in the Association of Southeast Asian Nations (ASEAN) in terms of ease of doing business.

Laws/Regulations of FDI

The basic legislation on investment includes the Investment Incentive Order 2001 and Income Tax (As Amended) Order 2001. Brunei does not yet have its own stock exchange, but a securities market order reportedly is under development. Brunei's constitution does not provide for judicial independence but in practice the court system operates without government interference. Brunei's legal system includes parallel systems, one based on Common Law and the other based on Sharia Law.

Brunei's national strategy, Wawasan (National Vision) 2035, emphasizes attracting FDI as an important driver of growth. The Brunei Economic Development Board (BEDB) seeks to diversify Brunei's economy and create employment opportunities for its people. The BEDB administers incentives and loans to encourage investment projects from abroad.

The Ministry of Industry and Primary Resources is the main coordinating agency for investment and industrial development in the primary sector, manufacturing, and tourism. The Ministry encourages and helps local and foreign investors to participate in ventures to produce goods and services for export and local markets and to satisfy national food security and employment needs.

Industrial Strategy

Through its Investment Incentives Order 2001, Brunei seeks to stimulate economic development by encouraging the establishment and expansion of specified industrial and economic enterprises. The authority to administer this legislation is currently vested in the Minister of Industry and Primary Resources, who is able to offer investment incentives in the form of tax relief for the following:

Pioneer Industries: Any limited company which has been granted a pioneer certificate will then be given pioneer incentives including exemption from the 30 percent corporate tax for a period ranging from five years for a fixed capital expenditure of B$500,000 to B$2.5 million (USD$397,000 to USD$1,987,000); eight years for an expenditure over B$2.5 million; and 11 years for a project located in a designated high-tech industrial park, with permitted extensions; exemption from taxes on imported duties on machinery, equipment, components parts, accessories or building structures; exemption from taxes on imported raw materials not available or produced in Brunei intended as feedstock for the production of Pioneer products; and carry forward losses and allowances.

Industries that have been declared as pioneer industries and pioneer products include:

Agribusiness (fertilizers and pesticides); **Agricultural, Construction, Building & Heavy Equipment** (cement finishing mill, manufacture of electrical industrial machinery and apparatus, rolling mill plant, sheet metal-forming); **Chemicals, Petrochemicals, Plastics & Composites** (plastics and synthetic, manufacture of non-metallic mineral products, gas);**Consumer Goods & Home Furnishings** (furniture, ceramic and potteries, tissue paper, toys); **Environmental Technologies** (related waste industry); **Food Processing & Packaging** (slaughtering, preparing and preserving halal meat, canning, bottling and packaging); **Health Technologies** (pharmaceuticals); **Information & Communication**(manufacture of radio, television and communication equipment and apparatus); **Industrial Equipment & Supplies**(glass, woodbase); **Marine Technology** (ship repair and maintenance, supporting services to water transport); **Metal Manufacturing & Products** (aluminum wall tile); **Services** (aircraft catering services); **Textiles, Apparel & Sporting Goods** (textiles).

Additional details are available at **http://www.bedb.com.bn/doing_incentives_pioneer.html**

Pioneer Service Companies: Pioneer service companies may be eligible for tax relief, depending on the fixed capital expenditure, for a period of 8 years with given extension not exceeding 11 years in total.

Activities that have been declared as pioneer services include:

Agribusiness (agriculture technology related services and activities); **Architecture & Engineering** (any engineering or technical services including laboratory, consultancy and research and development activities, development or production of any industrial design); **Automotive & Ground Transportation** (operation or management of any mass rapid transit system); **Education** (provision of education related services); **Finance** (business, management and professional consultancy services, financial services, venture capital fund activity); **Health Technologies** (medical services); **Information & Communication** (computer-based information and other computer related services, publishing services); **Media & Entertainment** (maintaining and operating a private museum, provision of leisure and recreation related services and activities); **Services** (services and activities related to warehousing facilities); **Travel**(services and activities relating to the organization or management of exhibitions and conferences)

Additional details are available at **http://www.bedb.com.bn/doing_incentives_pioneerservice.html**.

Production For Export: The Minister of Industry and Primary Resources may approve a company proposing to engage in specified activities either wholly or partly for export as an export enterprise. Certified companies may be exempted from income tax; from import duties on machinery, equipment, component parts, accessories or building structures; and from import duties on raw materials for a period of six to 15 years depending on the company's fixed capital expenditure and pioneer status.

Qualified activities have included:

Agribusiness (agriculture, forestry and fishery activities).

Additional details are available at **http://www.bedb.com.bn/doing_incentives_production.html**.

Service For Export: Specified services may be eligible for exemption from income tax and deduction of allowance and losses. The tax relief period of an export service company shall begin on its day of commencement and shall not exceed 11 years. Any given extension shall not exceed 3 years at one time and not exceed 20 years in total.

Qualified services have included:

Architecture & Engineering (technical services including construction, distribution, design and engineering services);**Education** (educational and training service); **Industrial Equipment & Supplies** (fabrication of machinery and equipment, and procurement of materials, components and equipment); **Information & Communication** (data processing, programming, computer software development, telecommunications and other related ICT services);**Services** (consultancy, management supervisory or advisory services relating to any technical matter or to any trade or business; professional services including accounting, legal, medical and architectural services.)

Additional details are available at **http://www.bedb.com.bn/doing_incentives_service.html**

Foreign Loan for Product Equipment

There is a 20% withholding tax for interest paid to non-resident lenders. However the government may grant a tax exemption for any approved foreign loan if the loan is utilized for the purchase of production equipment.

Additional information is available at **http://www.bedb.com.bn/doing_incentives_foreign.html**

Information on additional forms of business and investment incentives is available at**http://www.bedb.com.bn/doing_incentives.html**.

Limits on Foreign Control

There has been no restriction on total foreign ownership of companies incorporated in Brunei Darussalam. The Companies Act requires locally incorporated companies to have at least one of the two directors – or if more than two directors, at least two of them – to be ordinarily resident in Brunei Darussalam. The Companies Act allows the board to be totally non-resident; however, the company concerned would have to apply to the appropriate authorities for permission and show justifications for such decisions. Notwithstanding whether the company is locally or foreign owned and managed, the rates of corporate income tax is the same.

Privatization Program

Brunei's Ministry of Communication has made corporatization and privatization part of its Strategic Plans 2008-2017, which call for the Ministry to shift its role from a service provider to a regulatory body with policy-setting responsibility. In that role, the Ministry will develop specific policies through corporatization and privatization; establish a regulatory framework and business facilitation. Currently, the Ministry is studying initiatives to privatize and corporatize four state-owned agencies: the Ports Department, the Maritime and Port Authority of Brunei Darussalam, the Postal Services Department and Brunei International Airport management. These services are not yet completely privatized and there is no timeline for privatization, as the Ministry is still in the process of considering the initiative. Guidelines regarding the role of foreign investors and the bidding process are not yet available. The strategy can be found in**www.mincom.gov.bn**.

Screening of FDI

Post is informed that Brunei, through BEDB, has one or more processes to screen, review or approve foreign investments. The processes are kept confidential. Post has received no complaints from U.S. businesses about the screening process.

Competition Law

Brunei does not have any general competition legislation pertaining to the regulation of competition issues. Brunei formally started the process of drafting the Brunei Competition Order in May 2012, which reportedly emulates the legislation and best practices in the international jurisdiction including prohibitions against anti-competitive agreements, abuse of dominance, and anti-competitive mergers. It is not known when the law will be approved and implemented.

Investment Trends

Brunei is a participant in the Trans-Pacific Partnership (TPP) negotiations, through which the United States and its 10 Asia-Pacific partners are seeking to establish a comprehensive, next-generation regional agreement to liberalize trade and investment.

This agreement will advance U.S. economic interests with some of the fastest-growing economies in the world, act as an important tool to expand U.S. exports which are critical to the creation and retention of jobs in the United States, and serve as a potential platform for economic integration across the Asia-Pacific region. The TPP agreement will include ambitious commitments on goods, services, and other traditional trade and investment issues. It will also address a range of emerging issues not covered by past agreements, including trade and investment in innovative products and commitments to help companies operate more effectively in regional markets. In addition to the United States and Brunei, the TPP negotiating partners currently include Australia, Canada, Chile, Japan, Malaysia, Mexico, New Zealand, Peru, Singapore, and Vietnam.

Brunei's annual trade balance decreased by 16.8 per cent from BND$11,765.5 million (USD$9,488.31 million) in 2012 to BND$9,788.4 million (USD$7,830.72 million) in 2013. Meanwhile the total trade showed a decline of 8.9 per cent from BND$20,675.9 million (USD$16,672.11 million) in 2012 to BND$18,829.6 million (USD$15,063.68 million) in 2013. The U.S. goods trade surplus with Brunei was BND$676 million (USD$541 million) in 2013, a decrease of USD$470 million (BND$587 million) from 2012. U.S. goods exports in 2013 were USD$559 million (BND$699 million), up 254.4 percent from the previous year. Corresponding U.S. imports from Brunei were USD$17 million (BND$21 million), down 81 percent. Brunei is currently the 100th largest export market for U.S. goods. The stock of U.S. foreign direct investment (FDI) in Brunei was USD$42.64 million (BND$55 million) in 2011 (latest data available), down from USD$43.33 million (BND$57 million) in 2010.

Table 1: The following chart summarizes several well-regarded indices and rankings.

Measure	Year	Index or Rank	Website Address
TI Corruption Perceptions index	2013	(60 of 177)	http://cpi.transparency.org/cpi2013/results/
Heritage Foundation's Economic Freedom index	2013	(69 of 177)	http://www.heritage.org/index/ranking
World Bank's Doing Business Report "Ease of Doing Business"	2013	(59 of 189)	http://doingbusiness.org/rankings
Global Innovation Index	2013	(74 of 142)	http://www.globalinnovationindex.org/content.aspx?page=gii-full-report-2013#pdfopener
World Bank GNI per capita	2009	$31,590	http://data.worldbank.org/indicator/NY.GNP.PCAP.CD

2. CONVERSION AND TRANSFER POLICIES

Foreign Exchange

In June 2013 the Financial Action Task Force (FATF) announced that Brunei Darussalam is no longer subject to FATF's monitoring process under its on-going global Anti-Money Laundering/Countering the Financing of Terrorism (AML/CFT) compliance process. Brunei Darussalam will work with the Asia-Pacific Group (APG) as it continues to address the full range of AML/CFT issues identified in its Mutual Evaluation Report. The report cited Brunei's significant progress in improving its AML/CFT regime and noted that Brunei had established the legal and regulatory framework to meet its commitments in its Action Plan regarding the strategic deficiencies that the FATF had identified in June 2011.

For additional analytical, marketing, investment and business opportunities information, please contact
Global Investment & Business Center, USA
(202) 546-2103. Fax: (202) 546-3275. E-mail: rusric@erols.com

3. EXPROPRIATION AND COMPENSATION

There is no history of expropriation of foreign owned property in Brunei. There have been cases of domestically owned private property being expropriated for infrastructure development. Compensation was provided in such cases and claimants were given the opportunity to have claims heard.

4. DISPUTE SETTLEMENT

Onshore companies are governed by the Companies Act while offshore companies are governed by the International Business Companies Order of 2000. There are no specialized commercial courts. Brunei's constitution does not provide for judicial independence but in practice the court system operates without government interference. Post has received no complaints from companies regarding the judicial system.

Bankruptcy

Brunei's bankruptcy act is available at **http://www.agc.gov.bn/agc1/images/LAWS/ACT_PDF/cap067.pdf**.

Recent amendments to the act increased the minimum threshold for declaring bankruptcy from BND$500 to BND$10,000 and enabled the trustee to direct the Controller of Immigration to impound and retain the bankrupt's passport, certificate of identity or travel document to prevent him from leaving Brunei Darussalam. The amendments also saw the imposition of a number of duties on the bankrupt to deliver all his property under his possession, books, paper etc. to the trustee.

5. PERFORMANCE REQUIREMENTS AND INVESTMENT INCENTIVES

Investment Incentives

Companies producing goods and services for export can apply for a renewable 10-year tax exemption. Corporate tax relief of up to 5 years is available for companies that invest between B$500,000 to B$2.5 million (USD$385,000 to USD$1.9million) and up to 8 years for amounts exceeding B$2.5million (USD$1.9 million) in approved ventures. An 11-year tax break is offered if the venture is located in a high-tech industrial park. Businesses wishing to compete in domestic markets can qualify for tax breaks for up to eight years. Sole proprietorships and partnerships are not subject to tax. Individuals do not pay any capital gains tax and profits arising from the sale of capital assets are not taxable. Brunei has double-taxation agreements with Britain, Indonesia, China, Singapore, Vietnam, Bahrain, Oman, Japan, and Pakistan. Tax on petroleum operations is codified in the 1960 Income Tax enactment, which is similar to tax policies in other oil-producing nations.

6. RIGHT TO PRIVATE OWNERSHIP AND ESTABLISHMENT

All businesses in Brunei must be registered with the Registrar of Companies within the Attorney General's Chambers. Except for sole proprietorships, foreign investors can fully own incorporated companies, foreign company branches or representative offices. Partnerships generally require the participation of citizens. Foreign direct investments by multi-national corporations may not require local partnership in setting up a subsidiary of their parent company in Brunei. However, at least one company director must be a Brunei citizen or permanent resident in Brunei Darussalam.

A multinational company with an operating plant on an MIPR industrial park is required to have 30% of the companies' board represented by Brunei citizens and permanent residents.

7. PROTECTION OF PROPERTY RIGHTS

Real Property

Mortgages are recognized and enforced in Brunei, however only Bruneians can own land property in Brunei. Foreigners and permanent residents can only hold properties under strata tiles or long-term leasehold rights. Most banks have stopped granting housing loans to foreigners and permanent residents. The 2011 data from the International Monetary Fund (IMF) showed no foreign direct investment (FDI) for real estate, rentals and business activity. In 2009 and 2010, the sector saw B$3 million in FDI per year while in 2007 and 2008 it logged B$2 million of FDI value.

Amendments to the Land Code are in the works to ban past practices of proxy sale of land to foreigners and permanent residents using the power of attorney (PA) and Trust Deeds (TD). PA and TD are no longer recognized as viable mechanisms in land deals involving non-citizens. The move to ban the PA and TD was announced at the 8th Legislative Council meeting on March 12, 2012. The proposed laws will also have retroactive effect, converting all existing property owned through PA and TD into 60-year leases. The rationale for the restriction is to ensure sufficient land ownership by citizens. PA's are still in land development transactions allowing for only 5 year ownership for land developers and 25 year ownership for banks. The PA in these cases were allowed to be used as collateral.

Intellectual Property (IP) Rights

Brunei's IP protection and enforcement regime is still in development but is increasingly strong and effective. The country was removed from the Special 301 report in 2013, and stayed off the list in 2014, in recognition of its improving IPR protections, increasing enforcement, and efforts to educate the public about the importance of IPR.

Brunei's long-gestating Copyright (Amendment) Order 2013 was finalized and adopted in December 2013, a development long requested by the U.S. government. The change further enhanced enforcement provisions for copyright infringement by increasing penalties for offences; adding new offenses; strengthening the enforcement powers of the Royal Brunei Police Force and the Ministry of Finance Customs and Excise Department; and allowing for sanctioned private prosecution. The amendments are designed to deter copyright infringements with fines of BND$10,000 (USD$8,130) to BND$20,000 (USD$16,260) per infringing copy, imprisonment for a term up to five years or both. The new penalty is up to four times more severe than the previously existing penalty. Enforcement agencies are authorized to enter premises and arrest without warrant, to stop, search and board vehicles and also to access computerized and digitized data. The amendments further allow for admissibility of evidence obtained covertly and protect the identity of informants.

Brunei transferred its Registry of Trademarks from the Attorney General's Chambers (AGC) to the BEDB effective June 2013. The transfer expanded the BEDB Patents Registry Office's (PRO) capabilities to accept applications for the registration of trademarks in addition to patents and industrial designs. The office's name officially changed on July 1 to the Brunei Intellectual Property Office (BruIPO). The change created a national IP office, making policy coordination easier. The World Intellectual Property Organization's Singapore office described the move as a very positive step in terms of strengthening the IP protection efforts, because it provides comprehensive management of IP.

In September 2013, Brunei acceded to the Geneva (1999) Act of the Hague Agreement Concerning the International Registration of Industrial Designs to protect IP from industrial designs, making it the second ASEAN Member country, following Singapore, to accede. The accession emphasized Brunei's commitment under the ASEAN Intellectual Property Rights Action Plan 2011 – 2015. Brunei also plans and has publicly committed to acceding to other World Intellectual Property Organization's (WIPO) treaties including the Madrid Protocol for the International Registration of Marks and the WIPO Performances and Phonograms Treaty (WPPT). In addition, Brunei is actively negotiating the Trans-Pacific Partnership's IP chapter with the United States and other TPP participants. The Recording Industry Association of Malaysia, which in the past had criticized Brunei for a lack of support for IPR protection, opened its own office in Brunei in 2013.

For additional information about treaty obligations and points of contact at local IP offices, please see WIPO's country profiles at http://www.wipo.int/directory/en/.

For additional information about treaty obligations and points of contact at local IP offices, please see WIPO's country profiles at **http://www.wipo.int/directory/en/**.

Resources for Rights Holders:

Contact at Mission:

Matthew B. Stannard
Political/Economic/Consular Officer
+673 718-3583
stannardmb@state.gov

Local Business Lawyers:

FATHAN, RUDI LEE, ANNIE KON & ASSOCIATES
Advocates & Solicitors / Commissioners For Oaths
Unit A1-1 & A2-1, 1st Floor, Block A Shakirin Complex
Simpang 88, Kampung Kiulap, BSB BE1518
Tel: +673.223.5111
Fax: +673.223.4206
Email: *fralaw2@gmail.com*

***Services Provided**: adoptions, commercial/business law, foreign investments, trademarks, civil law, criminal law, damages, narcotics, collections, commerical law, contracts, corporations, foreign claims, estates, labor relations, immigration, auto/accidents*

PENGIRAN IZAD & LEE
Advocates & Solicitors / Commissioners For Oaths
6th Floor, Bangunan Hj. Ahmad Laksamana Othman
38-39, Jalan Sultan, BSB BS8811
Tel: +673.223.2945/6/7/8
Fax: +673.223.2944
Email: *pial@brunet.bn*

***Services Provided**: family law, insurance, banking/financial, commercial/business law, foreign investments, marketing agreements, patents/trademarks/copyrights, civil law, criminal law,*

For additional analytical, marketing, investment and business opportunities information, please contact
Global Investment & Business Center, USA
(202) 546-2103. Fax: (202) 546-3275. E-mail: rusric@erols.com

damages, collections, commerical law, contracts, corporations, aeronautical/maritime, foreign claims, estates, taxes, government relations, labor relations, immigration, auto/accidents

SANDHU & COMPANY
Advocates & Solicitors
Unit 3, 4 & 5, Block A, Simpang 150, Bangunan Habza
Kg. Kiarong, BSB BE1518
Tel: +673.222.0783
Fax: +673.224.1237
Email: *sandhuco@brunet.bn*

***Services Provided**: insurance, commercial/business law, patents/trademarks/copyrights, civil law, damages, commerical law, contracts, foreign claims, auto/accidents*

8. TRANSPARENCY OF THE REGULATORY SYSTEM

Brunei's foreign direct investment policies are not fully transparent, particularly with respect to limits on foreign equity participation, partnership requirements, and the identification of sectors in which foreign direct investment is restricted.

9. EFFICIENT CAPITAL MARKETS AND PORTFOLIO INVESTMENT

Brunei recently signed a Memorandum of Understanding (MOU) with the Securities Commission Malaysia (SCM) to boost cooperation in the capital markets. The MOU was designed to strengthen collaboration in the development of fair and efficient capital markets in the two countries. It also provided a framework to facilitate greater cross-border capital market activities and cooperation in the areas of regulation as well as capacity building and human capital development, particularly in the area of Islamic capital markets.

10. COMPETITION FROM STATE-OWNED ENTERPRISES (SOES)

Brunei operates state-owned monopolies in key sectors of the economy, such as oil and gas, telecommunications, transport, and energy generation and distribution. However, Brunei has not yet notified its state trading enterprises to the WTO Working Party on State Trading Enterprises. There is no published list of SOE's, but specific examples include:

Semaun Holdings, incorporated as a private limited company, is wholly owned by the Brunei Government. Its emphasis is on joint ventures with foreign investors, mainly in aquaculture, food processing, glass crystal, and hi-tech manufacturing industries which are currently not open for 100% foreign ownership.

Under the Telecommunications Order 2001, the Authority for Info-communications Technology Industry (AiTi) regulates the licensing of the telecommunications industry. The establishment, installation, maintenance, provision or operation of unlicensed telecommunication systems or services within Brunei is a punishable offence, resulting in imprisonment, and large fines. AiTi has not opened up the telecommunications industry for foreign participation. The telecommunications industry is dominated by Telekom Brunei (TelBru) and Data Stream Technologies (DST) Communications, both privatized state companies. Telbru is the sole provider of fixed lines. Its subsidiary company, B-mobile, provides 3G mobile services together with DST. DST is also the sole provider of Global Systems for Mobile communication (GSM) mobile phone service and the sole pay-television service provider.

The Brunei Investment Agency (BIA) manages the Government of Brunei's General Reserve Fund, and their external assets. Established in 1983, its assets are reportedly worth USD$30 billion. It has holdings in corporations, real estate, and currencies. BIA's activities are not publicly disclosed. It is ranked the lowest in transparency ratings by The Sovereign Wealth Fund Institute.

The Royal Brunei Technical Services (RBTS), established in 1988 as a wholly-government owned corporation, is responsible for managing the acquisition of a wide range of systems and equipment and maintaining those acquired systems and equipment.

Brunei National Petroleum Sendirian Berhad (PB) is the national oil company. PB is wholly owned by the Brunei Government and was incorporated on January 14, 2001 as a private limited company. The company was granted all the mineral rights in eight prime onshore and offshore petroleum blocks comprised of the deepwater offshore Blocks CA1 & CA2, inboard offshore Blocks N, P, Q, & B and onshore Blocks L & M totaling 20,552 sq. km. Currently, the company manages the production sharing contractors exploring the onshore and deepwater offshore blocks. The company is also working with the Block B operator in the development of the Maharaja Lela/Jamalulam Field.

11. CORPORATE SOCIAL RESPONSIBILITY (CSR)

Corporate social responsibility (CSR) is still a relatively new concept in Brunei, and there are no specific government programs encouraging foreign and local enterprises to follow generally accepted CSR principles. However there is a general awareness of corporate social responsibility among both producers and consumers, and individual private and public sector organizations have formalized CSR programs and policies.

There are no reporting requirements and no independent NGOs in Brunei that promote or monitor CSR.

12. POLITICAL VIOLENCE

Brunei has no recent history of political violence. The country experienced an uprising in 1962, when it was a British protectorate, which ended through the intervention of British troops. The country has been under emergency law ever since.

13. CORRUPTION

Brunei, since January 1, 1982 has enforced the Emergency (Prevention of Corruption) Act. In 1984, the Act was renamed the Prevention of Corruption Act (Chapter 131).The Anti-Corruption Bureau (ACB) was established on February 1, 1982 for the purpose of enforcing the Act. The Prevention of Corruption Act provides specific powers to the ACB for the purpose of investigating into complaints against corruption. The Act also provides power for ACB to investigate certain offences under the Penal Code and offences under other written laws, provided such offences were disclosed during the course of ACB investigation into offences under the Prevention of Corruption Act.

The ACB strives to ensure a corruption-free public service. Corrupt practices are punishable under the Prevention of Corruption Act. The Act also applies to Brunei citizens abroad. There are perceptions that corruption in the private sector is more prevalent than in the public sector. This has prompted the ACB to focus on the private sector, as the private sector plays a critical role in

Brunei's economic diversification. Brunei is a member of the International Association of Anti-Corruption Authorities.

In Transparency International's Corruption Perception Index (CPI) 2013, Brunei is ranked 60th out of 177 countries.

No U.S. company has identified corruption as an obstacle to conduct business in Brunei.

Resources to report corruption:

Government Point of Contact

Name: Hj Md Juanda Hj A. Rashid
Title: Director
Organization: Anti Corruption Bureau Brunei Darussalam
Address: Old Airport Berakas, BB 3510 Brunei Darussalam
Tel: +673 238-3575 / +673 238-3197
Fax: +673-2383193
Mobile: +673 8721002
Email: **info.bmr@acb.gov.bn**

There are no international, regional, local or nongovernmental organizations operating in the country/economy that monitor corruption.

14. BILATERAL INVESTMENT AGREEMENTS

Brunei is a member of the Association of Southeast Asian Nations (ASEAN), which has Free Trade Agreements (FTA) with Australia, New Zealand, China, India, and South Korea, and a Comprehensive Economic Partnership Agreement with Japan. Brunei is also a party to the Transpacific Strategic Economic Partnership Agreement.

Brunei currently has Bilateral Investment Treaties with China, Germany, India, the Republic of Korea, Oman, and South Africa.

Brunei was the ASEAN Coordinator in negotiations for the **ASEAN-Australia-New Zealand Free Trade Agreement**(AANZFTA), which was signed in Thailand on 27 February 2009 and entered into force on 1 January 2010. Brunei is a negotiating party to the TPP and the Regional Comprehensive Economic Partnership (RCEP).

Brunei was one of the original members of the Trans Pacific Strategic Economic Partnership Agreement (P4), a Free Trade Agreement between Brunei Darussalam, Chile, Singapore and New Zealand signed on 18 July 2005. The P4 later evolved into the Trans-Pacific Partnership (TPP) with the addition of new members, namely the United States, Australia, Peru, Vietnam and Malaysia. The TPP negotiations are currently ongoing.

15. OPIC AND OTHER INVESTMENT INSURANCE PROGRAMS

OPIC and other investment insurance programs are unlikely to operate in Brunei given the country's affluence.

16. LABOR

The 2011 labor force estimate was 185,900 persons with an unemployment rate of 1.7 per cent, according to the Brunei Darussalam Statistical Yearbook 2011.

Brunei relies heavily on foreign labor in lower-skill and lower-paying positions, with approximately 120,000 guest workers brought in to fulfill specific contracts. The largest percentage of those work in construction, followed by wholesale and retail trade and then professional, technical, administrative and support services. Most unskilled laborers in Brunei are immigrants from Indonesia, Malaysia and the Philippines on renewable two year contracts.

The skilled labor pool includes both immigrants on short term visas and Bruneian citizens and permanent residents, who often are well educated but who often prefer to work for the government, with its better benefits such as bonuses, education allowance, interest-free loans, housing allowance, and other benefits, rather than the private sector. Approximately 25% of the total Brunei citizen workforce is employed in the public sector.

Matters relating to labor conditions are covered under the Labor Act, Employment Order 2009 and Workmen's Compensation Act. Expatriate employment is controlled by a Labor Quota system from the Labor Department and the issuance of employment passes, by the Immigration Department.

The Brunei government is actively seeking to increase the number of Bruneians working in the private sector. Brunei's 2014 Energy White Paper calls for the number of persons employed in the energy sector to increase from 20,000 in 2010 to 50,000 in 2035, and for the number of locals employed in the sector to increase from 10,000 to 40,000 in the same period. To advance this goal, all companies competing for a tender in the oil and gas industry are required to have at least half of their employees Bruneians.

The law, including related regulations and statutory instruments, protects the right of workers to form and join unions. Under the Trade Unions Act, unions must be registered with the government. All workers, including civil servants other than those serving in the military and those working as prison guards or police officers, may form and join trade unions of their choice without previous authorization or excessive requirements. Foreign workers are excluded from most labor law protections, including freedom of association. The only union in the country was composed of Brunei Shell Petroleum workers. There were no other active unions or worker organizations.

While the law permits the formation of trade union federations, it forbids affiliation with international labor organizations unless there is consent from the minister of home affairs and the Department of Labor.

The government prohibits strikes, and the law makes no explicit provision for the right to collective bargaining.

The law prohibits employers from discriminating against workers in connection with union activities, but it does not provide for reinstatement for dismissal related to union activity.

There were no reports of government interference in union activity, and worker organizations were independent of the government. Employer discrimination against union members was not reported.

Various domestic laws prohibit the employment of children under age 16. Parental consent and approval by the Labor Commission are required for those under age 18. Female workers under age 18 may not work at night or on offshore oil platforms. The Department of Labor, which is part of the Ministry of Home Affairs, effectively enforced laws related to the employment of children. There were no reports of violations of child labor laws.

The law does not set a minimum wage, but most employed citizens commanded good salaries. Wages for employed foreign residents were wide ranging. Some foreign embassies set minimum wage requirements for their nationals working in the country.

The standard workweek is Monday through Thursday and Saturday, with Friday and Sunday off, allowing for two rest periods of 24 hours each week. The law provides for paid annual holidays, overtime for work in excess of 48 hours per week, and double time for work performed on legal holidays. The law also stipulates that an employee may not work more than 72 hours of overtime a month. Laws regarding hours were frequently not observed in practice.

Occupational health and safety standards were established by government regulations. The Labor Department inspected working conditions both on a routine basis and in response to complaints. There were approximately 40 labor inspectors in the Labor Department in 2013. The government usually moved quickly to investigate abuses, and abusive employers faced criminal and civil penalties. The Labor Department had the power to terminate the license of abusive employers and revoke their foreign labor quota. The majority of abuse cases were settled out of court through agreements where the employer paid financial compensation to the worker.

The government generally enforced labor, health, and safety regulations effectively, but enforcement in the unskilled labor sector was lax. This was true especially for foreign laborers at construction sites, where wage arrears and inadequate safety and living conditions were reported. The government may close a workplace where health, safety, or working conditions are unsatisfactory, but this did not happen during the year.

Government data from 2011, the most recent available, indicated approximately 85,000 foreigners lived in the country temporarily. The law protected the rights of foreign workers through inspections of facilities and a telephone hotline for worker complaints. Immigration law allows for prison sentences and caning for workers who overstay their work permits, for workers who fall into irregular status due to their employers' negligence, for irregular immigrants seeking work, as well as for foreign workers employed by companies other than their initial sponsor. The law also requires recruiting agencies to be registered.

Government mediation by the Labor Department continued to be the most common means used to resolve labor disputes. The commissioner responsible for labor had the additional authority to protect foreign worker rights. The government prosecuted employers who employed irregular immigrants or did not process workers' documents, rendering them irregular. When grievances could not be resolved, regulations require employers to pay for the repatriation of the foreign workers and all outstanding wages. By custom, particularly for low-skilled workers, some employers held employee passports and restricted employee activities during non-work hours.

Foreign workers who filed grievances sometimes did not receive their back wages. Foreign migrant workers often signed contracts with employment agents or other sponsors in their home countries that reduced their promised salaries through payments to the agencies or sponsors. The government forbade wage deductions to agencies or sponsors and mandated that employees receive their full salaries; nevertheless, foreign workers continued to pay high fees to manpower agents to obtain work in the country.

There were cases reported of nonpayment of salaries. The majority of cases involved domestic and construction workers. In many cases courts levied judicial penalties including convictions and fines against employers found guilty of nonpayment of wages.

17. FOREIGN TRADE ZONES/FREE PORTS

Muara Port is Brunei's main seaport with an established Free Trade Zone called the Muara Export Zone (MEZ), which was established to promote and develop Brunei Darussalam as a trade hub of the region. The establishment of the MEZ was an initial step towards developing other Free Trade Zones in the country.

18. FOREIGN DIRECT INVESTMENT AND FOREIGN PORTFOLIO INVESTMENT STATISTICS

Table 1. Foreign Direct Investment Statistics

		2011	2012	2013
ASEAN		7.0	39.3	(72.6)
	Malaysia	4.4	6.5	(57.8)
	Singapore	2.6	32.8	(14.8)
	Others	-		
EUROPEAN UNION		569.7	747.8	753.3
	Germany	-	(20.1)	19.0
	Netherlands	0.9	265.7	143.1
	United Kingdom	565.8	498.7	539.0
	Others	3.0	3.4	52.2
OTHER COUNTRIES		292.7	293.8	227.7
	Hong Kong SAR	17.2	108.8	116.4
	Japan	69.7	69.4	19.8
	USA	23.2	40.1	(6.7)
	Others	182.6	75.4	98.1
TOTAL		869.4	1,080.8	908.4

19. Contact Point at Post for Public Inquiries

Contact at Mission:
Matthew B. Stannard
Political/Economic/Consular Officer
+673 238-4616
stannardmb@state.gov

Foreign Direct Investment and Foreign Portfolio Investment Statistics

TABLE 2: Key Macroeconomic data, U.S. FDI in host country/economy

	Host Country Statistical source*		USG or international statistical source		USG or international Source of Data: BEA; IMF; Eurostat; UNCTAD, Other
Economic Data	Year	Amount	Year	Amount	
Host Country Gross Domestic Product (GDP) (Millions U.S. Dollars)	Insert (Year) 2013	Amount 16,108	Insert (Year) 2012	Amount 16.950	http://data.worldbank.org/country/brunei-darussalam http://www.depd.gov.bn/
Foreign Direct Investment	Host Country Statistical source*		USG or international statistical source		USG or international Source of data: BEA; IMF; Eurostat; UNCTAD, Other
U.S. FDI in partner country (Millions U.S. Dollars, stock positions)	Insert (Year) 2010	Amount 45.5	Insert (Year) 2012	Amount 116.0	(BEA) click selections to reach. Bureau of Economic Analysis Balance of Payments and Direct Investment Position Data U.S. Direct Investment Position Abroad on a Historical-Cost Basis By Country only (all countries) (Millions of Dollars)
Host country's FDI in the United States (Millions U.S. Dollars, stock positions)	Insert (Year)	Amount	Insert (Year) 2012	Amount -6.0	(BEA) click selections to reach Balance of Payments and Direct Investment Position Data Foreign Direct Investment Position in the United States on a Historical-Cost Basis By Country only (all countries) (Millions of Dollars)
Total inbound stock of FDI as % host GDP (calculate)	Amount 7.3%	Insert (Year) 2012	Amount	Insert (Year)	http://www.depd.gov.bn/

Summary - Sources for USG/International Statistics:

U.S. Bureau of Economic Analysis (**http://www.bea.gov/international/index.htm**) produces two types of direct investment statistics:

International transactions & direct investment position statistics

Activities of multinational enterprise statistics

Can be used to assess the effects of multinationals in local economies

http://www.treasury.gov/resource-center/data-chart-center/tic/Pages/index.aspx

Treasury International Capital (TIC) System collects data on portfolio investment – companion data to direct investment, less than 10% ownership.

Data collected on banking, securities, and non-bank assets and liabilities.
Country-level detail available.
http://cdis.imf.org/

IMF compiles data on direct investment from and to individual countries.
Publishes cross tabulations of data.
Users can see at a glance multi-country direct investment data.
Metadata, or methodology, also available.
One stop shopping for direct investment position data
Less detailed than BEA – only total, equity, and debt position data available.

For additional analytical, marketing, investment and business opportunities information, please contact
Global Investment & Business Center, USA
(202) 546-2103. Fax: (202) 546-3275. E-mail: rusric@erols.com

BRUNEI OIL, GAS, AND ENERGY SECTOR - STRATEGIC INFORMATION AND DEVELOPMENTS

OIL AND GAS SECTOR BASICS

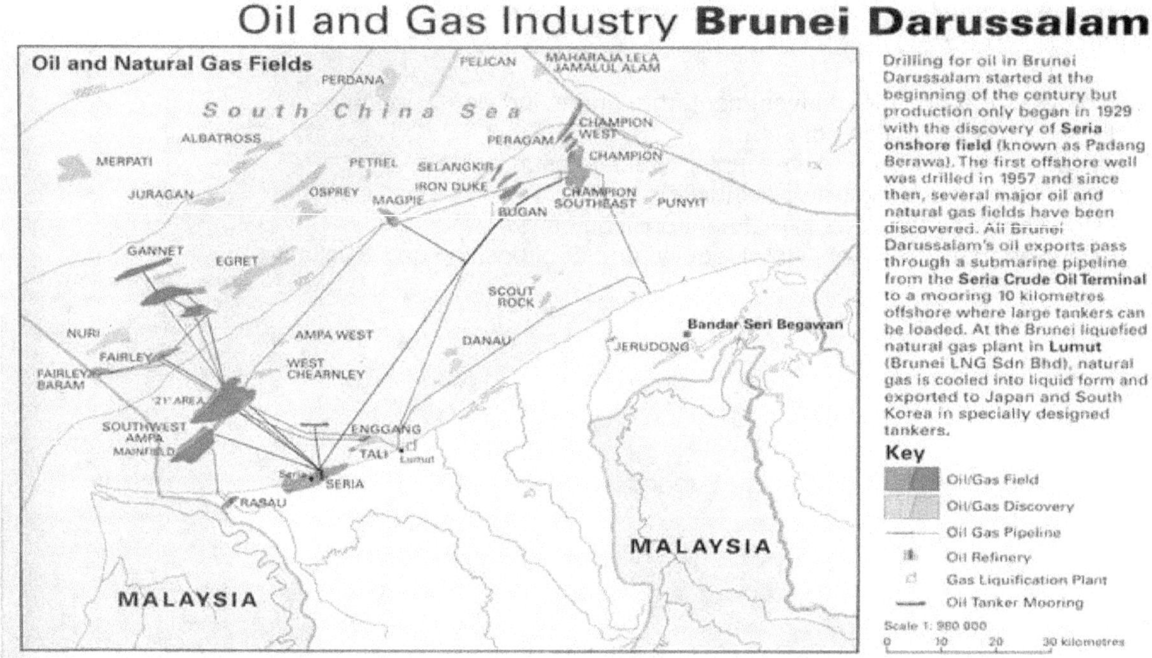

PETROLEUM AND OTHER LIQUIDS

Brunei's proved oil reserve estimate was 1.1 billion barrels as of the beginning of 2016, the fourth highest in Southeast Asia, according to the *Oil and Gas Journal*(OGJ). Through its long-standing joint venture with Royal Dutch Shell, Brunei has produced oil and natural gas for several decades, primarily from two large, mature fields - Southwest Ampa and Champion - in the offshore Baram Delta.

After reaching a peak of 221,000 barrels per day (bbl/d) in 2006, Brunei's petroleum and other liquids production has declined by nearly half to an estimated 125,000 bbl/d in 2015. Many of Brunei's currently-producing oil and natural gas fields are aging, and much of the shallow waters around the country have been explored. Also, several oil facilities have been undergoing refurbishment over the past few years. Maintenance of these facilities is scheduled to be completed by 2016 at the earliest, which could allow production to recover some recent losses.

Brunei has an interest in hydrocarbon development in the South China Sea (SCS), and it makes only one claim in the hotly contested Spratly Islands - the Louisa Reef, a small island that is part of the country's exclusive economic zone and is located in the southeastern part of the Spratly Islands. The Louisa Reef also lies within China's 'nine-dash line', a sizeable claim to the South China Sea which also encompasses all of the Spratly Islands. An offshore settlement with Malaysia in 2010 allows Brunei to explore untapped and formerly disputed deepwater areas in the Baram Delta (namely Commercial Areas 1 and 2) and issue more production sharing contracts to help prop up oil and natural gas production and offset declines from older existing fields.

Petronas of Malaysia and Brunei National Petroleum Company (Petroleum Brunei) signed a 40-year agreement in 2010 to jointly explore these two blocks. In 2013, PetroleumBrunei and Petronas of Malaysia signed several cooperation agreements for joint development of oil and natural gas fields in both countries' deepwater offshore areas. The national oil companies of both countries are actively exploring and anticipate hydrocarbon production in the joint commercial areas to begin by 2021.

Despite the recent decline in production, Brunei is the largest net exporter of petroleum liquids in the Asia-Pacific region given the country's minimal domestic consumption. In 2015, Brunei's net exports of total liquids were about 110,000 bbl/d, primarily crude oil sent to key Asian oil consumers, including Indonesia, Japan,South Korea, China, and Malaysia. Brunei plans to expand its refinery capacity, as Chinese company Zhejiang Hengyi Group has plans to construct a new refinery with a capacity of 148,000 bbl/d. However, the project has encountered several delays since 2011. If built, this new facility could shift the dynamics of the country's oil exports in favor of consuming more crude oil and exporting more petroleum products.

NATURAL GAS

Brunei's proved oil reserve estimate was 13.8 trillion cubic feet as of the beginning of 2016, according to the *Oil and Gas Journal* (OGJ). Brunei produced about 419 billion cubic feet (Bcf) of marketed natural gas in 2014, following a steady decline from a high in 2011 of 452 Bcf. Most of the natural gas output is from Southwest Ampa, Champion, and other fields associated with oil production. Although domestic gas demand has increased steadily in the past decade, Brunei still exports on average about three-quarters of its output. French major Total, made significant natural gas and condensate discoveries in Block B in 2010 which could bolster Brunei's natural gas reserve base, sustain its production levels, and support LNG exports over the next decade. The company plans to add about 30 Bcf/y of production from its second phase of production from the Maharaja Lela field development in 2016 to help offset natural declines and extend the field's output to 2035.

Brunei has been a stable and long-term liquefied natural gas (LNG) exporter to Japan and Korea from its 5-train, 950 million cubic feet per day Lumut LNG liquefaction plant. Brunei exported about 317 Bcf in 2015, a 6% increase from 2014. However, exports have not fully recovered after an 11% drop between 2013 and 2014 as a result of contract changes and growing domestic demands. South Korea and Japan renewed several of their long-term contracts in 2013 for significantly shorter terms, and Japan reduced its contracted volumes. These new contracts are set to expire by 2023. The drop in contracted LNG exports has prompted Brunei LNG to sell to other regional buyers and seek short-term contracts or spot cargo sales. Brunei LNG signed a 10-year contract with Petronas of Malaysia starting in 2013 and began sending spot cargoes to other Asian consumers, including India, China, and Taiwan. Brunei's increasing domestic demand for natural gas from the power and petrochemical sectors is likely to compete with LNG exports, and more of the country's gas production could shift to domestic needs.

The oil and gas industry remains the fundamental sector in Brunei's economy and it continues to play a dominant role even as the nation strives to diversify into non-oil industrialization.

The government's policy, initiated in 1988, is to conserve this natural resource by reducing production of crude oil to around 150,000 barrels per day (b/d).

At the same time, the search for new reserves and for alternative sources of energy is being intensified.

For additional analytical, marketing, investment and business opportunities information, please contact
Global Investment & Business Center, USA
(202) 546-2103. Fax: (202) 546-3275. E-mail: rusric@erols.com

Brunei Shell Petroleum Sendirian Berhad (BSP) announced a major gas discovery in July 1995 at Selangkir-1 well, which is about 12 kilometers west of the Champion Field.

BSP has seven offshore oil fields, including Champion. The others are Southwest Ampa, Fairley, Fairley-Baram (which is shared with Malaysia), Magpie, Gannet and Iron Duke -BSP's newest field which came on stream in 1992. Two more fields are situated onshore.

The Brunei Government is an equal partner with the Royal Dutch Shell Company. Besides Shell, another active concession holder is Jasra-Elf.

Based in Brunei Darussalam since 1986, the Jasra-Elf Joint Venture has been actively exploring for hydrocarbons offshore and has made some discoveries, in particular in the Maharaja Lela Field (Block B).

Having confirmed technically that there is a significant amount of oil and gas reserves in this field, the Joint Venture is presently concentrating its efforts towards the development and production of these reserves in the most efficient and optimized way.

The country's production of oil reached a peak of 250,000 b/d 1979 but in the Eighties, a ceiling of about 150,000 b/d was introduced. In 1991, production went up to 162,000 b/d, rising to 180,000 b/d in 1992 and falling slightly to 174,000 b/d in 1993.

At the current rate of extraction, it is estimated that the country's oil reserve would run out in about 27 years' time.

Some 40 per cent of the country's reserves are found in the Champion Field, which is situated in 30 meters of water about 70 km north-east of Seria. This field produces more than 50,000 b/d.

The oldest field is Southwest Ampa, 13 kilometers off Kuala Belait. It holds more than half of Brunei's total gas reserves and the gas production accounts for 60 per cent of the country's total output.

The onshore oilfield in Seria, which is the country's first oil well drilled in 1929, still produces around 10,000 b/d used mainly for domestic consumption. On the domestic market, unleaded petrol was introduced in 1992.

The main foreign markets for Brunei's crude oil are Thailand, Singapore, the Philippines, Australia, China, Japan, South Korea, Taiwan and the United States of America.

The contribution of crude oil to the country's Gross Domestic Product has seen a decline from 88 per cent in 1974 to 58 per cent in 1990. In terms of employment, the oil and gas sector's share of the total labor force was only 5 per cent in 1990.

This means it has the highest value-added ratio per worker and labor productivity remains highest among all sectors while its workers are among the highest paid in the country.

Brunei is the world's fourth largest producer of liquefied natural gas (LNG). The current gas production is approximately 27 million cubic meters per day, and 90 per cent of it is exported to Japan, namely the Tokyo Electric, Tokyo Gas and Osaka Gas Companies.

The Japanese companies and Brunei Coldgas of Brunei LNG signed a further 20-year contract in 1993. The new contract is believed to have raised the quantity and price of gas.

The Brunei Liquefied Natural Gas plant in Lumut, one of the largest in the world, was upgraded and expanded at a cost of around B$100 million in 1993.

The LNG from the plant is transported to Japan by a fleet of seven specially-designed 100,000-tonne tankers with a capacity of 73,000 cubic meters of LNG each. The sale of LNG has grown to be as important a revenue earner as oil exports.

The domestic market takes up only 2 per cent of the LNG produced.

At the current rate of production, the proven reserves of natural gas is estimated to last another 40 years.

However, the discoveries of new gas fields and the possibility of more finds will enable Brunei to benefit from the growing demand for LNG in Asia, which is needed primarily for power generation.

Despite the uncertainty that surrounds the global oil market, the hydrocarbon industry looks set to continue to be the beacon of Brunei's economy. The Brunei Petrochemical Industry Master Plan, completed in May 2001, has identified a number of potential petrochemical industries - both upstream and downstream - for development over the next decades.

Brunei has been described as "the next epicenter of deepwater activity in Asia." Deepwater exploration for oil and gas is going on strong in Brunei, with a number of offshore acreages awarded to major prospectors in the industry.
In 1982, Brunei made legal claims to its EEZ, allowing the Sultanate to take measures to tap the wealth potential of its offshore areas. But Brunei has been prospecting offshore for oil since the 1960s. The first offshore discovery was made in 1963, at the South West Ampa Offshore Field.

DEEPWATER DRILLING

Deepwater drilling allows:

1. for the full realisation of the country's potential oil and gas reserves
2. for the tapping of mature fields to their full potential, with the advent of new technologies
3. for the rejuvenation of existing fields and infrastructures

Deepwater prospecting in Brunei takes place in blocks located some 200 kilometres off the country's coastline, but still within its EEZ. Drilling would be conducted into waters between 1.5 to 2.5 kilometres deep.

Brunei is fortunate in that the waters of the South China Sea where the prospecting takes place is rather calm, posing very little or no threat at all to the safety of drilling rigs. Ultra deepwater drilling is, however, relatively new to Brunei. Thus far, only two ultra deepwater blocks - of 10,000 square kilometers each - had been awarded to drilling consortia, consisting of major players in the global oil and gas industry.

TotalFinaElf owns 60% of the consortium that operates in Block J, followed by BHP Billiton with 25% and Amerada Hess with 15%. The Block K group, meanwhile, consists of Shell (50%), Conoco (25%) and Mitsubishi (25%).

For additional analytical, marketing, investment and business opportunities information, please contact
Global Investment & Business Center, USA
(202) 546-2103. Fax: (202) 546-3275. E-mail: rusric@erols.com

An average of 50 producer and injection wells are anticipated for each drilling field, which should result in a massive drilling activity in the next 10 to15 years, involving a very high demand for specialised technology and engineering services.

It is hoped that deepwater-drilling endeavours in Brunei would also result in a transfer of new technology and skills to benefit locals. These activities are also expected to stimulate business activities in support services and create new job opportunities, as well as increase the number of local and international joint venture opportunities.

THE FUTURE OF OIL

Economic and social development in Asia over the next decades will fuel the need for power supply, vis-a-vis oil and gas, to drive generators. Worldwide demand for oil is expected to increase some 60% in the next 25 years, with an "economically buoyant" Asia to lead the rise, said industry experts during the OSEA 2002 oil and gas conference in Singapore in October 2002.

"Energy consumption continues to grow especially in the Asia-Pacific region," an industry captain said. "This growing trend shows a greater increasing demand for gas to be used for power generation and this will continue to fuel the development of offshore oil fields."

Rising demand for oil and gas will drive the sector in the medium and long term, especially in the "increasingly popular" field of deep-sea exploration for natural gas deposits, experts said.

By 2020, Asia will be the largest net importer of oil, "surpassing Europe and North America," said Singapore's Minister of State for Foreign Affairs and Trade, Raymond Lim at the conference. The demand for gas is projected to exceed the demand for oil as well by 2020.

All these bode well for the Brunei hydrocarbons industry, as it endeavours to tap its vast offshore oil and gas potential. The move to explore the deep waters of Brunei presents both risks and opportunities, wrote the Managing Director of TotalFinaElf John Perry in the magazine 'Asia Inc'.

"In their location and required technology, the deep water permits are literally at the frontier of exploration and production activities," he added. "Developing oil and gas fields in 2,000 metres of water is no easy business. It carries significant risk and huge costs, perhaps US$3-4 billion to develop a commercial discovery.

"Yet, the potential is there to succeed."

Success, he said, will take not just the form of a revenue stream for His Majesty's Government, but will also provide a "stable economic base, founded on a global commodity, to enable Brunei's economy to diversify beyond the oil and gas sector."

But the country is not going just upstream with its deepwater ventures. The afore-mentioned Petrochemical Industry Master Plan also has a number of downstream industries that could be developed to complement the new drilling activities in Brunei. For instance, the Plan mentioned methane-based industries like the production of ammonia, urea and methanol from hydrocarbon derivatives; olefins and aromatic derivatives from naphtha crackers, "with the possible integration with a refinery" and energy-intensive activities like aluminium smelting.

DOWNSTREAM ACTIVITIES

For additional analytical, marketing, investment and business opportunities information, please contact
Global Investment & Business Center, USA
(202) 546-2103. Fax: (202) 546-3275. E-mail: rusric@erols.com

Indeed, the Government has set aside two sites for use of such downstream industries. The 1,000sq km Pulau Muara Besar, located just across the Muara deepwater port, will be used for the development of integrated petrochemical projects in the mid-term. In addition, the 230 hectare Sungai Liang site is "readily available for development", complete with existing gas pipelines to the nearby Lumut BLNG plant, as well as the TFE onshore gas processing plant.

The Sungai Liang site is given "priority" for immediate development, especially for stand-alone projects.

The Government agency that oversees the oil and gas industry in Brunei is PetroleumBRUNEI. It was formed in 2001 to:
1. strengthen and to push, and to jointly spearhead the development of the local petroleum industry
2. play a more active role in the exploration and development of the petroleum industry
3. accelerate economic development based on the domestic petroleum industry

Still, "gas is the energy of the future," Perry wrote. The GASEX gathering in May 2002 - a "quality event" which attracted "quality delegates" - was an indication of the high regard Brunei is held in the gas industry.

The Minister of Industry and Primary Resources, Pehin Dato Hj Abd Rahman, in his capacity as chairman of the Brunei Oil and Gas Authority (BOGA), in 2001 said: "The Government of His Majesty continues to place a great importance on the long-term sale of LNG in generating revenue, while at the same time strengthening efforts in diversifying its economy from non-renewable resources.

"Having said that, the government has also ensured that sufficient gas will be made available to fulfil the nation's energy requirements well into the next millennium."

OIL & GAS ACTIVITIES & OPPORTUNITIES

UPSTREAM ACTIVITIES

Concession Areas

The Petroleum Unit, on behalf of the Government of His Majesty the Sultan and Yang Di-Pertuan of Brunei Darussalam, controls and oversees all activities that are carried out by concessionaires in relation to their concessions. At present, a total area of 11,000 square kilometres is being held by two concessionaires.

One of the concessionaires, Brunei Shell Petroleum, is a company jointly owned by the Government of His Majesty the Sultan and Yang Di-Pertuan of Negara Brunei Darussalam and Royal Dutch Shell.

Conservation Policy

Beginning 1981, Brunei Darussalam introduced a conservation policy whereby production was gradually reduced from a peak of 261,000 barrel per day (bpd) to 150,000 bpd. The said conservation level was reached in 1988.

For additional analytical, marketing, investment and business opportunities information, please contact
Global Investment & Business Center, USA
(202) 546-2103. Fax: (202) 546-3275. E-mail: rusric@erols.com

Export Destinations

Brunei crude oil is exported to various countries including several ASEAN countries, e.g., Indonesia, Singapore and Thailand. In year 2004, Thailand is the main export destination for Brunei Darussalam crude oil, i.e., 31.38% from the overall export. This is followed by Japan (17.73%), South Korea (14.66%), U.S.A (10.75%), Australia (8.75%), India (6.24%), Singapore (5.25 %), New Zealand (2.25 %), China (2.12 %) and Indonesia (0.86%).

Open Areas

There are currently more than 38,229 sq. km. of open areas available for future exploration activities. These areas, divided into blocks, include the Brunei Muara, Tutong, Temburong, rural area of Belait District and several areas of Brunei water up to 200 nautical miles within the Brunei Exclusive Economic Zone.

DOWNSTREAM ACTIVITIES

Oil Refinery

The Seria Oil Refinery, operated by Brunei Shell Petroleum and situated at the oil town of Seria in the Belait District, has a production capacity of 10,000 bpd each for its Crude Distillation Unit (CDU) and Reformer unit. This refinery produces unleaded motor gasoline, gasoil, Jet A1, and Kerosene.

LNG Plant

Natural gas produced from Brunei oil fields is exported as liquefied natural gas (LNG) to three buyers in Japan namely Tokyo Gas, Tokyo Electric, and Osaka Gas and one buyer

from South Korea, Korea gas Corporation. The LNG is processed at Brunei LNG Sdn. Bhd. Plant at Lumut, Seria. In year 2004, LNG exports amounted to 192 'B-Class' cargoes where 88.48% are exported to Japan and the rest (11.52%) are exported to South Korea.

Brunei Export Oriented Refinery

For additional analytical, marketing, investment and business opportunities information, please contact
Global Investment & Business Center, USA
(202) 546-2103. Fax: (202) 546-3275. E-mail: rusric@erols.com

The Government of His Majesty the Sultan and Yang Di-Pertuan of Negara Brunei Darussalam, through the Petroleum Unit, is actively promoting the setting up of export oriented oil refineries in the country. Several studies, made under Memorandum of Understanding between His Majesty Government and international consortiums are currently being carried out to study the feasibility of producing petrochemical by-products for exports to other countries in the region.

EXPLORATION

PetroleumBRUNEI was granted all mineral rights to prime petroleum blocks, covering a total of approximately 21,000 sq. km. The deepwater offshore blocks are Blocks CA1 and CA2, shallow offshore blocks are Blocks N, P, Q, and B while the onshore block are Block L and M. PetroleumBRUNEI's upstream business is conducted in Brunei and abroad including activities in the fields of exploration and production.

DOMESTIC - BLOCK A & B

PetroleumBRUNEI is an active partner in the operation of two blocks via its upstream subsidiary, PB ExPro Sdn Bhd. PB ExPro offers its own expertise to the operators and partners in its 46% equity in Block A and 27.5% equity in Block B.

Currently, exploration and potential development activities are actively being pursued in Block A. Meanwhile, Block B has been in production since 1999 and a new Maharaja Lela South (MLS) projects is being executed to increase in production level to approximately 33,000 boe per day by 2016.

INTERNATIONAL - BLOCK SK318, SARAWAK, MALAYSIA

PB ExPro has completed farm-in process for 10% equity into SK318 Block in October 2014. This project is one of the International investment in the upstream for exploration and production by PetroleumBRUNEI. The block is located offshore Sarawak, Malaysia some 250km North East of Bintulu. The partnerships are between Sarawak Shell Berhad, PETRONAS Carigali and PB ExPro for which Sarawak Shell Berhad is the Operator.

INTERNATIONAL - INTEGRATED SHALE GAS TO LNG PROJECT, BRITISH COLUMBIA, CANADA

PetroleumBRUNEI has acquired a 3 % interest in an integrated Shale Gas to LNG project in Canada on a 'stapled' basis, holding 3 percent interest in all the entities across the value chain. This is the first international venture for PetroleumBRUNEI.

INTERNATIONAL - BLOCK EP-1, MYANMAR

PetroleumBRUNEI was awarded Block EP-1, onshore Kyaukkyi-Mindon Area on 19 November 2013 after participating in the 2013 Myanmar Onshore Bidding Round.

The onshore Block EP-1 is located 250km north of Yangon covering an area of 1,135 km2. PetroleumBRUNEI will be the operator of the Block with 87.25% interest while the local partner IGE Pte Ltd holds an interest of 12.75%.

Block EP-1 is the key milestone for PetroleumBRUNEI as a full-pledge operator in its journey towards increasing international investments.

OIL AND GAS PRODUCTION SHARING CONTRACTS

Oil and gas production activities in Brunei are currently governed by the terms of Production Sharing Contracts (PSC).

The key components of Brunei fiscal regime for oil and natural gas development include Royalty, Cost Recovery, Profit Sharing and Income Tax. These are described below.

ROYALTY

In the 2000 model agreement, for onshore fields, the royalty rate is 12.5% and for deepwater developments, the royalty rate is 8%.

Under concessions awarded before the 2001 bidding round, the royalty rates depend on the location of the developments. The rate is 12.5% for onshore fields, 10% for discoveries between three and ten nautical miles offshore and 8% for discoveries more than ten nautical miles offshore.

COST RECOVERY

After Royalty, the contractors are allowed to recover costs from the Gross Revenue, subjected to a negotiated cost recovery ceiling. The cost recovery ceilings announced in the government's bid presentation on 23 October 2000 are 60% for oil discoveries and 70% for gas discoveries onshore and 80% for oil discoveries and gas discoveries in deepwater. Costs can be recovered under the Brunei PSCs include exploration and appraisal costs, development costs, operating costs, abandonment sinking fund and excess revenue payments. All costs are expensed and recovered immediately. Unrecovered costs are carried forward indefinitely until fully recovered but not beyond the duration of the contract.

PROFIT SHARING

The revenue remaining after Royalty and Cost Recovery is Profit Petroleum which is shared between the contractors and the State at negotiable rates on an incremental sliding scale depending on the production rate. The profit shares indicated in the government's bid presentation of 23 October 2000 are given inTable 45 and Table 46.

PROFIT SHARING IN BRUNEI ONSHORE PSCS

Production		Contractors' Profit Share
Oil	Gas (Tcf)	
0 – 10 Mbbl/d		50%
10 – 25 Mbbl/d		40%
> 25 Mbbl/d	–	30%
> 50 MMbbl cumulative production		50%
	0 – 2	50%
–	> 2	40%

PROFIT SHARING IN BRUNEI OFFSHORE PSCS

Production		
Oil	Gas (Tcf)	Contractors' Profit Share

0 – 50 Mbbl/d		75%
50 – 100 Mbbl/d		65%
> 100 Mbbl/d	–	60%
> 200 MMbbl cumulative production		50%
	0 – 4	60%
–	> 4	30%

INCOME TAX

The petroleum income tax rate in Brunei is 55%.

The deductions for income tax include exploration costs, operating costs, royalty and depreciation. Exploration costs and operating costs are immediately deductible. Capital costs are depreciated on a straight line basis over different periods of time depending on the category of expenditure.

SELECTED TENDER OPPORTUNITIES

Contract Title	Work Category	LBD Quadrant	Planned Tender Date	Closing Tender Date	Expected Contract Duration	Current Status
PPE Award	96AAAA - Fire/Safety/Envir. Eqp	Basic	7/7/2015	8/7/2015	3 years	Evaluation
Provision Of Integrated Fluid Management Services	Drilling Fluids Services	Core	9/1/2015	4/8/2016	3 yrs with (3x) 1 yr extension option	Evaluation
Supply Of Batteries	C&A/ Electrical	Highly Specialised	9/1/2015	10/1/2015	3 years	Awarded
Small Tools	Mechanical	Basic	9/1/2015	10/1/2015	3 years	Evaluation
Provision For Stimulation/Ctu Services	Coiled Tubing Services (Offshore)	Core	10/1/2015	1/11/2016	Package 1: 3 years with (2x) 1-year extension options Package 2: 5 years with (2x) 1-year extension options	Evaluation

For additional analytical, marketing, investment and business opportunities information, please contact
Global Investment & Business Center, USA
(202) 546-2103. Fax: (202) 546-3275. E-mail: rusric@erols.com

2015 Marine Vessel Tender	Marine	Development	11/1/2015	3/1/2016	2,3,5 years depending on vessel	Evaluation
Seabed Soil Sampling & Analysis	Geosciences	Highy Specialised	11/1/2015		3 yrs with 1 yr extension option	Evaluation
The Provision Of Safehouse Habitat and its associated services	Well Control Support Services	Highly Specialised	12/1/2015	3/1/2016	3 yrs with 2 yr extension option	Awarded
2015 Newbuild Vessel Tender	Marine	Development	12/31/2015	3/2/2016	10 years	Evaluation
Provision Of Beam Pump Equipment And Associated Services	Production String Components and Subsurface Pumps	Highly Specialised	1/1/2016	4/15/2016	2 years	Issued
Provision of Infrastructure, Utilities Field Facilities Maintenance Services	Civil Infrastructure	Development	1/10/2016	1/15/2016	3 years with extension options	Evaluation
Industrial Building Maintenance Services	Civil Industrial Building	Development	2/1/2016	3/1/2016	3 years with extension options	Issued
Provision of Security Personnel & Services	Security Services	Basic	2/20/2016	4/11/2016	5 years	Issued
Darat Gas Cofferdam	Civil Industrial Building	Development	2/26/2016	4/8/2016	1 year	Issued
Provision Of Well Abandonment Services	Well Abandonment Services	Development	3/1/2016	4/4/2016	4 years	Issued

SCOT OES SPM Replacement Strategy, Sourcing	Marine Equipment & Offshore Installation	Highly Specialised	3/1/2016	4/29/2016	22 months	Issued
Civil Domestic Maintenance Services	Civil Domestic	Basic	3/1/2016	4/1/2016	3 years with extension options	Issued
Business Travel Tender to Award	Corporate Services, Travel	Basic	4/1/2016	5/1/2016	3 years	Not Yet Issued
Provision Of H2S Equipment And Services	HSE Risk Assessment Services	Highly Specialised	4/1/2016	5/9/2016	3 years with 2 years extension option	Not Yet Issued
Provision Of Low & Medium Capacity Cranes	Land	Development	4/1/2016		5 years	Not Yet Issued
BSM Aviation Refuelling Liability Insurance	Corporate Services, insurance	Core	4/1/2016	5/1/2016	NIL	Not Yet Issued
Plant Air Conditioning And Commercial Refrigeration Equipment Maintenance Services	Air-Conditioning Gas Fired Unit, Package Chillers, Plant	Core	4/1/2016		TBA	Not Yet Issued
Provision Of RTOC & Mudlogging Services	Well Intervention Services	Core	5/1/2016		TBA	Not Yet Issued
Marine Vessel Tank Cleaning	Marine	Core	5/1/2016		TBA	Not Yet Issued
2016 Marine Tender	Marine	Development	5/1/2016	6/1/2016	3, 5 years depending	Not Yet Issued

					on vessel	
Onshore Maintenance, Operatios and Projects (OMOP)	Onshore Construction and Maintenance	Core	6/1/2016		5 years	Not Yet Issued
Restoration of Process Tanks	Onshore Construction and Maintenance	Development	7/1/2016		5 years	Not Yet Issued
HRL Training Services	Training, Technical	Highly Specialised	12/1/2016	12/1/2016	3 years	Not Yet Issued

OIL AND GAS SECTOR POLICY

The export of oil and gas has dominated Brunei's economy since the 1930s and the oil and gas sector accounts for over two thirds of nominal GDP and generates more than 90% of total export earnings and government revenues. Wealth from oil and gas provides Brunei's small population with a relatively high standard of living compared with its ASEAN neighbours.

PRODUCTION AND TRADE

Brunei is the fourth-largest oil producer in South East Asia and is the ninth-largest exporter of liquefied natural gas in the world. Brunei's economy has followed the swings of the world oil market; economic growth has averaged around 2.6% in the 2000s, heavily dependent on oil and gas production. Oil production averaged slightly over 200,000 barrels a day during the period under review. The output target is flexible, however, and production in 2006 was 219,000 barrels per day, up from average annual production of 201,000 b/d in 2005 and 206,000 b/d in 2004 (Table IV.2); this allowed Brunei to take advantage of the high oil prices in 2006, which rose to US$69.4/b up from US$57.7/b in 2005 and US$41.7/b a year earlier.

Petroleum and natural gas production, export and domestic consumption, 2001-07

	2001	2002	2003	2004	2005	2006	2007[a]
Production							
Petroleum ('000 barrels/ day)	195	203	207	206	201	219	197
Natural gas (MMscf / day)	1,133	1,143	1,236	1,214	1,191	1,259	1,195
Export							
Petroleum ('000 b/day)	189	199	199	196	193	206	..
LNG (MMBtu/day)	948,803	965,799	1.01 mn	1.00 mn	977,397	1.03 mn	..
Price							
Oil (US$/barrel)	24.67	24.82	30.52	41.72	57.72	69.44	..
LNG (US$/MMBtu)	4.4137	4.1745	4.5451	4.9110	5.6723	5.9131	..
Domestic consumption							
Mogas, diesel, Jet A-1, other ('000 barrels)	3,281	3,493	3,617	3,691	3,818	3,996	..
Gas (MMscf/day)	145	145	146	162	167	167	..

Not available.
a Estimates.
Source: Department of Economic Planning and Development, *Brunei Darussalam Key Indicators 2001-2006*; and data provided by the authorities.

In 2006, Brunei consumed an estimated 13,000 barrels/day of oil; most crude oil production is exported to other countries in the region. Oil exports of 206,000 b/d were recorded in 2006, up from 193,000 b/d in 2005. Despite Brunei's status as a net exporter of oil, it imports about half of the refined petroleum products it consumes, as has limited domestic refining capacity.

In 2006, Brunei produced over 1,200 million standard cubic feet (MMscf) of natural gas per day (Table IV.2), which translated into a liquefied natural gas output that has fluctuated at around 1,000 trillion btu (British thermal units) per day during review period.

Brunei's wealth is based on its hydrocarbon reserves, which were at 1.1 billion barrels of mainly low-sulphur oil in January 2007.

- 1 According to two reports, Brunei's oil reserves are expected to last 25 years or only another 10 years, at current rates of extraction.1 Brunei's gas reserves have been estimated at 390 billion cu metres, and are expected to last another 40 years. The Government aims to conserve resources and continue exploration to open new fields; in early 2006, a consortium led by Canada's Loon Energy was awarded a 2,253 sq km oil exploration block. A 3,011 sq km block covering most of Brunei's Belait district was also awarded to a consortium led by the UK-registered Valiant International Petroleum.

However, the development of offshore areas is hampered by a territorial dispute with Malaysia. In 2003, Malaysia disputed Brunei-awarded oil exploration concessions for offshore blocks J and K (Total and Shell, respectively), which led to a moratorium on exploration activities in the areas.

- 1 Negotiations in order to resolve the conflict are continuing.

According to export figures for the first half of 2006, Indonesia, Australia, and Korea took about 67% of Brunei's total crude exports; traditional customers Japan, the United States, and China each took between 5% and 8% (Table IV.3). Brunei is one of the world's largest producers of liquefied natural gas (LNG), the bulk of which (over 5 million tonnes) is purchased by three Japanese utility companies under a long-term contract signed in 1972 and extended for 20 years in 1993. The Japanese company Mitsubishi is a joint venture partner with Shell and the Brunei Government in Brunei LNG Sdn Bhd, Brunei gas Carriers Sdn Bhd, and Brunei Shell Tankers Sdn Bhd, which produce the LNG. The second largest market is South Korea

- 1, which accounts for around 10% of total LNG exports.

Oil and gas exports by destination (% share), 2002-06

(B$ million and per cent)

- [1] U.S. Energy Information Administration (2006).
- [2] EIU (2007), p. 9; and Rabobank, Economic Research Department (2007).
- [3] In April 2003, several naval patrol boats from Malaysia are alleged to have chased away a Total ship in the disputed area in the South China Sea. Malaysia has extended its territorial claims into seas that Brunei says are in its Exclusive Economic Zone.
- [4] Brunei started to export LNG to the Korea Gas Corporation (KOGAS) in 1994 (0.27 million tonnes); it signed a two-year contract with the KOGAS in 1994 for 0.7 million tonnes per year to be delivered in 1995 and 1996. A long-term contract was signed in 1997 to supply similar amounts for 16 years.

	2002	2003	2004	2005	2006[a]
Crude petroleum					
Total (B$ million)	3,140	3,759	4,913	6,536	4,197
Australia	18	17	20	15	17
China	13	14	7	6	5
Indonesia	2	5	11	30	33
Japan	12	12	13	13	8
Korea	14	16	15	16	17
Thailand	25	19	12	4	3
United States	11	8	6	8	7
Others	5	9	16	8	10
Natural gas					
Total (B$ million)	2,604	2,964	2,564	2,983	1,462
Japan	87	91	88	92	86
Korea	11	9	12	8	14
Others	2	-	-	-	-

aJanuary-June.

Source: Brunei Darussalam Key Indicators 2002-2006, Department of Statistics, Report of Economic Planning and Development; and Brunei authorities.

OIL AND GAS INDUSTRY

Brunei's oil industry is largely dominated by Brunei Shell Petroleum (BSP), a joint venture owned in equal shares by the Brunei Government and the Asiatic Petroleum Company Ltd. BSP had a monopoly on all upstream and downstream activities until 1999, when the Government awarded some exploration blocks to other companies, notably Total E&P Borneo BV

- 1, which started production from offshore Block B.

BSP is the leading oil and gas production company in Brunei and operates the only refinery, which meets domestic demand for most petroleum products. BSP, BLNG, Brunei Shell marketing Company Sdn Bhd (BSM) and BST together constitute the largest employer in Brunei after the Government (Table IV.4) with some 4,000 personnel, of which 90% are Bruneians.

- 1

Overview of Brunei Shell Petroleum, 2006

Company	Ownership	Operations	Daily/annual output	Staff
Brunei Shell Petroleum (BSP)	Jointly owned by Brunei Goverment 50% and Asiatic Petroleum (part	11 offshore and 4 onshore oilfields (South West Ampa, Fairley Baram, Fairley, Gannet, Egret, Champion,	Oil – 213.8 Kbbl/d Gas – 31.5 Mil m3/d	3,116

- [5] Previously Total Fina Elf.
- [6] Prime Minister's Office (2007).

For additional analytical, marketing, investment and business opportunities information, please contact
Global Investment & Business Center, USA
(202) 546-2103. Fax: (202) 546-3275. E-mail: rusric@erols.com

	of Royal Dutch Shell group) 50%	Champion West, Bugan, Iron Duke, Magpie, Peragam. Asam Paya, Rasau, Enggang, Seria) 645 producing reservoirs, 837 producing wells, 1,188 pipelines Brunei's only petrol refinery		
Brunei Liquefied Natural Gas (BLNG)	Jointly owned by Brunei Government 50%, Shell Overseas trading 25%, Mitsubishi 25%	World's 3rd commercial LNG plant Plant has 5 LNG trains with a capacity of 44 cu m/hour	..	514
Brunei Shell Tankers (BST)	Jointly owned by Brunei Government 50% and Shell 25% and Mitsubishi 25%	Owns 7 B-class LNG tankers chartered to BLNG to transport liquefied natural gas	..	300
Brunei Shell Marketing (BSM)	Jointly owned by Brunei Government 50% and Shell Overseas Holdings 50%	Supply and marketing of petroleum products[a] in Brunei supplied by BSP refinery 36 land-based retail stations and 3 riversine station storage facilities at Muara Port and Brunei International Airport	..	67
Total E&P Borneo BV	Jointly owned by Brunei Government, Total and Shell Deepwater	Block B Joint Venture's (BBJV) Maharaja Lela field	Oil – 5.5 Kbbl/d Gas – 3.94 Mil m3/d	..
Brunei Gas Carrier (BGC)	Jointly owned by Brunei Government 80%, Shell 10% and Mitsubishi 10%	Owns one A-class LNG tanker (owned by Brunei Gas Carriers[b] or BGC) named ABADI, chartered to BLNG to transport liquefied natural gas	..	15

Not available.
a End-user prices of petroleum products (gasoline, diesel, kerosene and bottled LPG) have been regulated since 1978 under Price Stabilization Agreement signed by the Government and BSM, under which the Government subsidizes end-user prices if the price of crude rises above a certain level.
b Established in 1998 and jointly owned by the Government of Brunei, Shell Gas and Mitsubishi.
Source: BSP Annual Review 2005; and Brunei authorities.

Natural gas is also used domestically for petroleum operators' own-use, power generation, liquefied petroleum gas (LPG) used domestically, and as a reserve for industrial purposes. Approximately 90% of Brunei's natural gas is exported as LNG by BLNG. Petroleum products for local consumption are marketed solely by BSM, jointly owned by the Government of Brunei and Shell Overseas Holdings Ltd. Retail/end-user prices of gasoline, diesel, kerosene, and bottled LPG have been regulated since 1978, under a Price Stabilization Agreement (PSA) between the Government and BSM, under which the Government subsidizes prices if the price of crude oil rises above a certain level. According to the authorities, the subsidization costs over B$200 million per year.

PETROLEUM REFINING AND OTHER DOWNSTREAM ACTIVITIES

The Government encourages diversification, including downstream activities related to the petroleum and natural gas sector. At present, around 93% of Brunei's petroleum and 90% of its natural gas output is exported as crude oil and LNG, respectively. The remaining crude oil output is refined for domestic use. Brunei's only refinery, located in Seria, has a capacity of 10,000 bpd for its crude distillation unit and 6,000 bpd for its reformer unit. The main products include unleaded gasoline, gasoil, Jet A1 fuel, and kerosene.

The Government is keen to encourage investment in downstream activities and has set aside a trillion cubic feet of gas for industrial use. In 2006, an MoU was signed for the Gas Sales and Supply Agreement between BSP Co. Sdn Bhd and a consortium comprising Itochu, Mitsubishi Gas Corporation and Petroleum Brunei; a marketing agreement was also signed for the methanol plant located at the Sungai Liang Industrial Complex.

Under the Income Tax (Petroleum) Act, Cap. 119 (Laws of Brunei revised edition, 1984), Brunei levies a corporate tax on petroleum and gas operations at a rate of 55%. Royalties and petroleum income tax are payable on both concessions and production sharing agreements.

POLICY

In 2002, the Government established the Brunei's first national oil company, the Brunei National Petroleum Company Sdn Bhd, also known as Petroleum Brunei. Petroleum Brunei is responsible for managing assets in designated areas (Blocks J, K, L and M). It has chosen to award private companies the exploration rights for the blocks it controls. Despite efforts to introduce competition, BSP is likely to remain the dominant oil producer by virtue of its control of Brunei's major oil and natural gas fields. In 2003, BSP signed an extension of the petroleum mining agreements with the Government for a further 19 years until the end of 2022.

The Petroleum Unit, established in 1982 under the Prime Minister's Department, is the principal regulator of the petroleum and gas sector in Brunei. The Petroleum Unit reports to the Minister of Energy, whose portfolio was created in May 2005. The Unit's responsibilities include: overseeing the exploitation of Brunei's petroleum and gas reserves, and promoting the development of downstream industries; fixing crude oil prices; and ensuring compliance with internationally acceptable technical, accounting, health and safety, and environmental standards.

Under the Petroleum Mining Act (Chapter 44 of the Laws of Brunei, revised edition 2002), investors, including foreign investors, may apply for petroleum mining agreements in respect of

[7] The agreements – the Onshore Petroleum Mining Agreement and the consolidated First and Second Offshore Petroleum Agreement

For additional analytical, marketing, investment and business opportunities information, please contact
Global Investment & Business Center, USA
(202) 546-2103. Fax: (202) 546-3275. E-mail: rusric@erols.com

state land, whether onshore or offshore; the applications are considered by the Sultan of Brunei in Council.

OIL AND GAS SECTOR - IMPORTANT LAWS AND REGULATIONS

PETROLEUM MINING ACT

AN ACT TO AMEND AND CONSOLIDATE THE LAW RELATING TO EXPLORATION PROSPECTING AND MINING FOR PETROLEUM

[S 5/02]

Commencement: 18th November 1963

CITATION.

1. This Act may be cited as the Petroleum Mining Act.

INTERPRETATION.

2. In this Act unless the context otherwise requires —

"Company" means the Brunei National Petroleum Company Sendirian Berhad referred to in Brunei National Petroleum Company Sendirian Berhad Order, 2002;

[S 5/02]

"designated area" has the meaning provided in the Brunei National Petroleum Company Sendirian Berhad Order, 2002;

[S 5/02]

"mineral rights" means the exclusive authority to explore, prospect and mine for petroleum within any State Land;

[S 5/02]

"Offshore State Land" means State Land within the area of the Continental Shelf;

"Onshore State Land" means State Land other than within the area of the Continental Shelf including the foreshores and submarine areas beneath the territorial waters of Brunei Darussalam;

"person" means and includes any individual or group of individuals and any company, corporation or other body;

"petroleum" means any mineral oil or relative hydro-carbon and natural gas or casinghead petroleum spirit existing in its natural condition in strata but does not include coal or bituminous shales or other stratified deposits from which oil can be extracted by destructive distillation;

[S 5/02]

"petroleum mining Agreement" means an agreement with regard to exploration, prospecting and mining for petroleum or any of them that the State Party enters into under this Act. For the avoidance of doubt, petroleum mining Agreements shall include, without limitation, any licences, leases, concessions, production sharing agreements and service agreements with regard to exploration, prospecting and mining for petroleum or any of them entered into by the State Party in accordance with this Act;

[S 5/02]

"State Land" means land within Brunei Darussalam and includes the foreshores and submarine areas beneath the territorial waters of Brunei Darussalam and also the area of the Continental Shelf being the sea-bed and its sub-soil which lies beneath the high seas contiguous to the territorial waters of Brunei Darussalam;

"State Party" means —

(a) His Majesty in Council;

(b) the Government or any of its lawful authorities (including, without limitation, the Clerk to the Council of Ministers or a Minister) designated by His Majesty to act on behalf of His Majesty in Council; or

(c) as empowered by His Majesty in Council in respect of any designated area under the Brunei National Petroleum Company Sendirian Berhad Order, 2002, the Company or any of the Company's representatives acting on its behalf.

[S 5/02]

OWNERSHIP OF PETROLEUM.

2A. The entire ownership of any petroleum extracted from any State Land shall vest in the holder of mineral rights unless otherwise expressly provided in any petroleum mining Agreement.

MINERAL RIGHTS.

2B. Mineral rights shall not be granted or otherwise transferred or assigned, unless expressly provided in any other written law or in any petroleum mining Agreement.

RESTRICTION ON PROSPECTING OR MINING FOR PETROLEUM.

3. (1) Save as provided in subsection (2), any person found to be exploring, prospecting and mining or any of them for petroleum upon any State Land or doing any act with a view to such

For additional analytical, marketing, investment and business opportunities information, please contact
Global Investment & Business Center, USA
(202) 546-2103. Fax: (202) 546-3275. E-mail: rusric@erols.com

exploring, prospecting and mining or any of them upon any State Land and without having received lawful authority so to do under any of the provisions of this Act or in breach of any of the conditions thereof, shall be guilty of an offence: Penalty, imprisonment for 5 years, a fine or both, and all machinery, tools, plant, buildings or other property together with any minerals or other products which may be found upon or proved to have been obtained from the State Land so unlawfully explored, prospected or mined shall be liable to forfeiture, and if the offence is a continuing one to a further fine not exceeding $100,000 for every day or part of a day during which the offence has continued.

(1A) In determining any fine to be imposed under subsection (1), the court shall take into consideration any loss, injury or damage, or whatsoever nature, caused to or sustained by the Government, the public generally or any section of the public, or any person, whether or not such loss, injury or damage is of a nature to admit of being quantified or fully expressed in terms of money.

(2) Nothing in this Act shall invalidate any exploration licence, prospecting licence or mining lease issued by the lawful authority of the Government of Brunei Darussalam before the passing of this Act or abrogate any of the rights or privileges expressly conferred thereby:

Provided that every such right or privilege shall be limited to the extent prescribed by such licence or lease.

INVITATION TO BID.

4. The State Party may invite persons to bid for a petroleum mining Agreement in respect of any Onshore State Land or Offshore State Land for the purposes of exploration, prospecting for and the mining of petroleum or any of them, and any person so bidding shall conform to such terms and conditions as are imposed by the State Party in the invitation to bid. Any person so bidding is referred to in the Act as "the applicant".

INFORMATION CONFIDENTIAL.

5. All information comprised in, or furnished to the State Party in pursuance of, a bid made under section 4 shall be treated by the State Party as confidential.

6. *Repealed. [S 34/92]*

LAPSE OF APPLICATION.

7. If a petroleum mining Agreement is not executed within 6 months after approval of the application by State Party or the period agreed between State Party and the applicant the right of the applicant to such petroleum mining Agreement shall be deemed to have lapsed, unless State Party considers that the delay is not attributable to the fault of the applicant.

AREAS AND FORM OF AGREEMENT.

8. (1) State Party may —

(a) enter into a petroleum mining Agreement in respect of any area of State Land for which application has been made as herein provided;

For additional analytical, marketing, investment and business opportunities information, please contact
Global Investment & Business Center, USA
(202) 546-2103. Fax: (202) 546-3275. E-mail: rusric@erols.com

(b) at the request of the licensee or lessee, enter into one or more petroleum mining Agreements in substitution for and in respect of the same area or areas as are covered by any one or more exploration licence, prospecting licence or mining lease which was valid and subsisting (or which may be accepted by State Party as if it had been valid and subsisting) on 18th November 1963.

(2) His Majesty in Council may by regulations prescribe the terms and conditions of a petroleum mining Agreement:

Provided that until any such terms and conditions have been so prescribed, a petroleum mining Agreement made on or after 31st October 1992, shall contain such terms and conditions as may be agreed between State Party and the applicant.

[S 5/02]

(3) A person with whom a petroleum mining Agreement and any collateral agreement or agreements is made shall be entitled to all the rights thereby expressed to be granted.

9. *Repealed. [S 34/92]*

GRANT OF MORE THAN ONE AGREEMENT.

10. Nothing in this Act shall prevent more than one petroleum mining Agreement being made with the same person.

EXECUTION.

11. The Clerk to the Council of Ministers or the Minister designated by His Majesty shall have power to execute for and on behalf of His Majesty in Council any petroleum mining Agreement and any collateral Agreement or Agreements which His Majesty shall direct to be executed:

Provided that any petroleum mining Agreement and any collateral agreement or agreements in respect of any designated area shall be executed for and on behalf of the Company by a duly authorised representative of the Company.

NOTIFICATION.

12. The State Party shall, as soon as may be after the execution, surrender, determination, or assignment of any petroleum mining Agreement or the right thereunder under this Act, issue a public notification of the fact stating the name of the person with whom the petroleum mining Agreement was made, the name of any assignee and the situation of the area concerned.

LIABILITY OF DIRECTORS ETC. *[S 34/92]*

12A. Where a body corporate is guilty of an offence against this Act, every director and other person concerned in the management of the body corporate shall be guilty of the like offence unless he proves that the offence was committed without his consent or connivance and that he exercised all such diligence to prevent the commission of the offence as he ought to have exercised having regard to the nature of his functions in that capacity and to all the circumstances.

For additional analytical, marketing, investment and business opportunities information, please contact
Global Investment & Business Center, USA
(202) 546-2103. Fax: (202) 546-3275. E-mail: rusric@erols.com

RULES.

13. His Majesty in Council may from time to time make and when made vary, alter, amend, revoke or cancel rules generally for carrying out the provision of this Act, and, without prejudice to the generality of the foregoing, to provide for —

(i) the appointment, duties, privileges and powers of persons to enforce the provisions of this Act or any petroleum mining Agreement made thereunder;

[S 34/92]

(ii) the prescribing of fees to be paid in respect of anything to be done in accordance with the provisions of this Act or any petroleum mining Agreement made hereunder.

Saving.

14. Nothing in the Emergency (Petroleum Mining Act) (Amendment) Order, 1992 (S 34/92) shall invalidate any exploration licence, prospecting licence, mining lease or petroleum mining Agreement issued or entered into by the lawful authority of the Government before 31st October 1992 or abrogate any of the rights or privileges expressly conferred thereby:

Provided that every such right or privilege shall be limited to the extent prescribed by such licence, lease or Agreement and that the same shall not be extended upon expiry.

For additional analytical, marketing, investment and business opportunities information, please contact
Global Investment & Business Center, USA
(202) 546-2103. Fax: (202) 546-3275. E-mail: rusric@erols.com

ENERGY SECTOR DEVELOPMENT AND OPPORTUNITIES

BASIC INFORMATION

Total installed electricity capacity (2008): 759 MW
Thermal: 100%

Total primary energy supply (2008): 3,629 ktoe
Natural gas: 78.2%
Oil and products: 21.8%

Brunei Darussalam basically depends totally on fossil fuels for its energy needs. The efficient use of fossil fuel has been recognized as the most cost-effective measure in mitigating emissions of greenhouse gas and to prolong the fossil fuel reserve. Increasing energy efficiency also contributes towards better air quality, reduction in energy costs, and moderating the growth in energy consumption.

Brunei Darussalam has a national target on the reduction of national energy intensity at 25 per cent by 2030 (with 2005 as the base year), which is in line with the pledges by APEC leaders in the 2007 Sydney Declaration.

Within the Brunei National Energy Research Institute the government is looking into the establishment of research on alternative energy.

In 2008, the economy generated 3,423 GWh of electricity, entirely from thermal sources, namely natural gas and oil. The electricity generated from natural gas amounted to 3,390 GWh and that from oil was 33 GWh.

BD has been a net exporter of oil and gas. The country significantly reduced its imports of the refined petroleum products, which was high owing to the limited domestic refining capacity, to 6% in 2008. Oil and gas production of 9,838 ktoe and 11,288 ktoe respectively, amounted to 21,126 ktoe in 2008, an increase of 1.4% from 2007 production (20,834 ktoe). Brunei Darussalam exported 82.3% of its oil and gas production in 2008.

The electricity networks extend throughout the Sultanate, providing power to almost the entire population. According to figures from the Department of Statistics, the country had electricity coverage of 99.7% in 2008, with 0.3% accounted for by remote communities, most of which have their own generators.

The three main grids are operated by two utilities, the governmental Department of Electrical Services, and the Berakas Power Company Private Limited (BPC). BPC supplies around 40% of the total generation in Brunei.

BD is launching prepaid cards, 'powercard', for electricity usage top-up at homes and business in October 2011. Following the introduction of the prepaid cards, all post-paid electronic meters in private households will be replaced to pre-paid meters free of charge. In addition, the electricity tariff has been reviewed in order to encourage the public to conserve electricity as well as to benefit the lower income groups.

For additional analytical, marketing, investment and business opportunities information, please contact
Global Investment & Business Center, USA
(202) 546-2103. Fax: (202) 546-3275. E-mail: rusric@erols.com

CAPACITY

Compared to the international target of approximately 10–12%, the Bruneian electricity supply industry showed high system losses of about 20%. One of the targets of the current Power Development Policy is; "To plan, design and commission a low loss transmission and distribution system". In 2008, the loss was decreased to 4.79%.

Brunei's current reliance on oil and gas as the sole sources of energy to generate income and provide a ready surplus of energy for the citizens of Brunei is not sustainable in the long term, without proper energy efficiency and conservation measures. Brunei consumes a disproportionate amount of energy in relation to its small population. The usage of energy for transportation and electricity consumption per capita are among the highest in Asia.

RENEWABLE ENERGY

SOLAR ENERGY

Brunei has considerable potential for solar energy, and photovoltaics/solar thermal technologies have been the most investigated renewable energy application in the country. Average daily insolation is in the region of 400 to 500 W/m2, with peaks of over 1000 W/m2. A solar diesel hybrid electric power system with a 2.4kW solar array and an 80kVA diesel generator was installed in 2000 at Ulu Belalong National Park in the Temburong district, as an initial foray into solar technology. Despite the potential of the photovoltaics technology, the technology will be used as an alternative or add up power resource by the Government to the national grid or as an individual system for only small scale applications, rather than for much needed air-conditioning, which requires a large and costly photovoltaics system for individual users. Solar thermal energy could be used for low and medium temperature applications such as solar water heaters, but not for high temperature applications as the direct component of solar radiation to be concentrated is not available throughout the day (Malik 2011: 435).

Wind energy

Measurements taken by the Department of Physics at the University of Brunei Darussalam indicate annual average wind speeds of 5 m/s in coastal regions, suggesting the potential for power generation from wind energy in the country. The first wind turbine to be installed in the country will be at the Ministry of Development, and further studies are being conducted in order to ascertain the potential for further wind energy utilisation. The calculation based on the offshore wind data, theoretical possible annual potential offshore wind power is 372 MW (Malik 2011: 430).

HYDROPOWER

While the high rainfall in BD provides a potential for the generation of hydropower, the running water in the rivers does not have a sufficient head which could be utilised to produce hydropower without building a storage dam. However, because of the small size of the country, it is difficult to find a location to build a dam. Measurements taken by the Department of Electrical Services (DES) indicate that the Temburong Basin has an estimated hydro-electric potential of 300 GWh per year, equivalent to 70-80 MW of installed hydropower capacity. The negative environmental impacts in the construction of hydropower installations are a barrier to further studies of this resource.

For additional analytical, marketing, investment and business opportunities information, please contact
Global Investment & Business Center, USA
(202) 546-2103. Fax: (202) 546-3275. E-mail: rusric@erols.com

OCEAN ENERGY

Ocean power is another option to be studied. The potential for power generation from tidal energy has also been investigated in the country. Whilst it is theoretically possible to generate approximately 335 kW of tidal energy annually, it may not be economically viable owing to the location of the country. Ocean thermal energy conversion is not possible due to the small temperature gradient between the top and bottom layers of the ocean. The potential of wave energy depends on the month, with December providing the maximum power. Provided that approximately 269km of the coastline in BD could produce 15-126 GW of wave energy, the annual theoretical potential of the wave energy in BD is 66 x 1010 W.

BIOMASS ENERGY

Brunei has considerable forest resources, with an average of 382 tonnes of wood potential per hectare across the country. The proper cultivation of rainforest for energy production has been identified as a priority for increasing the utilisation of renewable energy sources in the country, provided that an integrated total system design was used to prevent undue damage to the nation's forest resources. In addition, with the increasing population and the six landfill sites in BD, the country should be able to produce landfill gas for power generation as a by-product of the decomposition of solid waste.

GEOTHERMAL ENERGY

Whilst the potential for geothermal energy utilisation has been proposed in Brunei, no dedicated study has yet been conducted into the theoretical and economically viable potentials for geothermal power generation.

ENERGY EFFICIENCY

In 2008, BD's total final energy consumption was 1,606 ktoe, almost doubled from 810 ktoe in 2007. The sectoral shares of final energy consumption saw a significant increase in the industrial sector, which consumed 55.8%, followed by the transportation sector (23.7%) and the residential, commercial and non-energy sectors combined (18.0%). By energy source, gas contributed the largest share, accounting for 50.1% of consumption, followed by oil (33.0%) and electricity (16.8%). Natural gas accounts for 99% of the fuel use to generate electricity, with only 1% being generated by diesel fuel.

As part of Brunei's Wasawan (Vision) 2035, a national energy efficiency study is being prepared by the Mitsubishi Corporation. In addition, a "Handbook on Energy Management" has been produced by the Energy Division of the Prime Minister's Office, detailing strategies for improving public and private-sector energy efficiency. Nonetheless, because of the regressive electricity tariff, there is little economic incentive to conserve electricity or to be energy efficient; and the power demand id rapidly growing at about 7-10%. Passive solar architecture should be encouraged in order to reduce the need for air-conditioning and to give natural day light in buildings.

OWNERSHIP

ELECTRICITY MARKET

Electricity is supplied by the Department of Electrical Services (DES, www.des.gov.bn) and the Berakas Power Management Company Sdn Bhd (BPMC). The BPMC is in effect owned by the Brunei Investment Agency (BIA), but operates as a private limited company, which owns four power stations, including Berakas 1, Berakas 2, Gadong and Jerudong, and supplies 40% of the national electricity requirement. It supplies power to important sites, such as royal palaces, hospitals and military facilities. The DES owns four power generating plants, including three gas-fuelled and one diesel-fuelled plants (Malik 2011: 428). Metering and cable supply has been privatised. Both the DES and BPC are state-owned, the division between them dating back to 1992. While the DES is a service provider as a utility, BPMC is solely a utility, with its billing services run by the DES, which also has most of the functions of the sector authority.

The DES is the government utility in charge of the generation, transmission, and distribution of electricity in the country. The DES also sets the standards for the usage of electricity in public buildings, and oversees their overall electro-mechanical maintenance.

OIL AND GAS MARKET

Brunei Shell Petroleum (BSP, www.bsp.com.bn) dominates the production of natural gas and crude oil from both onshore and offshore fields, and owns the Brunei Refinery. BSP produces 90% of its oil and all its commercial gas from seven offshore fields. The Government of BD and the Asiatic Petroleum Company Limited are equal shareholders. Liquefied Natural Gas (LNG) activities are carried out by Brunei LNG (BLNG, www.blng.com.bn), a joint venture between the government of Brunei (50%), Mitsubishi (25%), and Shell (25%). BLNG receives most of its natural gas supplies from BSP, although from the beginning of 1999, it began receiving small amounts of natural gas from Total's offshore production facilities.

The Brunei National Petroleum Company (PetroleumBRUNEI) is the state-owned utility in the field of oil exploration and production, as well as mining.

COMPETITION

There is hardly any competition in the generation and retail of power in Brunei. There is no specific legislation governing the electricity sector.

BD has a large extent of vertical integration. The DES is under the Ministry of Energy in the Prime Minister's office, and it is in charge of operating the electricity sector. The DES is both a department and an integrated electric utility monopoly. As a utility, it is responsible for planning future generation and distribution requirements, while as a service department it sets standards and implements electricity usage plans in public buildings.

The BPC supplies power to users in the Brunei Maura district exclusively, and is owned by the state, but has autonomy of operation.

ENERGY FRAMEWORK

BD implements five-year economic development plans known as the National Development Plans. Currently, the ninth National Development Plan (2007–2012) is in force. In line with this plan, the economy has also launched a long-term development plan, the Brunei Vision 2035. The plan states that the economy's major goal for the next three decades is economic diversification, along with strengthening of the oil and gas sector. The latter is to be achieved by expanding the sector's oil and gas reserves through ongoing exploration, both in existing areas, and in new deep-sea locations.

BD's energy policy is centred on its oil and gas industry. In 1981, the Oil Conservation Policy was introduced when oil production peaked at 239,000 barrels per day (bbl/d) in 1980. The policy aimed to prolong the life of the economy's oil reserves. As a result, oil production gradually declined to around 150 bbl/d in 1989. In November 1990, the government reviewed the policy and removed the production ceiling, resulting in production of 219 bbl/d by 2006.

In 2000, the Brunei Natural Gas Policy (Production and Utilisation) was introduced. The policy aimed to maintain gas production at 2000 rates in order to adequately satisfy export obligations. It aimed to open new areas for exploration and development, and encourage increased exploration by new and existing operators. Under the policy, priority is always given to domestic utilisation of gas, especially for electricity generation.

The Brunei National Petroleum Company Order, introduced in January 2002, empowers the Brunei National Petroleum Company Sdn Bhd (PetroleumBRUNEI) to act as the economy's oil company. Among others, PetroleumBRUNEI is given designated Areas for which the company has the right to negotiate, conclude and administer petroleum sharing agreements.

The Energy Efficiency and Conservation (EE&C) goals submitted to the 5th East Asia Summit Energy Ministers Meeting, held on 20 September 2011 in BD, state that the country uses Energy Intensity (TPES/GDP) as the EE Indicator, and aims at 25% improvement by 2030 from 2005 level. The action plans to achieve the EE&C goals above are mostly formulated in 2010, including the voluntary basis EE 5-star labelling for commercial and residential sectors, the establishment of "Energy Club" in secondary schools, the declaration of "Energy Day" (24 May) to inculcate EE&C culture, and National EEC Initiative Award Competition. The enhancement of supply side management in power sectors has been added in 2011 in order to increase efficiency and reduce use of energy, with a specific goal of more than 45% of efficiency through combined cycle and co-generation.

The Energy Labelling and Standards for electrical products to the national market through the Energy Labelling and Standards Task Force (ELSTF), which was established in September 2008 in the Energy Division, is one of BD's EE&C Initiatives. The Energy Labelling Scheme was launched as a voluntary basis scheme on 26 May 2008 preliminary for single-phase non-deducted room air conditioners and will be extended to other appliances in the later stage.

BD, as a member of the Association of Southeast Asian Nations (ASEAN), has signed the ASEAN Petroleum Security Agreement. Under the agreement, the country has agreed to cooperate closely on energy security relating to oil supply with other member states. The ASEAN Plan of Action on Energy Cooperation of 2010-2015 and a number of activities and programmes under the umbrella of the ASEAN Ministers on Energy Meeting (AMEM) are central to the drive towards achieving among others the region's energy security, efficiency and conservation. For example, Brunei Darussalam is working with other ASEAN members on the Trans-ASEAN Gas Pipeline project and the ASEAN Power Grid project to promote and enhance energy security through energy market integration in the region. During the 29th AMEM, held in BD, ASEAN and the IEA signed a Memorandum of Understanding on Cooperation on Energy.

In August 2007, BD ratified the United Nation Framework Convention on Climate Change (UNFCCC) and subsequently ratified its Kyoto Protocol on 20th August 2009.

INPORTANT DEVELOPMENTS

In August 2008, a Memorandum of Understanding (MoU) was signed between the Energy Division of the Prime Minister's Office (EDPMO) and the Mitsubishi Corporation (MC) to construct a 1.2 MW PV power generation demonstration project, Tenaga Suria Brunei (TSB), for evaluating the performance of six types of photovoltaic panels. The TSB is the largest solar power demonstration plant in Southeast Asia, which aims to increase public awareness on the potential of solar as a source of clean and renewable energy. The construction of the solar plant started in 2009, and the system was connected to the national grid in 2010, making the first introduction of renewable energy being connected to the national power grid. It was completed on 31 July 2010, and the inauguration of the TSB was held on 26 May 2011. The TSB is expected to determine the most suitable solar panel, whether the panels should be set vertically or horizontally and the most efficient way in maintaining the facilities for the tropical climate conditions in BD in three years.

An energy white paper to outline strategies to squeeze out more profits from oil and gas industries will be published in 2011. The document will address the country's current energy-related challenges by calling for more upstream and downstream "growth", maximising economic spin-offs from the industry and ensuring "secure, reliable and efficient supply and use of energy" through making use of key performance indicators (KPI).

The government is actively promoting energy efficiency and conservation in various sectors in the economy. These activities include public education awareness campaigns, publications on energy efficiency & conservation issues, and talks, as well as a voluntary energy labelling scheme for air-conditioners. In addition, the economy is also enhancing its human capacity building through seminar-workshops on energy management, energy auditing and energy education in schools.

Brunei Energy Expo (BEE) 2011 (www.bee2011.gov.bn/) was held between 21-23 September 2011, in conjunction with the 29th ASEAN Ministers on Energy Meeting, to showcase energy development in the local, regional and international arena as well as to provide a platform for various representatives from many countries to interact and share knowledge on the prevailing energy technologies and initiatives.

The Government is assessing the viability of large-scale PV electricity generation. To promote this effort, the government has initiated a solar energy demonstration project known as Tenaga Suria Brunei, with a capacity of 1.2 MW. The plant first connected to the power grid of the Department of Electrical Services in May 2010, and is now operating at full capacity after completing a 3-month testing period.

On 23 June 2009 Brunei became a Signatory State of the International Renewable Energy Agency (IRENA).

ROLE OF GOVERNMENT

On 24 May 2005, the government created the post of, and appointed, the Minister of Energy at the Prime Minister's Office. The Minister of Energy presides over energy matters in the country, including those of petroleum and electricity. Upon the creation of the post, the Energy Division at the Prime Minister's Office was also formed. The Petroleum Unit and the Department of Electrical Services were brought under the purview of the Minister of Energy in the same year.

The Energy Division advises the Minister of Energy on pertinent matters concerning energy and its administration. The energy matters that are handled by the Energy Division range from petroleum and electricity matters, to energy policy and sustainable energy issues.

In July 2011, the Energy Minister announced the merger of the Energy Division and the Petroleum Unit at the PMO into the Energy Department at the PMO, retaining the division's former acronym, EDPMO, in order to achieve the KPIs in the energy white paper.

GOVERNMENT AGENCIES

The Brunei Energy Association (BEnA), created in 2002, plays a major role in the development of the energy industry, and in improving the dissemination of knowledge and emphasis on energy conservation and efficiency.

A current challenge is the trend in the level of national electricity energy consumption, which is equal to the consumption levels in highly developed countries, and to which the main contributions are from residential users. BEnA will be responsible for the drive to increase participation in the preservation, conservation and efficient use of energy.

The Energy Efficiency Conservation Committee (EECC) promotes public awareness in the importance of energy efficiency and conservation.

ENERGY PROCEDURE

The Brunei Darussalam Centre for Strategic and Policy Studies (CSPS) and the Energy Division have commissioned teams of consultants to conduct studies on An Energy Efficiency and Conservation Plan for Negara Brunei Darussalam and a Nationwide Feasibility Study on Alternative Energy Sources and to Formulate a Roadmap Towards Achieving Energy Security and Sustainability for Brunei Darussalam".

Canadian consultants Powertech Labs Inc carried out the alternative energy study which looked at bioenergy, hydroelectricity, hydrogen, nuclear, ocean, solar and wind. Three alternative energy sources, namely bioenergy, hydrogen and ocean, were found to be the most feasible when looking at a medium-capital, low-risk and short-term solution and were suggested for long-term development projects.

The EEC study carried out by the Mitsubishi Research Institute (MRI) underlines transport and cooling as primary reasons for energy usage in BD. It pinpoints the regulation of the fuel economy and the setting of appliance standards as the start of more energy-efficient usage in the country.

The full results and recommendations from these two studies are to be released and discussed at a national conference on 'Energy Efficiency and Conservation and Alternative Energy: Policy Option for Wawasan 2035' on 27 July 2011. The CSPS wants to see a multi-energy solution to the whole thing in considering the Wawasan 2035 Vision. Towards these objectives, various initiatives are being undertaken:

Energy Efficiencies
BD depends totally on fossil fuels for its energy needs. The efficient use of fossil fuel has been recognised as the most cost-effective measure in mitigating emissions of greenhouse gases, and in prolonging the nation's fossil fuel reserves. Increasing EE also contributes towards better air quality, reduction in energy costs, and moderating the growth in energy consumption. Brunei has a national target for the reduction of national energy intensity by 25% by 2030 (with 2005 as the base year), which concurs with the pledges by Asia-Pacific Economic Co-Operation (APEC) leaders in the 2007 Sydney Declaration. EE&C initiatives have been developed in BD to:

- Promote public awareness and encourage the adoption of EE technologies and best practices;
- Establish and develop EE&C regulations and guidelines to encourage practice;
- Improve energy efficiency in the supply, transportation and utilisation of energy;

- Develop energy efficiency labelling and standards to encourage procurement of energy efficient appliances; and
- Strengthen collaborations with local and international institutions, to develop and enhance human capacity building and sustain energy efficiency efforts.

Bukit Panggal Power Station

The Bukit Panggal Power Station was a project under the 8th National Development Plan with a budget of about B$170 million. Construction work began in 2005, and the plant was operational by January 2008 where it uses the 'Combined Cycle' concept which is the first of its kind owned by the DES.

Bukit Panggal Power Plant has a designed thermal efficiency of 47%, whereas the designed efficiency of existing generators using the 'Simple Cycle' is only, on average, 28%. The Bukit Panggal Power Station is based on a 140 hectare wide piece of land, where 75 hectares have been developed for phase one of its long term planning, with a capacity of 500MW.

BD, through the Energy Division at the Prime Minister's Office, is promoting energy efficiency & conservation. Human capacity development workshops on energy management and energy audit were organised in collaboration with local and international institutions. Energy clubs in schools were launched in 2009, so as to inculcate an energy efficient culture. The 24th May was declared, in 2007, as the Energy Day, to promote a more energy-conscious mindset and encourage the populace to adopt more environmentally sustainable lifestyle choices.

The National Development Plan for 2007–2012 proposes that the three power grids currently operating independently will be interconnected by 2012. Utilisation of the Temburong Basin's hydro-electric potential is also covered under this plan.

ENERGY REGULATOR

No dedicated energy regulator exists in the country. Regulatory functions are fulfilled by the DES, established in 1921, whose mission includes the management and development of the electricity sector.

DEGREE OF INDEPENDENCE

The DES is a government body, directly subsidiary to the Ministry of Energy of the Prime Minister's Office. The organisation is headed by a Director, with no governing board. Financing for the organisation comes partly from tariffs imposed on consumers for the company's operations in the electricity service sector.

REGULATORY FRAMEWORK

Brunei does not currently have a dedicated policy framework for renewable energies. The current regulatory framework for the electricity sector dates back to 1973, with the Electricity Act, and its subsequent amendment in 2002. The act details the role of the DES in the electricity sector as a service provider and a governing body, as well as prescribing the conditions necessary for the granting of licenses to use electrical equipment, and the responsibilities of the DES to the electricity sector, including the department's regulatory responsibilities.

The Energy Division will work with the Ministry of Development (MoD) to incorporate energy efficiency and conservation (EE&C) features into the existing National Building Code. The

For additional analytical, marketing, investment and business opportunities information, please contact
Global Investment & Business Center, USA
(202) 546-2103. Fax: (202) 546-3275. E-mail: rusric@erols.com

existing National Building Code will be updated to include EE&C features, applicable to house construction.

REGULATORY ROLES

The DES undertakes most of the functions of the sector authority, for example:

1. Advise the government/minister on policies and strategies relating to energy issues that are specific to power, and on matters pertaining to the regulatory body,
2. Advise the government/minister on matters relating to the generation, transmission, distribution, trading, retail, and use of electricity,
3. Exercise and enforce the Electricity Act, as well as regulations.
4. Address the interest of stakeholders and utilities with regards to:

- The prices charged and other terms for the supply of electricity,
- The security, reliability, availability and continuity of electricity supply,
- The electricity services provided,

5. Promote the efficient use of electricity (potentially through demand side management),

6. Recommend a regulatory framework with respect to the generation, transmission, and possible import and export of electricity,

7. Protect the public from dangers arising from the generation, transmission, supply or use of electricity,

8. Coordinate various activities with regard to supply infrastructure planning (such as supply security & sufficiency) & implementation, efficiency..

ENERGY REGULATION ROLE

The Ministry of Energy is responsible for formulating the energy policy of the country, including the setting of laws such as the Electricity Act. As the controlling body of the DES, the Ministry also has final control over all actions of the company as a government department.

REGULATORY BARRIERS

Numerous barriers exist to the improvement of energy regulation. The disassociation of electricity service company and regulator would help improve the fairness of regulation, but is yet to occur in BD. The lack of experience in sustainable energy and its regulation could be overcome through further capacity building.

For additional analytical, marketing, investment and business opportunities information, please contact
Global Investment & Business Center, USA
(202) 546-2103. Fax: (202) 546-3275. E-mail: rusric@erols.com

CLEAN ENERGY INITIATIVES[8]

1. INTRODUCTION

Brunei Darussalam, a small country with area of 5,765 sq. km and a population of about 406,200 in 2009. Brunei Darussalam is endowed with rich resources of fossil fuels. Crude oil and natural gas industries are the dominant industry in Brunei Darussalam. Brunei Darussalam's gross domestic product (GDP) in 2008 was estimated at B$20,397.9 million.

Brunei Darussalam is currently embarking on its long-term development plan called Wawasan 2035 to achieve its industrialization and economic diversification aspirations. Energy, a crucial necessity in the sustainable development of Brunei Darussalam, must meet the needs of today and the future without adverse effects to the environment.

2. ENERGY AUTHORITIES

The Ministerial post on Energy at the Prime Minister's Office was first created in May 2005 by the Government of His Majesty The Sultan and Yang Di-Pertuan of Brunei Darussalam. Subsequent to the creation of the Energy Ministerial post, an Energy Division at the Prime Minister's Office was established to advise the Minister of Energy on matters concerning energy and its administration. Under the purview of the Minister of Energy are the Petroleum Unit and the Department of Electrical Services.

The Petroleum Unit oversees exploitation of Brunei's reserves, monitors the development of downstream activities, regulates domestic oil/gas matters and ensures that internationally acceptable standards on technical, accounting, health and safety and environmental grounds are adhered to.

The Department of Electrical Services (DES) is a government authority and utility mandated to look after and responsible for the operation and development of the electricity sector. As a utility, it is responsible for management and administration of generation, transmission, distribution and retailing of electricity; while as a service provider it sets the necessary standards for the usage of electricity by the public and private sectors.

3. CLEAN ENERGY INITIATIVES

Brunei Darussalam recognizes the importance in ensuring energy security and environmental sustainability in fueling the economic growth. Environmental policy directions are embedded in the 2035 Long Term Development Plans, which includes amongst others:

- Implementing the highest environmental standards for existing and new industries in accordance with established international standard and practices.
- Strictly enforcing appropriate regulations regarding the maintenance of environment that affect public health and safety.
- Supporting global and regional efforts to address trans-border and regional environmental concerns.

The Brunei Darussalam Centre for Strategic and Policy Studies has recently just commissioned teams of consultant to conduct studies on "An Energy Efficiency and Conservation Plan or

[8] Brunei government report

Roadmap for Negara Brunei Darussalam" and "Nationwide Feasibility Study on Alternative Energy Sources and to Formulate a Roadmap Towards Achieving Energy Security and Sustainability for Brunei Darussalam".

Towards these objectives, various initiatives are being undertaken:

A) Energy Efficiencies

Brunei Darussalam basically depends totally on fossil fuels for its energy needs. The efficient use of fossil fuel has been recognized as the most cost-effective measure in mitigating emissions of greenhouse gas and to prolong the fossil fuel reserve. Increasing energy efficiency also contributes towards better air quality, reduction in energy costs, and moderating the growth in energy consumption.

Brunei Darussalam has a national target on the reduction of national energy intensity at 25 per cent by 2030 (with 2005 as the base year), which is inline with the pledges by APEC leaders in the 2007 Sydney Declaration.

EE&C initiatives have been developed in Brunei Darussalam to:

- Promote public awareness and encourage the adoption of energy efficient technologies and best practices;
- Establish and develop Energy Efficiency & Conservation regulations and guidelines to encourage energy efficiency and conservation practices;
- Improve energy efficiency in the supply, transportation and utilization of energy;
- Develop energy efficiency labelling and standards to encourage procurement of energy efficient appliances; and
- Strengthen collaborations with local and international institutions to develop and enhance human capacity building to sustain energy efficiency efforts.

Bukit Panggal Power Station

The Bukit Panggal Power Station was a project under the Eighth National Development Plan with a budget of about B$170 million. Construction works began in 2005 and the plant was operational by January 2008 where it uses the 'Combined Cycle' concept which is the first of its kind owned by the Department of Electrical Services (DES).

Bukit Panggal Power Plant has a designed thermal efficiency of 47 per cent where-as the designed efficiency of existing generators using the 'Simple Cycle' is only at 28 per cent.

The Bukit Panggal Power Station is based on a 140 hectare wide piece of land where 75 hectares have been developed for phase one of its long term planning with a capacity of 500MW.

I. Electrical Energy Consumption

The recorded average usage of electricity for the past five years has shown that 48 per cent are consumed by the domestic sector, 25 per cent for commercial sector, 17 per cent for government sector and 10 per cent for the Oil and Gas Sector.

Brunei Darussalam through the Energy Division at Prime Minister's Office is actively promoting energy efficiency & conservation in various sectors in the economy, including nationwide public education awareness campaigns, briefings, publications as well as voluntary energy labeling scheme for air-conditioners.

On enhancing human capacity development, seminar-workshops on energy management and energy audit were organized in collaboration with local and international institutions. Energy clubs in schools were launched in 2009 so as to inculcate an energy efficient culture from the grass-root level.

24th May was declared in 2007 as the Energy Day of Brunei Darussalam with the aims to inculcate a more energy-conscious mindset both in the young and old and encourage them to adopt more environmental sustainable lifestyle choices.

II. Petroleum Product Quality

The transport sector is the dominant sector in the Final Energy Consumption. The 2007 Brunei Darussalam Energy in Brief 2007's indicated that the transport sector alone is responsible for more than 50% of the total energy consumption in the country between the years 2000 and 2006.

Brunei's sole local refinery, with a production capacity of around 12,000 barrels per day, was built in Seria in 1983. It is able to produce among other grades, motor gasoline quality standard equivalent to Euro II to cater for domestic demand for petroleum products.

Most ASEAN countries including Brunei Darussalam follows the European Union product specification standard (Euro I, II, III, IV and V) for the vehicle emission standards. ASEAN is planning to move towards cleaner fuels i.e. Euro 5 vehicle emission standard by 2015. Brunei Darussalam is also currently studying into upgrading the existing refinery to meet the higher EURO standard requirement.

b) Renewable Energies

Brunei started looking into the potential of renewable in 1994 when a pre-feasibility study was carried out in the Temburong District to identify its hydro potential. The project was however not pursued due to the environmental concerns at the time. Other than hydro, Brunei Darussalam also has looked into potential of solar energy as Brunei Darussalam is located in the tropical region with plenty of solar radiation. A solar diesel hybrid electric power system with a 2.4kW solar array and 80kVA diesel generator was installed in 2000 at Ulu Belalong National Park in the Temburong district.

In August 2008, a Memorandum of Understanding (MoU) was signed between Energy Division at the Prime Minister's Office (EDPMO) and Mitsubishi Corporation (MC) to construct a 1.2 MW PV power generation demonstration project, Tenaga Suria Brunei (TSB), for evaluating the performance of six types of photovoltaic panels. TSB is expected to be completed in July 2010.

On the research and development of clean and renewable energies, Brunei Darussalam will continue to facilitate and encourage the research and development of clean and renewable sources of energy. Local higher institutions are encouraged to carry out research works and collaborations with international institutions on information sharing, capacity building and transfer of technologies.

For additional analytical, marketing, investment and business opportunities information, please contact
Global Investment & Business Center, USA
(202) 546-2103. Fax: (202) 546-3275. E-mail: rusric@erols.com

C) FOSTERING INTERNATIONAL CO-OPERATIONS

In August 2007, Brunei Darussalam ratified the United Nation Framework Convention on Climate Change (UNFCCC) and subsequently ratified its Kyoto Protocol on 20th August 2009.

On 23 June 2009 Brunei Darussalam also become a Signatory State of International Renewable Agency (IRENA).

4. CONCLUSION

Through technology advances and its growing wide applications, the clean energy initiatives are hope to become more technologically viable and affordable. Brunei Darussalam will continue its efforts in its clean energy initiatives. This is seen as part of the drive to sustain the country's socio-economic development now and for the generations to come.

BRUNEI ENERGY SECTOR STRATEGY - PLANS AND DEVELOPMENTS[9]

THE ENERGY SECTOR IN BRUNEI DARUSSALAM

Oil and Gas sector contributes >60% to GDP

Oil and gas production about 400,000 BOEPD

806 MW of installed capacity in power generation

Energy is a core pillar of Brunei Darussalam's economy. It includes oil and gas exploration and production, petrochemical and refineries, fuel, power, energy efficiency and conservation and renewable energy. The energy sector accounts for more than 60 percent of Brunei Darussalam's Gross Domestic Product (GDP). It currently provides steady employment to 24,000 people. It also contributes to a significant portion of Government revenue, allowing the Government to invest these revenues in the social and economic development of our nation.

The energy sector in Brunei Darussalam traces its roots back to the first oil discovery in 1910[1]. The first commercial oil production in Brunei Darussalam started in 1929 from the onshore Seria field, reaching its peak production at 115,000 barrels per day in 1956. Oil development activity spurred development in other sectors of the economy; first in supporting infrastructure and services and later, as the economy developed, on a more diversified basis.

In the 1970s, the first oil crisis led to increased efforts to explore and produce in Brunei Darussalam. This led to increased oil production which thus reached a peak of 254,000 barrels per day in 1979 before the Government imposed a strict conservation policy on production at 150,000 barrels per day in 1981. The Government has since then revised the policy which resulted in an increase of production at availability. In 2006, Brunei Darussalam achieved an oil production level of 219,000 barrels per day. Currently, Brunei Darussalam is producing around 372,000 barrels of oil equivalent per day (BOEPD) for both oil and gas.

The presence of significant associated natural gas and the discovery of giant offshore gas fields enabled Brunei Darussalam to play a pioneering role in the nascent Liquefied Natural Gas (LNG) industry back in 1972. Brunei Darussalam's LNG production grew rapidly to a peak in 2006. The natural gas produced also enabled the development of downstream industries like the Brunei Methanol Company (BMC) (refer to Exhibit 2.1 for the historical oil and gas production).

For Brunei Darussalam's 2013 total domestic energy consumption, oil was the most consumed fuel type accounting for 65.6 percent, followed by electricity at 32.2 percent and town gas at 2.2 percent respectively. Thermal power stations generated 99.95 percent of total power generation, while 0.05 percent was generated by the solar power plant Tenaga Suria Brunei.

As the country developed and industrialized, there was also an increasing need for power to generate lighting and electricity for industrial and residential uses. From the first fuel oil plants

---

[9] ENERGY DEPARTMENT PRIME MINISTER'S OFFICE BRUNEI DARUSSALAM BRUNEI DARUSSALAM ENERGY WHITE PAPER

For additional analytical, marketing, investment and business opportunities information, please contact
Global Investment & Business Center, USA
(202) 546-2103. Fax: (202) 546-3275. E-mail: rusric@erols.com

built in 1935[2], Brunei Darussalam now has about 806 MW of installed capacity in power generation and the ability to generate 3.5 million MWh of energy for electricity and other uses.

1 Drilling activities began as early as 1899. The first commercial find was made in 1929 at Seria, Belait.

2 The Electric Office (predecessor of the Department of Electrical Services) began supplying electricity to its first customer (Wireless and Telegraph Department) in 1921. In 1935, the first diesel-powered generator began operations and by 1953, power was supplied to the entire Brunei Town.

To drive Brunei Darussalam's economy into a sustainable future, Brunei Darussalam supports the implementation of strategies related to energy security, diversification of supply, energy efficiency and conservation. The Government is working to achieve the country's target while exploring plans to diversify the energy mix through a concerted effort and promotion of alternative and renewable energy sources for power generation. The potential of non-conventional energy resources and power transmission interconnection for energy exchange or power transactions will need to be exploited fully to create the additional power generation capacity. It is expected that the economy's venture into renewable energy along with its work to upgrade and expand existing electricity-generating facilities will help to ensure the economy's energy security.

For additional analytical, marketing, investment and business opportunities information, please contact
Global Investment & Business Center, USA
(202) 546-2103. Fax: (202) 546-3275. E-mail: rusric@erols.com

Global energy demand will grow more than 30% by 2035

THE GLOBAL ENERGY CONTEXT

In 2012, the world consumed approximately 90 billion barrels of oil equivalent (BOE) of energy[3]. This is approximately 40 percent more than the consumption two decades earlier. Going forward, the world's thirst for energy is expected to continue to grow significantly. A range of external publications by the US Energy Information Administration (EIA), International Energy Agency (IEA) and BP suggest that the global energy demand in 2035 could grow more than 30 percent to around 125 - 140 billion BOE.

The key features of the World Energy Outlook 2013 from IEA are:

Over 90 percent of this growth is driven by emerging economies – mainly in Asia and the Middle East, and increasingly in Africa and Latin America.

World electricity demand will account for more than 60 percent of the growth over the period 2011 - 2035.

Coal will remain as the leading fuel for power generation, although its share of total power output will decline from 41 percent in 2011 to 33 percent in 2035.

The declining trend in coal share benefits renewable energy as their share is expected to increase from 20 percent in 2011 to 31 percent by 2035.

The substantial growth in global primary energy demand by 2035 poses significant challenges on supply, as much of this energy supply needs to be developed against the background of dwindling production of oil and gas from existing oil and gas fields (a consequence of the maturity of these fields).

The key features of global energy supply in the next two decades according to IEA are:

Cumulative investments of USD 15.1 trillion (in year-2012 dollars) is needed in upstream oil and gas supply activities between 2013 and 2035.

About 62 percent of total investment in upstream oil and gas supply activities will take place in non-OECD countries, where demand is expected to increase most.

The projected rising electricity demand imply a need for cumulative global investment in power sector of USD 8.5 trillion (in year-2012 dollars). More than 60 percent of the investment is needed in non-OECD countries.

North America's emergence as a net exporter accelerates the eastward shift in trade. Rising supplies of unconventional gas and LNG help to diversify trade flows, putting pressure on conventional gas suppliers and oil-linked pricing mechanisms.

Despite international efforts, billions of people still lack electricity. Many developing countries have made progress in their electrification. Nonetheless, more than half billion people remain un-

For additional analytical, marketing, investment and business opportunities information, please contact
Global Investment & Business Center, USA
(202) 546-2103. Fax: (202) 546-3275. E-mail: rusric@erols.com

electrified in developing Asia, representing an impressive market especially for off-grid renewable applications.

The need for electricity in emerging economies drives a 70 percent increase in worldwide demand, with renewables accounting for half of the new global capacity. However, electricity prices are set to increase with the highest prices persisting in the European Union and Japan, well above those in China and the United States.

3 Equivalent of 496 quadrillion British thermal units (QBtu) under the assumption of 6.1 GJ/BOE

In 2011, Asia and Australia contributed to approximately 39 percent of global primary energy demand. The external forecast from IEA predicts the demand in 2035 to increase by 70 percent from 2010 levels, thereby increasing its global share to approximately 45 percent. The growth is mainly expected from increased use of coal in power generation and use of gas in industry and buildings. The share of renewable in primary energy demand is expected to increase by 3 percent from 14 percent in 2010 to 17 percent by 2035.

Despite the tragic accident at the Fukushima-1 Nuclear Power Station in March 2011, many nations recognise the importance of the safe and secure uses of peaceful nuclear energy to diversify their energy mix, satisfy growing energy demand and reduce greenhouse gas emissions. Cooperation includes sharing knowledge and experience on nuclear technologies and safety at nuclear power stations and related facilities i.e. improvement of safety standards, coordination of emergency response and preparedness mechanisms.

Even though energy efficiency practices in many developing countries are still in its infancy stage, there is evidence that the energy intensity - the amount of energy used to produce each dollar of Gross Domestic Product (GDP) - in some regions has steadily declined. For example, between 2005 and 2011, ASEAN countries reduced their energy intensity by 6.8 percent, bringing them closer to reducing regional energy intensity by at least 8 percent from 2005 levels in 2015.

Governments have to take the lead in furthering energy efficiency. Several countries have existing policies and market incentives to promote energy efficiency, but need to ensure better enforcement and development of the requisite monitoring and evaluation systems. Two-thirds of the economic potential to improve energy efficiency remains untapped in the period up to 2035. Economically viable energy efficient measures can cut energy demand growth by half by 2035.

Independent of the supply and demand scenario one chooses, the world will continue to need significantly more oil and gas exploration and development to make up for decline in production from maturing existing fields, as well as to account for incremental demand growth.

The growth in primary energy demand will also spur growth in many parts of the industry including alternative and renewable energy and oil field services. Policymakers nowadays face critical choices in reconciling energy, environmental and economic objectives. Changing outlook for energy production and use may redefine global economic and geopolitical balances. As climate change slips off the policy radar, the "lock-in" point moves closer and the costs of inaction rises. The gains promised by energy efficiency are within reach and are essential to underpin a more secure and sustainable energy system.

Increasing Challenges in Upstream Production

The technical complexity of oil and gas exploration, development and production is increasing as the world develops ever more complex and mature reservoirs including greater water depths and in more demanding and harsh environments. Brunei Darussalam is a case in point: ongoing exploration in the deep offshore areas are in water depths ranging from 1000 to 2750 meters. Significant efforts are also being made in Brunei Darussalam to increase the recovery from oil and gas fields by deploying advanced technologies. This increase in complexity, as seen globally, is resulting in increased demand for oil and gas services – the sector is expecting total capital expenditure to grow at around 5 percent globally per year between 2010 and 2020.

Shale "revolution" technologies increase commercial value of oil and gas production

In addition, coal met 45 percent of the growth in global energy demand over the past decade. The IEA forecast that over three-quarters of the next two decades growth in coal demand will be associated with power generation.

Global Climate Change

One of the physical phenomena that concerns the energy sector is global warming caused by higher anthropogenic emissions and concentrations of greenhouse gases in the atmosphere. The concentrations of carbon dioxide in the atmosphere have risen rapidly from the pre-industrial levels of 278 parts per million to more than 400 parts per million in May 2013. The current global mean temperature has continued to increase and now estimated to be around 0.8°C above pre-industrial levels. Global mean temperature beyond 2°C above pre-industrial levels are considered to cause severe drought, major floods and heat waves in many regions with serious impacts on human systems, ecosystems, and associated services. Small island developing states and least developed countries (LDCs) however consider 1.5°C global warming to have serious threats to their own development. While all countries are vulnerable to the impacts of climate change, the world's poorest regions that have the least economic, institutional, scientific, and technical capacity to cope and adapt would experience the brunt of global warming. The global community in 2010 agreed to limit the global temperature rise to 2°C at the end of 21st century.

New international commitments to further reduce greenhouse gas emissions would be imperative to meet this global warming target. Though technically feasible, achieving the 2°C target would be challenging. The energy sector is at the core of this challenge since it contributes around two-thirds of the global greenhouse gas emissions and that fossil fuels account 80 percent of the total energy use.

While waiting for climate change negotiators to frame up new international commitments, the IEA identified key policies that could be pursued by each country to keep on track of the 2°C global warming trajectory. These policies could contribute significant emissions reductions from the energy sector in 2020 and would rely mainly on existing technologies that were adopted and proven in many countries, and that their widespread adoption would not harm economic growth of any country or region. These are:

Adopting specific energy efficiency measures

Limiting the construction and use of the least-efficient coal-fired power plants

Minimising methane (CH_4) emissions from upstream oil and gas production

Accelerating the (partial) phase-out of subsidies on fossil-fuel consumption.

In addition to mitigation measures, countries need to improve the resiliency of energy systems to climate change. Frameworks should be implemented to encourage adaptation and ensuring that the private sector considers climate change risks and impact as part of their investment decisions.

Shale "Revolution"

Another phenomenon currently having significant influence on the oil and gas production outlook is the successful application of technologies to develop oil and gas resources that are trapped in shale rock formations. It has been known for decades that the shale formations spread across the world contained significant volumes of hydrocarbons. Until less than a decade ago, however, there were no development options available to produce significant quantities of this resource at economically attractive conditions.

In the last decade, the successful application of horizontal drilling technology and of hydraulic fracturing has made the development of oil and gas trapped in shale economic for the first time. The first breakthrough occurred in shale gas production in the United States of America. From almost no production a decade ago, the United States in 2010 supplies almost a fifth of its gas demand from domestic shale gas production – and production is set to continue growing.

As a result of the increased ability to develop shale gas in a commercially viable manner, the domestic gas reserves in the United States have nearly doubled from 5-10 years ago and are now sufficient to cover current production rates for nearly a hundred years. This has made the United States self-sufficient in their gas supply and also increases the prospects of United States LNG exports. As of 10 March 2014, the United States Department of Energy (DOE) has approved 35 long-term applications to export lower-48 state LNG to countries with which the United States has Free Trade Agreements (FTAs) that require national treatment for trade in natural gas. Furthermore, DOE has granted 1 final and 5 provisional long-term authorisations to export domestically-produced lower-48 state LNG to non-FTA countries. The current over-abundant supply of natural gas in North America, as a result of the surge in shale gas production, has reduced gas prices significantly (from USD8-12/MMBtu five years ago to about USD4/MMBtu in 2013).

North American producers are now experiencing early successes applying the same technologies to tight oil-bearing rock formations. This has created an anticipation that a similar "revolution" could occur in the production of oil as what occurred with gas.

Based on the success in North America, attention has focused on this resource globally, and it is expected that significant amounts of unconventional gas could be developed worldwide, using the same technologies. The wider dispersion of shale gas reserves, compared with oil reserves, implies a strong potential of shale gas to be as a major alternative source of energy. A 2011 EIA survey of global unconventional resources singles out China, Poland and Argentina, among other geographies, as having significant potential. Most industry analysts expect, however, that large-scale development of these resources will not occur before the 2020s.

Continued Growth of LNG

Global LNG demand has grown dramatically in the last decade, from approximately 100 mtpa in 2000 to approximately 220 mtpa in 2010; an annual growth rate in excess of 8 percent. The global financial crisis and the growth of United States shale gas reduced the rate of growth temporarily, but this was followed by a significant resurgence in 2010. Demand growth in 2011

For additional analytical, marketing, investment and business opportunities information, please contact
Global Investment & Business Center, USA
(202) 546-2103. Fax: (202) 546-3275. E-mail: rusric@erols.com

also received an unexpected additional boost following the Tsunami and ensuing nuclear power accident in Japan.

The base case outlook for LNG demand remains strong for the rest of the decade and into the next, with most industry observers expecting annual demand growth in the 5-6 percent range this decade. More than two-thirds of the demand growth is expected to come from new and emerging LNG markets. The most significant and visible downside risk to demand growth in the near to medium term comes from Europe.

While the demand outlook remains strong for this decade as well as the next, the medium-to-long term (2020+) demand outlook has more uncertainties than the near term. An important factor in this uncertainty is the impact of unconventional gas on global LNG demand. "US-like" developments of shale gas in China, Europe and Latin America could impact price levels for gas in important regional markets and possibly also reduce LNG demand growth from some major demand centres in the next decade. Visibility on the magnitude of the impact will improve as we learn more on the exact nature of the resource and possible development options. Demand growth from emerging markets in the medium-to-long term may also add upside surprises to global LNG demand.

Due to the long construction lead time for LNG liquefaction projects, the rate of supply growth is relatively predictable in the near term. There was approximately 260 mtpa of installed LNG liquefaction capacity worldwide in 2010 (adjusted for average plant availability). Supply will grow significantly by 2015-2017, taking account of significant LNG projects that will come onstream in the meantime. By 2017, there should be as much as 320 mtpa of available capacity (an annual supply growth rate of approximately 3 percent). Significant additional capacity additions are on the drawing board beyond this initial supply window. Significant gas discoveries in East Africa (Mozambique and Tanzania) have led to expectations that LNG projects will be developed there too.

A third and potentially significant new source of supply is LNG supply from North America. The significant supply additions from shale gas production in North America, coupled with an unprecedented gas price difference between North America gas markets and Asian and European LNG markets is making its export potentially attractive for developers. LNG export projects look likely to be developed provided that price risk between markets can be managed and that political and policy support exists for these projects to obtain the needed permits and licenses.

In addition to the potential new supply projects mentioned above, it is possible for Qatar, one of the world leaders in gas production, to create additional supply on top of its already world leading production. Qatar has proven large gas resources, and the installed infrastructure would allow them to increase capacity through debottlenecking of existing trains as well as through incremental trains.

Emerging Markets and Downstream Outputs

Downstream processing (refining and petrochemicals) looks set to continue adding capacity to satisfy the growing demand, especially for the supply of emerging markets. Between 2012 and 2015, 6,400 mtpa of petrochemical capacity additions and 3.7 million barrels of refinery distillation capacity have been announced with more than 60 percent coming from the Middle East and Asia. Significant investments will be required to increase capacities. As has been the case historically, investments in downstream occur in cycles rather than consistently over time.

The downstream development in emerging economies, with increasing standards of living and rapid urbanization, also leads to an increased need for capacity and reliability of power generation, transmission and distribution infrastructure.

Growing Awareness of Sustainability

The large scale of development and growth in the energy sector occurs amidst increased awareness of and concern around the need to develop the planet in a sustainable manner. Governments and citizens around the world are attempting to ensure continued economic growth while recognising challenges related to carbon emissions and the need to preserve resources and the living environment for future generations. This awareness has spurred significant innovation in energy efficient technologies as well as renewable energy technologies, amongst others.

Progress is being made to achieve "grid parity" for renewable energy resources such as waste-toenergy, solar and wind power. Grid parity is when energy from renewable resources are generated at a competitive cost with conventional resources without Government subsidies. Significant innovation also plays an important role in reducing the high cost of renewable energy technologies.

In line with the global efforts on enhancing sustainable growth, APEC economies, including Brunei Darussalam, have set an ambitious regional goal of a 45 percent energy intensity reduction by 2035 versus a 2005 baseline. This would heighten the importance of natural gas, given it is 'cleaner' than alternatives such as crude oil and coal, which could generate up to 50 percent higher carbon dioxide emissions.

Brunei Darussalam Context

Despite the increased focus on energy efficiency and sustainability, demand for energy will continue to grow at a frenetic pace for the next 30 to 50 years. Given the sheer scale of demand growth, fossil fuels will continue to remain as the primary source of supply to meet this energy demand. This creates many opportunities for an oil and gas producing nation like Brunei Darussalam. With our impeccable credentials of reliability and safety, our long positive track record of partnership with key consuming nations and being in the heart of Southeast Asia, Brunei Darussalam is in a favourable position to continue as a leading upstream producer, particularly natural gas, and growing the downstream industry.

Brunei Darussalam recognises the importance of a low carbon economy in strengthening energy security, creating green jobs and generating new sources of economic growth to help achieve our energy intensity goal. The intensification of greenhouse gas emissions reduction efforts will place increased emphasis on utilisation of cleaner fuels such as natural gas and renewable forms of energy.

To enhance energy security and sustainability, improve energy efficiency and accelerate deployment of renewable energy and clean energy supply for Brunei Darussalam, concerted efforts and partnership among all stakeholders are imperative.

WAWASAN BRUNEI 2035

BRUNEI DARUSSALAM'S ENERGY SECTOR TO PLAY A PIVOTAL ROLE

Brunei Darussalam today enjoys one of the most advanced standards of living in Asia. Its per capita income is one of the highest in Asia, the standards of education and health are among the best in the developing world and it has already achieved almost all of the targets outlined in the Millennium Development Goals. This has largely been the result of political stability created by the Government of His Majesty, investment of its oil and gas revenues in the development of its infrastructure and far-reaching programs on social welfare.

Wawasan Brunei 2035

As current prosperity cannot be taken for granted, the National Vision 2035 - known as Wawasan Brunei 2035 - has been launched with 3 main goals for Brunei Darussalam:

To make Brunei Darussalam a nation which will be widely recognised for the accomplishment of its educated and highly skilled people as measured by the highest international standards.

To achieve quality of life that is among the top 10 countries in the world.

To build a dynamic and sustainable economy with an income per capita among the world's top

10.

Exhibit 2.3

Brunei Darussalam's energy sector will contribute BND 42 billion to the 2035 GDP

3 Strategic Goals of Brunei Darussalam's energy sector and 10 KPIs have been developed by EDPMO

For additional analytical, marketing, investment and business opportunities information, please contact
Global Investment & Business Center, USA
(202) 546-2103. Fax: (202) 546-3275. E-mail: rusric@erols.com

To ensure the accomplishment of these goals, 8 strategies have been identified in the Wawasan Brunei 2035, in ensuring that all aspects of development are being implemented systematically and effectively, covering among others, education, economic development, local business development and environment strategy. Additionally, the government is currently conducting a study to increase productivity in all sectors in Brunei Darussalam, including the energy sector.

The Role of the Energy Sector: Targets and Priority Areas

All sectors have a role to play in the realisation of the Wawasan Brunei 2035. Growth of other sectors such as tourism, banking, finance and insurance and info-communication technology, will bring increasing diversity to the economy. At the same time, the energy sector still has a pivotal role to play. It will continue to act as a catalyst for investment, education and infrastructure development. As such it will provide some of the "fuel" for Brunei Darussalam's continued economic success.

Achieving the objectives of Wawasan Brunei 2035 will require a significant increase in the activity level of the energy sector. The aspiration for growth in the broader energy sector (including upstream, downstream energy services and power sub sectors) is for the sector to grow at approximately 6 percent per annum in real terms, from a GDP contribution of BND 10 billion in 2010 to BND 42 billion in 2035 (refer to Exhibit 2.3).

Brunei Darussalam's energy sector is entering an era with new challenges. We need to boost upstream production by maximising the potential of our mature fields and venturing into further exploration and development activities. We also need to go further downstream to maximise the value creation potential of these upstream assets. In doing so, we must ensure that locals are highly educated and technically skilled which will match the highly skilled and specialised jobs as required by these industries. All of these objectives must be achieved in a sustainable manner that ensures secure, reliable and efficient use of energy. This will require proactive management and initiatives on the part of the EDPMO as well as other public and private sector stakeholders.

We need to set ambitious, yet realistic goals, track them, debottleneck issues as they arise and then put in place key enablers such as an optimal regulatory environment and a talented local workforce to attract the right investments and ensure delivery on our commitments.

The growth in the energy sector is being addressed by outlining three strategic goals:

Strategic Goal 1 – Strengthen and Grow Oil and Gas Upstream and Downstream Activities

Strategic Goal 2 – Ensure Safe, Secure, Reliable and Efficient Supply and Use of Energy

Strategic Goal 3 – Maximise Economic Spin-Offs from Energy Industry – Boost Local Content and Secure High Participation of Local Workforce

The EDPMO has developed 10 key performance indicators (KPIs) (as shown in Exhibit 2.4) in order to address needs across the different segments and parts of the value chain in the energy sector. An initial set of supporting initiatives have also been identified in order to ensure that the energy sector delivers its targets by 2035, thus ensuring a sufficient buffer period to take into account any final additional or mitigating actions needed to attain the set targets.

To ensure that this transformational step-up in the energy sector is achieved, change needs to stem from an increased ability to compete and openness to investment and knowledge. While leveraging critical regulatory support and government oversight to accelerate results, we need to educate and train our people and grow the capabilities of our industries.

Hence, 4 key enablers have been identified to ensure that Brunei Darussalam grows in a manner that is competitive and sustainable. These are:

Enabler 1 – Implementing supportive policy and regulatory frameworks

Enabler 2 – Growing Bruneian human capital

Enabler 3 – Attracting investment to fuel growth

Enabler 4 – Ensuring delivery on our commitments

The attainment of these goals for the energy sector will support and ultimately achieve the goals under the Wawasan Brunei 2035. The initiatives developed to achieve these goals, are part of a journey, and not a one-off effort. The EDPMO, the entirety of the Government, public and private investors in our energy sector and the public at large will labour diligently over the next two decades to continuously improve our success in the energy sector and to ensure that we achieve our goals.

The current assessment and supporting initiatives for each of these strategic goals, KPIs and enablers are elaborated in the subsequent sections.

Green Growth: Brunei Darussalam's Perspective on a Green Industry and Green Jobs

Brunei Darussalam recognizes the importance of green growth in promoting a clean, low carbon and green economy for sustainable development. A green industry promotes sustainable methods of production and consumption i.e. energy efficient, low-carbon and minimize waste with less pollution. Among others, the initiatives include effective energy management, green transportation and green energy technologies that are responsibly managed throughout their lifecycle.

The greening of industries will become one of the core determinants of economic competitiveness and sustainable growth for Brunei Darussalam's future industrial development. This will play a role in green job creation especially for small medium enterprises (SMEs) as well as increase competitiveness through the reduction of operation costs, increase efficiency and production.

Exhibit 2.4

3 STRATEGIC GOALS AND 10 KPIS BRUNEI DARUSSALAM'S ENERGY SECTOR IN 2035

For additional analytical, marketing, investment and business opportunities information, please contact
Global Investment & Business Center, USA
(202) 546-2103. Fax: (202) 546-3275. E-mail: rusric@erols.com

Ratio of expectation reserves added eachOil and Gas Reserve1 year and annual production volume (oil and Ratio 0.5

>1 >1Replacement Ratio

gas) Barrel Oil Equivalent2 Oil and Gas Production Gross production of oil and gas 408,000 430,000 650,000

(BOE) per day

Downstream Economic BND Million3 Revenue from sales of products 300 3,000 5,000Output per year

Number of major accidents for the energy Number per4 Ensure safe operations 0 0 0industry year Ton oil equivalent Ratio of primary energy demand for all per USD5 Energy Intensity 390 320 215 sectors and GDP

Million of GDP (2005 baseline)

Renewable Energy in Total Power generation from renewable sources 6 MWh 808 124,000 954,000Power Generation Mix of energy

Reliable Energy -Power Number of incidents of power outages of Number per7A >300 100 <50Outage (>1 hour) more than 1 hour duration in a year year

Number of incidents where there is a supply Reliable Energy interruption for transportation fuel for 7B Interruption in supply of general public consumption at more than Number 0 0 0 Transport fuel 50% fuel stations at any district in a given day

Contribution from local industries and Local Content Spending in workforce in the provision of goods and8 % 15 50 >80Energy Industry

services supplied to the energy sector in Brunei Darussalam Number of employment in the energy Number 20,000 30,000 50,000industryEmployment in Energy9 Industry Number of locals working in the energy Number 10,000 20,000 40,000industry

Number of local companies that have atLocal Companies10 least 40% of sales of goods and services Number 0 8 30Development generated from overseas market

The green industry will grasp the potential for industries to achieve higher economic growth and revenues with less resource use and pollution. Green industries will be creative and innovative, constantly developing new ways of improving national economic, environmental and social performance, while the government policies for supporting green industry will be undertaken.

For additional analytical, marketing, investment and business opportunities information, please contact
Global Investment & Business Center, USA
(202) 546-2103. Fax: (202) 546-3275. E-mail: rusric@erols.com

Creating green jobs in Brunei Darussalam are not out-of-reach. In these circumstances, the transition to green growth and job creation can go hand-in-hand. Green jobs can take place in energy sector, agricultural, manufacturing, research and development (R&D), administrative, and service activities that contribute substantially to preserving or restoring environmental quality. This includes jobs that help to protect ecosystems and biodiversity; reduce energy, materials, and water consumption through high-efficiency strategies; de-carbonize the economy; and minimize or altogether avoid generation of all forms of waste and pollution.

Referring to a World Bank study published in March 2012[4], the green industry in Brunei Darussalam could create job opportunities up to at least 2,000 jobs by 2035.

BNERI: A Think Tank through Policy Design and Strategic Solutions

The newly established Brunei National Energy Research Institute (BNERI) aspires to become an international centre of excellence on energy that will support the Wawasan Brunei 2035.

Its strategic objective is to support and promote Brunei Darussalam's energy security, economic growth and environmental sustainability through policy research and design, including policy implementation on renewable and alternative energy, energy efficiency and conservation, power and oil and gas.

BNERI shall recommend and accelerate the energy strategies by providing policy research solutions, information, expertise and capacity building to ensure that over the long term, necessary energy development policies and programs are in action and harmony with the economic growth and the environmental sustainability of Brunei Darussalam under Wawasan Brunei 2035.

The ambition is to make BNERI a centre of excellence on energy in Brunei Darussalam with plans to make it an institute of at least 10 - 15 researchers over the next three years. BNERI is currently governed by a Statutory Board and advised by an International Advisory Board. The Boards are chaired by the Minister of Energy at the Prime Minister's Office of Brunei Darussalam. BNERI is headed by a Chief Executive Officer (CEO) who reports to the Statutory Board.

The study suggests that green jobs creation in industries providing environmental services accounted about 1% of total employment.

3 KPIs to support Brunei Darussalam's energy sector to further strengthen the country's economy by sustaining the upstream industry and further diversifying the downstream industry

THREE STRATEGIC GOALS TO REALISE BRUNEI DARUSSALAM'S ENERGY VISION

STRATEGIC GOAL 1: STRENGTHEN AND GROW OIL AND GAS UPSTREAM AND DOWNSTREAM ACTIVITIES

The energy sector, mainly driven by exporting crude oil and LNG, has been the primary driver of overall GDP for the country and will continue to retain primacy as a key measure of the contribution of the energy sector to Brunei Darussalam's economic development. Growing the downstream industry will help Brunei Darussalam diversify its energy sector, strengthen its resilience to primary energy shocks and maximise the value of upstream oil and gas through the development of higher value added downstream industries. In order to further strengthen the country's economy by sustaining the upstream and further diversifying the downstream industry, the EDPMO has set three KPIs to achieve this goal:

Oil and Gas Reserve Replacement Ratio (RRR): Ratio of expected reserve addition to production volumes. The target is to continue to maintain an RRR of 1 or greater. This will ensure that Brunei Darussalam continues to benefit from production in the energy sector in the long-term and is able to sustain its reliance on self-produced oil and gas.

Oil and Gas Production: Gross production of Brunei Darussalam's oil and gas (both conventional as well as unconventional). The target is to grow production from 400,000 BOEPD in 2010 to about 430,000 BOEPD by 2017 and to more than 650,000 BOEPD by 2035. EDPMO will continuously monitor external variables that could require refining the target in order to i) maximise output from the fields, ii) account for global supply and demand fluctuations and oil price movements, and iii) ensure sustainability and conservation of oil and gas fields to optimise long term production.

Downstream Economic Output: the revenue from current and future domestic downstream industries and its sales is and will continue to be tracked across all downstream sub-industries - refinery, chemicals and petrochemical plants. Brunei Darussalam seeks to increase its downstream economic output from about BND 300 million in 2012 to BND 3 billion by 2017, and reach BND 5 billion by 2035.

Current Assessment

The Reserve Replacement Ratio (RRR) from the two major producing concessionaires has been in the range of 0.3 to 0.7 over the last decade. Recent RRR has been higher; above 1 in last five years. The major concessionaires have developed plans to ensure that the success of the past few years is sustained for the rest of this decade, with significant exploration programmes in place. Existing plans, if successful, together with findings from offshore blocks, are expected to deliver 3.5 billion BOE cumulative expected reserves addition by 2035 (representing a RRR of above 1). In the event that the RRR is below the target threshold, we will adjust the upstream production target to ensure long term sustainability and conservation of oil and gas reserves.

Priority Initiative 1: Exploration of Unlicensed Acreage

To increase reserves, the EDPMO seeks to ensure the expansion of exploration in areas that are yet unlicensed including the frontier areas. "Unlicensed acreage" refers to new unexplored areas, areas that are explored but not currently contracted for operations and relinquished areas.

The EDPMO will review existing energy legislation and draft new energy legislation as required to facilitate exploration activities. Among the legislation to be introduced is the Hydrocarbon Data Order (HDO) that culminates in the establishment of a Hydrocarbon Data Centre (HDC) and an entity called the Hydrocarbon Data Management and Information Services (HDMIS). The HDO acts as a framework to expand and streamline the management of domestically acquired hydrocarbon data with an ultimate aim of creating an environment conducive to conducting an efficient and cost-effective exploration ventures in the country through the access of hydrocarbon data at the HDC.

For additional analytical, marketing, investment and business opportunities information, please contact
Global Investment & Business Center, USA
(202) 546-2103. Fax: (202) 546-3275. E-mail: rusric@erols.com

The implementation of such initiatives is expected to draw earnest players with strong expertise and broad experience, that may also include new and independent but competitive players, to spur high exploration activities in the country. Such vital partnership is envisaged to accelerate the development of these unlicensed acreages, shorten the lead time between discovery and production, while actualising the implementation of innovative but proven technologies (e.g. broad-band and multi-azimuth seismic surveys, Controlled Source Electromagnetic (CSEM) and in other areas that includes production systems e.g., floating operations for offshore unlicensed acreage) to speed up operations.

Priority Initiative 2: New Field Development

The EDPMO will also facilitate the execution of new field development projects and the increase in new reserves through:

Accelerating the study of maturing fields ("Scope For Recovery") to enable booking of new reserves, and

Developing unconnected marginal oil and gas fields through a cluster development approach.

Priority Initiative 3: Exploration of New Resources

The EDPMO will also continue to explore the availability and development potential of new sources of energy. Common categories include tight gas, requiring a large number of horizontal wells and hydraulic fracturing to produce economically; coal bed methane (CBM), where the gas is produced from and stored in low permeability coal streaks; and

A target of Reserve Replacement Ratio >1 by 2035 Oil and Gas Production >650,000 BOEPD by 2035 shale gas, where gas is found in very low permeability shale deposits, again requiring many horizontal fractured wells for economic production.

Coal Development - The Government of Brunei Darussalam via EDPMO is currently assessing the potential of coal resources. From preliminary assessments, Brunei Darussalam has significant thermal coal endowment within the country's interior. Hurdles to commercial development include the potential impact on the Heart of Borneo area.

CBM Development -Alternatively, if the development of CBM from Brunei Darussalam's coal deposits proves feasible, it could potentially add 0.35 billion BOE of gas resource by 2035. CBM could potentially be utilised for domestic power purposes.

Unconventional Gas -Globally, unconventional gas are generally considered to be those hydrocarbon volumes situated in rocks of very low permeability (<1millidarcy) and generally developments are concentrated onshore due to the high cost. In Brunei Darussalam, early efforts in unconventional plays, studies and pilots are ongoing for low-resistivity pay and lower permeability gas reservoirs in current producing concessionaires.

Current Assessment

For additional analytical, marketing, investment and business opportunities information, please contact
Global Investment & Business Center, USA
(202) 546-2103. Fax: (202) 546-3275. E-mail: rusric@erols.com

Two major concessionaires are currently operating in Brunei Darussalam and covers 6,320 square kilometres of concession areas. Together, both areas achieved a gross oil and gas production of 372,000 BOEPD in 2013, with an approximate 40 to 60 percent split between oil and gas. In a scenario of "no further activity" (i.e. no significant additional investments are made to develop new fields or ensure increased recovery from maturing fields), the production from these fields is expected to halve (i.e. 200,000 BOEPD) by 2035 as a result of natural field decline.

Improved oil recovery (IOR) or enhanced oil recovery (EOR) and near field exploration techniques are currently being developed to sustain the production level from existing fields. This could potentially increase the oil recovery (percentage of the oil recovered over the total amount of oil originally in place in the field) to about 40 percent from the current 30 percent.

Local and international exploration and production (E&P) operators, including the Brunei National Petroleum Company (PetroleumBRUNEI), are exploring oil and gas development in awarded onshore and offshore acreage. This has the potential to add up to 450,000 BOEPD by 2035. In early 2001, Brunei Darussalam embarked on one of the largest single three-dimensional (3-D) seismic surveys in the world (acquisition of approximately 10,000 square kilometre 3-D seismic data over deepwater offshore areas in the Brunei Darussalam Exclusive Economic Zone). As a result, two deepwater offshore blocks covering an area about 5,000 square kilometres each were awarded to consortiums. Additional oil and gas volumes from these blocks could help Brunei Darussalam further develop its downstream industry. If successful, these initiatives put together will help Brunei Darussalam achieve, and potentially exceed, the target of 650,000 BOEPD by 2035. To plan for a scenario where deepwater offshore blocks deliver less incremental production than the forecasted potential, Brunei will undertake several initiatives to stimulate production, such as the following:

Priority Initiative 1: Rejuvenate Existing Fields

A core focus area in upstream will be the rejuvenation of our current producing assets to enhance recovery from these fields and maximise production. 'Ever-greening' of our macro-assets will at first require conducting a full field review and acquiring new, deeper data as well as conducting additional geological research to identify the potential actions to be taken. Global best practices demonstrate that the deployment of new technology, coupled with the right incentives for mature field (re)development can create the conditions to increase the recovery (percentage of the oil recovered over the total amount of oil originally in place in the field) from a global average of less than 30 percent to 40 percent or more.

The EDPMO currently encourages operators to deploy state-of-the-art subsurface IOR and EOR technologies in Brunei Darussalam, to maximise the recovery from existing fields. The EDPMO will review regulatory measures that could help boost the use of these modern technologies. Such techniques could potentially increase production by 10 to 20 percent, which would mean increasing recovery to about 45 percent in those fields.

Priority Initiative 2: Maximise Economic Recovery from New Discovered Fields

As initiatives to ensure the hydrocarbon resources of Brunei Darussalam are appropriately explored, developed and managed in the new discovered field, the EDPMO requires all operators to submit field development plans (FDP) with an objective of maximising economic ultimate recovery of the total hydrocarbon including evaluating the complete full life cycle opportunities which encompasses secondary and tertiary recovery schemes. In addition, the operators also need to justify why remaining volumes are deemed unrecoverable.

For additional analytical, marketing, investment and business opportunities information, please contact
Global Investment & Business Center, USA
(202) 546-2103. Fax: (202) 546-3275. E-mail: rusric@erols.com

Priority Initiative 3: Review Potential Solutions for Development of Small and Unconnected Fields

Development of small and unconnected fields faces the challenge of economic viability. Small field developments often lack the scale needed to make the economic returns attractive. The EDPMO will review measures, which other countries have adopted in similar situations, to make these small and unconnected fields economically viable. Some of the measures that the Government could potentially leverage are:

Promote the sharing of infrastructure, including straddled fields development to spread infrastructure cost among the various players through clustering approach with opportunity of early production. Industry best practices indicate that third party access to infrastructure can bring on-stream discoveries for new and smaller players. Such practices include, for example, upholding infrastructure safety and integrity, protecting the environment and support-negotiated access in a timely manner. Brunei Darussalam is pursuing similar development concepts to promote sharing of infrastructure and leveraging existing facilities.

Adoption of advanced technology, such as 4D seismic survey sub-sea solutions for minor discoveries and discoveries in offshore, sub-sea tie backs and extended reach drilling for various small and large oil fields.

Fallow acreage policy schemes to develop small fields (for fields that are smaller than a certain materiality threshold), where blocks with no activity for a certain number of years can be re-auctioned to new players. This allows new licensees to leverage the seismic information available and deploy the best of their technologies to develop the fields. The UK, for example, has managed to develop fields with less than 30 MMBOE in reserves through this policy, resulting in the relicensing of 180 blocks or subareas since 2002.

The 2035 Target of Downstream Economic Output is BND 5 billion

Production and reserves are closely linked, as an increase in discovery of reserves implies an increase in production, provided that these reserves could be extracted. Hence, the initiatives listed in the previous section will also impact production.

Priority Initiative 4: Upstream International Ventures

Brunei Darussalam has the potential to grow an international presence in the oil and gas industry. With its long-standing experience and expertise in oil and gas, Brunei Darussalam has the capability to build a strong portfolio of international assets whether it be in the upstream or downstream sector. Possible areas of focus include Asia, Africa and North America.

Strategies to building this portfolio could be done through PetroleumBRUNEI or government investment companies and through their collaboration with reputable energy companies. In the upstream, one investment strategy is to develop a well-balanced portfolio consisting of new acreage, new discoveries, new development and production enhancement of existing fields. In the mid and downstream sectors, there will be a focus on the development of natural gas and LNG related projects covering the whole LNG chain including power generation. Our aspirational target in international ventures investment is to achieve around 100,000 BOEPD by 2035 as part of the overall target.

For additional analytical, marketing, investment and business opportunities information, please contact
Global Investment & Business Center, USA
(202) 546-2103. Fax: (202) 546-3275. E-mail: rusric@erols.com

Current Assessment

The existing downstream industry in Brunei Darussalam comes from methanol produced by the Brunei Methanol Company (BMC) which is targeted to contribute about BND 300 million to the economy annually. Both EDPMO and Brunei Economic Development Board (BEDB) are working closely to develop integrated chains in a range of downstream industries to boost value addition and wealth creation of the energy sector. This will also promote overall resilience by expanding beyond the reliance on sales revenue from crude oil and LNG.

In order to increase the downstream economic output, there is a need to attract investors to develop and diversify additional downstream opportunities such as gas-based petrochemicals, crude and condensate based petrochemicals. These prospects would be spurred on by the successful commercialisation of the offshore gas assets. An expanded downstream industry would create jobs and business opportunities across a wide range of sectors.

The relevant Government agencies will provide the appropriate support and incentives to secure the investments in these downstream industries and also to improve the competitiveness of Brunei Darussalam's industry in by reducing production costs and thus gaining access to the world's market.

Initial projects have already been identified and are currently being assessed such as refining and the production of basic and specialty chemicals and fertilizers. In attracting investments in downstream sectors, this will maximise the total GDP across the full energy value chain (upstream and downstream) and this will be balanced with other core Government priorities such as employment diversification and improving energy efficiency. The economic output from this set of initiatives is estimated to amount to approximately BND 21 billion in an un-risked (i.e. not risk weighted) assessment scenario (see Exhibit 3.1).

In addition to Sungai Liang Industrial Park (SPARK) in Sungai Liang, Pulau Muara Besar (PMB) will soon be established as a petrochemical industrial hub. Both SPARK and PMB are forecasted to attract additional foreign investors. It is expected that refined finished products will be produced such as motor gasoline and diesel as well as petrochemicals such as paraxylene, benzene and other such materials.

Priority Initiative: Evaluate Feasibility of Downstream Derivatives

The EDPMO has conducted a preliminary review of a range of options to further diversify the downstream industry in Brunei Darussalam. These options include leveraging natural gas and other potential high value adding energy industrial development options (refer to Exhibit 3.2).

Five different options have been identified and is based on either natural gas or crude oil as the starting building block. This would include the addition of a new refinery, the setting up of ammonia and urea derivatives, the extension of chemical and petrochemical chain and aluminium.

An initial assessment indicates that three potential downstream derivatives should be further explored. The economic and technological feasibility, along with the impact on other macroeconomic objectives such as employment and sustainable energy development, needs to be analysed in further detail.

■ Extension of Petrochemical Chain to include Ethylene and Propylene Building Blocks

The EDPMO would consider opportunities to extend the petrochemical chain. Some options are:

a) Gas and naphtha based ethylene crackers and downstream derivatives such as LDPE, HDPE, ethylene di-chloride, should the gas from offshore blocks possesses high concentrations of ethane. The plant could be configured to run either on gas or naphtha fuel.

b) Conversion of methanol to propylene using a recently developed technological breakthrough in China and further downstream derivatives such as polypropylene and acronitrile. A pilot plant on this design has already been successfully launched, with China announcing plans to increase propylene capacity by 3 mtpa.

c) Specialty chemicals from methanol chain such as Vinyl Acetate Monomer (VAM).

d) Creation of spin offs from the existing methanol facility in Brunei Darussalam. The SPARK is a 271 hectare piece of land that is home to a methanol plant operated by BMC. Methanol is widely used in the manufacturing of chemicals such as formaldehyde and polyoxymethylene (POM). Developing alternative industries from this chain will offer more values to the socio

- economic benefit of the country.

The feasibility of these options will have to be assessed, taking into account factors such as the provision of gas and the presence of logistics or port infrastructure to facilitate the export of the final end products across the region to potential markets. Furthermore, there will be keen competition coming from cheaply produced products from other countries which are able to

For additional analytical, marketing, investment and business opportunities information, please contact
Global Investment & Business Center, USA
(202) 546-2103. Fax: (202) 546-3275. E-mail: rusric@erols.com

leverage on lower cost coal-based technologies and subsidised natural gas (about USD 1/MMBtu).

■ Development of Aluminium Derivatives

The demand for aluminium as an end product is projected to grow at 2 to 4 percent per annum from 2010 to 2020 in major Asian markets. This is mainly driven by the transportation, electronics, communication and construction industries. The EDPMO will assess the feasibility of setting up the midstream derivatives of an aluminium smelter (such as die casting, forging and extrusion) to produce higher value-added aluminium derivatives. Discussions are currently underway to develop new industries requiring natural gas and electricity. The focus within the next few years will be to ensure that these projects are implemented and commissioned.

■ Pioneering New Low Carbon Technologies such as Hydrogen Fuel

A variety of efficient end use technologies and alternative fuels have been proposed to address energy-related environmental or supply security challenges in fuel use. Recently, hydrogen have received increased attention world wide because it offers a long term potential to radically reduce several important societal impacts of fuel.

STRATEGIC GOAL 2: ENSURE SAFE, SECURE, RELIABLE AND EFFICIENT SUPPLY AND USE OF ENERGY

he oil and gas industry, is classed as a major hazards industry. With significant operations located both onshore and offshore, the key focus of the national safety and health policy is to continuously improve safety and health standards in the entire supply chain of this sector. Due to aging infrastructure, a key focus area for the oil and gas industry is asset integrity. Maintaining

For additional analytical, marketing, investment and business opportunities information, please contact
Global Investment & Business Center, USA
(202) 546-2103. Fax: (202) 546-3275. E-mail: rusric@erols.com

asset integrity, is not only a key enabler to achieving good safety performance, it also plays a very important role in maximising the country's oil and gas production.

The KPI that relates to the health and safety of oil and gas sector is:

- Ensure Safe Operations: The priority for safety performance is to ensure that high risk activities are effectively managed and controlled; and all reasonably practicable measures necessary to prevent major accidents have been taken to limit the consequences to persons, assets and the environment. The target is therefore to have zero major accidents.

Climate change and other environmental concerns are becoming more important in the national agenda especially in the effort to ensure domestic economic and energy securities. An energy sector that does not compromise the environment is thus a prerequisite. Significant steps toward this is decarbonisation of the primary energy demand and supply through energy conservation and renewable energy resources respectively.

The KPI which track the low-carbon primary energy demand and supply are:

Energy Intensity: An indicator used to assess the performance of energy efficiency that is measured by the ratio of primary energy demand to the country's GDP value contribution measured in 2005 real terms. The target is to reduce energy intensity by 45 percent by 2035 in line with Brunei Darussalam's commitment to APEC.

Renewable Energy in Total Power Generation Mix: Renewable energy is energy that comes from resources that can be naturally replenished such as solar and waste-to-energy. Currently, Brunei Darussalam produces about 1,700 MWh of solar energy per year. The target is to increase the share of renewable energy in the total power generation mix by 2.7 percent or 124,000 MWh by 2017 and by 10 percent or 954,000 MWh by 2035.

Reliability of domestic power and fuel supplies is an important component that makes up Brunei Darussalam's energy security. These supplies are very much vulnerable to any disruptions that cause power outages and insufficient domestic fuel supply. Therefore, it is important to increase the reliability of these supplies in order to lessen the country's vulnerability and economic risks

Ensure Safe Operations, zero major accidents

Energy Intensity decreasing to 215 toe per USD Million of GDP by 2035

associated with interrupted power and fuel shortages. The two KPIs relevant to reliability of energy supply in Brunei Darussalam are:

Power Outages: An incident of unscheduled power outages that lasts for more than one hour resulting from technical failure, human error and severe weather. This does not include scheduled power outages for maintenance purposes. The target is to reduce power outages frequency to less than 100 per year by 2017 and to less than 50 per year by 2035.

Interruption in Supply of Transport Fuel: An incident whereby there is a supply interruption on gasoline (Premium 97, Super 92 and Regular 85) or diesel at more than half of the total pump stations in the respective districts in one day. The target is to achieve zero interruptions in transportation fuel supply.

For additional analytical, marketing, investment and business opportunities information, please contact
Global Investment & Business Center, USA
(202) 546-2103. Fax: (202) 546-3275. E-mail: rusric@erols.com

Current Assessment

Health, Safety, Security and Environment remains as the top priority as Brunei Darussalam continues to develop its main economic activity. Regulating health and safety in a high-risk oil and gas industry has proven to be challenging for the Government, but has at the same time triggered the drive towards achieving a zero major accident in the industry.

Priority Initiative: Develop Safety and Health Regulatory Framework

In order to set the required standard for Brunei Darussalam and to provide a common framework for the energy industry, the Government has introduced the Control of Major Accident Hazards (COMAH) regulations. The COMAH Regulations 2013 underpin and support the overarching safety and health requirements of the Workplace Safety and Health Order 2009 (formally enacted on 1 August 2013 by the Ministry of Home Affairs). The COMAH regulations impose a duty, on those in control of premises where hazardous substances are present, or where drilling activities are taking place, to ensure that the premises are being operated safely and all major accident hazards have been identified and risk control measures implemented. The COMAH regulations define what is a Major Accident. Further, companies in the energy sector will be stimulated to have a good safety and health culture and a proper consequence management system to ensure we can reduce all safety and health accidents to as low as is reasonably practicable. The target of this KPI is to have zero major accidents year-on-year.

The COMAH regulations cover new projects as well as existing facilities. A refinery project that is currently under construction at Pulau Muara Besar, requires to be in compliance with the COMAH Regulations. Under this regulation, the duty holder of the refinery is required to submit a detailed design notification to EDPMO and a Safety Case prior to operation for approval.

The project execution on Pulau Muara Besar will be closely monitored by a Project Compliance Team, consisting of experienced personnel, throughout the various project stages commencing from the design, construction, commissioning until operation so as to assure the best engineering practice are being followed so that the risks are controlled to as low as it is reasonably practicable.

Current Assessment

In line with APEC aspiration, Brunei Darussalam is working towards an ambitious goal of a 45 percent energy intensity reduction by 2035 (with 2005 as the base year). For 2005, at GDP of USD 6,864 million and population of 370,000, Brunei Darussalam energy intensity was at 390 ton oil equivalent per US$ Million GDP. In 2012, Brunei Darussalam's energy intensity was at 346 ton oil equivalent per US$ Million GDP at a GDP of USD 9,895 and population of 401,000. Anticipated increase in power requirements from the development of Brunei Darussalam's emerging downstream industry and other economic activities will increase domestic energy demand, while new oil and gas discoveries are expected to boost the country's GDP. Significant measures thus need to be carried out as to ensure the reduction of the country's energy intensity.

Priority Initiative: Evaluate Range of Options to Reduce Energy Intensity

For additional analytical, marketing, investment and business opportunities information, please contact
Global Investment & Business Center, USA
(202) 546-2103. Fax: (202) 546-3275. E-mail: rusric@erols.com

In achieving the energy intensity target, concerted efforts and close coordination among relevant stakeholders such as those of Government agencies, industry and individuals are instrumental. Government agencies work together in evaluating legislative, financial and fiscal policy measures that promote energy efficiency and low-energy intensive industries. Industries role include identification of technical levers that reduce energy usage over time while individuals shift consumption behaviour towards energy efficiency that includes making choices on high energy efficient appliances (refer to Exhibit 3.3).

The EDPMO is currently in the process of enacting a regulatory framework on Energy Efficiency and Conservation (EEC) through the National EEC Committee, a platform that coordinates EEC efforts with various stakeholders at a high-level and oversees the implementation the EEC Plan of Actions on four major sectors namely residential, commercial, industrial and transportation. This Committee is co-chaired by the Minister of Energy at the Prime Minister's Office, the Minister of Development and the Minister of Communication.

Residential and commercial buildings: Measures include applying "smart" tariffs, application of high-energy efficient technologies in buildings, installation of smart meters and evaluation of feasibility of altering tariff structure that promotes efficient consumption behaviour. Implementation of the initiatives set out in the residential sector would reduce energy consumption to 36 percent from the Business-As-Usual (BAU) scenario which is about 16.2 percent of the total targeted energy intensity reduction by 2035. Similar measures in commercial sector could result up to 41 percent reduction which is about 18.5 percent of the total targeted energy intensity reduction by 2035.

Industrial Sector - Implementation of the EEC initiatives set out under the industrial sector would reduce energy consumption to 10 percent from the Business-As-Usual (BAU) scenario which is about 4.5 percent of the total targeted energy intensity reduction by 2035.

Transport: Under the jurisdiction of Ministry of Communications, measures towards energy intensity reduction include promotion of fuel efficient technologies, the use of hybrid cars for private transportation and introduction of fuel economy standards. These efforts are set to reduce about 13 percent of energy consumption from the Business-As-Usual (BAU) scenario which is about 5.9 percent of the total targeted energy intensity reduction by 2035. The Government through Centre of Strategic and Policy Studies (CSPS) has introduced a Brunei Land Transport Masterplan that promotes modal shift towards public transportation and will play a role in further reducing energy consumption in the sector.

Power generation: The Department of Electrical Services (DES) and Berakas Power Management Company (BPMC) have set out plans to increase efficiency in the power generation from 23 percent to more than 45 percent. Plans include implementation of combined cycle turbine and co-generation powerplant, reduction of partial load operation, improvement of transmission and distribution losses, mandate an energy efficiency standard for new power plants and reduction of gas consumption through integration of renewable and alternative energy as to meet domestic power demand.

In realising all the above initiatives, a number of legislative measures are under consideration by the EDPMO, Ministry of Communications, Ministry of Development and Ministry of Education. In 2009, the Centre for Strategic and Policy Studies (CSPS) has conducted a Brunei Energy Efficiency and Conservation Study on the Roadmap Formulation and Policy Advice via a consultant firm which as a result, designed seven key policies that come with the following recommendations:

Policy 1: Appliance Energy Efficiency Standards and Labeling

Establishing legal framework for energy efficiency standards.

Setting up minimum energy efficiency standards for air conditioners in the first phase, followed by refrigerators, lightings and other appliances in the subsequent phases.

Designing the types of energy efficiency indicators and rating scale to be adopted for each appliance.

Introducing energy labeling for selected electrical appliances.

Policy 2: Building Regulation

Under the jurisdiction of Ministry of Development, initiatives include:

– Establishing legal framework for Building Energy Efficiency.

– Introducing energy efficient or green building labels or certificates.

– Demonstrating green buildings

Policy 3: Energy Management

Introducing the energy management process that is compatible with international standards such as ISO 50001.

Introducing energy audit policy for buildings and industries

Promoting Energy Service Company (ESCO)

Policy 4: Fuel Economy Regulation

Under the jurisdiction of Ministry of Communications measures include:

– Evaluate the possibility of implementing fuel economy regulations.

– Promoting the utilisation of hybrid and electric vehicles.

Policy 5: Electricity Tariff Reform

Expanding the current progressive electricity tariff for residential sector to other sectors when appropriate.

Evaluating feasibility of altering tariff structure to promote desired consumption behaviour.

Conducting regular surveys to understand the optimum tariff schedule through understanding the relationships between household income and electricity usage.

Policy 6: Financial Incentives

– Introducing appropriate incentives for energy efficient appliances and vehicles.

Policy 7: Awareness Raising

Setting up EEC curriculum in national education system to increase awareness at the grassroot level.

Introducing annual awards to incentivise individual and corporation to practice energy management.

Conducting energy exhibitions, roadshows, workshops and seminars for general public to demonstrate the potential for EEC.

Educate young generation through the establishment of Energy Clubs in secondary schools and sixth form centres.

Regularly publishing energy consumption of major energy users to inform end users and induce their behavioural change.

Conducting regular survey on energy consumption pattern in different sector to spur an informed-based decision making process.

Current assessment

Brunei Darussalam has more than 1.2 MW installed renewable power capacity from

The target of Renewable Energy production in Total Power Generation Mix is 954,000 MWh by 2035 the Tenaga Suria Brunei Photovoltaic Demonstration Project and from other small scale grid-connected and off-grid solar projects. A recently completed waste-to-energy assessment study estimated between 10 to 15 MW could be developed from the country's production of municipal solid waste. The Government aims to generate at least 10 percent of its total power generation mix from renewable energy sources by 2035.

Priority Initiative 1: Introduce Renewable Energy Policy and Regulatory Frameworks

Establish renewable energy policies and regulatory frameworks.

Introduce support mechanisms to stimulate private sector investments.

Establish clear market and grid access rules and procedures.

Priority Initiative 2: Scale-up Market Deployment of Solar PV and Promote Waste-to-Energy Technologies

Establish grid-connected solar PV development targets taking into account variable nature of the solar energy.

Adopt the most efficient and state-of-art waste-to-energy technologies taking into account source of waste generation, collection, sorting and recycling systems.

Create policy framework for public private partnership to accelerate the implementation of solar PV and waste-to-energy projects.

Priority Initiative 3: Raise Awareness and Promote Human Capacity Development

Carry out public awareness programs through roadshows, forums, exhibitions to increase the awareness concerning renewable energy.

To utilise Tenaga Suria Brunei (TSB) as a training facility for best practice project development to stimulate replication and scale up solar PV investments.

Strengthen higher learning institutions and industry stakeholders in promoting renewable energy education, capacity building and entrepreneurships.

Priority Initiative 4: Support Research, Development and Demonstration (RD&D) and Technology Transfer

Promote RD&D of RE Technologies that have potential for commercialisation in the country and for exports.

Promote transfer of technologies and facilitate linkage between international research institutions and private companies and local entities.

For additional analytical, marketing, investment and business opportunities information, please contact
Global Investment & Business Center, USA
(202) 546-2103. Fax: (202) 546-3275. E-mail: rusric@erols.com

Current Assessment

EDPMO targets to reduce the number of power outages that lasts for more than 1 hour in a year to less than 100 by 2017, and to less than 50 by 2035. Causes for the outages have been mainly attributed to ageing assets and the need to improve maintenance services and staff competency.

Power Development Plan will be continously reviewed to meet the increase in power demand which is expected to grow organically at 4 percent year-on-year as well as meeting power requirement from future industries. Additionally, sufficient and reliable supplies of gas to power generating plants will be needed to meet the anticipated growth in demand.

The Government will focus on improvements in the following areas: structured replacement, rejuvenation and modernisation program of the ageing assets, organisational change and competency development. The EDPMO has developed plans to address capacity and upgrading needs. These include:

Rejuvenation, capacity upgrade and efficiency enhancement of power generating stations.

Strengthening of national grid including sub-transmission network and provisions of future regional connectivity.

Reinforcement of distribution system assets-primary and secondary substations and distribution networks.

Installation of a new state-of-the-art Energy Management System which includes load dispatch centre and supervisory control and data acquisition (SCADA) system.

EDPMO will undertake three priority initiatives to further evaluate options to transform the way Brunei Darussalam's power system is managed and operated.

Priority Initiative 1: Improve Power System Reliability

Diagnose failure modes, carry out root cause analysis for each major outage and implement the recommendations of the analysis.

Benchmark network performance System Average Interruption Duration Index (SAIDI) and System Average Interruption Frequency Index (SAIFI) in line with Electricity Supply Industry's best practices.

Maximise the use of Computerised Maintenance Management System (CMMS) to plan and execute routine, preventive and corrective maintenance work.

Timely implementation of assets modernisation program.

Priority Initiative 2: Improve Operational and Technical Efficiency of Power Supply System

Introduce power sector structural reforms and improve the competency of the staff to enhance organizational effectiveness.

Improve efficiency of power plants through conversion or replacement of existing open cycle generation plants to more efficient systems.

Optimise power supply system operation through introduction of an energy management system.

- Priority Initiative 3: Adopt Advanced Power Supply and Equipment Technologies

– Identify and adopt state-of-the-art key equipment in the power supply chain.

– Use of latest technology to enhance people and process efficiency.

–

Explore implementation of smart grid system.

Current Assessment

There has not been a major incident of fuel shortages in the history of Brunei Darussalam

Reliable Energy:

To reduce power outage (> 1 hour) to less than 50 times per year by 2035

Zero major incidents of interruption in supply of transport fuel so far. With the population expected to increase by 40 percent by 2035 however, the demand for transportation fuel is set to significantly surge and put pressure on the current transportation fuel supply infrastructure. In order to keep the record of fuel shortages at zero, it is necessary to put in place measures for a continued reliable supply of fuel. A national disruption of transportation fuel has been defined as a disruption of 50 percent or more of the fuel stations at the respective district

i.e. Belait, Tutong, Brunei-Muara and Temburong as the number of fuel stations varies significantly across districts (e.g. two stations in Temburong vs. 25 stations in Brunei Muara) and the average travelling distance of half of the stations within a district is about 30 km (refer to Exhibit 3.4).

The Government will embark on four priority initiatives across the value chain to secure uninterrupted supply of transportation fuel.

Priority Initiative 1: Secure fuel supply

Brunei Darussalam currently imports about 40 percent of total transportation fuel due to the recent increase in demand. With planned refinery initiatives, the domestic fuel production capacity will be 3 to 4 times higher and will surplus projected demand after 2017. This will enhance national fuel sufficiency.

For additional analytical, marketing, investment and business opportunities information, please contact
Global Investment & Business Center, USA
(202) 546-2103. Fax: (202) 546-3275. E-mail: rusric@erols.com

Priority Initiative 2: Storage Capacity to Meet Projected Fuel Demand

Current and planned storage capacity is also sufficient to meet the projected demand growth in transportation fuel. The Government will continue to monitor closely the demand of fuel and will consider adding new capacity as and when the utilisation of storage capacity is expected to approach 90 percent level.

Additionally, the EDPMO will assess potential incentives or regulations that could be introduced to encourage stations to keep a fuel buffer. This would reduce the probability of fuel outages in case of any supply or logistical disruptions.

Priority Initiatives 3: Review Petroleum Product

A Government and Industry Taskforce is also currently being formed to prepare and plan for the reliability and efficiency of petroleum products. The taskforce will conduct an in-depth analysis of the entire petroleum product supply value chain in order to recommend improvements that may be necessary in the system to adequately and efficiently meet current and projected petroleum product demand, in terms of quantities, quality, pricing, consumption, imports and stock levels. By assessing current and projected vulnerabilities to the petroleum product supply, the taskforce will recommend the actions needed to respond to the range of possible disruption scenarios which will enhance the petroleum product supply security.

The output from this taskforce will be in the form of a comprehensive masterplan entitled "Brunei Darussalam Petroleum Product Security Masterplan" which will guide co-ordinated government and industry in their decision-making and action to optimise the reliability and security of petroleum product supply, in a manner that adequately and efficiently fulfills consumer needs, while maximising value for all stakeholders and the country.

Priority Initiative 4: Review The Distribution Network

The EDPMO will continuously monitor and review the need to upgrade or enhance the distribution network, for example, fleet capacity and network optimisation.

STRATEGIC GOAL 3: MAXIMISE ECONOMIC SPIN-OFF FROM ENERGY INDUSTRY - BOOST LOCAL CONTENT AND SECURE HIGH PARTICIPATION OF LOCAL WORKFORCE

s initiatives to scale up and diversify the energy sector are developed, it is important that Brunei Darussalam's local industries and its people contribute to and benefit from the growth of the country. This is at the heart of the national energy agenda – ensuring that the sector's further development creates employment and business growth opportunities for locals.

The basis of growth will be one, which promotes fair competition on a level playing field. Hence, the maximisation of local industry contribution will be premised on the foundation of strong local companies, with the ability to compete successfully and fairly for domestic contracts. These "Truly Bruneian Businesses" are ones that are fully owned, and managed by Bruneian and can imbed and practice strong governance as well as demonstrate strong performance in HSSE, Technical know-how, able to compete commercially and can support other SME's to grow. As the local industries develop a strong domestic presence, it is then important for these local companies to establish a regional or international footprint to strengthen resilience and competencies.

Local business growth will be tracked as follows:

Local Content: The contribution from local industries and workforce in the provision of goods and services supplied to the energy sector in Brunei Darussalam. The target is to have local industry contribution grow from 15 percent in 2010 to 50 percent by 2017 and to more than 80 percent by 2035.

Total Employment: The total employment in the industry to grow to 30,000 by 2017 and to 50,000 by 2035, with the target for total Bruneians employed in the energy sector is set at 20,000 by 2017 and 40,000 by 2035.

Local Content Spending in Energy Industry

Goods & Services Spending >80% of local industry contribution by 2035

Employment spending for 50,000 jobs until 2035

A core component of building local industries lies in securing employment and participation by the local workforce. This is to maximise job creation benefits to Bruneians, thereby building a strong and skilled workforce able to sustain and lead the energy sector in Brunei Darussalam.

These local employment targets will be driven by increasing the size and skill level of the local energy labour force, to ensure that Bruneians are employed based on merit, i.e. strong qualifications and industry relevance.

For additional analytical, marketing, investment and business opportunities information, please contact
Global Investment & Business Center, USA
(202) 546-2103. Fax: (202) 546-3275. E-mail: rusric@erols.com

■ Companies Venturing Overseas: The target is to have at least 8 local companies go international by 2017 and a total of 30 local companies to have gone international by 2035. The local companies can be considered venturing overseas when these local companies have more than 40 percent of total sales of goods and services generated from overseas market.

Today, there are approximately over 400 local oil, gas and energy service companies directly or indirectly supplying to operators in Brunei Darussalam. Preliminary estimates indicate that local companies providing energy goods and services account for approximately 15 percent of the total expenditure of the energy sector in 2010.

Energy expenditure is expected to grow to approximately BND 8.8 billion by 2035, based on projects identified in the upstream, downstream and other energy industries. To attain targets of 80 percent local industry contribution by 2035 would mean an increase of greater than 10 times the baseline amount at the local contribution estimate, as shown in Exhibit 3.5

Local content refers to the sum of value added or created in the Bruneian economy through the use of local employment, goods and services. As part of the definition and for calculation purposes:

Employment spend in country is defined as any costs of locally-based staff (local and non-local) including Employees Trus Fund (TAP), Supplemental Contributory Pensions, all subsistence costs and any other costs. It is assumed that the contribution towards employment spent is 100 percent of costs for local staff and 50 percent of costs for non-local staff.

For additional analytical, marketing, investment and business opportunities information, please contact
Global Investment & Business Center, USA
(202) 546-2103. Fax: (202) 546-3275. E-mail: rusric@erols.com

Goods and services spend in country is defined as spending on any services rendered/purchases of materials/equipment in Brunei Darussalam, monies paid to subcontractors or suppliers in Brunei Darussalam.

Subcontracts is total spend on contractor's first tier sub contractors.

At present, there is limited local manufacturing of energy equipment, but rather a significant emphasis on sub-contracting to, or resale from, foreign vendors. This indicates a significant opportunity for local companies to grow in scale and skill. A number of manufacturing and support industries could also be further developed as a spin-off from main Oil and Gas contracting activities. Furthermore, the current production and operation activities in the matured area and the field rejuvenation projects and the future exploration and production activities expected from the deepwater blocks presents an immediate large opportunity for local businesses to develop new technologies and services required.

As these upstream and downstream initiatives are deployed, direct employment will be created to execute the projects and run the operations, as well as indirect employment through the creation of opportunities for companies supplying goods and services to the operators. Employment in the energy sector includes professionals and other skilled or semi-skilled employees in upstream, downstream, goods supply and services, and power. Similarly, initiatives to increase power capacity upgrade, power facilities and expand the scale and scope of renewable energy production will generate jobs in the energy sector.

In order to reach the 2035 target of 50,000 jobs available in the energy sector, identified initiatives in the upstream, downstream and energy service industries need to be realised. Hence, the fulfillment of the target is largely dependent on the ability to reach target production from the offshore blocks, grow the midstream and downstream businesses, upgrade power infrastructure, develop energy-related goods and services industries and so on. Furthermore, local companies need to genuinely and actively recruit and employ locals as well as create a conducive working environment for locals to succeed.

Imperative to the creation of employment is to ensure that there is a steady supply of professional and other skilled local workforce to capture these job opportunities. Out of the 50,000 employments in 2035, 80 percent or 40,000 of the employment are targeted for local Bruneians, with 5,000 jobs filled by qualified professional local workforce.

Qualified professional local workforce are those who have attained Higher National Diploma qualifications and above including a bachelor's degree and a master's degree. Skilled local workforce are those who have attained skills training either formally via

A target for total employment in the energy industry at 50,000 by 2035 with a total locals at 40,000 (80%) by 2035

training institutes or via on the job training provided by companies as part of their staff development program.

To address the need to produce qualified and skilled workforce, and grow Brunei Darussalam's human capital, the EDPMO in collaboration with other relevant Ministries has implemented the following:

For additional analytical, marketing, investment and business opportunities information, please contact
Global Investment & Business Center, USA
(202) 546-2103. Fax: (202) 546-3275. E-mail: rusric@erols.com

■ *ESTABLISHMENT AND IMPLEMENTATION OF ENERGY INDUSTRY COMPETENCY FRAMEWORK (EICF)*

The Energy Industry Competency Framework (EICF), established in July 2013, is a joint collaboration between the EDPMO, the Ministry of Education and the energy industry. The EICF provides another alternative pathway for secondary school leavers to receive training that meets industrial standards and have the right competency to start work once they completed their training. The individuals can also have the option to continue on from this vocational training to higher education if they wish to. Thus, the objectives of the EICF are to:

Define the competencies required to perform jobs and roles in the workplace (Energy Industry);

Create alignment between training providers and industry requirements; and

Increase employability by up-scaling the skills required by the energy industry.

To facilitate the implementation of the EICF, a Joint Implementation Group was formed which reports directly to the EICF Steering Committee chaired by the Minister of Energy at the Prime Minister Office and Deputy Minister of Education as the deputy chairman. The Joint Implementation Group supported by four taskforce working groups consists of the following (as shown in Exhibit 3.6):

Competency Development Technical Group (CDTG)

Workforce Development Planning Group (WDPG)

Energy Industry Quality Agency (EIQA)

Registered Training Organisation Network (RTON)

The above taskforce groups comprise members of senior government officials, industry leaders, technical experts and representatives from training providers. They coordinate the following key aspects of national employment and skills development for the energy industry;

a. The development and implementation of a comprehensive industry workforce development plan;

b. The establishment and monitoring of effective industry led quality assurance including National Standards and qualification in the energy industry;

c. Raising the standard and co-ordination of training provision for the industry; and

d. Ongoing review and incorporation of appropriate industry endorsed qualifications, skill sets and units of competencies for the industries.

The competency framework further describes competency requirements that can be used by relevant stakeholders as a formal guide to allow companies to establish or align their own competency requirements against the national framework. The companies will have to articulate the skills required to perform the work so that effective screening can take place. This would also demand the need to strengthen the quality of education and training institutions to be in line with the framework standards. As for the candidates, this would present a career path for their development in the energy industry.

Exhibit 3.6

By providing these standards, the framework will not only become a valuable tool for increasing public confidence in the energy sector, it will also address local employment and unemployment issues by using the framework to create new business opportunities. Exhibit 3.7 shows the various elements of the framework, expected outcome and benefits.

Furthermore, there are also several key enablers that have been identified and implemented by the taskforce to ensure effective operation and implementation of the EICF. These, amongst others, include the following:

Skill and career pathway.

Industry commitment and contribution.

Youth Engagements.

Skilled Workers Apprenticeship Scheme.

Workforce Planning.

For additional analytical, marketing, investment and business opportunities information, please contact
Global Investment & Business Center, USA
(202) 546-2103. Fax: (202) 546-3275. E-mail: rusric@erols.com

Phase 2 of EICF programs is targeted to be introduced in Q3 2014. Phase 2 EICF programs include

Exhibit 3.7

EICF implementation will be done in phases. Under phase 1 (first intake), 9 EICF programs have been introduced as follows:

Higher National Technical Certificate (HNTec): Plant Engineering, Electrical Engineering, Instrumentation and Control Engineering, Mechanical Engineering.

National Technical Certificate (NTec): Plant Engineering.

Industry Skilled Qualification (ISQ): Scaffolder, Welder, Marker/Fitter, Rigger.

For additional analytical, marketing, investment and business opportunities information, please contact
Global Investment & Business Center, USA
(202) 546-2103. Fax: (202) 546-3275. E-mail: rusric@erols.com

The plan is for 800-1000 intake of EICF students annually for the next five years under EICF phase 1 programs. With the demand profile from the industry produced by EICF taskforce groups, all the students who graduates from the EICF phase 1 programs can be absorbed by the industry (refer to Exhibit 3.8).

programs such as Mason and Carpenter, Engineering Services, Logistic and Warehouse Management, Drilling and Well-Service programs. Students who graduate from the new programs will further contribute to the local workforce to fill more than 1000 positions that are currently either vacant or filled by expatriates in the energy industry. Further new EICF program will be developed based on new requirements by the industry.

- *ESTABLISHMENT OF BRUNEI MARITIME ACADEMY (BMA)*

The marine industry, which provides services to Brunei Darussalam's oil and gas industry spends more than BND 500 million annually, operating more than 100 vessels of various types and purposes and employing more than 2,000 individuals, including 1,500 positions as seafarers. It has been projected that this sector will continue to grow with the increasing offshore activities including future deepwater explorations.

For additional analytical, marketing, investment and business opportunities information, please contact
Global Investment & Business Center, USA
(202) 546-2103. Fax: (202) 546-3275. E-mail: rusric@erols.com

However, only 10 percent of the human resources in this sector are currently filled by local Bruneians. In addition, seafarers are needed by Brunei Gas Carriers (BGC) to deliver LNG to buyer terminals.

The Brunei Maritime Academy (BMA), established in 2013, under the purview of the Ministry of Education and supported by the EDPMO and the Ministry of Communication, will be one of the centres of excellence under the new Brunei Technical Education (BTE) system. The academy will produce industry ready Bruneians as maritime professionals and seafarers, approved and recognised by the International Maritime Organization (IMO) to work in the maritime industry of Brunei Darussalam as well as internationally. This formation is also in line with EDPMO objective towards supporting Local Business Development (LBD) to increase local content including local employment in the marine sector.

In collaboration with Singapore Maritime Academy (SMA), the academy will offer a range of industry and internationally accredited competency-based qualifications training for the maritime industry. The assistance provided by SMA amongst others, will include building training capabilities, training of trainers and to help establish an academic quality assurance system in accordance with the standards for Quality in Maritime Education and Training (QMET).

BMA will start its operation in April 2014 and plans to take in approximately 200 students annually. Collaboration with the marine industries including vessel service contractors is critical to ensure the availability of student placements during their required sea times training and also eventual permanent employment upon graduating from the academy.

- *CONDUCTING ANNUAL OIL AND GAS EVENTS (CAREER ROADSHOWS AND JOB FAIRS)*

Since 2012, EDPMO has been conducting annual oil and gas event such as Career Roadshows and Job Fairs with objectives of among other to instill the interest of young Bruneian in the energy industry, promoting the oil and gas career as well as providing opportunities for job seekers to find suitable vacancies in the energy industry and also facilitating between the job seekers and the potential employers in the energy industry.

Meanwhile, EDPMO in collaboration with the energy industry has annual Job Fair to ensure there is a continuous effort and focus in recruiting locals in the energy Industries. EDPMO has set annual target of local recruitment in the energy industry. It is targeted for local employment to increase to 20,000 by 2017 and to 40,000 by 2035. All the above initiatives are aligned with the EDPMO's strategic goals to increase local content and ensure greater participation of local Bruneian in the energy industry workforce.

Capacity building programs and initiatives will be developed via the LBD framework aim to develop and grow "Truly Bruneian Businesses" in a sustainable manner. This includes creation of new entrepreneur with a structure industry sponsored and supported program, involvement of new companies into the industry and creation of local companies that can compete regionally and internationally.

For additional analytical, marketing, investment and business opportunities information, please contact
Global Investment & Business Center, USA
(202) 546-2103. Fax: (202) 546-3275. E-mail: rusric@erols.com

The ultimate objective of Local Companies Development is to have competent local companies undertaking services in the country and also venturing overseas (defined as Brunei established local companies with average revenue from overseas for the year of greater than 40 percent).

To build the foundation for the above, EDPMO will also track the development of local companies based on additional elements as follows;

New Local Companies in Oil and Gas Industry, is the number of Brunei established local companies awarded with contract for the first time in Oil and Gas Industry.

Companies in Incubator and Energy Business Academy, is the number of Brunei established local companies undergoing in BSJV Incubator and Energy Business Academy Programs.

As more local companies grow and strengthen their competencies, their competitiveness will also grow. In order to ensure a fair level playing field and maintain a competitive environment, the LBD framework ensures no monopoly in any market segment.

Thus, in order to grow further, it is estimated that the top performing 5 percent from the total number of active local companies will have to internationalise in order to strengthen resilience, spur further growth and access newer and potentially larger markets. Currently, there are several local companies that are starting to penetrate regional market – though the revenue generated is still relatively low.

Internationalisation requires companies to expand the scale, scope and competitiveness of their business. For the top performing active local companies, the Government of Brunei Darussalam intends to provide support for them in their international forays. Similarly, these top performing truly Bruneian businesses need to heed galvanisation efforts, take initiative and optimise the support available.

EDPMO is working with the relevant authorities such as the Ministry of Finance and Authoriti Monetari Brunei Darussalam (AMBD) to develop and enhance corporate governance, financial management and reporting. Furthermore, current local companies development programs will be further enhanced to provide more focus on local business development, local content and capacity building. The Government would seek to evaluate the potential elements of support, which could include:

Capital: Develop financing and fiscal incentives to best support overseas expansion. This will be collaboration between various parties such as EDPMO, Ministry of Finance, AMBD, BEDB and the Brunei Association of Banks.

Capabilities: Set up global entrepreneurship, training and development programs for the industry. Currently there are a number of programs undertaken by various agencies like BEDB and main operators of oil and gas offering programs relating to development of local companies capabilities. This is aimed at providing structured assistance for truly Bruneian businesses to enhance their capabilities and competitiveness in order to venture overseas.

Catalysts: Establish a "market insight agency" which will provide a repository of best practices, techniques and tools to develop a suitable international business model and branding strategy. The agency will also host and offer a professional network of mentors, business training and advisory services to help companies refine market entry and expansion strategies. Currently, in a bid to provide further opportunities openly to local vendors, a list of Tender Opportunities from all

Major Oil and Gas Operators is regularly updated on the EDPMO Website (www.energy.gov. bn). Moving forward, other catalysts will be implemented by such as hosting conferences, trade forums and establishing an association of local energy companies.

Connections: Countries around the world use "bridge offices" in key overseas markets to connect companies with local knowledge and networks. These overseas stations will gather information on local needs and trends, the best way to navigate systems (such as tax, accounting and other government regulations) and provide link-ups with potential customers, partners and influencers in the country. With assistance from relevant agencies e.g. BEDB, a programme will be suggested to these local vendors, where assistance will be given to gain access to various business networking opportunities and overseas markets via participation in trade expo's and international tenders.

Conditions: The Government will facilitate industry reorganisation or foreign investment that is required to turbo-charge local companies with the scale and scope to compare well with other multinational companies. In line with this, the Ministry of Finance has introduced several tax incentives that are aimed at assisting growth of local companies and further drive international trade (e.g. streamline export licensing and improve port efficiencies). In order for businesses to

expand, the provision of land for businesses to be set up and also to allow expansion of current business activities is also being conducted with assistance from BEDB, Ministry of Industry Primary Resources and Ministry of Development.

These levers are summarised in Exhibit 3.9. While the Government could provide the springboard to support companies in expanding overseas, the onus to internationalise would fall mainly on the ambitions and growth plans of local companies. Local companies should fully leverage Government support to diversify their business and elevate business excellence.

There are 5 Priority Initiatives the Government is embarking on, which require close industry cooperation and commitment, in order to build local industry capabilities.

Priority Initiative 1: Identify the pools of local companies, which could potentially win in the domestic market

To build strong local companies, the first step is to identify the product or service areas where local companies already have existing capabilities, and leveraging these capabilities to capture the large value pools going forward.

The EDPMO has commenced on this effort through the "Local Business Development" (LBD) Framework (as shown in Exhibit 3.10). This framework considers the value ("total approved contract value") and technical complexity ("technology") of the product or service area in determining the required local content target. It seeks to focus on the high value contracts, beginning with a higher target for those of lower technical complexity to ensure targets are feasible and focused on core areas.

As a next step, the Government will work closely with foreign and domestic operating companies to develop potential priority areas within the "Development" and "Core" categories in Brunei Darussalam (e.g. drilling, casing supply, geological services, etc.). This will also involve how to grow or evolve these targets with time, and how the Government can support companies to continuously grow their value add.

Industry engagement and involvement is paramount - scaling local competencies could potentially involve the formation of consortiums, mergers and acquisitions, and/or collaborations or joint investments with international players. Opportunities must be provided via suitable oil and gas projects, tenders and subcontracting activities. Government can support with financing, and can facilitate industry reorganisation or foreign investment efforts, but the primary motivation and driving force for change need to be owned and generated from the industry.

Priority Initiative 2: Establish and imbed feasible local content targets and supporting legislations, directives, policies and regulations into long term business planning

The LBD framework establishes local content targets for each quadrant. To make these targets actionable and relevant, the Government will seek to set local content targets specific to each respective placement of the good and service categories in the quadrants based of these targets and will monitor the progress of actual performance against targets over the prime period of the contract. Active engagement of operators will be required to involve industry early in the process and obtain commitment to these targets.

Additionally, all companies operating in the Brunei Darussalam Oil and Gas Industry will be required to submit four types of reports regarding local content achievements. "LBD Reporting" is necessary to ensure that LBD is properly incorporated and embedded into local businesses. Formal reporting mechanisms also allow "measure of success" of local content development and capacity building in Brunei Darussalam. Where it is lacking, other suitable LBD initiatives and capacity building program

Exhibit 3.9

will be developed. The EDPMO will review the institution and/or mechanisms to ensure accuracy of these reports, including performing verification audit.

Exhibit 3.10

companies

companies.

The reports include:

LBD Business Plan - This report includes assurances or progress on the implementation of an LBD Management system in the Operators, Contractors and Sub-Contractors' process and procedures. This report is due annually at the start of the financial year.

Local Content Opportunity Framing report - This report is applicable to any new projects to be undertaken by an Operator. This report is to be submitted prior to any final investment decisions.

LBD Performance Report -This report will cover the performance to date of the Operators, Contractors and Sub-contractors on the Local Employment, Local Content, etc. This report shall be submitted three times per year, i.e. 30th April, 31st August and 1st December via the online reporting tool on the Energy LBD website (www.EnergyLBD.gov.bn) of each year.

Deviations to the Framework - This report to include any deviations proposed or have been taken, any difficulties or issues faced by the Operators, Contractors and Sub-Contractors in fulfilling the requirements. This report is due annually at the end of the financial year.

The Government intends to work with industry to ensure that the structuring of all contracts for goods and services is done in a manner that provides opportunities for competitive local players to compete and bid for these contracts. Activities included here intend to facilitate interactions between buyers and suppliers to find out the optimal way to level the playing field for local

Priority Initiative 3: Set up mechanisms and relevant infrastructure to support and ensure compliance to policies

To ensure that local content figures reported are faithfully represented, the Government has established a unit with the mandate to promote LBD. This unit is charged with the task of putting together a taskforce to manage, assist and enforce local content development and reporting. It will also define the criteria and procedures for the activities to be carried out and engage with the industry to ensure all aspects of the rules and regulations are fully communicated and understood. This includes conducting regular site visits to company's facilities, as well as conducting various capacity building sessions in collaborations with other Government agencies, industry and other key stakeholders. A proposal on a central registration system to promote establishment of local businesses and create competitive supplier base will also be developed. The EDPMO will further evaluate and develop an optimal design and operational choices for enforcing local content.

The EDPMO is currently developing two new industrial sites in Sungai Duhon, Kuala Belait for marine industries and at Bukit Panggal, Tutong to provide a convenient infrastructure to develop good and service activities in this sector. The EDPMO will also continue to evaluate the new manufacturing and service activities to support, build or develop to facilitate growth of local capabilities.

Priority Initiative 4: Coordinate with relevant industries to organise "allied" labour pools

In view of the pressing need to quickly scale local industries, Brunei Darussalam could explore industries with complimentary functional capabilities. The workforce in other industries as well as ex military such as navy, seafearers, construction, IT, mechanic and machinery repair could yield skills that with additional training, could become relevant for the energy sector.

The Government plans to collaborate with members of these organisations to examine the potential for labour conversion or mobility programs. These programs aim to train these workers in skills that would allow them to participate in the energy sector, leveraging the relevant expertise that they already have. The design of these programs should not, however, compromise the needs of other industries. This will merely serve as an interim measure to boost the local energy sector workforce.

EDPMO will also conduct annual Job Fairs on an industry level, engagements with the unemployed and other recruitment initiatives to further encourage, provide and secure employment for locals.

Priority Initiative 5: Encourage IOCs to make significant contribution to local capabilities

The Government will evaluate incentives and regulations to ensure international oil companies (IOCs) to continue to contribute to building local capabilities.

BOTTOM LINE: MEASURING LOCAL CONTENT DEVELOPMENT VIA GDP CONTRIBUTION FROM THE ENERGY SECTOR

verall GDP reflects the value addition, or wealth creation, generated for the country and the citizens by the energy sector. It serves as a broader measure of the impact of the energy sector on the Bruneian economy.

The EDPMO has identified initiatives across the priority areas - i.e. covering upstream, downstream, energy services and related industries - are expected to generate approximately BND 42 billion in an unrisked assessment (Exhibit 3.11). Upstream oil and gas sales (including LNG sales) will drive most of the growth, expected to contribute approximately 90 percent of total GDP from the energy sector in 2035. This is based on an oil price growing within the range from USD 120 - USD 145 per barrel of oil by 2035, per International Energy Agency and the U.S Energy Information Administration estimate, and assuming an exchange rate of 1.3 BND per USD.

- Attracting investment to fuel growth

- Ensuring delivery to our commitments

KEY ENABLERS FOR THE ENERGY VISION

he EDPMO will work with the relevant Government agencies to ensure that the key enabling factors for this transformational step-up in the energy sector are in place. Four areas in particular will receive attention;

Implementing a comprehensive set of supportive policy and regulatory frameworks to help boost upstream production, secure employment for Bruneians, ensure high safety standards and provide attractive value propositions for companies to develop downstream chains.

Growing Bruneian human capital by building the skills and capabilities needed for the energy sector.

Attracting investment in core areas requiring growth and developing synergistic fit with investors.

Ensuring realisation of our commitments through a relentless focus on the delivery of outcomes.

Enabler 1: Implementing supportive policy and regulatory frameworks

RELEVANCE

With maturing assets, enhanced focus on offshore exploration and production, and increased downstream activities, it is critical to have a comprehensive policy and regulatory framework to support the strategic objectives set out for the energy sector. Amongst others, the EDPMO has identified four key regulatory policies and frameworks and will seek to develop further regulations as required. The development will consider stakeholder consultation during the formation of these regulatory policies. These four regulatory policies aim to boost upstream production, diversify and

For additional analytical, marketing, investment and business opportunities information, please contact
Global Investment & Business Center, USA
(202) 546-2103. Fax: (202) 546-3275. E-mail: rusric@erols.com

grow the downstream industry, ensure and monitor LBD, and foster a world-class health, safety, security and environment (HSSE).

POTENTIAL LEVERS AND IDEAS

■ Supporting measures to boost upstream production (as per Upstream Directive no 1/2011 on Field Development Plan For Maturing Hydrocarbon Development Projects)

Based on the experience of other countries that have faced similar issues with maturing assets, the Government will implement several measures to boost upstream production. The Government is ensuring that the right supporting measures are present to increase the attractiveness of potential projects in existing assets (e.g. asset rejuvenation) and new offshore opportunities, including a regulatory framework for sharing of infrastructure to attract more investment in small fields and guaranteed off-take for additional complex field developments.

■ Implementation of key LBD Initiatives

To date LBD Framework have been issued to ensure that there is a fair and level playing field and building of "Truly Bruneian Businesses" that imbed, uphold and practice strong business principles.

There are three main objectives of LBD:

To increase the country's economy through use of local goods and services.

To create employment opportunities for Bruneians and ensure employment of locals.

To develop truly Bruneian businesses that are able to compete regionally.

Under the LBD framework, targets are proposed for the use of local goods and services, and local employment. Based on this framework, all companies will be guided by EDPMO. Furthermore, in order to be transparent about opportunities and business information, EDPMO has developed an "Energy LBD website" (www.EnergyLBD. gov.bn) to make such information widely available to all parties. Regularly updated information helps the Government to improve investment climate in our oil and gas sector.

The Government will consider potentially instituting a regulatory body to monitor the local content requirement in the bidding process for contracts from operators. The regulatory body will develop methodologies to calculate local content of goods and services, audit attainment of targets, and set up incentives and penalties. Additionally, the regulatory body will also promote the participation of small companies and foster geological and geophysical services applied to oil exploration through stipulating significant revenues on R&D.

A proposal on a central registration system to promote establishment of local businesses and create competitive supplier base will also be developed. The EDPMO will further evaluate and develop an optimal design and operational choices for enforcing such local content regulations.

Further directives and policies may be developed to cover compliance to previous initiatives where penalties for non-compliance may be stipulated. The central registration system will be a key tool in determining suitable penalties when applicable. Moving forward, all current and future contracts with all Brunei oil and gas operators must incorporate new terms and conditions to enable this.

■ Health, Safety, Security and Environment (HSSE) framework

The Government considers attainment of the highest standards on Health, Safety, Security and Environment (HSSE) as a non-negotiable "must" for the energy sector. Compromises on this front can have significant and damaging costs on the economy, society and environment. The EDPMO has introduced and enforced the Control of Major Accident Hazards (COMAH) regulations that underpin and support the overarching safety and health requirements of the Workplace Safety and Health Order (WSHO) 2009.

Under WSHO, all employers have a duty to ensure the safety and health of their employees, and the safety and health of others affected by their (the employers) activities. Employees also have a direct duty not to put themselves at risk and to co- operate with their employer.

In addition, leaders of oil and gas companies will be directly accountable and responsible for ensuring all major accident hazards have been identified and relevant controls have been implemented to reduce risks to persons, assets and environment as low as is reasonably practicable. This will avoid delegation of such roles to their subordinates. Companies in the energy sector will also be strongly stimulated to have a good HSSE culture and a proper consequence management system in place to ensure we deliver on our commitment of having zero major accidents every year.

Enabler 2: Growing Bruneian human capital

RELEVANCE

For Bruneians to co-create the future of Brunei Darussalam's energy sector, it is imperative to create a robust pipeline of high-quality labour force equipped to fulfill the requirements of jobs in the industry. The pipeline of skilled labour should address 3 key elements:

Quantity: Are there adequate numbers of professional and vocational graduates with relevant qualifications relevant to capture job opportunities in the market?

Value-proposition: Are these qualified graduates attracted to seek jobs in the energy sector?

Quality: Are these job seekers of high quality and readily employable in a full-time position?

A supply-demand analysis of labour pools indicates that Brunei Darussalam needs to significantly bolster the current education infrastructure to meet the 2035 local employment target.

Exhibit 4.1 summarises the labour supply situation vis-à-vis expected job creation (demand) from the energy sector. With the present pool, Brunei Darussalam needs to increase supply of specialised technical professionals including those in petrochemicals, HSSE, geology and marine engineering. For energy-related generic professionals such as mechanical, electronic and IT where alternative career options abound in other sectors, the value proposition of the energy sector has to be considerably enhanced. Vocational education institutes will also require substantial scale up, especially in national diplomas relating to specific skilled operational roles like seafarers, scaffolders and welders.

Increasing the employability and quality of the workforce is also critical, as Brunei Darussalam seeks to develop offshore development expertise, create research niches and explore alternative sources and technologies in energy such as small field development, EOR techniques and renewable energy. Therefore, increasing the scale and skill level of Bruneian labour supply to the energy sector is paramount in other to achieve our aspirations.

POTENTIAL LEVERS AND IDEAS

In addition to the above initiatives and in order to grow Brunei Darussalam's human capital, the EDPMO has currently identified a few potential ideas to evaluate:

- *ESTABLISH REGULATORY REFORMS AND INCENTIVE SCHEMES TO DRIVE WORKPLACE TRAINING*

In order to encourage the provision of training for existing employees and apprenticeships for students, the Government would evaluate potential regulatory reforms. Across the world, Governments utilise incentives (direct and indirect) and training levies to encourage training. For example, to promote development of apprentices, the Government could encourage high quality training such as providing incentives for the industry to train apprentices in roles that require the use of more complex or specialised equipment. Often, the rights and obligations of the apprentice are unclear, especially when it comes to contentious issues such as rights to insurance and work safety claims. The Government needs to legislate the standardisation of apprentice contracts, in order to facilitate the development of apprenticeship activities.

As an initial step, EDPMO, with support from the industry has introduced the National Energy Graduate Apprenticeship Scheme (NEGAS). NEGAS, among others aims to provide opportunities for unemployed HND graduates and above a real working experience in the energy sector, for a period of up to 12 months, with structured training, development and assessment programs to enable them to eventually acquire the experience to compete in the job market. It is planned that the NEGAS will enrol up to 100 unemployed graduates annually.

- *DEVELOP A FORMAL NETWORK OF CAREER COUNSELLING*

The Government will evaluate options to increase the amount of career guidance for students to broaden the awareness and knowledge of career opportunities and pathways available. One option is to build a strong network of career counsellors, either as full-time specialists or trained school staff, to draft and communicate compelling career pathways in the energy sector. These career counsellors could help students craft, evaluate and refine their portfolio of skills and learning experiences based on their interests. Career counsellors would have to involve educators, parents and the business community in the process to align all the support required for students talented and interested in energy.

Interaction with and guidance for students could vary from large career fairs or events, targeted talks and group sessions, to one-on-one discussions. Career Roadshows to create awareness amongst students about careers in energy have regularly operated since early 2012.

- *GROWING PRIVATE REGISTERED TRAINING ORGANISATION (RTO)*

With the growth in the number of students intake annually participating in the EICF Programs, EDPMO has also opened up the opportunity to grow and develop not only the current public Registered Training Organisations (RTO) such as our vocational and technical educational

Exhibit 4.1

institutions but also private RTOs. Through the EICF, we have opened up opportunities for new local training providers to be registered and qualified as private RTOs to provide programs such as Welders, Scaffolders, Riggers, and Marker/Fitters.

All the RTOs must comply with the RTO standards and registration criteria to provide students with training resulting in qualifications that are recognised and accepted by the energy industry and at the same time the RTOs should satisfy the requirements of the EICF (including Energy Industry Quality Agency - EIQA). EDPMO will facilitate the setting up of these private RTOs with collaboration with the Ministry of Education.

- *DEVELOP STANDARDS AND PROGRAMS TO INCREASE QUALITY OF EDUCATION AND TRAINING*

In order to ensure that a high quality of teachers is maintained, providers should develop selective recruitment processes focused on core required skills. Teachers and trainers should be required to undergo continual training and upgrading themselves in order to keep abreast of the latest knowledge. Teachers in schools and trainers in the industry have in-depth skills that are complementary to one another. The main challenge in vocational education and training (VET) experience in many countries relates to the fact that teachers have inadequate or outdated industry experience. Conversely, trainers in the workplace are not equipped with the skills to deliver instruction and support trainee development. Learning partnerships between industry and providers would help teachers and industry trainers exchange complementary skills, as shown in Exhibit 4.2. Through the EICF, we have started to see teachers from vocational school

Exhibit 4.2

undergo training in the industry and vice-versa trainers from the industry attending pedagogical programs in education institution.

The Government could further provide support by mandating minimum qualifications and work experience for vocational teachers and trainers respectively. Some countries have also used an enforcement mechanism to ensure workplace training is of high quality. Quality standards or checklists are developed, and only certified companies will be issued "quality licenses". Inspectors will carry out random audits by reviewing processes and conducting interviews with trainees.

- *CREATE INDUSTRY-EDUCATOR MOBILISATION AND TRAINING SCHEMES*

Government and providers need to find a way to encourage members of the industry to be guest-speakers or faculty (part-time or full-time) at schools. Particularly, there are many industry retirees in Brunei Darussalam, who should be mobilised to impart industry knowledge at schools. Once

For additional analytical, marketing, investment and business opportunities information, please contact
Global Investment & Business Center, USA
(202) 546-2103. Fax: (202) 546-3275. E-mail: rusric@erols.com

the pool of industry experts is mobilised, training programs should be established to equip experts with the skills on delivering instruction and managing student development.

The Government cannot work alone to revamp the education and training system. Active involvement by industry and providers on all the proposed initiatives is a pre-requisite for success. Additionally, providers and institutions have to thrive for excellence in productivity to ensure full optimisation of the education infrastructure. Companies also have a role to play in developing attractive career development pathways and performance incentives to enhance employee retention.

Enabler 3: Attracting investment to fuel growth

RELEVANCE

Attracting investments is an essential pillar to grow Brunei Darussalam's energy sector, be it in the development of EOR technologies, development of small and marginal fields, building of new downstream industries, boosting the local energy goods and service industries, developing renewable energy and so forth. Brunei Darussalam will actively seek to engage world-class companies and talents to jointly transform the energy sector, and ensure that carefully planned quality investments are deployed to bring mutually beneficial investments for the partners involved.

In order to achieve its GDP target, we anticipate that Brunei Darussalam needs to attract approximately BND 70 to 80 billion in cumulative investment from 2011 to 2035. This represents average annual investment level of about BND 3 to 4 billion in the next two decades, which is more than twice the recent investment level. Doubling the average annual investment level is a challenging task as this requires sustaining an average investment growth rate of 6 to 7 percent for a two-decades time frame. However, there are several countries around the world which have achieved high investment growth rates over a long period of time. Singapore, South Africa and Costa Rica, for example, managed to achieve annual investment growth rate of 5 to 7 percent in the previous two decades. Similarly in Qatar, the government has actively sought to promote international investment in core sectors such as energy. This has helped it increase the share of FDI to total GDP from 1 percent in 2000 to 3.5 percent by 2011.

The Government is fully dedicated to provide the necessary support including capital, infrastructure, business environment and regulatory reform to attract and sustain investment in priority areas of the economy and harness synergistic effects from these projects.

POTENTIAL LEVERS AND IDEAS

Based on the successful best practices in investment attraction, the Government will evaluate 4 main ideas:

Building a strong and competent team of investment officers to approach high priority investors. These investment officers will assess which are the key investors, proactively pitch deals and build and manage the relationship with the client.

Designing customised value propositions to pitch investors. Investment officers will utilise investment pitch books customised to the business and priorities of the investor. This ensures a synergistic fit between the investment requirements and needs of the investor.

For additional analytical, marketing, investment and business opportunities information, please contact
Global Investment & Business Center, USA
(202) 546-2103. Fax: (202) 546-3275. E-mail: rusric@erols.com

The remaining two initiatives will focus on providing key supporting enablers:

Investing strategically in key supporting infrastructure and providing incentives to attract world class investors, particularly in the downstream industry as Brunei Darussalam's aspires to move from being largely an upstream exporter to a sophisticated downstream player of scale. This would continue Brunei Darussalam's tradition of building infrastructure of significant scale and surrounding facilities, such as the world class petrochemical hub SPARK and Telisai-Lumut Highway, will allow investors to set up and ramp up operations quickly. The Government also plans to strategically provide incentives to investors in priority industries such as strategic income tax reliefs and agreements.

Creating a business friendly environment and a cosmopolitan society to attract foreign talent to live and work in Brunei Darussalam. The Government could explore options to improve the ease of doing business, as well as develop a social eco-system that embraces the diverse needs of foreign investor personnel. This is beneficial not only to the energy sector, but the Brunei Darussalam's economy at large, and would require coordinated efforts from various Government entities and members of the industry.

Enabler 4: Ensuring delivery on our commitments

RELEVANCE

The EDPMO has set big, bold aspirations to achieve by 2035. For example, upstream production has to grow to more than 1.5 times, downstream value-add has to grow to more than 10 times and local content has to grow by more than 10 times as well.

Delivering impactful outcomes will involve mobilisation of the civil service and the private sector, domestic and foreign, on an unprecedented scale. High public expectations and scrutiny raises the pressure to achieve big outcomes quickly and the need for the highest order of transparency.

POTENTIAL LEVERS AND IDEAS

To meet the challenges of delivering aspirations of this large magnitude, there are three core levers in delivery the Government will seek to develop:

- *EXTENSIVE ENGAGEMENT WITH KEY STAKEHOLDERS TO DRIVE IMPLEMENTATION*

The EDPMO will orchestrate and manage engagement with a broad set of stakeholders to drive the development of implementable solutions and to ensure strong support to drive execution. Key stakeholders include:

a) *Other Government ministries and agencies.* Establish strong links with the Ministry of Education, Ministry of Finance, BEDB and DEPD, amongst others, on topics such as workforce planning, budgeting and resource allocation and national economic planning.

b) *Companies in the industry.* Work closely with all relevant companies in the energy sector across upstream, downstream, power, energy goods and services and others to coordinate and strengthen the capabilities of local companies.

c) *Academia and research.* Engage schools, training facilities and BNERI to coordinate labour supply, research focus and increasing the skill level and employability of local labour supply. d)

For additional analytical, marketing, investment and business opportunities information, please contact
Global Investment & Business Center, USA
(202) 546-2103. Fax: (202) 546-3275. E-mail: rusric@erols.com

Investors. Proactively pursue quality investments through close contact and negotiations with major domestic and foreign investors.

e) *International companies and institutes.* Close collaboration and cooperation with IOCs and international research institutes and agencies to leverage specialised knowledge and expertise required to build local capabilities.

■ *DEVELOP A RIGOROUS RHYTHM OF PERFORMANCE MANAGEMENT*

The EDPMO intends to drive the delivery effort with robust performance management processes to ensure timely achievement of outcomes along the journey. These processes would aim at establishing clear accountabilities, constructive performance dialogues and consistent use of differentiated, meaningful rewards and consequences for dedicated leaders and the front-line who could most directly influence specific outcomes. Additionally, the EDPMO will examine the most appropriate reporting and escalation process, focused on constructive interventions to address shortfalls, to monitor performance.

■ *BUILD STRONG MOMENTUM OF PLANNING AND EXECUTION OF PLANS*

In order to ensure a continuing drive and enthusiasm around delivery of plans, the Government will need to elevate these targets and initiatives as national imperatives. Additionally, the Government will source for talents in the public and private sector with the passion and skills to ensure delivery happens. A disciplined process of structured interactions and touch-points to communicate and gather input on the progress achieved and plans in place would also secure commitment for the entire journey.

The energy sector requires a robust state of initiatives and processes to produce outcomes and impact

CALL TO ACTION

Delivering the Vision: Concerted effort from all stakeholders

The vision set out for the energy sector requires robust initiatives and processes to produce outcomes and impact. Driving these initiatives will require a concerted effort across all stakeholders to engage, leverage and support the initiatives identified, and propose new ideas that could accelerate growth.

Each part of the engine for success needs to be in place, whether it be the necessary regulations, Government support, education and training, labour supply planning, organisation and galvanisation of local companies, the development of new technologies, investments by international and domestic companies and so on. The multiple Government agencies, companies in the industry, members of academia and research, domestic and foreign investors, international organisations and the public at large have a significant role to play in building and operating the gears to drive the energy agenda.

The energy sector in Brunei Darussalam is embarking on a journey of unprecedented significance and aspirations. To deliver on these aspirations, we require substantial growth and stronger resilience in our energy sector, and the country's economy at large. Now is the opportune time for domestic and international stakeholders to be involved and jointly create a thriving and dynamic future for energy in Brunei Darussalam.

GLOSSARY

ABS Acrylonitrile butadiene styrene, a common type of thermo-plastic. AMBD Autoriti Monetari Brunei Darussalam (Monetary Authority of Brunei Darussalam) APEC Asia Pacific Economic Cooperation BEDB Brunei Economic Development Board BGC Brunei Gas Carriers BND Bruneian Dollar

BOE Barrel of oil equivalent, a unit of energy based on the approximate energy released by burning one barrel of crude oil.

BMC Brunei Methanol Company Sendirian Berhad (BMC), a joint venture company between Mitsubishi Gas Chemical Company, Inc., PetroleumBRUNEI and ITOCHU Corporation. Established on 13th March 2006 to diversify the energy industry, it is Brunei's first Methanol manufacturing and exporting plant.

BNERI Brunei National Energy Research Institute. Established in January 2012.

BOEPD Barrel of oil equivalent (BOE) per day

CBM Coal Bed Methane, a form of natural gas extracted from coal bed mostly found in

US and Canada as well as in parts of Asia and Australia.

CDTG Competency Development Technical Group

DES Department of Electrical Services

EDPMO Energy Department, Prime Minister's Office

EEC Energy Efficiency and Conservation

EIA US Energy Information Administration, the statistical and analytical agency within the U.S. Department of Energy. EIA collects, analyses, and disseminates independent and impartial energy information to promote sound policymaking, efficient markets, and public understanding of energy and its interaction with the economy and the environment.

EICF Energy Industry Competency Framework

E&P Exploration and Production

EOR Enhanced oil recovery, is a generic term for techniques for increasing the amount of crude oil that can be extracted from an oil field, for instance, gas injection, chemical injections, cyclic steam injections, etc.

Energy LBD website www.EnergyLBD.gov.bn

Energy Website www.energy.gov.bn

For additional analytical, marketing, investment and business opportunities information, please contact
Global Investment & Business Center, USA
(202) 546-2103. Fax: (202) 546-3275. E-mail: rusric@erols.com

EU European Union

FDI Foreign Direct Investment - direct investment by a company in production located

in another country either by buying a company in the country or by expanding operations of an existing business in the country

FTE Full Time Employment

GDP Gross Domestic Product - market value of all officially recognised final goods and services produced within a country

HDPE High density polyethylene, a type of thermoplastic made from petroleum.

HSSE Health, Safety, Security and Environment

IEA International Energy Agency, a leading agency on energy policies, energy security, economic development and environmental protection. It is an autonomous intergovernmental organisation established in the framework of the Organisation for Economic Co-operation and Development (OECD) in 1974, and acts as a policy adviser to its member states, as well as to non-member countries, especially China, India and Russia.

IMO International Maritime Organization

IOC International Oil Company

IOR Improved Oil Recovery. See "EOR".

JPKE Jabatan Perancangan dan Kemajuan Ekonomi (Department of Economic Planning

and Development), Prime Minister's Office

KPI Key Performance Indicator

kV Kilo Volts (Thousand Volts)

LBD Local Business Development

LDPE Low density polyethylene, a type of thermoplastic made from petroleum.

MMBOE Million barrels of oil equivalent (BOE). See "BOE".

Mtpa Million tonnes per annum

MMbtu Million British thermal unit (btu) A btu is a measure of energy consumption – refers to the amount of heat required to increase the temperature of a pint of water (which weighs exactly 16 ounces) by one degree Fahrenheit.

MW Megawatts, a measure of the rate of energy conversion.

For additional analytical, marketing, investment and business opportunities information, please contact
Global Investment & Business Center, USA
(202) 546-2103. Fax: (202) 546-3275. E-mail: rusric@erols.com

MWh Megawatts hour. A MWh is a unit of energy equivalent to one Megawatt of power expended for one hour of time.

MV Mega Volts (Million Volts)

NFA No Further Action

OECD Organisation for Economic Co-operation and Development

PTA Purified Terephthalic Acid, a chemical mainly used in the production of polyester products.

RRR Reserve Replacement Ratio, a metric used by investors to judge the operating performance of an oil and gas exploration and production company. It measures the amount of proved reserves added to a company's reserve base during the year relative to the amount of oil and gas produced. The ratio must be at least 1 for the company to sustain its business in the long-term.

SAIDI System Average Interruption Duration Index, the total time without power for the average customer per year, measured in minutes and a measure of service unavailability

SAIFI System Average Interruption Frequency Index, the frequency of sustained interruptions or how often the average customer's lights are out, measured in times per year

SSC Sector Skills Council, a government and industry linked organisation which coordinates labour through standardisation of qualifications and accreditation and through facilitation of information flows between the industry and education or training institutes.

TAP Tabung Amanah Pekerja (Employees Trust Fund)

TOE Tonne of oil equivalent, a unit of energy based on the approximate energy released by burning one tonne of crude oil.

TSB Tenaga Suria Brunei Project, a photovoltaic (solar) power generation joint-project between the Government of Brunei and Mitsubishi Corporation.

USACEP U.S - Asia Pacific Comprehensive Energy Partnership

USD United States Dollar

VAM Vinyl Acetate Monomer, an important industrial polymer.

VET Vocational Education and Training. As defined by OECD, vocational education prepares participants for direct entry, without further training, into specific occupations. Successful completion of such programmes leads to a labour-market relevant vocational qualification.

WEO World Energy Outlook

For additional analytical, marketing, investment and business opportunities information, please contact
Global Investment & Business Center, USA
(202) 546-2103. Fax: (202) 546-3275. E-mail: rusric@erols.com

APPENDIX

■ KEY ASSUMPTIONS

GDP contribution from the energy sector assumes oil price (in real terms, 2010) growth from about USD 85 per barrel in 2010 to USD 133 per barrel of oil in 2035. This is based on estimates by a leading energy authority, the International Energy Agency (IEA) and is in line with projections of the U.S. Energy Information Administration (EIA) (refer to Exhibit A1 below). An exchange rate of 1.3 BND per USD was applied based on the current exchange rate regime.

Over the past decade, the real prices and volatility of commodities (food, agricultural products, metals and oil) have increased significantly (Exhibit A2). Heightened uncertainty surrounding the global financial markets and economies and the supply of energy have significantly contributed to volatility of prices. Increasing demand due to the growth of emerging markets, especially China, also pushed up real prices.

■ RISKS AND UNCERTAINTY

There are risks that unforeseen future events or circumstances will cause oil price to deviate from projections. The EDPMO will have to react to changes in the oil prices as we progress through the transformation journey, tailoring our initiative plans and targets accordingly.

Additionally, there are business and commercial risks associated with the expected production and materialisation of the initiatives identified. Hence, further examination of economic viability and the optimisation of prioritised objective functions (e.g., economic value-add, employment and diversification) is critical.

Dynamic factors and changes in industry and world trends would have to be continually scanned to ensure that prudent revisions and decisions are made in each step of the journey.

■ Upstream Directive 1/2011: - Field Development Plan For Maturing Hydrocarbon Development Projects

BRUNEI ENERGY EFFICIENCY STRATEGY - IMPORTANT DEVELOPMENTS

PEER REVIEW ON ENERGY EFFICIENCY IN BRUNEI DARUSSALAM Final Report November 2013 Report or the APEC Energy Working Group

BASIC TRENDS

Brunei Darussalam is one of the few economies in the APEC region that is self-sufficient when it comes to energy. The economy is blessed with an abundance of oil and gas resources. With the small population, total overall energy consumption constitutes a small share of its energy production and the economy is able to export the bulk of its resources to generate revenue. Its current GDP per capita is one of the highest in the region. Based on APERC's projections in the *APEC Energy Demand and Supply Outlook 5th Edition*, Brunei Darussalam is likely to remain an energy exporter beyond the year 2035. The economy's wealth from the oil and gas industry is generously shared with its citizen in various forms; ranging from absence of tax on income; free education (up to university level and overseas scholarships); reduced prices for staple food (sugar and rice), housing, medical and health care services; as well as subsidised energy and utility prices (petrol products, electricity, water).

For most APEC economies, especially economies with limited energy resources, expensive energy imports are a powerful motivator for energy efficiency and conservation (EEC) measures. Given the wealth and secure energy situation of this economy, the PREE Review Team was curious as to why Brunei Darussalam was motivated to undertake a Peer Review on Energy Efficiency; after all, motivation is a fundamental criterion in ensuring that EEC implementation is successful and sustainable for the long term. The government officials interviewed during the visit were very clear and passionate about this subject. Several reasons were cited, ranging from the recognition that the oil and gas resources on which Brunei Darussalam has built its wealth upon may not last forever; the extremely high energy consumption per capita especially when compared to other economies in the region; the benefits of saved energy for export; the social and environmental costs of energy wastage; and the unsustainably high energy subsidies.

With these motivations in mind, Brunei Darussalam has decided to implement a number of EEC initiatives in pursuit of its energy savings goal. In an effort to first understand the consumer habits in the economy, in 2010, the Centre for Strategic and Policy Studies of Brunei Darussalam engaged a consultant to conduct a comprehensive study on EEC that critically evaluates energy consumption across all major sectors and identifies measures and recommends appropriate policy options to achieve high energy efficiency in each of these sectors. Eight key policy options were identified, namely appliance standards, labelling, building regulation, energy management, fuel economy regulation, electricity tariff reform, financial incentives and awareness-raising.

By the time of the PREE Review Team's visit in June 2013, the electricity tariff reform policy option has already been successfully implemented since January 2012 while the awareness-raising policy option is now a continuous, on-going process under the responsibility of the Energy Department, Prime Minister's Office (EDPMO) and the Ministry of Education. As for the other key policy options, Brunei Darussalam is currently conducting in-depth evaluation for each option to design the most appropriate method of implementation that best suits the economy's circumstances (i.e. institutional capacity, legislative and regulatory frameworks, private and public sector costs and savings, social impact and feasibility, timeframes).

For additional analytical, marketing, investment and business opportunities information, please contact
Global Investment & Business Center, USA
(202) 546-2103. Fax: (202) 546-3275. E-mail: rusric@erols.com

The PREE Review Team highly commends and appreciates Brunei Darussalam's positive attitude and endeavours in planning innovative EEC measures and incentives that suits the economy's unique situation. At the same time, the PREE Review Team strongly believes that these EEC measures and initiatives should be integrated into an overarching national EEC strategy with well-defined, sector-specific targets and clear implementation plans. This will enable the economy to prioritise resources allocation and designate responsibilities for EEC program implementation, monitoring and evaluation.

From the institutional context, while EDPMO and other government agencies have been tasked with implementing specific EEC measures in concert with other stakeholders it is important that there is strong leadership and coordination at the ministerial level to oversee the overall planning and effective implementation of EEC programs in order to ensure national targets can be achieved. To this end the National Energy Efficiency & Conservation Committee (NEECC) was established in 2011 and is co-chaired by the Minister for Energy, Minister of Development and Minister of Communication.

The PREE Review Team also believes that the EEC data collection and monitoring should be a priority for Brunei Darussalam as a first step towards providing real and useful information on energy usage. This is vital in the initial design process of appropriate EEC programs and policies. In the future, information on energy consumption will enable EDPMO to monitor progress and modify EEC initiatives accordingly.

Under the current energy pricing mechanism, motivating the people of Brunei Darussalam to voluntarily apply EEC measures is admittedly a challenge as the usual market incentives are not the main driving force in this economy. Therefore, PREE Review Team strongly recommends that Brunei Darussalam initiate a detailed market research to identify the EEC messages and incentives that would be most likely to appeal to different consumer groups, and customize communication strategies accordingly. Additionally, other novel EEC approaches that the PREE Review Team believes would be suitable for implementation in Brunei Darussalam have been included in this report. Two examples of innovative approaches are the Opower Home Energy Reports that applies a social incentive approach to electricity billing and the demand-responsive transport model to replace the traditional fixed-route public transport model.

At the same time, it is essential that certain policy options are backed up by the necessary legislative measures to ensure compliance. Specifically, the appliances and equipment minimum energy performance standards and labelling, EEC Building Codes and fuel economy regulations are policy options that require legislative and regulatory measures in order to ensure a minimum standard is achieved across the board. Legislative measures are also necessary in establishing the EEC-related institutions and financial frameworks proposed in this report, otherwise, the EEC institutions proposed may not have sufficient authority to carry out its EEC mandate.

The PREE Review Team is concerned that implementation of EEC policy actions may be hampered by the shortage of qualified EEC practitioners and experts in the economy as EEC has only recently been made a priority area in Brunei Darussalam. The PREE Review Team proposes that Brunei Darussalam conduct accelerated capacity building workshops on EEC data collection and management, EEC compliance, energy facility management, energy auditing and energy financing to quickly overcome this shortage.

On the other hand, the PREE Review Team was favourably impressed with the many initiatives that Brunei Darussalam has implemented to EEC awareness for the general public, especially the School Energy Clubs and designated Energy Day.

For additional analytical, marketing, investment and business opportunities information, please contact
Global Investment & Business Center, USA
(202) 546-2103. Fax: (202) 546-3275. E-mail: rusric@erols.com

In summary, Brunei Darussalam has already identified the key policy options that should be implemented in order to achieve the economy's goal of 45% reduction in energy intensity by 2035 (using 2005 levels as the base line). The PREE Review Team agrees that these policy options are essential and will likely result in vast reductions in energy consumption, especially for the major consuming sectors. The recommendations made in this report are tailored towards aligning policy options under a unified framework and sharing best practices and innovative approaches from around the world, while concurrently identifying and addressing issues that may hinder EEC implementation in the economy. Brunei Darussalam has great potential to become one of the most efficient economies in APEC, and it is hoped that the recommendations in this report will help the economy to realize this potential and achieve its EEC goals.

RECOMMENDATIONS

INSTITUTIONAL CONTEXT

Recommendation 1: The National Energy Efficiency & Conservation Committee (NEECC) should oversee not only the implementation but also the planning of prioritized energy efficiency and conservation (EEC) plan of actions. This committee should be overseen by the Prime Minister.

Recommendation 2: The Government of Brunei Darussalam should enact necessary legislative measures to promote EEC. In addition, a comprehensive EEC Law should be considered in order to systematize necessary legislative measures.

Recommendation 3: The Government of Brunei Darussalam should establish the proposed innovative financing program, Brunei Energy Efficiency Fund (BEEF), in order to facilitate EEC projects in the private sector.

Recommendation 4: The Government of Brunei Darussalam should consider implementing gradual energy pricing reforms which draws on successful approaches used in other countries.

ENERGY EFFICIENCY GOALS, TARGETS AND STRATEGY

Recommendation 5: Identify appropriate incentives to further enhance EEC measures.

Recommendation 6: Establish a national energy efficiency sub-target which measures energy efficiency improvement in the economy and ensures that it has a significant role in achieving the energy intensity target.

Recommendation 7: Apply a clear implementation plan (roadmap) to accelerate appropriate technologies to meet or exceed Brunei Darussalam's EEC targets. This plan should be announced to the public as a national agenda.

ENERGY DATA COLLECTION AND MONITORING

Recommendation 8: Define a structured energy efficiency data collection framework and ensure regular implementation.

Recommendation 9: Introduce a data evaluation, monitoring and verification (EMV) protocol to ensure energy efficiency data is credible and accurate.

Recommendation 10: Publish energy efficiency indicators monitoring reports periodically to evaluate progress and encourage continuing efforts in energy efficiency improvements.

Recommendation 11: Establish a Brunei Energy Data Management Centre (BEDMC) that reports directly to the Minister of Energy.

POLICY MEASURES – RESIDENCE, COMMERCIAL, GOVERNMENT AND INDUSTRIAL SECTORS

Recommendation 12: Brunei Darussalam should conduct a detailed market research to identify which EEC messages would appeal the most to different consumer groups.

Recommendation 13: School Energy Clubs should be enhanced by developing an energy efficiency curriculum to reach all students in all levels of education.

Recommendation 14: An energy conservation and promotion fund (ECPF) should be established to be used for funding the EEC promotion program such as partial subsidies for EEC project investment, rebate, labelling, capacity building and demonstration programs, research and development grants, etc.

Recommendation 15: An Energy Conservation Centre Brunei (ECCB) should be legally established.

Recommendation 16: To demonstrate the effectiveness of energy management systems, a number of government, commercial and industrial facilities should be selected to participate in an energy management pilot program in line with ISO 50001 criteria. This can be further supplemented with detailed guidelines for establishing and implementing energy management systems, which could be distributed to the target organizations.

Recommendation 17: Brunei Darussalam should develop an energy management law adopting appropriate parts of the ISO 50001: 2011 Energy Management System, particular emphasis should be given to energy management system training.

Recommendation 18: In support of the energy management law, a sufficient number of qualified external auditors should be trained to conduct monitoring and verification exercises to ensure compliance.

Recommendation 19: Appropriate incentives should be designed to motivate facility managers and operators, particularly those in government-owned facilities, to apply EEC improvements that minimize operation costs.

Recommendation 20: The proposed EEC Building Code should include a strong foundation for EEC elements (along with existing fire, safety, construction and health) and be a unified document that clearly defines the jurisdiction of all agencies.

Recommendation 21: EEC Building Code should include passive or partial-passive cooling and lighting design, and construction using low thermal mass and insulated materials for new residential, government and commercial buildings. In doing so, cooperation with a research centre, such as the Energy Research Group of Universiti Brunei Darussalam (UBD), is highly recommended.

Recommendation 22: EDPMO should develop a compliance enforcement program to be effective once the EEC Building Code comes into force.

Recommendation 23: Build local capacity for addressing the EEC elements of the Building Code.

Recommendation 24: Energy efficiency improvement in the oil and gas industry should be focused on heat recovery, and this should be also applied for any new oil and gas plant designs.

Recommendation 25: Consider replacing small gas turbines with new gas engine sets for power generation in oil and gas industries.

Recommendation 26: Conduct a study on the efficiency of the gas transmission line, to check whether there might be gas leakage along the gas pipe line. Then, identify and implement energy efficiency measures that could reduce gas wastage.

Policy Measures – Transport Sector

Recommendation 27: Continue developing a database of fuel efficiency of light vehicles in the Brunei Darussalam fleet to be the basis on which vehicle fuel efficiency policies and initiatives, including consumer information, can be designed and monitored.

Recommendation 28: Provide consumer information on vehicle fuel consumption through the implementation of a vehicle labelling programme and energy efficient driver behaviour.

Recommendation 29: Incorporate fuel efficiency into new driver education and driver licensing.

Recommendation 30: Set CO2 emissions based vehicle acquisition or taxation policies which encourage both fuel efficient vehicles and lower carbon fuel vehicles, such as gas vehicles, electric vehicles and plug-in hybrids.

Recommendation 31: Continue to periodically survey daily vehicle usage patterns (range of trip distances, range of daily driving distances and trip purpose) to increase understanding of travel patterns to assist in the design of future policies and initiatives.

Recommendation 32: Investigate information technology based, demand responsive transit models which may be more suitable to Brunei Darussalam's population size and urban density than traditional fixed-route public transport and better meet customers' needs.

Recommendation 33: Encourage greater coordination between the infrastructure functions of the Ministry of Development and the transport functions of the Ministry of Communications.

Policy Measures – Electricity Sector

Recommendation 34: The Department of Electrical Services (DES) should develop a roadmap to improve overall power systems efficiency.

Recommendation 35: DES should work closely with the Ministry of Finance to ensure that a well structured finance plan is put in place to provide the capitalization needed to finance the roadmap.

For additional analytical, marketing, investment and business opportunities information, please contact
Global Investment & Business Center, USA
(202) 546-2103. Fax: (202) 546-3275. E-mail: rusric@erols.com

Recommendation 36: DES should implement ISO 50001 in all of its power generating stations.

Recommendation 37: Continue to implement progressively increasing tariffs over a specified long-term schedule, similar to what is currently being practiced in Japan and California.

Recommendation 38: Consider using other innovative tariffs such as "time of use (TOU) tariffs" to encourage consumers to increase their use of energy efficiency and lower overall system consumption.

Recommendation 39: Install smart meters for enhancing both demand side and supply side operations and programs.

Recommendation 40: Accelerate efforts to implement demand-side measures such as those being implemented for air conditioning units, chillers and lighting and consider Building Management Systems (BMS) for the commercial sector.

Recommendation 41: Consider implementing an energy efficiency (and water saving) program for drinking water and waste water treatment facilities.

Recommendation 42: As part of the efforts to supply electricity to the eco-tourism Temburong area, conduct a feasibility study that applies intensive energy efficiency measures integrating small-scale renewable energy supply (keeping the diesel generation facility as a back-up if needed).

POLICY MEASURES – APPLIANCES AND EQUIPMENT

Recommendation 43: The EDPMO and BNERI should accelerate the development of the National Standard and Labelling Regulation, in order to achieve a more rapid transformation of the energy efficiency market in Brunei Darussalam.

Recommendation 44: Benchmark Brunei Darussalam's standards to established international or other regional standards.

Recommendation 45: Enforcement of the set standards should be a priority. Therefore, plan resources to ensure that stringency is maintained and enforcement is carried out.

Recommendation 46: Allow a grace period for sellers to sell out their existing inventory of inefficient products and limit their ability to import such products prior to the standards' effective date.

Recommendation 47: Develop a product label that is easily identifiable by consumers and uses a simple rating system.

PART I: BACKGROUND INFORMATION

The background information contained in this report has been contributed by Brunei Darussalam. This information is intended to provide some context to the recommendations of the PREE Review Team. The first section discusses the trends in Brunei Darussalam's energy consumption. The second section provides information on Brunei Darussalam's energy efficiency institutions, current policies and objectives and energy efficiency programs.

For additional analytical, marketing, investment and business opportunities information, please contact
Global Investment & Business Center, USA
(202) 546-2103. Fax: (202) 546-3275. E-mail: rusric@erols.com

1. STATISTICS, FORECASTS AND TRENDS IN ENERGY CONSUMPTION

1.1 BRUNEI DARUSSALAM'S ENERGY SITUATION IN 2012

Brunei Darussalam enjoys a high standard of living with a GDP per capita of BND 52,315, which is among the highest in the region; thanks to the oil & gas sector that contributes about 67.6% of the BND 20.5 Billion Brunei Darussalam's GDP (in 2011). Oil & gas sector also constitutes about 95.6% of the BND 15.6 Billion total export and also about 91.4% of the Government's revenue. The oil & gas sector has for a long time been the determining factor for Brunei Darussalam's economy and is expected to remain the dominant contributor to the economy's revenue and source of energy in the foreseeable future.

Total final energy consumption in Brunei Darussalam is around 2.5 ton of oil equivalents (toe) per capita (2012). For production of electricity, 99% of the generation mix comes from natural gas and the other 0.999% is coming from oil (diesel) and 0.001% from solar energy. Most of the power plants in Brunei Darussalam are still using single cycle gas turbines, which have low efficiency. The single cycle gas turbines burn more fossil fuel and emit more carbon dioxide to the atmosphere. In 2012, an average of 39% of the electricity generated goes to residential sector, 27% to commercial sector, government sector takes an average of 18% and the remaining 16% is supplied to the oil & gas industrial sector (Figure 1).

Figure 1 – Average Electricity Consumption by Sector in Brunei Darussalam for 2012

Air conditioning is the leading consumption of electricity. Air conditioner accounted for almost 60% of electricity consumption in a building. This is prevalent in almost all homes, government buildings and commercial buildings in Brunei Darussalam. With the relatively low electricity tariff, the population have enjoyed cheap and relatively high usage of air conditioning to create "cool" environment in both home and office.

Transportation sector is the third largest spender in fuel expenditure, accounted B$ 521 Million or 25% of total energy expenditure in Brunei Darussalam (2010). Meanwhile excessive fuel is burnt given that the average efficiency of motor transport in Brunei Darussalam is only 10%. The number of in-use private and commercial is estimated at 200,000 vehicles travelling on 2,775 km

For additional analytical, marketing, investment and business opportunities information, please contact
Global Investment & Business Center, USA
(202) 546-2103. Fax: (202) 546-3275. E-mail: rusric@erols.com

of paved roads (2010). This makes Brunei Darussalam one of the highest in the world as far as car ownership is concerned, equivalent to more than 2 vehicles per licensed driver.

1.2 TRENDS IN ENERGY SUPPLY

Brunei Darussalam is well endowed with conventional energy resources such as oil and gas and renewable energy sources such as solar energy may also have some potential.

In 2012, the total primary energy supply of Brunei Darussalam was 3,425 kilotonnes of oil equivalent (ktoe) as shown in Table 1. Natural gas and oil accounted for most of the supply whereas natural gas represents about 77.9% and the rest was from oil (22%) and solar - photovoltaic (>1%).

Table 1: Brunei Darussalam Energy Supply and Consumption for 2012

	2012
Primary Energy Supply (ktoe)	
Indigenous Production	20,201
Net imports and other	-17032
Total PES	3,425
Coal	0
Oil	756
Gas	2,669
Other	0.14
Final energy consumption (ktoe)	
Industry	250
Transport	452
Other sectors	310
Total FEC	1,012
Coal	0
Oil	666
Gas	26
Electricity and other	320
Power Generation (GWh)	
Total	3,930
Thermal	3,929
Hydro	0
Nuclear	0
Other	1.2

Brunei Darussalam's domestic oil production occurs both offshore and onshore. The Brunei Darussalam's oil and gas production in 2012 was 20,201 ktoe, a decline of 2.95% from 2011, where crude oil /condensate and petroleum products production was around 8,616 ktoe and 17 ktoe respectively. Natural gas production and other (solar) production were around 11,568 ktoe and 0.14 ktoe respectively.

Historically, Brunei Darussalam is the net exporter of oil and natural gas. The crude oil and condensate export was around 151 thousand barrels per day. Net oil and gas exports account for

For additional analytical, marketing, investment and business opportunities information, please contact
Global Investment & Business Center, USA
(202) 546-2103. Fax: (202) 546-3275. E-mail: rusric@erols.com

more than 80% of Brunei Darussalam's production. The main export destinations were the ASEAN countries, South Korea, India, Australia, New Zealand, Japan, China, and USA. The majority of natural gas was exported as liquefied natural gas (LNG) to Japan and the rest to South Korea.

On the other hand, Brunei Darussalam also imported 379 ktoe of energy, primarily in the form of motor gasoline, diesel, Jet A-1, bitumen and lubricant.

1.3 TRENDS IN ENERGY CONSUMPTION

The final energy consumption in 2012 was around 1,012 ktoe, whereas petroleum products contributed the largest share around 666 ktoe (65.8%), electricity 320 ktoe (31.6%) and the rest was natural gas at around 26 ktoe (2.6%). The total final energy consumption in 2012 increased slightly around 6.5% compared to 2011. Figure 2 shows Brunei Darussalam's final energy consumption.

Brunei Darussalam Final Energy Consumption

Figure 2 – Brunei Darussalam's Historical Final Energy Consumption

Energy Consumption by sector

Historically, the shares of the three main sectors still remain unchanged. In 2012, the transportation sector was the largest final energy end user at 452 ktoe, or 44.7% of total final energy consumption, followed by the commercial and residential sector at 310 ktoe, or 30.6% and the industrial sector at 250 ktoe, or 24.7%.

a) Residential and Commercial Sectors:

The residential and commercial sector is the second largest energy consumer in the country. In the year 2012, this sector consumed 310 ktoe of energy. Residential & commercial sectors accounted for an average of 48% and 25% respectively in terms of electricity consumption for the

For additional analytical, marketing, investment and business opportunities information, please contact
Global Investment & Business Center, USA
(202) 546-2103. Fax: (202) 546-3275. E-mail: rusric@erols.com

past 5 years. In the past few years, significant efforts have been implemented towards saving energy in the residential and commercial sectors. Measures include applying "smart" tariffs in the residential sector which was launched on the 1st January 2012 and using high-energy efficiency technologies in buildings. Technologies like air-conditioners with 'inverter' technology, chillers, lighting equipment (i.e., compact fluorescent lamps, LEDs) and lighting system controls, automatic control equipment occupancy sensor and photo sensor unit at the offices to control brightness, penetration of solar water heaters and "Smart" power meters at the main switchboard to continuously monitor consumption are used by leading green energy organizations. According to a preliminary study, promoting these energy conservation initiatives in residential sector could result in up to 50% reduction in energy from Business-As-Usual (BAU) case in 2035 with three quarters of this contribution from high efficiency air conditioners and 7% from high efficiency lamps. Similar measures in commercial buildings could result in up to 44% reduction in energy from BAU case in 2035 with half of the total contribution from high efficiency air conditioners and a quarter of the total contribution from high efficiency chillers.

b) Transport Sector:

Gasoline cars and diesel cars account for 52% and 27% (or collectively 79%) of energy consumption in this sector respectively. Energy saving measures that have been implemented include promoting technologies, like the optimized gear box, the use of hybrid cars, electric vehicles and fuel efficient vehicle (FEV) to the public and evaluation of imposing the EU equivalent standards of fuel economy by 2025 for all the new vehicles (i.e. 21.3 km/l). This could result in about 40% lower energy needs than the BAU scenario by 2035. In collaboration with Ministry of Communication (MoC), the EDPMO will also evaluate how to improve the public transportation system (by adding capacity, optimizing routes and upgrading infrastructure) and the potential use of hybrid or electric vehicles for public transportation. Furthermore, EDPMO and MoC will seek to promote behavioral levers such as planning destination routes upfront and car-pooling to minimize the number of vehicles on the road.

c) Industrial sector:

The industrial sector accounts for 250 ktoe of energy, approximately one quarter of the total final energy consumption. By practicing energy efficiency, the industrial sector could not only optimize energy usage and abate CO_2 emission, but also reduce operational costs. In Brunei Darussalam, industrial sector is dominated by oil and gas industry which account for an average of 10% in terms of energy consumption for the past 5 years. In the oil & gas industry, the CO_2 emissions mostly come from the combustion of fossil fuel from auto-producer power plant facilities. Various initiatives have been undertaken in the oil & gas industry sector by the local operators to improve their operational efficiencies and reduce greenhouse gas emission. There has been a steady decrease of greenhouse gas emissions over time especially from 1998 onwards. The main contribution to the reduction of greenhouse gas emissions has primarily been from the reduction in venting and flaring emissions through rationalization projects and improvements in operational efficiencies in producing oil & gas fields. With significant reductions having been achieved in venting and flaring emissions, fuel gas (for gas compression and power generation) becomes the main contributor to greenhouse gas emissions in the order of about 50%. Efforts are now focused on energy efficiency of compression and auto-producer power plant facilities. The opportunities identified include upgrading or replacement of aged and inefficient equipment (e.g. compressors and control systems) in improving operational reliability and efficiency.

Energy Price and Subsidies

a) Fuel Prices

For additional analytical, marketing, investment and business opportunities information, please contact
Global Investment & Business Center, USA
(202) 546-2103. Fax: (202) 546-3275. E-mail: rusric@erols.com

Brunei Darussalam's fuel prices are fixed and set as follows:-

Table 2: Fixed Fuel Prices

Fuel Type	Cost
Premium Ron 97	B$0.53 cents/litre
Regular Ron 95	B$0.36 cents/litre
Diesel	B$0.31 cents/litre

b) Electricity Tariff

Brunei Darussalam's current electricity tariffs are structured as follows:

Table 3: Residential Electricity Prices

Units	Rates
1 to 600 units	B$0.01 cents/kWh
601 to 1500 units	B$0.08 cents/kWh
1501 to 4000 units	B$0.10 cents/kWh
4001 units above	B$0.12 cents/kWh

Table 4: Commercial/ Industrial Premises Electricity Prices

Units	Rates
First 10 units	KVA x B$0.20 cents/kWh
Next 60 units	KVA x B$0.07 cents/kWh
Next 100 units	KVA x B$0.06 cents/kWh
Remaining units	KVA x B$0.05 cents/kWh

The tariff for domestic sector was changed on 1 January 2012 from a regressive to a progressive structure, however the tariff for commercial and industrial premises remain unchanged.

c) Gas Subsidy to DES/BPC

The price of gas delivered to the Department of Electrical Department (DES) and Berakas Power Company (BPC) gas power stations are lower than the market price.

Energy Intensity

In line with other APEC economies, Brunei Darussalam is working towards an ambitious goal of a 45% energy intensity reduction by 2035 (using 2005 as the base year). Historically, there has been a severe irregularity in terms of energy intensity trend in Brunei Darussalam from 2005-2012 primarily as a result of inconsistent trend of both Gross Domestic Product (GDP) and Total Primary Energy Supply (TPES) – see Figures 3 and 4. Presumably, the trend will remain analogous for the next few years due to the development of downstream industry and additional production from offshore blocks which will further increase the energy usage in the region. However, due to the disproportionately higher increase in GDP contribution from the upstream industry, the overall energy intensity will drop to about 215 toe / USD Million GDP. This

For additional analytical, marketing, investment and business opportunities information, please contact
Global Investment & Business Center, USA
(202) 546-2103. Fax: (202) 546-3275. E-mail: rusric@erols.com

corresponds to a 45% reduction from 2005 baseline, indicating significant efforts need to be undertaken to help Brunei Darussalam reduce its energy intensity.

Currently, Brunei Darussalam is using TPES/GDP as a reference indicator to calculate energy intensity (EI) reduction in line with the reference indicator being used by APEC member economies. However, this indicator does not seem to be the right tool to measure the amount of reduction for energy consumption because it has no direct impact on, and is perhaps not solely related to, energy efficiency improvement. In view of this, ASEAN member states (AMSs) are planning to use a reference indicator of TFEC/GDP for ASEAN long-term energy intensity reduction target. Brunei Darussalam is in full support to use TFEC/GDP as a reference indicator to be used on long-term EI reduction target for all AMSs. In the meantime, Brunei Darussalam calculates EI reduction using both reference indicators (TPES/GDP & TFEC/GDP) as shown in Tables 5 and 6.

2. ENERGY EFFICIENCY INSTITUTIONS, POLICIES AND MAJOR PROGRAMS

2.1. INSTITUTIONAL FRAMEWORK

2.1.1 The Energy Department, Prime Minister's Office (EDPMO)

The EDPMO is under the purview of the Minister of Energy at the Prime Minister's Office co-headed by the Permanent Secretary (Upstream) at the Prime Minister's Office and the Permanent Secretary (Downstream & Power) at the Prime Minister's Office.

Figure 5 – Organisation Structure of Energy Department, Prime Minister's Office

The Department envisions a "sustainable energy for Brunei prosperity" with a mission to "drive Brunei economy into sustainable future". Its goals include to strengthen and grow oil and gas upstream and downstream activities, ensure safe, secure, reliable and efficient supply and use of energy, and maximize economic spin-offs from energy industry.

Under the EDPMO, the relevant entities for EEC policy planning and implementation are as follows:-

1) The Energy Efficiency & Conservation Unit

The Energy Efficiency & Conservation (EEC) Unit is entrusted to implement all necessary plans of action which help to reduce energy consumption towards more efficient use of energy nationwide. The unit shall manage all initiatives and projects for the development of energy efficiency & conservation, in particular but not limited to the following:

i.	Promoting and developing allconservation (EEC) nationwide.	plans and programs	related	to energy	efficiency	&
ii.	Ensuring the implementation of energy efficiency & conservation (EEC) projects. These are not just limited to the projects planned by the Energy Department itself, but also include all projects being planned by other agencies or organizations including secondary schools through their Energy Clubs.					
iii.	Develop and establish energy efficiency & conservation policies and laws and to ensure all agencies, organizations and individuals are fully obliged in implementing those policies and laws.					
iv.	Undertake an audit at government and commercial buildings in order to monitor the energy consumption patterns and will make recommendations towards energy efficiency improvements.					
v.	Providing advice on matters directly related to Energy Efficiency & Conservation (EEC) to public including school students.					

2) National Energy Efficiency & Conservation Committee (NEECC)

A comprehensive approach on EEC initiative taken by the EDPMO is the formation of National Energy Efficiency and Conservation Committee (NEECC) in 2011 at the Ministerial level. This committee, which is co-chaired by the Minister of Energy, Minister of Development and Minister of Communication, is tasked to oversee the implementation of prioritized EEC plan of actions as outlined in the EEC Roadmap. The EEC Roadmap was developed in 2011 from four major sectors namely residential, commercial, transportation & industrial sectors. The NEECC will also be in charge of the execution of projects and coordination with various stakeholders. Moreover, in line with the realization of energy intensity target in the future, the committee will also need to set standards for industries (especially for the new upcoming downstream) on the production process that would comply with the minimum energy consumption policy to ensure the national level of energy intensity can be achieved.

2.1.2 Department of Electrical Services

The Department of Electrical Services (DES) is a government department under the Prime Minister's Office mandated as a regulator and service provider in the areas of:

i. The generation of electricity.

ii. The transmission of electric power.

iii. The distribution of electricity to the end-users.

iv. The use of electricity in Brunei Darussalam The DES also provides technical and essential services to the consumers in the form of:

i. Controlling the standard of electrical works in buildings;

ii. Technical advisory services to the end users;

iii. Installation, operation and maintenance of street lighting.

DES has five power stations; namely Gadong 1A Power Station, Gadong 2 Power Station, Bukit Panggal Combined Cycle Power Plant, SOASSKW Lumut Co-Generation Power Plant and a diesel powered power station at Belingus in the Temburong District. All power stations are strategically located close to the load centres. Lumut Power Station is located in the Belait District, Bukit Panggal Power Station is located in Tutong District and Gadong I & Gadong II Power Stations are located in the Brunei Muara District.

The existing total capacity for electricity generation by DES power stations stands at 442 MW. The DES generation peak load is 313 MW. This accounts for 60% of the total peak load for Brunei Darussalam.

2.1.3 Other Related Agencies

In order to realize the energy intensity target, EDPMO will require coordinated effort from all stakeholders (government and private sectors) who will jointly evaluate legislative measures to promote energy efficiency & conservation. The four (4) important Ministries which are also the core members of NEECC are the Ministry of Development, Ministry of Communication, Ministry of Education and Ministry of Finance.

1) Ministry of Development

Under the Ministry of Development (MoD), there are two Departments that play major roles in achieving nationwide EE&C goals:-

i. Department of Mechanical and Eletrical (DME), Public Works Department

ii. Authority for Building Control & Construction Industry (ABCi).

The Ministry of Development via ABCi and DME, in collaboration with EDPMO, are responsible for the development of the EEC Building Regulation/Code as outlined in EEC's roadmap with an objective to establish energy efficiency and conservation standards and a regulatory mechanism for buildings in Brunei Darussalam.

Meanwhile, the Department of Environmental, Park & Recreation (DEPR), which is also one of the departments under the Ministry of Development, plays an important role on subjects related to climate change. EDPMO has been working very closely with DEPR towards the reduction of carbon emission from various energy sectors in the country.

2) Ministry of Communications

The Ministry of Communications (MinCom) with the vision of being a 'Service Hub 2004" has a mission for the "provision of a safe, efficient, accessible and secure transport and communication services" or SEAS. Part of the role of the Transportation Section in the Ministry of Communication is to be responsible for managing and administering the land-based transport in the country, both private and public. It enforces the policy and regulations for transport management.

Land Transport Department as one of department under the Ministry of Communication is also responsible for sustainable development of public transport system and promoting widespread usage of modes of transport to ensure public transport service operators provide a more integrated, efficient and safe transport system in the country.

In terms of EEC initiatives in relation to transportation, the EDPMO has been working together with the Ministry of Communication in introducing and promoting the use of hybrid cars, electric vehicles and Fuel Efficient Vehicle (FEV) in the country. This is again another initiative being undertaken by the EDPMO in collaboration with Ministry of Communication to reduce the energy intensity to 45% via transportation sector as well as to push towards a cleaner, greener and more sustainable transportation system and a better living environment in Brunei Darussalam by 2035.

3) Ministry of Education

Another important initiative being undertaken by the EDPMO (in cooperation with STEP Centre, Ministry of Education) is the establishment of Energy Clubs in schools since 25 May 2009. The objective is to inculcate the culture of energy efficiency and conservation at grassroots level (at schools) so that young people would become EEC ambassadors.

Currently, there are 30 Energy Clubs in Brunei Darussalam. This number is expected to rise as there are several schools that have conveyed their interest to establish Energy Clubs in their schools. Since its establishment, Energy Clubs have conducted quite a number of EEC and renewable projects. Some of these projects were showcased in big, energy-related events nationwide, including Brunei Energy Expo & Energy Week.

4) Ministry of Finance

The Ministry of Finance, in collaboration with EDPMO, plays an important role in introducing effective financial incentives for energy efficient products and technologies. Financial incentives such as tax reductions or perhaps tax exemption are often used for prevailing energy efficient equipment that initially has high costs. This financial support will aid in reducing the cost differences that may be incurred when purchasing more efficient equipment.

Discussion have been going on between EDPMO and relevant departments under the Ministry of Finance to explore several options in setting up an appropriate financial incentive mechanism or framework; i.e, for energy efficient cars such as electric vehicles (EV), hybrid vehicles and EV infrastructure in transportation sector as well as incentives for energy efficient equipment/technologies for example; air-conditioning, lightings, photovoltaic, HP water heaters and solar water heaters in residential and commercial sectors.

Support from the Ministry of Finance in making endorsements and approving financial incentives would be vital for the success of EEC promotion initiatives in Brunei Darussalam.

5) Brunei National Energy Research Institute

The Brunei National Energy Research Institute (BNERI) is a think-tank that provides policy advice to the Government of Brunei Darussalam on energy matters including those of Energy Efficiency and Conservation. BNERI will play an important role in imparting the best EEC policies into Brunei Darussalam's current institutional framework.

2.2. BRUNEI DARUSSALAM ENERGY WHITE PAPER

In order to secure the future of Brunei Darussalam's energy sector, Energy Department in the Prime Minister's Office (EDPMO) has set 3 strategic goals in the Energy White Paper (EWP) to drive the energy sector forward and realize the National Vision:

Strategic Goal 1 – Strengthen and Grow Oil and Gas Upstream and Downstream Activities
Strategic Goal 2 – Ensure Safe, Secure, Reliable and Efficient Supply and Use of Energy
Strategic Goal 3 – Maximise Economic Spin-off from Energy Industry - boost local content

and secure high participation of local workforce More details of the Energy White Paper will be available when it is launched (date to be confirmed).

3. ENERGY EFFICIENCY AND CONSERVATION ROADMAP

3.1 ROADMAP FOR POWER SECTOR

Proposed integration of renewables into the grid sometime in 2020 by implementing feed-in tariff (FIT). New fossil fuel fired power plants does not need to be built in the next 20 years as electricity demand will not grow due to energy savings made in the residential and commercial sectors and the integration of renewables, including the proposed Sarawak inter-connections. Tariff reform is a very effective method to incentivize energy savings in residences and offices and has already been implemented on 1 January 2012.

Figure 6 – Roadmap for Power Sector

3.2 ROADMAP FOR TRANSPORTATION SECTOR

The key measure is to introduce fuel economy labelling to allow fuel efficient vehicle to be sold in Brunei Darussalam. The fuel economy regulation of 39.97 MPG by 2020 and 49.48 MPG can be effectively introduced by 2025. Electric vehicles (EV) were first introduced in Brunei Darussalam in 2011 during the Brunei Energy EXPO 2011 and have since been utilized by the government as a pilot demonstration project. Until now, EVs have not been expanded for registered public use. There is a proposal to study and develop EV charging infrastructure to ease the transition from conventional vehicles to EVs and this will support the target for diffusion for EV by 2022. Additionally, there is also a proposal to consider providing subsidy for EV as part of incentives for both charging station and EVs by 2020. On public transportation, it is proposed to undertake feasibility study as early as 2012, followed by financial assistance for infrastructure. The introduction of public transport is proposed to be implemented by 2018.

Figure 7 – Roadmap for Transportation Sector

3.3 - ROADMAP FOR INDUSTRIAL SECTOR

On the improvement of equipment efficiency, pilot projects and subsidies can be an effective policy options towards improving energy efficiency by 2035. The dissemination of newly developed technologies is also an important factor in energy efficiency improvement. On recovery of waste energy, the adoption of subsidy schemes is a prospective policy option which can be introduced by 2020. Meanwhile, in a survey for potential for change of energy, a subsidy for installation is again the preferred policy option to be introduced by 2020. On operational improvement, the introduction of energy advisor is an important policy option for Brunei Darussalam by 2020. On structural change of energy management, an introduction of energy managers as well as awareness-raising would be an important policy option at least by 2020.

For additional analytical, marketing, investment and business opportunities information, please contact
Global Investment & Business Center, USA
(202) 546-2103. Fax: (202) 546-3275. E-mail: rusric@erols.com

Figure 8 – Roadmap for Industrial Sector

3.4 - ROADMAP FOR RESIDENTIAL AND COMMERCIAL SECTORS

In order to improve the energy efficiency of cooling in Brunei Darussalam, it is highly important that the use of energy efficient air conditioners such as inverter air conditioners & inverter chiller should be introduced. Compact fluorescent and LED lamps should also be used and installed in building and houses as early as 2012. Appliances Standard & Labeling would be the preferred policy to be implemented for both cooling system and lamps to prohibit low energy efficiency products from entering the market and hence people would purchase energy efficient products and appliances.

Figure 8 – Roadmap for Residential and Commercial Sectors

In order to realize these initiatives as discussed above, a number of legislative measures are under consideration by the EDPMO, Ministry of Communications, Ministry of Development, Ministry of Education and Ministry of Finance. From a comprehensive study undertaken by a consultant firm in 2011, 8 key policies have been identified to be implemented in order to effectively support all EEC initiatives to be undertaken. Those 8 key policies are summarized as follow:

Policy 1 - Appliance Standards

Implementation of appliance standards.

Prioritizing implementation of high energy efficiency air conditioners, chillers and lamps.

Setting up a minimum energy efficiency target.

For additional analytical, marketing, investment and business opportunities information, please contact
Global Investment & Business Center, USA
(202) 546-2103. Fax: (202) 546-3275. E-mail: rusric@erols.com

Designing the types of metrics (i.e., efficiency standards such as rating scale) to be adopted for each appliances.

Policy 2 - Labeling

In order to reduce the energy consumption of appliances, it is crucial to raise public awareness of energy conservation. A labeling scheme is regarded to be one of the most important measures to raise awareness and provide information to the public regarding the energy efficiency of products. The main objectives of labeling schemes are described as follows:

Introduce energy labeling for consumer to compare the energy efficiency of products and information on reducing energy cost.

Inform end users of the importance of energy conservation and to raise awareness.

Inform end users that energy efficient products can reduce energy costs dramatically and that initial costs will eventually be returned through energy savings.

The objective of producing policy 1 & 2 (the National Standard & Labeling Regulation) are to halt the importation of the non-efficient electrical appliances & products (air conditioning & lightings) into the country and concurrently to educate and encourage people to opt to a more energy-efficient electrical appliances & products.

- Policy 3 – Building Regulation

It is highly effective to develop energy efficiency regulations for buildings so as to improve the energy efficiency of buildings in Brunei Darussalam. It is crucial to establish Brunei Darussalam's specific building regulations according to its climate with the following criteria:

Standards to reduce solar heat gains.

Standards for insulation.

Standards for air leakage.

Temperature setting.

Policy 4 – Energy Management

Implementing the energy management process that is compatible with international standards such as ISO 50001.

Installing equipment such as Building Automation Systems (BAS), Controllers (i.e. demand controllers) and Building Energy Management Systems (BEMS).

Policy 5 – Fuel Economy Regulation

For additional analytical, marketing, investment and business opportunities information, please contact
Global Investment & Business Center, USA
(202) 546-2103. Fax: (202) 546-3275. E-mail: rusric@erols.com

Adopting EU equivalent fuel economy regulations by setting a target at 39.97 MPG (Mile Per Gallon) (17.2 km/l) by 2020 (EU 2016 target equivalent) and at 49.48 MPG (21.3 km/l) by 2025 (EU 2020 target equivalent).

Electric, hybrid and Fuel Efficient Vehicles should also be utilized.

Policy 6 – Electricity Tariff Reform

Continue to implement progressively increasing tariffs, similar to what is currently being practiced in Japan and California.

Conducting a survey to understand the optimum tariff schedule through understanding the relationships between household income and electricity usage.

Installing smart meters to allow more flexible tariff mechanism.

Policy 7 – Financial Incentives

Introducing the appropriate incentives for energy efficient cars such as electric vehicles (EV), hybrid vehicles and EV infrastructure in transportation sectors.

Introducing appropriate energy efficient equipments/technologies incentives for example; air-conditioning, lightings, photovoltaic, HP water heaters and solar water heaters in residential and commercial buildings.

Policy 8 – Awareness Raising

Setting up EEC curriculum in national education system to increase awareness.

Introducing yearly awards to incentivize people and corporation to practice energy management.

Conducting Energy Expo, Roadshows, Workshops and seminars for general public to demonstrate the potential for EEC.

Educate young generation through the establishment of Energy Club in schools.

4. MAJOR PROGRAMS FOR THE PROMOTION AND IMPLEMENTATION OF ENERGY EFFICIENCY

a) Early last year, His Majesty the Sultan and Yang Di-Pertuan of Negara Brunei Darussalam has consented for the review of the electricity tariff structure in the residential sector which has taken into effect on the 1st January 2012. It is followed by the replacement of post-paid to pre-paid meters as the first steps toward encouraging energy savings amongst the public. The main objective of the introduction of the new electricity tariff is to correct the old tariff, which suit today's environment. In the old structure, those who consumed less were charged at a higher rate and

For additional analytical, marketing, investment and business opportunities information, please contact
Global Investment & Business Center, USA
(202) 546-2103. Fax: (202) 546-3275. E-mail: rusric@erols.com

were paying more on average per kWh compared to those who consumed more. The new tariff structure moves to being progressive from regressive. Up to a certain level, example for a consumption of 2000 kwh/month, consumers will be paying the same or less than what they are paying before (with the old tariff).

b) Improving our overall existing power generation efficiency to greater than 45% by 2020 by replacing simple cycle power plant with more efficient combined-cycle or co-generation plant and by having a structured maintenance programme in place. Two major projects have been initiated at two of the major power plants in the country – the Lumut Co-Gen which will have an overall efficiency of greater than 60 per cent through the application of combined heat and power integration or Co-Generation. The other project at Bukit Panggal power plant has already reached an efficiency of about 47% using "Combined Cycle" concept. This is a significant difference compared to the efficiency level of other existing generators using the "Simple Cycle" concept which is only around 26%.

c) On legislation, Energy Department in collaboration with Brunei National Energy Research Institute (BNERI) is currently developing a National Standard and Labeling regulation for electrical appliances which are the air-conditioner and lightings. This is a follow-up from the work which has been developed by a consultant firm on standard appliances and labeling scheme which was completed end of last year. The objective of producing the National Standard & Labeling Regulation is to halt the importation of the non-efficient electrical appliances & products (air conditioning & lightings) into the country and concurrently to educate and encourage people to opt to a more energy-efficient electrical appliances & products. The air-conditioner accounted for almost 60% of electricity consumption in a building. This is prevalent in almost all homes, government buildings and commercial buildings in Brunei Darussalam. Hence, with the later implementation of this regulation, it is hoped that consumers will have a better understanding on which product has a better efficiency rate to be purchased and hence will reduce the energy consumption nationwide.

d) Energy Department is also currently working with a consultant firm to develop Energy Efficiency and Conservation Program in Brunei Darussalam. The objective of the project is to pursue the development of Energy Efficiency and Conservation Program for government and commercial buildings in the country. In addition, the Energy Department is also preparing a paper for the establishment of the Energy Manager for all buildings belong to government ministries in Brunei Darussalam. The Energy Manager is responsible for assessing how, when and why energy use in buildings through energy audit or review. All Energy Managers will undergo training and courses for certification to be an accredited Energy Manager from the ASEAN Energy Manager Accreditation Scheme (AEMAS).

e) Energy Department in collaboration with the Ministry of Development via the Authority for Building Control and Construction Industry (ABCi) and the Department of Mechanical and Electrical (DME) is also currently in the process of developing the EEC Building Code with an objective to establish energy efficiency and conservation standards and a regulatory mechanism for buildings in Brunei Darussalam. Joint working committee has been established between Energy Department and Ministry Development to facilitate the formulation of EEC Building Code through consultant service as well as to recommend the best option in terms of EEC Building Code frameworks and contents.

f) On transportation sector, Energy Department is currently working together with the Ministry of Communication to introduce utilization of hybrid cars and electric vehicles in the country. This is again another initiative being undertaken by the Energy Department towards green environment.

g) Another important initiative being undertaken by the Energy Department in corporation with STEP Centre, Ministry of Education is the establishment of Energy Clubs in schools on the 25th May 2009. The objective is to inculcate the culture of energy efficiency and conservation at grassroots level (at schools) so that young people would become EEC ambassadors.

h) Energy Department will continuously conducting the awareness raising programmes to all community level by organizing Energy Week, Energy Expo and roadshows, workshops and seminars on capacity building and also educate younger generation through the establishment of Energy Clubs in schools. EDPMO is also from time to time conducting a seminar on energy savings to newly appointed government officers and staff, organized by the Institute for Public Service Institute, Prime Minister's Office. The seminar on energy saving is also planned to be extended to rural communities so that they will be given equal opportunity to learn EEC.

i) Another significant project which will be undertaken by the Energy Department is the replacement of the existing High Pressure Sodium Vapour (HSPV) street lighting to low wattage and better light intensity lighting. The benefit of the project would be a saving of approximately USD134 million over a period of 11 years. The government is currently in the high level discussion with one potential company for project kick-off.

j) While efforts are made to increase efficiency in electricity usage, Energy Department has also taken steps and will continue to put emphasis on the introduction of alternative and renewable energy into the energy mix for Brunei Darussalam. In 2011, Brunei Darussalam has commissioned its first photovoltaic solar power plant, that is, the Tenaga Suria Brunei (TSB), in Seria. At 1.2 MW it is supplying power to about 200 homes. It is small but an important first step in the development of renewable energy sources. In addition to solar power, the Energy Department in co-operation with Brunei Economic Development Board (BEDB), Economic Planning & Development Department (JPKE) and the Department of Environment, Park & Recreation (DEPR) is also looking at the possibility of having a Wasteto-Energy facility at Sungai Paku, Seria. This facility would be able generating up to 25 MW of power. The Government has an aspiration to generate at least 10% (50 MW) of the total power generation from new and renewable resources. With the continuous drive to use energy efficiently and with the introduction of renewable energy, it will eventually help to reduce the consumption of natural gas which can either be exported or use as a feedstock to downstream industries, creating thousands of employment opportunities for the people of Brunei Darussalam while ensuring environmental and economic development sustainability.

Figure 9 is showing the EEC's legislative measures that will be developed and implemented in Brunei Darussalam. The implementations of a set of policy measures are very important to comprehend Brunei Darussalam's EEC roadmap. Three measures are to be implemented into the residential and commercial sectors which include; an appliance standard & labeling under the responsibility of EDPMO and building regulation under the responsibility of the Ministry of Development. Meanwhile, measure to be implemented into the industrial sector is the energy management i.e. energy management building and energy monitoring which is again EDPMO as responsible agency. As for the transportation sector the fuel economy regulation is an effective energy savings measure under the responsibility of Ministry of Communication and EDPMO is responsible agency on tariff reforms under power sector which can potentially contribute to savings in electricity consumption. Sector-wide measures include subsidies and tax implementations are again under the responsibility of EDPMO alongside awareness raising initiatives such as education and events which are under the responsibility of Ministry of Education.

For additional analytical, marketing, investment and business opportunities information, please contact
Global Investment & Business Center, USA
(202) 546-2103. Fax: (202) 546-3275. E-mail: rusric@erols.com

Figure 9 - Legislative Measures: Set of policy recommendation & contribution from other government agencies.

IMPOTANT TRENDS AND DEVEOPMENTS

1.1 ACHIEVEMENTS AND CHALLENGES

A discussion on Brunei Darussalam's energy efficiency institutional context should be prefaced with some review on the energy situation in the economy. It should be recognized that Brunei Darussalam enjoys a high GDP per capita that is among the highest in the region due to the economy's abundant oil and natural gas resources. This has enabled Brunei Darussalam to implement a very generous energy pricing mechanism for its citizens. Unfortunately, this generous energy pricing mechanism, made possible by the abundance of indigenous fossil fuel resources, are the reason for the substantial barriers to energy efficiency in the economy. This may not be sustainable in the long-run as reserves begin to deplete. On the other hand, prioritizing energy efficiency initiatives will benefit the economy in the long-run as these initiatives will free up more oil and natural gas for exports that will increase or prolong national revenue.

As International Monetary Fund (IMF) stated in its report published in 2013, *Energy Subsidy Reform: Lessons and Implications*[1] , "energy subsidies are pervasive" in the world and is not limited in Brunei Darussalam, and "energy subsidies have wide-ranging economic consequences". However, the level of energy subsidies in Brunei Darussalam is relatively high in the APEC region, especially for petroleum products. According to the IMF report, Brunei Darussalam's pre-tax subsidy[2] for petroleum products is the second highest after Indonesia in terms of per cent of GDP. The role of the pre-tax subsidy for petroleum products in encouraging excessive energy consumption is readily apparent in Brunei Darussalam's rapid motorization.

For additional analytical, marketing, investment and business opportunities information, please contact
Global Investment & Business Center, USA
(202) 546-2103. Fax: (202) 546-3275. E-mail: rusric@erols.com

One of the results of this energy pricing mechanism is Brunei Darussalam's large consumption of fossil fuels; the economy currently ranks fourth in the world for Greenhouse Gas (GHG) emission on per capita basis. This fact also became a driver for Brunei Darussalam to promote energy efficiency initiatives more rigorously.

As for achievements in the Institutional Context, the Energy Efficiency & Conservation (EEC) Unit was established under the Energy Department, Prime Minister's Office (EDPMO). The EEC Unit takes the lead in coordination among government agencies related to energy efficiency and conservation (EEC) in implementing EEC measures including the National Standards and Labelling initiative, the EEC Building Code initiative, the Electricity Tariff Reforms and EEC Awareness Raising.

In addition, a National Energy Efficiency & Conservation Committee (NEECC), co-chaired by the Minister of Energy, Minister of Development and Minister of Communication, was established in 2011. The committee is in charge of the execution and coordination with various EEC stakeholders (government agencies, industries and individuals). Mainly, the committee is tasked to oversee the implementation of prioritized EEC plan of actions and ensure the national level of energy intensity can be achieved. However, prioritized EEC plan may need to be revised to cope with rapidly changing energy and economic situations in Brunei Darussalam. In order to facilitate timely and speedy revisions of prioritized EEC plan, NEECC should oversee not only the implementation, but also the planning, of prioritized EEC plan. For the same purpose, this committee should be overseen by the Prime Minister in order to avoid possible discord among co-chairing three Ministers. In Brunei Darussalam's legislation, relevant government agencies have already initiated joint evaluation of legislative measures to promote EEC, such as the National Standard and Labelling regulation and the

[1] Available at http://www.imf.org/external/np/pp/eng/2013/012813.pdf [2] The IMF report defines two components for consumer subsidies, a *pre-tax subsidy* (if the price paid by firms and households is below supply and distribution costs) and a *tax subsidy* (if taxes are below their efficient level).

EEC Building Code (see Chapter 4 and 7 for more detailed information). On top of each legislative measure, it is important to create the necessary legal framework that will allow EEC laws to be effective.

Along with government institutions and legislation, financial Incentives are also a part of the institutional basis for energy efficiency initiatives. While EEC projects by government agencies can be financed by the government budget, with the inexpensive energy prices, there will be no incentives for private entities to pursue EEC measures. The most serious challenge is to obtain the Ministry of Finance's approval for the proposed innovative "Brunei Energy Efficiency Fund (BEEF)". BEEF is expected to facilitate EEC projects by incentivizing private financial institutions and also reducing expenditures by the Ministry of Finance. In addition to BEEF, other financial instruments can be further developed for energy efficiency projects, which will be discussed in Chapter 4 on the policy measures for residential, commercial, government and industrial sectors.

1.2 RECOMMENDATIONS

Recommendation 1: *NEECC should oversee not only the implementation but also the planning of prioritized EEC plan of actions. This committee should be overseen by the Prime Minister.*

Recommendation 2: *The Government of Brunei Darussalam should enact necessary legislative measures to promote EEC. In addition, a comprehensive EEC Law should be considered in order to systematize necessary legislative measures.*

Recommendation 3: *The Government of Brunei Darussalam should establish the proposed*

innovative financing program, Brunei Energy Efficiency Fund (BEEF), in order to facilitate EEC projects in the private sector.

Recommendation 4: *The Government of Brunei Darussalam should consider implementing gradual energy pricing reforms which draws on successful approaches used in other countries.*

Example: The IMF *Energy Subsidy Reform: Lessons and Implications* report contains a section on "Lessons Learned from Experience" based on case studies of successful and unsuccessful reform exercises by economies around the world.

Other case studies and recommendations are also available at the Global Subsidies Initiatives Website[3]; including a series of *Citizen Guides to Energy Subsidies* by economy to engage public interest on energy subsidies and reform measures.

[3] Available at http://www.iisd.org/gsi/

2. ENERGY EFFICIENCY GOALS, TARGETS AND STRATEGY

ACHIEVEMENTS AND CHALLENGES

Brunei Darussalam attaches great importance to energy efficiency. In line with other APEC economies, the economy is working towards an ambitious goal of a 45% energy intensity decline by 2035 (using 2005 as the base year) while identifying energy efficiency improvement and renewable energy development as major approaches to realize this goal. Many coordinated efforts from all the stakeholders (government agencies, industries and individuals) have been conducted or in the process of being conducted.

As described in the draft *Energy White Paper of Brunei Darussalam,* "Ensure Safe, Secure, Reliable and Efficient Supply and Use of Energy" is now prioritized as one of the three national energy strategic goals[4]. This has been laid down as an essential basis for improving energy efficiency and promoting energy conservation in Brunei Darussalam towards 2035.

In 2011, a comprehensive study on energy efficiency, entitled *Brunei Energy Efficiency and Conservation Study: Roadmap Formulation and Policy Advice,* was published. The study was commissioned by the Brunei Darussalam government to investigate various possible pathways from major sectors (residential, commercial, power, transportation, and industrial) to realize its energy efficiency goals. Based on the results of this study, several energy efficiency and conservation (EEC) measures have been identified to ensure that the national level of energy intensity can be achieved. These are summarized in the table below.

Table 2-1: EEC Measures to Achieve Brunei Darussalam's National Level of Energy Intensity

Sector Measures

Residential and Commercial Sectors

Transport Sector

Applying "smart" tariffs

Promote use of high-energy efficiency technologies in buildings. Proposed technologies include energy efficient air-conditioners, chillers, lighting equipment (i.e., compact fluorescent lamps, LEDs) and lighting system controls, automatic control equipment occupancy sensor and photo sensor unit at the offices to control brightness, penetration of solar water heaters and "Smart" power meters at the main switchboard to continuously monitor consumption.

Promoting technologies, like the optimized gearbox, the use of hybrid cars, electric vehicles and fuel-efficient vehicle (FEV) to the public and evaluation of imposing the EU equivalent standards of fuel economy by 2025 for all the new vehicles (i.e. 21.3 km/l).

Evaluate how to improve the public transportation system (by adding capacity, optimizing routes and upgrading infrastructure) and the potential use of hybrid or electric vehicles for public transportation.

Promote behavioural levers such as planning destination routes upfront and car-pooling to minimize the number of vehicles on the road.

[4] The other two national energy strategic goals from the draft *Energy White Paper of Brunei Darussalam* are "Strengthen and Grow Oil and Gas Upstream and Downstream Activities" and "Maximize Economic Spin-off from the Oil and Gas Industry".

Power Sector • Increase efficiency in the power generation from 23% to 45% by implementing energy-saving technologies – the combined cycle turbine, reducing partial load operation and transmission and distribution losses, mandating an energy efficiency target for any new power plant, installing smart meters (i.e. dynamic pricing based on energy consumption).

Evaluating feasibility of altering tariff structure to promote desired consumption behaviour.

Integration of renewable energy to meet the demands on power in Brunei Darussalam and reduce gas consumption.

Industrial • In Brunei Darussalam, fuel gas is the main contributor to greenhouse gas

Sector emissions. Efforts are now focused on improving energy efficiency and reliability of compression and auto-producer power plant facilities. Opportunities identified include upgrading or replacement of aged and inefficient equipment (e.g. compressors and control systems).

Prior to 1998, the main contribution to greenhouse gas emission comes from the combustion of fossil fuel from auto-producer power plant facilities. It is encouraging that with the various initiatives undertaken in the oil and gas industry sector by the local operators, there has been a steady decrease of greenhouse gas emissions over time especially from 1998 onwards. This was achieved mainly through rationalization projects and improvements in operational efficiencies in producing oil and gas fields which resulted in reduction in venting and flaring emissions.

For additional analytical, marketing, investment and business opportunities information, please contact
Global Investment & Business Center, USA
(202) 546-2103. Fax: (202) 546-3275. E-mail: rusric@erols.com

It should also be noted that energy intensity in Brunei Darussalam has shown some fluctuations since 2005. However, largely due to economic improvements, overall energy intensity in 2012 is lower than the base year of 2005 by more than 10% (mainly as a result of increase in oil and natural gas export in recent years), which is in line with the expected pace of progress towards achieving its energy intensity decline target by 2035.

Brunei Darussalam has identified 8 key policies to be implemented in order to effectively support all EEC Measures identified in Table 2-1, these policies are summarized in the next table.

Table 2-2: Implementation of Key EEC Policies

Policy	Rationale	Implementation
Policy 1: Appliance Standards	--	• Implementation of appliance standards. • Prioritizing implementation of high energy efficiency air conditioners, chillers and lamps. • Setting up a minimum energy efficiency target. • Designing the types of metrics (i.e., efficiency standards such as rating scale) to be adopted for each appliance.

Policy 2	In order to reduce the energy	• Introduce energy labelling for consumer
Labelling	consumption of appliances, it is crucial to raise public awareness of energy conservation. A labelling scheme is regarded to be one of the most important measures to raise awareness and provide information to the public regarding the energy efficiency of products.	to compare the energy efficiency of products and information on reducing energy cost. • Inform end users of the importance of energy conservation and to raise awareness. • Inform end users that energy efficient products can reduce energy costs dramatically and that initial costs will
	At the same time, like the appliance standards, labelling schemes will halt importation of non-efficient appliances and products into the country and concurrently to educate and encourage people to opt to a more energy-efficient electrical appliances and products.	eventually be returned through energy savings.
	It is highly effective to develop	Criteria to be included in Brunei
	energy efficiency regulations for	Darussalam's building regulations:
	buildings so as to improve the energy efficiency of buildings in	-Standards to reduce solar heat gains.
	Brunei Darussalam.	-Standards for insulation.
	With its hot climate, Brunei	-Standards for air leakage.
	Darussalam requires high cooling	-Temperature setting.
	loads throughout the year so it is	
	crucial to establish Brunei	
	Darussalam's building regulations	
	according to its specific	
	requirements.	
Policy 4 –	The use of energy management is	• Implementing the energy management
Energy	a fundamental approach to	process that is compatible with

Management	promoting EEC in companies,	international standards such as ISO
	governmental organizations,	50001.
	schools etc. When EEC is promoted properly, it is essential that the actual status of energy consumption is known, and that an appropriate plan and selection	• Installing equipment such as Building Automation Systems (BAS), Controllers (i.e. demand controllers) and Building Energy Management Systems (BEMS).
	of measures is employed.	
	An energy management provides	
	such an appropriate base for EEC.	
	Generally, energy management is	
	implemented by a PDCA (Plan,	
	Do, Check, Act) cycle.	

–	There are currently no policies to regulate fuel economy and CO_2 emissions in Brunei Darussalam. However, the introduction of such policies will make it possible to achieve energy conservation within the transportation sector.	• Adopting EU equivalent fuel economy regulations by setting a target at 39.97 MPG (Mile per Gallon) (17.2 km/l) by 2020 (EU 2016 target equivalent) and at 49.48 MPG (21.3 km/l) by 2025 (EU 2020 target equivalent). • Electric, hybrid and fuel-efficient vehicles should also be utilized.
Policy 6 –	A reform of Brunei Darussalam's	• Continue to implement progressively
Electricity	tariff mechanism will offer the	increasing tariffs, similar to what is
Tariff Reform	opportunity to create and provide incentives for Bruneians to use energy more efficiently.	currently being practiced in Japan and California. • Conducting a survey to understand the optimum tariff schedule through understanding the relationships between household income and electricity usage. • Installing smart meters to allow more flexible tariff mechanism.
	Financial measures such as tax	• Introducing the appropriate incentives
	reductions and subsidies are	for energy efficient cars such as electric
	often used for the prevailing	vehicles (EV), hybrid vehicles and EV
	energy efficient equipment that	infrastructure in transportation sectors.
	has a higher price than existing standard products.	• Introducing appropriate energy efficient equipment/technologies incentives for
		example; air-conditioning, lightings, photovoltaic, HP water heaters and solar water heaters in residential and commercial buildings.
Policy 8 –	In order to maximize the	• Setting up EEC curriculum in national
Awareness	effectiveness of energy saving	education system to increase
Raising	measures, it is very important that each person in Brunei Darussalam understands the importance of energy savings.	awareness. • Introducing annual awards to incentivize people and corporation to practice energy management.

For additional analytical, marketing, investment and business opportunities information, please contact
Global Investment & Business Center, USA
(202) 546-2103. Fax: (202) 546-3275. E-mail: rusric@erols.com

	Even if energy efficient	
	equipment is installed, individuals need to be made aware of how to use the equipment effectively, to its full potential. Therefore awareness-raising is the key to a successful EEC.	• Conducting Energy Expo, Roadshows, Workshops and seminars for general public to demonstrate the potential for EEC. • Educate young generation through the established Energy Clubs in schools.

Figure 2-1 shows the detailed information of EEC potential and its clear benefit to Brunei Darussalam. Under BAU scenario, energy consumption is projected to increase by 89% from 2009 to 2035, which is equivalent to 1,389 thousand toe increase. However under EEC scenario, a potential of 63% reduction from BAU, which is equivalent to 1,863 thousand toe, would be achieved by 2035 primarily from a reduction of fossil fuel supply for inland energy use via four major sectors, namely commercial, residential, transportation and industrial sectors. This will allow Brunei Darussalam to export more oil and natural gas. The overall benefit of this EEC scheme is calculated to be around BND 523 million per year by 2035, with additional investments of around BND 255 million per year in achieving and maintaining the EEC scheme.

Most APEC economies are facing the twin challenges of limited domestic energy resources and expensive energy prices. These challenges are less urgent in Brunei Darussalam; as a result, there are less financial incentives to implement EEC measures. Therefore, finding the correct, alternative incentives for consumers to engage in EEC actions is a particular challenge in Brunei Darussalam.

Presently, the oil and gas sector contributes more than 60% of the total national GDP in Brunei Darussalam. Fluctuations in price for oil and natural gas at international market (export price) will result in fluctuations in Brunei Darussalam's GDP, which will in turn influence energy intensity. In order to realize Brunei Darussalam's 2035 energy intensity reduction target, more detailed analysis in defining energy efficiency indicators will be required to reflect EEC efforts. Considering their importance of energy activities in Brunei Darussalam, clear energy efficiency indicators serving as disaggregated goals for energy efficiency improvement are especially required for power generation sector, commercial sector, residential sector, transportation sector and industrial sector. Moreover, identification and implementation of pragmatic countermeasures in these key sectors is another challenge for Brunei Darussalam towards realizing its energy intensity reduction target.

[5] Mitsubishi Research Institute (2011), *Brunei Energy Efficiency and Conservation Study: Roadmap Formulation and Policy Advice.*

2.2 RECOMMENDATIONS

Recommendation 5: *Identify appropriate incentives to further enhance EEC measures.*

One possible incentive can be based on the fact that "oil and natural gas conserved through EEC initiatives can expand export (hence achieve more GDP) at current level of oil and natural gas production" as this fits well with the interest of sustainable development by keeping more reserves of oil and natural gas for longer-term utilization.

Most efficiency programs apply financial incentives (rebates, discounts, financing or other forms of subsidies) for the purchase or installation of specific energy efficiency measure. It is also possible to apply non-financial incentives to encourage energy efficient behaviour. For instance, implementing energy efficiency measures can create a barrier known as the "hassle factor" where consumers do not have the time or expertise to work through all the steps required in the process.

Two non-financial incentives that can help mitigate this problem are the information services and technical services incentives. Information services like brochures and training can help educate consumers on basic EEC information such as how to determine how efficient their homes/businesses are, what their EEC options might be and how to evaluate these EEC options. Technical support and assistance can help customers to reduce the hassles of implementation, thus increasing installation rates[6]. Brunei Darussalam may also consider using social incentives as in the following example.

Example: Social incentives can also be a good motivator for energy behaviour at the consumer level. A US company, Opower, provides consumers with a Home Energy Reports that delivers information about household energy usage, tips that lead to quick energy savings and info-graphics showing the household energy use in comparison with similar households in their neighbourhood.

According to a Business Week Report, one million households received these monthly Home Energy Reports in 2009, and customers in the program have reduced annual energy usage by an average of 2.8%, or the equivalent of 280 kilowatt-hours per year[8].

Recommendation 6: *Establish a national energy efficiency sub-target which measures energy efficiency improvement in the economy and ensures that it has a significant role in achieving the energy intensity target.*

Additionally, the PREE Review Team strongly believes that there should be targets developed for each sector that is in line with the national energy efficiency sub-target. Setting individual sectoral targets will allow Brunei Darussalam to focus and tailor policies and programs specific to each sector, determine if the national energy efficiency sub-target is being met, and understand where more aggressive measures are needed.

At the same time, the PREE Review Team noted that this might be a long process due to unavailability of baseline data and collecting data for this purpose may need a few years. During this process, there may be a need for capacity building in data decomposition.

Example: Indonesia, Korea, New Zealand, Peru, the Philippines, Chinese Taipei, Thailand and the United States have specific sectoral goals that are in line with the overall national energy efficiency target[9].

Recommendation 7: *Apply a clear implementation plan (roadmap) to accelerate appropriate technologies to meet or exceed Brunei Darussalam's EEC targets. This plan should be announced to the public as a national agenda.*

Technological advancement is a key instrument to improving energy efficiency in Brunei Darussalam. The PREE Review Team recommends that Brunei Darussalam establish an appropriate technology roadmap by considering the existing research findings, including inter alia, the energy efficiency reports by the Mitsubishi Research Institute, International Energy Agency (IEA) and APEC. These should be adopted by Brunei Darussalam to encourage rapid uptake of energy efficiency technologies.

3. ENERGY DATA COLLECTION AND MONITORING

3.1 ACHIEVEMENTS AND CHALLENGES

Brunei Darussalam already has a framework in place for collecting, compiling and analysing energy data related to the production and overall consumption of oil, natural gas, petroleum products and electricity. The department responsible for this task is the Strategy, Planning, Economic and Intelligence (SPEI) unit of the Energy Corporate Division under the Energy Department. The Energy Department is under the Prime Minister's Office. The SPEI unit is also responsible for handling data requests from all government agencies and third parties, some of which are shown in Figure 3-1, and includes many international organizations like the Asia Pacific Economic Cooperation (APEC), United Nations (UN) and the International Energy Agency (IEA) as well as reputable publications like the Oil and Gas Journal.

For additional analytical, marketing, investment and business opportunities information, please contact
Global Investment & Business Center, USA
(202) 546-2103. Fax: (202) 546-3275. E-mail: rusric@erols.com

Usually, the SPEI Unit collects data on a monthly basis. Oil and gas data are provided by oil and gas operating companies/stakeholders including Brunei National Petroleum Company Private Limited (PetroleumBRUNEI), Brunei Shell Petroleum (BSP), Brunei LNG Sdn. Bhd. (BLNG) and Brunei Shell Marketing (BSM). Electricity data is sourced from the Department of Electricity Services (DES). Data reporting follows the format for the JODI and APEC questionnaires, if the requests differ from these formats, the data will be re-calculated and adjusted accordingly.

It is worthwhile to note that SPEI Unit has excellent cooperation and relationship with the stakeholders providing energy data, thus enabling the unit to easily request and access available data and provide timely reports as required.

Brunei Darussalam's current energy data collection framework has not been designed to collect data for energy efficiency analysis at sectoral level. In 2010, Brunei Darussalam contracted a consultant to conduct an Energy Efficiency and Conservation (EEC) Study. Under this study, energy consumption for major sectors were estimated based on statistical data obtained from interviews with 23 organizations, including governmental organizations, and questionnaire surveys with 100 households. This is a commendable achievement as it gave a good indication of the current energy supply and consumption structure in Brunei Darussalam and enabled the formulation of an EEC roadmap that is in line with the Wawasan Brunei 2035. However, this was a one-off study, and more consistent collection and analysis of disaggregated energy end-use

For additional analytical, marketing, investment and business opportunities information, please contact
Global Investment & Business Center, USA
(202) 546-2103. Fax: (202) 546-3275. E-mail: rusric@erols.com

data will be required in order to continually measure and improve energy efficiency initiatives in the economy.

3.2 RECOMMENDATIONS

Recommendation 8: *Define a structured energy efficiency data collection framework and ensure regular implementation.*

Data collection is an important component for any EEC initiative as this will provide a good basis for understanding energy use in different sectors of the economy which is essential to help policy makers decide on effective strategies policy instruments to improve energy efficiency.

As part of this proposed framework:

A set of quantifiable energy efficiency indicators should first be developed, in line with Brunei Darussalam's energy efficiency targets. Examples of useful energy efficiency indicators are energy intensities by sector and sub-sector (kWh/BND or toe/BND), specific energy consumption by physical units (kWh/appliance, litre/100 km, toe/employee).

Data requirements should be defined in accordance with the energy efficiency indicators.

Relevant stakeholders/agencies responsible for providing the data should be identified.

Based on the identified requirement, a clear and concise data reporting procedure may be developed to standardise and simplify the data collection process.

Report submission by stakeholders/agencies must be made a mandatory, periodic exercise with appropriate penalties for non-compliance.

Example: The IEA has conducted a workshop on Energy Efficiency Indicators that covers how to develop and utilize energy efficiency indicators to support energy efficiency initiatives[10]. A detailed guideline for Russia was also produced in 2011[11].

Information available in both the workshop materials and the report should serve as a useful example for Brunei Darussalam on the how to develop its own set of energy efficiency indicators, the stakeholders that should be involved and the reporting procedures that can be implemented.

[10] International Energy Agency (2012), *Energy Efficiency Indicators Workshop*

http://www.iea.org/workshop/energyefficiencyindicatorsworkshop-6-70612.html

[11] International Energy Agency (2011), *Development of Energy Efficiency Indicators in Russia,*

http://www.iea.org/publications/freepublications/publication/Russia_En_Eff_Ind.pdf

Recommendation 9: *Introduce a data evaluation, monitoring and verification (EMV) protocol to ensure energy efficiency data is credible and accurate.*

A well-designed EMV protocol will help Brunei Darussalam to:

For additional analytical, marketing, investment and business opportunities information, please contact
Global Investment & Business Center, USA
(202) 546-2103. Fax: (202) 546-3275. E-mail: rusric@erols.com

Accurately measure energy savings achieved and evaluate effectiveness of policy instruments; this enables policy makers to adjust policy instruments to become efficient and effective.

Ensure the credibility of reports on outcomes for energy efficiency investments, thus increasing investor confidence in energy efficiency projects which in turn will enhance the chances of more energy efficient projects of being financed.

Highlight public co-benefits of energy efficiency initiatives, including improved community health, reduced environmental degradation and increased employment.

Therefore, Brunei Darussalam should strongly consider introducing a data EMV protocol in conjunction with the energy efficiency data collection framework.

Example: Guidelines from Ecofys Netherlands[12] and Efficiency Valuation Organization (EVO)[13] may be useful starting points for Brunei Darussalam.

Recommendation 10: *Publish energy efficiency indicators monitoring reports periodically to evaluate progress and encourage continuing efforts in energy efficiency improvements.*

Periodic dissemination of monitoring reports will enable stakeholders to consistently evaluate the progress and success of EEC improvements, thus elevating the level of confidence and commitment and garnering support for further energy efficiency initiatives, particularly for initiatives that require funding. Dissemination may be done either monthly or quarterly through printed publications or online. Sharing the reports with the general public is strongly recommended to encourage widespread public participation in EEC initiatives.

Example: Several APEC Economies are already publishing their energy use statistics online, including New Zealand[14] and Thailand[15]. Another excellent example is Brunei Darussalam's own Public Works Department's Green Building Initiatives Website[16]. The website allows users to analyse monthly data on energy consumption at selected government buildings before and after the adaptation of Green Building Initiatives.

[12] Ecofys (2006), *Guidelines for the Monitoring, Evaluation and Design of Energy Efficiency Policies*, http://www.aid-ee.org/documents/000Guidelinesforthemonitoringevaluationanddesign.PDF

[13] Efficiency Valuation Organization (2013), *International Performance Measurement and Verification Protocol (IPMVP)*, http://www.evoworld.org/index.php?option=com_content&view=article&id=272&Itemid=397&lang=en

[14] New Zealand Energy Efficiency Conservation Agency, *Energy End-Use Database*,

http://enduse.eeca.govt.nz/default.aspx [15] Thailand Energy Policy and Planning Office, *Energy Statistics*, http://www.eppo.go.th/info/ [16] Brunei Darussalam Public Works Department, *Green Building Initiatives Website*,

http://www.pwd.gov.bn/dme/Default.aspx?ObjectId=AS-C02

Recommendation 11: *Establish a Brunei Energy Data Management Centre (BEDMC) that reports directly to the Minister of Energy.*

The introduction of this centre is based on the need to ensure a strong focus on data collection and analysis in order to monitor progress towards EEC improvement goals. The introduction of a single organisation or authority will help to streamline and simplify data collection and EMV efforts.

Examples of Energy Data Management Centres in other APEC economies:

In the United States, the US Energy Information Administration (EIA) is the statistical and analytical agency within the US Department of Energy that collects, analyses and disseminates independent and impartial energy information to promote sound policymaking, efficient markets, and public understanding of energy and its interaction with the economy and the environment.

In Indonesia, the Centre for Data and Information (PUSDATIN) under the Secretary General of the Ministry for Energy and Mineral Resources is responsible for Indonesia's centralised and coordinated energy data and information collation, storage and dissemination.

Brunei Darussalam may establish this proposed BEDMC either:

As an entity under the Brunei National Research Institute (BNERI) that reports directly to the Minister for Energy.

As a new department directly under the Ministry of Energy. Enhancing the functions of the SPEI Unit would be a practical step if Brunei Darussalam decides to pursue this option. Under the current organizational framework, the SPEI unit resides under Permanent Secretary (Upstream) (please refer to Figure 3-2). To create independence, the new BEDMC should be relocated to a new position directly under the Minister of Energy.

The PREE Review Team strongly suggests that the proposed BEDMC should have the following characteristics:

The BEDMC should be all-inclusive but with separate units that compiles data on hydrocarbons, electricity sector, oil and gas downstream sector and energy use for different demand sub-sectors.

Capacity building workshops should be held to train both the officers in this centre and agencies providing data to ensure high quality data.

Data reporting must be a periodic, mandatory exercise.

For additional analytical, marketing, investment and business opportunities information, please contact
Global Investment & Business Center, USA
(202) 546-2103. Fax: (202) 546-3275. E-mail: rusric@erols.com

4. POLICY MEASURES – RESIDENTIAL, COMMERCIAL, GOVERNMENT AND INDUSTRIAL SECTORS

4.1 OVERALL DEMAND SECTOR INITIATIVES

4.1.1 Achievements and Challenges

A number of energy efficiency improvement measures for residential, commercial, government and industrial sectors have been formulated by Energy Department, Prime Minister's Office

For additional analytical, marketing, investment and business opportunities information, please contact
Global Investment & Business Center, USA
(202) 546-2103. Fax: (202) 546-3275. E-mail: rusric@erols.com

(EDPMO) in conjunction with other stakeholders, including other government agencies, industries and individuals. These include applying smart (pre-paid) meter and new tariffs and using high-energy efficiency technologies in buildings. Technologies like energy efficient air-conditioners, chillers, lighting equipment (i.e., compact fluorescent lamps, LEDs) and lighting system controls, automatic control equipment occupancy sensor and photo sensor unit at the offices to control brightness, penetration of solar water heaters and "Smart" power meters at the main switchboard to continuously monitor consumption are used by leading green energy organizations.

In addition, several energy efficiency and conservation (EEC) related studies and activities have also been conducted in the economy as follows:

A study on energy efficiency financing models has been commissioned by EDPMO and undertaken by Sustainable Development Capital Limited. From the PREE expert team observations, the proposed models relies more on external financing rather than internal financing.

A feasibility study on a standards and labelling scheme was commissioned by EDPMO and undertaken by the Mitsubishi Research Institute (MRI). The final report, titled *Brunei Energy Efficiency and Conservation Study: Roadmap Formulation and Policy Advice,* was published at the end of 2011. This study also included the results from a survey of energy end-users to clarify how much energy is consumed by each major sector, and in what way. The major sectors covered are the power sector, transport sector, industrial sector, residential sector and commercial sector[17].

EDPMO in collaboration with Brunei National Energy Research Institute (BNERI) is currently in the process of developing a National Standards and Labelling Regulation and associated implementation documents.

An online website has been developed by the Public Works Department that publishes the energy consumption and performance of several government buildings monthly since 2011[18].

Energy Club for Schools has been established since 2009. The objective is to generate awareness of energy conservation at the grassroots level, and engage students to be ambassadors for energy saving awareness. By the end of May 2013, 30 Energy Clubs would have been established.

Review and restructure of the electricity tariff in the residential sector have been made and the new electricity tariff structure has been in effect since 1 January 2012. The new tariff structure shifted from regressive to progressive rate.

The Public Service Institute regularly organises 'Energy Savings Seminars' for government officials to disseminate energy savings culture in offices. This year, the 'Energy Saving Seminars' will be extended to schools and rural communities to further promote the awareness on EEC to the general public.

24th May has been designated as 'Energy Day' for Brunei Darussalam since 2007 to foster the culture of energy saving and efficiency. Each year, various events are organised in conjunction with this day, including mass prayers, presentation of EEC awards, distribution of car stickers bearing tips on saving energy, energy forums and expos as well as energy camps and competitions for school children.

In 2010, EDPMO introduced the Energy Efficiency and Conservation Initiatives Awards with categories for the education sector, government sector, commercial sector and industry sector.

Based on Brunei Darussalam's national energy balance from 2008 to 2012, electricity accounts for about 56-60% of the final energy consumption for residential, commercial, government and industrial sector. At present, Brunei Darussalam does not monitor or collect electricity consumption statistics from each economic sector or sub-sectors, instead energy consumption data is aggregated as either under Industry Sector or Other Sector (As in Table 4-1). On the other hand, according to the MRI's Report, for 2009, electricity accounted for 82% and 92% of energy consumption in residential and commercial sectors respectively (p. 78), and 27% of industrial sector energy consumption (p. 63). For both residential and commercial sectors, air-conditioners accounted for the bulk of electricity use.

While statistical information on household electricity consumption is not yet available at present, the number can be derived based on the MRI report findings and available Brunei Darussalam statistic reports. From Table 4-1, total electricity consumed in 2011 was 3,389 GWh. Based on the MRI report; it can be assumed that 48% of this total was consumption by the residential sector, which is 1,627 GWh. From the Brunei Darussalam *Population and Housing Consensus 2011*, there were a total of 68,208 households in the economy that same year. Therefore, the average household electricity consumption can be estimated at 23,849kWh/year or 1,987kWh/month, which is considerably high; almost triple that of Singapore[20]. It is likely that the low electricity tariffs works as a disincentive in this economy. Most households are probably not aware of how to rationally and efficiently use electricity as there are currently no financial incentives to do so.

[19] Statistics from EDPMO's *PREE Background Report for Brunei Darussalam* [20] The Energy Market Authority's *Singapore Energy Statistics 2012* reported that in 2011, the average monthly household electricity sales for private housing was 784 KWh/month. This is more than double of the public housing monthly average of 369 KWh/month.

In fact, referring to the next table on the ASEAN Electricity Tariffs, Brunei Darussalam's electricity price is ranked as the lowest among ASEAN economies at BND 0.06/kWh; half of the next lowest economies (Lao PDR, Thailand and the Philippines) and almost one-tenth of the highest ranked economy, Myanmar.

Table 4-2: Average ASEAN Electricity Tariff[21]

Countries		Brunei Cents/kWh
1	Myanmar	50
2	Singapore	27
3	Cambodia	23
4	Indonesia	19
5	Malaysia	18
6	Vietnam	13
7	Lao PDR	12
8	Thailand	12
9	Philippine	12
10	Brunei Darussalam	6

Therefore, while the PREE expert team applauds Brunei Darussalam's efforts to implement new tariffs that are progressive and still protects the welfare of low-income households, it is still important to acknowledge that the low electricity prices may encourage wasteful energy use.

From the presentation on New Electricity Tariffs during the PREE expert team visit, the majority of consumers (79%) are unaffected by the tariff change. It is possible that the 12.4% reduction in 2011 electricity consumption achievement may not be due to the tariff reform, but rather mainly the application of pre-paid meters.

kWh	Old Tariff	New Tariff
600	$36.00	$6.00
1500	$90.00	$78.00
1600	$96.00	$86.00
2000	$120.00	$118.00
2050	$123.00	$123.00
3000	$180.00	$218.00
4000	$240.00	$318.00
4800	$288.00	$414.00

Given the high average household electricity consumption, especially when compared to other economies of similar size and, climate conditions, there are many opportunities for applying energy efficiency measures for the residential and commercial sectors.

Based on the MRI report, under Business-as-usual (BAU) scenario, energy consumption in 2035 has been projected to increase by 1,389 kTOE, or 89% from the baseline year 2009. But under EEC scenario, the energy consumption in 2035 would be reduced by 474 kTOE, or 30% from the year 2009, resulting in an energy saving potential of 1,863 kTOE, or 63% reduction from the BAU scenario in 2035. The leading energy saving potentials would be in the commercial and residential sectors, 41% and 36%, followed by transportation and industrial sectors, 13% and 10% from the BAU scenario respectively.

If these EEC improvements can be achieved in all of the major consuming sectors, then the fossil fuel supply for inland energy use can be significantly reduced. This will allow for more oil and gas exports which would translate to increased revenue for Brunei Darussalam, estimated to be around BND 523 million in 2035; after taking into account the investments required for achieving and maintaining the EEC measures.

For additional analytical, marketing, investment and business opportunities information, please contact
Global Investment & Business Center, USA
(202) 546-2103. Fax: (202) 546-3275. E-mail: rusric@erols.com

From Figure 4-2, it is evident that the residential and commercial sectors have by far the largest EEC potential, and as electricity is the main fuel in these sectors, most of the potential will be from electricity savings. More detailed analysis of energy saving potential by each sector is as illustrated in the figures below.

It was estimated that for the residential sector, there would be up to 52% overall reduction in energy consumption from BAU scenario in 2035. Most of this savings is contributed to the

For additional analytical, marketing, investment and business opportunities information, please contact
Global Investment & Business Center, USA
(202) 546-2103. Fax: (202) 546-3275. E-mail: rusric@erols.com

diffusion of more efficient appliances and equipment, particularly air-conditioners (76%) and lamps (7%), under the upcoming National Standards and Labelling Regulations.

For the commercial sector, up to 44% overall reduction in energy consumption from BAU scenario in 2035 is expected. As space cooling is a major use of energy for this sector, the bulk of savings is expected to come from the increased penetration of high efficiency air-conditioners and chillers.

The PREE Review team foresees that realizing these EEC potentials will be a major challenge for Brunei Darussalam, given the comparatively low electricity prices, the lack of historical base for promoting energy efficiency, and the lack of awareness among consumers as to the benefits of being energy efficient or what steps the consumer can take to become more energy efficient.

4.1.2 Recommendations

Recommendation 12: *Brunei Darussalam should conduct a detailed market research to identify which EEC messages would appeal the most to different consumer groups.*

It is clear that with its comparatively low electricity prices, market mechanism is not a good driver for energy efficiency initiatives in Brunei Darussalam. Instead new and innovative methods should be designed to better impart the EEC message to all segments of the population. This is where market research comes in, this exercise will help Brunei Darussalam to identify the values and motivators of each population segment, and how to successfully market EEC initiatives and instil EEC behaviour.

Examples of EEC Market Research Reports:

A report by the California Institute of Energy and Environment (CIEE)[22] evaluates how market segmentation can be applied to utility demand-side management programs to achieve energy

For additional analytical, marketing, investment and business opportunities information, please contact
Global Investment & Business Center, USA
(202) 546-2103. Fax: (202) 546-3275. E-mail: rusric@erols.com

reducing goals. In this report, residential consumers are segmented demographically (e.g. age, family size, income level, education level, etc.), and geographically. Businesses are segmented by similar end-use technologies, ownership patterns, economic characteristics and other associated behaviours. Energy efficiency programs and strategies are then crafted to address segment-specific problems. For example, hotels are segmented under the hospitality sector, and a useful program that addresses specific need is to provide direct installation of sensors that regulate air-conditioning in vacant rooms. Further examples on identifying and strategizing for different market segments are provided in the report.

The World Energy Council's publication *Innovative Communication Campaign Packages in Energy Efficiency*[23] highly recommends that EEC campaigns be based on market segmentation which allows better focus, use of tailored instruments and more efficient use of resources. The publication details several case studies on targeted EEC campaigns worldwide. For instance, Cuba's Energy Revolution and Chile's Good Energy Initiatives campaigns specifically addressed schoolchildren. Identifying target groups also enables campaigners to choose the best communication channels for reaching its target groups, while television and radio are still the most common medium, new social media like Facebook, Twitter and YouTube are also becoming more popular.

Recommendation 13: *School Energy Clubs should be enhanced by developing an energy efficiency curriculum to reach all students in all levels of education.*

In addition, posters, pamphlet, stickers of guidance for rational and efficient use of electricity at home, school, office, and commercial buildings should be published and distributed to the public as an EEC campaign, along with advertisement via TV and newspaper.

As before, market research will enhance understanding of Brunei Darussalam's market segments, enabling more effective planning of EEC campaign materials, communication channels and messages.

[22] California Institute of Energy and Environment (2008), *Market Segmentation and Energy Efficiency Program Design,* http://www1.eere.energy.gov/buildings/betterbuildings/neighborhoods/pdfs/market_seg.pdf

[23] World Energy Council (2010), *Innovative Communication Campaign Packages on Energy Efficiency*, http://www.worldenergy.org/documents/ee_case_study__communication.pdf

Therefore, such market research should be conducted regularly. Monitoring and evaluation of such a program should be conducted to get a feedback participation assessment.

Example: As Islam is the official religion in Brunei Darussalam, one way to reach the Muslim segment of the population is to collaborate with religious authorities to help spread the EEC message. The *Muslim Green Guide to Reducing Climate Change*[24] booklet is a good example of Islamic-related energy saving guidelines.

Recommendation 14: *An energy conservation and promotion fund (ECPF) should be established to be used for funding the EEC promotion program such as partial subsidies for EEC project investment, rebate, labelling, capacity building and demonstration programs, research and development grants, etc.*

The purpose of the ECPF is to fund energy conservation and energy efficiency activities initiated by the government. ECPF might be collected from any sources where appropriate and it is important to investigate the most practical and suitable way to provide for this ECPF fund.

For additional analytical, marketing, investment and business opportunities information, please contact
Global Investment & Business Center, USA
(202) 546-2103. Fax: (202) 546-3275. E-mail: rusric@erols.com

Possible methods include direct funding by the Ministry of Finance, levies from oil and gas export revenues and levies from energy users. The pros and cons of these funding methods must be explored fully to ensure sustainability of the fund.

Example: Thailand and Malaysia both apply a small levy on their energy prices to fund energy efficiency and renewable energy projects. In the case of Malaysia, a 1% levy is applied to consumers whose electricity usage exceeds 300kWh/month for the Renewable Energy Fund[25]. In the case of Thailand, this levy comes from the sale of specified fuels like gasoline, diesel, fuel oil, and kerosene[26]. This method is both sustainable and has the co-benefit of raising awareness and encouraging rational use of energy.

ECPF should be legally established under the jurisdiction of a committee that can legally protect the fund from being used for other purposes than EEC activities. The ECPF covers a much bigger scope compared to the BEEF revolving fund discussed in earlier section. BEEF can be partially funded from the ECPF, and be administered by local financial institutions under the supervision of the government. The purpose of BEEF would be to specifically finance EEC development projects proposed by the private sector.

Example: In Thailand, two types of fund are available, the EE Revolving Fund and ESCO Fund. Both are initially allocated from the ECPF.

• The EEC Revolving Fund provides a line of credit to local financial institutes or banks to provide low interest rates to developers of EEC and some types of renewable energy projects. The participating banks manages the loans, thereby minimizing government involvement in the financing process, but reports to the government authority[27] on project progress, thus ensuring real energy savings. This program has successfully helped to build local banks' understanding

[24] Islamic Foundation for Ecology and Environmental Sciences (2008), *Muslim Green Guide to Reducing Climate Change,* http://fathi.co.uk/booklet.pdf [25] Sustainable Energy Development Authority Malaysia (2011), *1% levy for electricity users from next month*, http://www.seda.gov.my [26] Center for Clean Air Policy (CCAP),*Revolving and Esco Funds for Renewable Energy and Energy Efficiency Finance: Thailand,* http://ccap.org/assets/CCAP-Booklet_Thailand.pdf [27] In this case, the Thailand Ministry of Energy's Department of Alternative Energy Development and Efficiency (DEDE).

and capacity to finance EEC projects on their own, therefore enabling Thailand to begin phasing out the EEC Revolving Fund since 2011[28].

• The ESCO Fund was established as a source of revenue capital for energy services companies to jointly invest with private investors through various channels; namely equity investment, ESCO venture capital, equipment leasing, carbon credit trading, technical assistance and credit guarantee facilities[29]. The fund is managed by government appointed, non-profit foundations. Projects are monitored during development, construction and operation

Recommendation 15: *An Energy Conservation Centre Brunei (ECCB) should be legally established.*

ECCB should take the lead role in implementing national EEC programs and should build its internal capacity to be able to effectively promote and incentivize EEC initiatives, standards and labelling, local capacity building and demonstration programs, etc.

For additional analytical, marketing, investment and business opportunities information, please contact
Global Investment & Business Center, USA
(202) 546-2103. Fax: (202) 546-3275. E-mail: rusric@erols.com

Examples of Energy Conservation Centres in APEC Economies:

> The Energy Conservation Center, Japan (ECCJ) was established under the Japanese Energy Conservation Act, with a mandate to promote energy conservation though out economic sectors in Japan, including control of energy management in commercial and industrial sectors to be compliance with the law. ECCJ has received a strong support from private sector, particularly industries since their inception, and partial support from the government in term of project basis.
>
> The Energy Conservation Center of Thailand (ECCT), on the other hand, was established as a joint government and private sector project under the cabinet approval. ECCT's mandate is to promote energy efficiency and conservation programs and provide energy efficiency advisory services to both government and private sectors. ECCT received an initial financial support from the government for their first five years of operation with a commitment to be self-reliant after that period, by generating their own income from providing energy solutions services. The government still provides partial support to ECCT, on project basis.

4.2 ENERGY MANAGEMENT SYSTEM INITIATIVE

4.2.1 Achievements and challenges

Brunei Darussalam is considering adopting an energy management system that is compatible with the ISO 50001. This system is to be implemented in commercial, government and industrial sectors. Building owners will be encouraged to introduce management systems that include equipment to monitor energy consumption such as the Building Automation Systems (BAS), Controllers (i.e. demand controllers) and Building Energy Management Systems (BEMS). The MRI report has also recommended the adoption of an energy manager scheme to monitor energy consumption and develop EEC plans and activities.

EDPMO, in collaboration with a consultant firm, is currently developing an Energy Efficiency and Conservation Program for government and commercial buildings. At the same time, EDPMO is also preparing a paper for the establishment of the Energy Manager for all buildings belonging to government ministries in Brunei Darussalam in line with the MRI recommendations. All Energy

[28] Same as CCAP. [29] APERC (2010), *Peer Review on Energy Efficiency in Thailand*,

http://aperc.ieej.or.jp/file/2010/9/26/PREE20100414_Thailand.pdf

Managers will be required to undergo training and courses for certification to be an accredited Energy Managers from the ASEAN Energy Manager Accreditation Scheme (AEMAS).

The PREE expert team found that energy savings is not usually designated as a critical part of productivity in Brunei Darussalam. Furthermore, there are no incentives for managers or operators to improve energy efficiency; even if applied energy savings help to lower operating cost for the business or facility, this usually does not translate to any additional benefit for the managers or operators.

The PREE expert team also believes that the ISO 50001 may be too complex for full-scale adoption by Brunei Darussalam. One concern is that there may not be sufficient numbers of technical persons in each organization to meet the requirements of implementing the energy management system.

For additional analytical, marketing, investment and business opportunities information, please contact
Global Investment & Business Center, USA
(202) 546-2103. Fax: (202) 546-3275. E-mail: rusric@erols.com

4.2.2 Recommendations

Recommendation 16: *To demonstrate the effectiveness of energy management systems, a number of government, commercial and industrial facilities should be selected to participate in an energy management pilot program in line with ISO 50001 criteria. This can be further supplemented with detailed guidelines for establishing and implementing energy management systems, which could be distributed to the target organizations.*

Recommendation 17: *Brunei Darussalam should develop an energy management law adopting appropriate parts of the ISO 50001: 2011 Energy Management System, particular emphasis should be given to energy management system training.*

Example: In Thailand, the Energy Minister issued a Ministerial Regulation governing Energy Management in designated buildings and factories under the Energy Conservation and Promotion Act. The Ministerial Regulation defines standards, criteria, and methodology for energy management system (compatible with ISO 50001) to be implemented by designated facilities. Designated factory and buildings may adopt the full ISO 50001 voluntarily as one of their operation standards, mostly with the view towards enhancing their business competitiveness.

Recommendation 18: *In support of the energy management law, a sufficient number of qualified external auditors should be trained to conduct monitoring and verification exercises to ensure compliance.*

Intensive training programs with expert facilitators should be provided to accelerate this capacity building process.

Recommendation 19: *Appropriate incentives should be designed to motivate facility managers and operators, particularly those in government-owned facilities, to apply EEC improvements that minimize operation costs.*

Acknowledging EEC success can take many forms ranging from formal written commendations and certificates, plaques presented at award ceremonies, bonuses and salary increases[30].

[30] US Environmental Protection Agency, *Teaming up to Save Energy*, http://www.energystar.gov/ia/business/guidelines/continuous_improvement/Teaming_Up_To_Save_Energy.p df

4.3 EEC BUILDING CODE INITIATIVES

4.3.1 Achievements and Challenges

The first building guideline and standards in Brunei Darussalam, the Piawai Brunei Darussalam 12 or PBD 12 – Building Guidelines and Requirements, was issued in 1994, and contains only building guidelines and standards for development purposes (earthwork and building construction). This was later revised in 2008 to take into account additional requirements from the Ministry of Health and the Brunei Fire and Rescue Department, but does not include energy efficiency requirements.

EDPMO in collaboration with the Ministry of Development (MOD) via the Authority for Building Control and Construction Industry (ABCi) and the Department of Mechanical and Electrical (DME) are in the process of developing the EEC Building Code with the objective to establish an EEC

For additional analytical, marketing, investment and business opportunities information, please contact
Global Investment & Business Center, USA
(202) 546-2103. Fax: (202) 546-3275. E-mail: rusric@erols.com

standards and a regulatory mechanism for buildings in Brunei Darussalam. Currently, the joint working committee with officials from EDPMO and MOD are working with a consultant service to identify the best options formulating the EEC Building Code framework and contents.

Based on the discussions during the visit, the PREE expert team has recognized several barriers that may hinder this EEC Building Code formulation process:

Insufficient indigenous human resources to develop and implement the EEC Building Codes.

The EEC Building Code should include guidelines on maximizing EEC potential through passive solar design and building orientation. However, according to EDPMO and MOD, the tools and data to determine solar and wind profiles, solar heat gain and building orientation are currently unavailable in Brunei Darussalam.

Jurisdiction among the government agencies responsible has not been clearly defined.

Compliance and enforcement issues have not been adequately addressed yet.

In addition to collaborating with EDPMO on the EEC Building Code formulation, the Public Works Department (PWD) under MOD has also begun its own EEC initiatives. This includes awareness raising programs within the ministry and department buildings such as the temperature setting (at 22-23°C), No-Lift Sundays and Rainwater Harvesting Pilot Project.

PWD is also conducting the Green Buildings Initiatives program for government buildings. Under this initiative, energy audits are conducted to detect excessive consumption or wastage, and potential EEC measures are identified. The effectiveness of these measures is monitored periodically and the actual energy consumption for each building audited is published online each month on the PWD website. Since 2011, nine buildings have been audited, and each building has shown reductions in energy consumption following the implementation of EEC measures.

According to Dr Rohaniyati Salleh's presentation during the PREE meetings, MOD has developed a Green Building Roadmap that will eventually lead to a National Green Building Certification Scheme for Brunei Darussalam. This roadmap adopts Singapore Building and Construction Authority's (BCA) Green Mark Scheme and will be applied for new and existing buildings. The implementation is still in early stages; and the PWD is currently reviewing current maintenance practices and collecting data for the benchmarking of existing buildings.

4.3.2 Recommendations

Recommendation 20: *The proposed EEC Building Code should include a strong foundation for EEC elements (along with existing fire, safety, construction and health) and be a unified document that clearly defines the jurisdiction of all agencies.*

Mandate of each agency involved could be defined in the main body of the code, but details of their specific requirements may be elaborated in separate documents that can be updated at different times, such as standards, guidelines, directives or annexes.

Example: The New Zealand Building Code sets out performance standards that must be met by all new buildings, and covers aspects such as structural stability, fire safety, access, moisture control, durability, services and facilities. Building consent is issued only if the building plans and specifications comply with the Building Code. However, detailed information on building materials, design or construction are not provided in the Building Code, instead, this information is provided in the Compliance Documents, which is under the purview of the Ministry of Business, Innovation and Employment[31].

EDPMO should be given the responsibility of reviewing and implementing the EEC elements of the Building Code every three years.

Recommendation 21: *EEC Building Code should include passive or partial-passive cooling and lighting design, and construction using low thermal mass and insulated materials for new residential, government and commercial buildings. In doing so, cooperation with a research centre, such as the Energy Research Group of Universiti Brunei Darussalam (UBD), is highly recommended.*

UBD is already working on EEC research projects for local content. One of the projects is on developing a database for local conditions (climate, building size and occupancy, building materials) for a standard energy efficiency/renewable energy building simulation software which will later enable users to model the building energy use under local Brunei Darussalam conditions. Collaborating with UBD researchers will beneficial for both EDPMO and UBD.

To further support the implementation of EEC elements in the code, EDPMO may also consider:

Conducting demonstrations for housing developers on integrating and constructing EEC design elements like passive cooling and lighting.

Setting up a building material testing laboratory, preferably at UBD to build local expertise in this field.

Offering financial and tax incentives for both housing developers and consumers.

Recommendation 22: *EDPMO should develop a compliance enforcement program to be effective once the EEC Building Code comes into force.*

The compliance enforcement program should include:

The design of the proposed building should meet the mandatory code requirements before receiving a building permit. Also, designated officials have to be given access during and after construction in order to verify compliance with the code.

Efficient methods for verifying compliance such as through site surveys, audits, submission of building plans and software tools[32].

[31] New Zealand Ministry of Business, Innovation and Employment, *About the Building Code,* http://www.dbh.govt.nz/bcr-about-the-building-code

[32] The US Department of Energy lists several software and web tools that can clarify compliance with energy codes and standards that simplify the process of verification. The list is available at http://www.energycodes.gov/compliance

3. Penalties for non-compliance; for instance civil fines and fees for minor infractions, revoking/suspension of license/certification or criminal prosecutions for major noncompliance.

For additional analytical, marketing, investment and business opportunities information, please contact
Global Investment & Business Center, USA
(202) 546-2103. Fax: (202) 546-3275. E-mail: rusric@erols.com

Example: The European Union has innovative examples of strategies for code enforcement including professional architect certification that can be revoked if a building is found to be out of compliance with the code. Denmark uses a two-stage compliance process – first providing permission to build based on code compliance of the building design and second, providing permission for occupancy based on the construction meeting the design requirements. Sweden requires a follow-up report two years AFTER construction to verify the predicted performance of each building.

Recommendation 23: *Build local capacity for addressing the EEC elements of the Building Code.*

Capacity building should be provided for all stakeholders at all stages of building construction; ranging from regulators (ministry officers responsible for building and maintaining the EEC Building Code), housing developers (including architects, engineers, contractors, project managers, etc.), compliance inspectors (local officers with the authority to issue building and occupancy permits) and building owners themselves. This can be done through training seminars, workshops, demonstrations and pilot projects.

4.4 INDUSTRIAL SECTOR INITIATIVES

4.4.1 Achievements and Challenges

In Brunei Darussalam's oil and gas industry, carbon dioxide emission mostly comes from the combustion of fossil fuel from auto-producer power plant facilities. Various initiatives have been undertaken by the local operators to improve their operation efficiencies and reduce greenhouse gas emission. There has been a steady decrease of greenhouse gas emissions over time especially from 1998 onwards. The main contribution to the reduction of greenhouse gas emissions has primarily been the reduction in venting and flaring emissions through rationalization projects and improvements in operational efficiencies in producing oil and gas fields. With significant reductions having been achieved in venting and flaring emissions, fuel gas (for gas compression and power generation) becomes the main contributor to greenhouse gas emissions in the order of about 50%. Efforts are now focused on energy efficiency of compression and auto-producer power plant facilities. The opportunities identified include upgrading or replacement of aged and inefficient equipment (e.g. compressors and control systems) in improving operational reliability and efficiency.

Based on Brunei Darussalam's background report, fuel gas in industrial plants is not used optimally. Typically, there is a tremendous heat loss with temperature over 500 °C in gas production process, particularly in the gas compression system, which could be converted to mechanical power for electricity generation, or for additional gas compression, or as a heat source for heating and cooling processes.

If waste heat is utilized for power generation, then this would reduce the amount of gas burned for electricity production. In the case of offshore gas producers, waste heat can be utilized to generate steam and drive an additional steam gas compressor to produce more volumes of gas. The latter method may be the more attractive measure since both energy efficiency and productivity improves.

Example: A pre-feasibility study in an offshore gas production platform in the gulf of Thailand revealed that the waste heat from operating the existing gas compressors, 22 MW x 3 units, could be converted into 18 MW of mechanical power.

For additional analytical, marketing, investment and business opportunities information, please contact
Global Investment & Business Center, USA
(202) 546-2103. Fax: (202) 546-3275. E-mail: rusric@erols.com

From this 18 MW of power, 6 MW is used in steam turbine generators to generate electricity, which is sufficient to meet the electricity demand of the whole plant. The rest, 12 MW, is utilized in a new steam gas compressor to produce additional gas volume for raising revenue.

Alternatively, the 18 MW mechanical power may be used solely to drive a new 18 MW steam gas compressor to generate more gas.

Brunei Darussalam estimates that it is possible for the industrial sector to achieve 23% reduction in energy from Business-As-Usual (BAU) case in 2035 by improving equipment efficiency and operational processes, implementing waste heat recovery, switching energy sources, and introducing energy management system. To support the implementation of these measures, it is likely that an investment of BND 37 million will be required.

4.4.2 Recommendations

Recommendation 24: *Energy efficiency improvement in the oil and gas industry should be focused on heat recovery, and this should be also applied for any new oil and gas plant designs.*

Feasibility study on whether it is converted into electricity or steam for powering steam gas compressor or used as a heat source for heating and cooling processes, should be conducted, taking into account technical barriers such as space availability, loading capacity, installation, extension or building a new platform etc., (in case of offshore gas production).

Recommendation 25: *Consider replacing small gas turbines with new gas engine sets for power generation in oil and gas industries.*

This option should be considered whenever there is a need to overhaul existing gas turbines. Replacement with new gas engines of equivalent size may or may not be cheaper, but operation costs will be lower as gas engines have higher efficiencies than gas turbines, especially when running at partial load.

For additional analytical, marketing, investment and business opportunities information, please contact
Global Investment & Business Center, USA
(202) 546-2103. Fax: (202) 546-3275. E-mail: rusric@erols.com

Example: A case study on replacing 3MW x 4 units of gas turbines with gas engine sets of the same size and units at an offshore gas production platform in the gulf of Thailand revealed that the project could reduce fuel gas consumption by up to 40%.

Recommendation 26: *Conduct a study on the efficiency of the gas transmission line, to check whether there might be gas leakage along the gas pipe line. Then, identify and implement energy efficiency measures that could reduce gas wastage.*

5. POLICY MEASURES – TRANSPORT SECTOR

5.1 ACHIEVEMENTS AND CHALLENGES

Transport is the largest energy end use sector in Brunei Darussalam, accounting for around half of all energy used by consumers, as shown in Figure 5-1[33]. This proportion is very high by international comparison. The vast majority (97%) of transport energy is used for road transport.

a. Energy End-use by Sector b. Transport Sector Modal Share

Brunei Darussalam has a good quality road infrastructure. The vehicle fleet is relatively modern with 65% of registered vehicles under 9 years old. In 2012, there were around 190,000 registered vehicles with a diverse fleet comprising around 190 different models. There is ready access to light vehicles with vehicle ownership rates being one of the highest rates in the world, given Brunei Darussalam's population of just under 400,000 people. Ownership rates are equivalent to more than two vehicles per licensed driver. Vehicle numbers are growing at around 4% per year, although it should be noted that with the number of vehicles exceeding the number of licensed drivers, increasing vehicle numbers may not necessarily translate into a corresponding increase in transport energy demand.

The government is considering fuel economy regulations and other policies and strategies to promote the uptake of energy efficient vehicles in the Sultanate. Brunei Darussalam has already started compiling a database of the fuel efficiency of vehicles entering the fleet.

For additional analytical, marketing, investment and business opportunities information, please contact
Global Investment & Business Center, USA
(202) 546-2103. Fax: (202) 546-3275. E-mail: rusric@erols.com

There is an existing fixed-route public bus network in Brunei Darussalam, but patronage is relatively low. A five-year roadmap to enhance public transport was announced earlier this year and lays out plans to increase bus frequency, extend operating hours, revise routes, develop kerbside infrastructure (designated bus stops and shelters) and revise fare systems.

Despite these achievements, the low price of transport fuels enjoyed by the people of Brunei Darussalam remains one of the significant challenges for improving transport energy efficiency. At the time of our visit in June 2013, petrol was retailing at BND 0.53 per litre. The World Bank ranked

[33] Mitsubishi Research Institute (2011), *Brunei Energy Efficiency and Conservation Study: Roadmap Formulation and Policy Advice.*

Brunei Darussalam as the eleventh cheapest in the world for the pump price of petrol (in USD equivalent) in 2012[34].

Brunei Darussalam's relatively low urban density, small population and high car ownership rates make it difficult for conventional, fixed-route public transport to meet the needs of potential customers and attract their ridership. These factors also provide challenges for other alternatives to private vehicle transport such as carpooling, walking and cycling.

Based on observations, it appears that traffic movements and parking management around commercial developments could be better integrated at the time of planning to reduce localized congestion.

5.2 RECOMMENDATIONS

Recommendation 27: *Continue developing a database of fuel efficiency of light vehicles in the Brunei Darussalam fleet to be the basis on which vehicle fuel efficiency policies and initiatives, including consumer information, can be designed and monitored.*

Private car transport is likely to remain the dominant mode of transport in Brunei Darussalam in the future due to existing high car ownership rates, low fuel prices in comparison with other economies and low urban density. Brunei Darussalam should therefore focus on transport energy efficiency initiatives on improving the energy efficiency of the vehicle fleet and encouraging more energy efficient driver behaviour. Increasing the understanding of the nominal fuel efficiency of the national light vehicle fleet (comprising cars, Special Utility Vehicles (SUVs), pick-ups, vans and multi-purpose vehicles) is the foundation on which vehicle fuel efficiency can be designed, implemented and monitored. Such a database is a pre-requisite for vehicle fuel economy labelling to provide consumer information to help people select the most fuel efficient vehicle that meets their requirements.

Brunei Darussalam does not have a domestic vehicle manufacturing industry and so is able import the latest technology vehicles from around the world. Consequently, the economy is positioned to readily take advantage of energy efficiency technology improvements as these are introduced to the market. Due to Brunei Darussalam's small population and wide range of imported vehicle models it would not be cost effective for Brunei to conduct vehicle fuel economy tests itself. Brunei Darussalam should use data from testing in other regions, backfilling the database as far as possible with fuel economy figures for existing light fleet vehicles.

For additional analytical, marketing, investment and business opportunities information, please contact
Global Investment & Business Center, USA
(202) 546-2103. Fax: (202) 546-3275. E-mail: rusric@erols.com

Recommendation 28: *Provide consumer information on vehicle fuel consumption through the implementation of a vehicle labelling programme and energy efficient driver behaviour.*

There is considerable variation between the fuel consumption of vehicles which otherwise appear similar and have similar engine displacement (cc rating). Providing vehicle buyers with fuel consumption information helps them determine which vehicles can meet their requirements on a total cost of ownership basis, rather than vehicle purchase price alone. The advantages of energy efficient technology advances, such as hybrid[35] vehicles, modern turbocharged diesel engines and

[34] The World Bank (2013), *Pump price for gasoline (US$ per liter)*, http://data.worldbank.org/indicator/EP.PMP.SGAS.CD/countries/1W?display=default, accessed June 2013. [35] Hybrid vehicles ('hybrids') use a combination of a petrol or diesel engine, a battery and an on-board electric motor to improve overall energy efficiency. The battery in a hybrid vehicle is charged by the engine and regenerative braking. This means that hybrids do not plug in to an electricity supply to recharge, their only source of energy is the fuel used by the engine.

engine stop-start systems, can also be more readily understood by vehicle buyers with fuel consumption labelling.

Brunei Darussalam should require all new vehicles to display a label giving standardised fuel consumption information at the point of sale. The requirement should ideally cover vehicles offered for sale via the internet and promoted in other traditional and non-traditional media. Co-promotion of fuel economy information with safety ratings for vehicles will help ensure that fuel economy is not promoted at the expense of vehicle safety (safety is usually a core function of transport agencies).

Brunei Darussalam has also expressed an interest in promoting natural gas vehicles and electric vehicles and so consideration should be given to how consumers can readily compare energy consumption between vehicles with different fuel/energy and prime mover technologies. Annual or five-year total running costs for a standardised annual distance may be one way to approach this, and also direct potential buyers into thinking about energy costs in terms of the length of time they will own and operate the vehicle.

Monitoring consumer awareness of the label and the degree to which fuel consumption is a factor in vehicle purchase decisions will help evaluate the benefits of the labelling programme.

Example: Vehicle fuel economy labels are used for petrol and electric vehicles in New Zealand to allow consumers to more easily understand the significant difference in energy costs between these two types of vehicles. Examples of the labels are shown in Figure 5-2. The label for electric vehicles also provides important additional consumer information about the range the EV will travel on one charge.

Recommendation 29: *Incorporate fuel efficiency into new driver education and driver licensing.*

The education and subsequent test that new drivers have to sit in order to be awarded a driver license is an opportunity for encouraging fuel efficient driver behaviour. Fuel efficient driver behaviours, such as anticipating traffic flow to avoid heavy braking and checking tyres are inflated correctly, are also safe driver behaviours. Teaching these skills from the start is always much easier than trying to get driver to change ingrained habits.

For additional analytical, marketing, investment and business opportunities information, please contact
Global Investment & Business Center, USA
(202) 546-2103. Fax: (202) 546-3275. E-mail: rusric@erols.com

Example: In Finland, fuel efficient driver training was first introduced in 1995 and became part of the driving test in 1998[36] (CIECA, 2007). Fuel efficient driving is also included in testing in Germany, the Netherland, Switzerland and Sweden.

Continuing driver education around energy efficiency should also be considered, particularly for commercial drivers of taxis, buses and freight vehicles. Government could lead the way by introducing continuing driver education for employees using government fleet vehicles. Such initiatives have been shown to save not only on fuel but also on accident-related costs, and their implementation may attract lower cost insurance premiums for drivers.

Recommendation 30: *Set CO2 emissions based vehicle acquisition or taxation policies which encourage both fuel efficient vehicles and lower carbon fuel vehicles, such as gas vehicles, electric vehicles and plug-in hybrids.*

Brunei Darussalam is already considering fuel economy regulations and other policies and strategies to promote the uptake of energy efficient vehicles. The economy is also interested in encouraging electric vehicles and natural gas vehicles. The two aims could be integrated into one by considering fuel economy regulation or incentives based on "well-to-wheel" CO2 emissions per km. This would allow diesel, gasoline, natural gas, electric vehicles and plug-in hybrids[37] (plus other vehicle fuel/technologies) to be compared using a common metric. For example, a policy could require the fleet average CO2 emissions of vehicles first entering the national fleet to meet a set maximum level which is signalled to gradually reduce over time, with the government specifying the emissions factors that apply for different fuel types. The requirement should fall on vehicle importers (as there is no vehicle manufacturing industry in Brunei Darussalam). Given the size of the market, vehicle importers should be allowed to "trade" requirements amongst each other to achieve the overall aim of a fleet average target.

While annual registration taxes for vehicles are very low in Brunei Darussalam, import duties are levied at a much more influential rate. They are applied on the basis of engine displacement (cc) for petrol and diesel vehicles, as shown in Table 5-1, which will help encourage vehicles with smaller engines which are generally more fuel efficient.

Table 5-1: Import duties for motor vehicles in Brunei Darussalam[38]

Fuel Type	Engine displacement	Import duty rate
Petrol Motor Vehicle	Not exceeding 1,000 cc	40%
	Exceeding 1,000 but not exceeding 2,000 cc	60%
	Exceeding 2,000 but not exceeding 3,000 cc	80%
	Exceeding 3,000 but not exceeding 4,000 cc	100%
	Exceeding 4,000 cc	200%
Diesel or semi	Not exceeding 2,000 cc	40%
diesel motor vehicle	Exceeding 2,000 but not exceeding 4,000 cc	80%
	Exceeding 4,000 cc	200%

[36] International Commission for Driver Testing, CIECA (2007), *Internal Project on 'Eco-Driving' in Category B Driver Training and the Driving Test*

[37] Generally the term electric vehicle refers to cars that are partly or wholly powered by an external source of electricity typically stored in batteries. The main variants are battery electric vehicles (BEVs), which are wholly powered by an external source of electricity, and plug-in hybrid

electric vehicles (PHEVs), which are vehicles that operate on a combination of external electricity and other fuels.[38] ASEAN, *Brunei Darussalam Tariff and Duty Rates,* http://www.asean.org/communities/asean-economiccommunity/item/brunei-darussalam-6

Brunei Darussalam could consider setting vehicle import duties on the basis of fuel efficiency or CO2 emissions instead of engine capacity, to better incentivise energy efficient vehicles and alternative energy vehicles such as electrical vehicles. Linking import duties with climate change measures may be seen as more acceptable than the status quo in terms of border measures.

One of the questions raised during the PREE Review Team's visit to Brunei Darussalam was whether electric vehicles, including plug-in hybrids, should be encouraged in Brunei Darussalam, given that current electricity generation is relatively inefficient. As well as diversifying energy types for transport, electric motors are inherently significantly more energy efficient than internal combustion engines as a vehicle prime mover. Figure 5-3 below illustrates a comparative analysis of the energy losses for a typical petrol vehicle, including losses associated with petrol refining and supply, with losses for a typical electric vehicle, including losses associated with electricity generation, transmission and distribution.

Two scenarios are presented for the electric vehicle analysis. The first, in light purple, is based on the current average generation efficiency in Brunei Darussalam of 23%[39]. The second, in dark purple, is based on the planned future average generation efficiency of 45% once upgrades from single cycle gas turbine generators are implemented, along with other efficiency initiatives. The analysis also includes the lower losses from electric vehicles in use when compared with conventional vehicles; electric vehicles are able to capture, through regenerative breaking, some of the losses associated with braking and coasting, and avoid losses by not consuming energy while stationary in congested traffic.

This analysis shows that even with the current relatively low average efficiency of gas generation in Brunei Darussalam of 23%, an electric vehicle would have an overall "well-to-wheel" efficiency slightly better than that of a typical internal combustion engine. As planned generation efficiency improvements are realised, this will increase the energy efficiency benefits of electric vehicles further. For an average planned generation efficiency of 45%, electric vehicles in Brunei Darussalam will be twice as efficient as internal combustion engine vehicles on a "well-to-wheel" basis. Brunei Darussalam does not need to wait until these electricity sector improvements are underway to start promoting the use of electric vehicles.

Electric vehicles also offer other co-benefits, such as improved air quality, reduced noise and increased comfort. Pre-cooling of electric vehicles while they are parked and plugged into a charger is an innovation which also provides energy efficiency benefits, as vehicle air conditioning is likely to be significant factor in actual fuel use for vehicles in Brunei Darussalam. For example, there is a smartphone application for the Nissan Leaf which allows drivers to send a message to the car to start it cooling ahead of use, using electricity direct from the local network. Such innovations may make electric vehicles appealing to consumers in Brunei Darussalam, as well as contributing to efficiency.

The question of a lack of recharging infrastructure for electric vehicles was also raised. Practical experience in other countries has shown that electric vehicles are typically charged overnight at home or, for company owned vehicles, at workplaces. The world's largest EV use monitoring project, The EV Project sponsored by the US Department of Energy, has shown that even when public recharging facilities are widely available, 88% of recharging happens at home[40] (Level 2 charging) and only 3% of recharging events occur at fast recharging stations (Level 3 charging). Brunei Darussalam's 230V network means that fully depleted electric vehicle batteries can be completely charged at home overnight in less than 6-8 hours while people are sleeping (Level 2 charging), providing at least 100km of daily driving range, with considerably higher ranges possible depending on vehicle type[41]. Given Brunei Darussalam's physical size and typical daily travel patterns, an overnight charge should be more than adequate for over 90% of travel needs.

Overnight charging can occur when daily electricity demand is at its lowest in Brunei Darussalam, between the hours of 11 pm to 7 am as shown in Figure 5.4. Increased night-time demand for electricity for electric vehicle charging, as part of overall energy efficiency improvements, will contribute to increased off-peak utilisation of generation and transmission/distribution assets improving their overall return on investment in these assets.

The fact that there are two cars for every licensed driver in Brunei Darussalam suggests that an alternative vehicle may be available for those occasions when a pure electric vehicle is not suitable. Plug-in hybrids should also be promoted which allow for electric powered driving for most situations, and hybrid driving for long-distance travel (e.g. to Malaysia).

Simply having an electrical vehicle recharger at the owner's home should be sufficient infrastructure for successful electric vehicle deployment. Installation of such rechargers is straightforward and usually comes as part of an electric vehicle purchase package. However, it may be helpful to install some Level 2 public recharging facilities in premium, high visibility parking locations, such as at the airport, to overcome the initial perceptions around "range anxiety" and raise awareness of electric vehicles.

Government purchase and use of electric vehicles will help promote this technology through leading by example.

[40] The EV Project (2013). Q1 2013 Report. http://www.theevproject.com/cms-assets/documents/113177646795.q1-2013-rpt.pdf

[41] Some electric vehicles now on the international market have a range of over 450 km on a single charge.

Recommendation 31: *Continue to periodically survey daily vehicle usage patterns (range of trip distances, range of daily driving distances and trip purpose) to increase understanding of travel patterns to assist in the design of future policies and initiatives.*

Increased knowledge of daily vehicle usage patterns will help with the improvement of public transport as a viable alternative to private car use, and will also improve understanding of how new technologies, such as electric vehicles, could potentially be encouraged in Brunei Darussalam.

Recommendation 32: *Investigate information technology based, demand responsive transit models which may be more suitable to Brunei Darussalam's population size and urban density than traditional fixed-route public transport and better meet customers' needs.*

Improving the bus system remains important to provide an alternative to private car use, particularly for those members of society who cannot afford a private car, those who cannot drive or who choose not to drive. Information technology and widespread uptake of mobile phones provides an opportunity for Brunei Darussalam to leapfrog to a more intelligent and flexible public transport system which suits the country's small population, low urban density and low public transport demand levels. This approach, termed "demand responsive transport" and sometimes known as "dial-a-ride" public transport, could provide an alternative to some of the current and proposed traditional fixed public transport routes, particularly on feeder routes or at off-peak periods.

[42] Figure from the Department of Electrical Services (DES) presentation during the PREE Review Visit to Brunei Darussalam

Example: This type of shared "taxi-bus" public transport has been growing in popularity over the last couple of decades and is in operation in parts of the UK, France, Germany, Canada, Australia and many other economies. Transport Scotland has published a good overview of how it works there[43].

Brunei Darussalam should investigate not only existing demand responsive transport operations but investigate the emerging use of intelligent transport systems and mobile telecommunications technology to increase the customer responsiveness of this type of public transport.

Recommendation 33: *Encourage greater coordination between the infrastructure functions of the Ministry of Development and the transport functions of the Ministry of Communications.*

The increased integration of land use planning with transport, both for individual commercial developments and residential/mixed-use developments, is a vital factor in ensuring overall transport energy efficiency improvements in the long term. Proposed developments should be required to provide a transport impact analysis, including parking management plans, with any mitigations identified being a required part of the approvals for the development. New developments should ideally be sited around existing or planned public transport routes. Provision of quality walking and cycling infrastructure should also be improved.

[43] Transport Scotland (2009), *A further review of demand responsive transport in Scotland,*

http://www.transportscotland.gov.uk/files/documents/public-transport/Demand_Responsive_Transport.pdf

6. POLICY MEASURES – ELECTRICITY SECTOR

6.1 ACHIEVEMENTS AND CHALLENGES

The Department of Electrical Services (DES) and the Berakas Power Management Company (BPMC) are the two major electric utilities in Brunei Darussalam. The electricity sector in Brunei Darussalam has an installed capacity of 895 MW and can generate more than 3.9 TWh per year. It has achieved the ability to produce significantly more power than is needed on a daily basis, for example, it has a peak capacity of more than 700 MW and in 2012 its highest peak demand was only 540 MW. The economy has a spinning reserve of approximately 25% and the ability to interconnect with another electricity generator in the case of a major loss of capacity.

For additional analytical, marketing, investment and business opportunities information, please contact
Global Investment & Business Center, USA
(202) 546-2103. Fax: (202) 546-3275. E-mail: rusric@erols.com

The economy uses an indigenous fuel, natural gas, for 99% of its generation with less than one per cent diesel generation and a solar generating station on the order of 1 MW. Consequently, it has achieved an enviable energy security position and a fairly clean generation profile from a climate change/greenhouse gas emission viewpoint.

Another achievement is that the DES is developing initiatives to increase efficiency in the power generation from 23% to 45%. Plans include implementing a number of smart policies and measures including energy-saving technologies[44] – the combined cycle turbine, reducing partial load operation and transmission and distribution losses, mandating an energy efficiency target for any new power plant, installing smart meters (i.e. dynamic pricing based on energy consumption), evaluating feasibility of altering tariff structure to promote desired consumption behaviour and reduction in gas consumption through integration of renewable energy to meet the demands on power in Brunei Darussalam.

Furthermore, Brunei Darussalam recognized that there is a need for electricity tariff reforms as a means to promote energy efficiency. Early last year, His Majesty the Sultan and Yang Di-Pertuan of Negara Brunei Darussalam consented for the review of the electricity tariff structure in the residential sector and a new electricity tariff was implemented. The new tariff corrected the old tariff which was regressive and incentivized the wasteful use of electricity. By implementing a reverse block rate and keeping the cost for the first 600 kWh extremely low (BND 0.01), the new tariff ensures that low income citizens would not be adversely impacted. A pre-paid meter system was also installed. After the first year, the DES achieved excellent results; it reduced electric consumption by 12.4% and saved more than BND 21 million.

Nevertheless, the electricity sector does face some challenges. Brunei Darussalam's electricity consumption is around 8,300 kWh per capita in 2008. An average of 48% of the electricity generated goes to residential, 25% is consumed by the commercial sector, the government sector consumes 17% and the remaining 10% is used by the oil and gas industrial sector

Brunei Darussalam ranks fourth in the world for highest CO2 emissions on a metric ton per capita basis[45] . While some of this emissions may be attributed to the production and flaring of natural gas, a portion of the emissions may well be attributed to the inefficiency of the gas turbines used in electricity generation. Most of the power plants in Brunei Darussalam are still using single cycle gas turbines, which have low efficiency, burn more fossil fuel and emit more carbon dioxide to the atmosphere than the combined cycle gas turbines (CCGT) commonly used in new power plant construction today. However, replacement of all the existing gas turbines in Brunei Darussalam is an expensive proposition. A financial plan to pay for the replacement needs to be developed to ensure the viability of DES and still keep rates to consumers as low as possible.

[44] Two major projects have been initiated at two of the major power plants in the country – the Lumut Co-Generation Power Station which has an overall efficiency of greater than 60% through the application of combined heat and power (CHP) integration or Co-Generation. The other project at Bukit Panggal Combined Cycle Power Station has already reached an efficiency of about 47% using "Combined Cycle Gas Turbine" technology to increase efficiency by more than one-third.[45] The World Bank Database, http://data.worldbank.org/indicator/EN.ATM.CO2E.PC/countries

Nonetheless, the Bukit Panggal Power Station is an excellent example of the increased efficiency attributable to new technologies and is the only non-simple cycle turbine generator in the economy's generating portfolio. This generating station is a CCGT plant in which the CCGT technology added one third more capacity (approximately 32 MW) more than if the plant had been just two simple cycle gas turbines. But the major benefit to the economy was that the plant

For additional analytical, marketing, investment and business opportunities information, please contact
Global Investment & Business Center, USA
(202) 546-2103. Fax: (202) 546-3275. E-mail: rusric@erols.com

produces an additional 32 MW of electricity with no additional need for natural gas fuel; thereby saving approximately BND 36 million in fuel costs per year (or if taken from the perspective of the government, the natural gas not burned at the plant was able to be exported and brought an additional BND 36 million in revenues to the economy).

Energy management is another area where improvements in efficiency can be made. The ISO 50001 is a well-recognized international standard that provides guidelines to the best practices in energy management. It recommends that each facility (of a certain size) have an energy manager at each site to ensure that all operational measures are optimized at all times. For example, if the equipment is not maintained or operating at its prescribed settings, then all the other measures are compromised – adoption of ISO 50001's energy management requirements by the utility sector would ensure that equipment is operating at optimal levels. The Bukit Panggal Power Station already performs some regular maintenance activities which result in increased energy efficiency, for example, online and offline washing of compressors significantly increases production efficiency up to 5%.

In addition, the hot and humid weather of Brunei Darussalam drives consumers in both the residential and commercial sectors to utilize significant amounts of air conditioning all year long. Air-conditioning is the leading consumer of electricity in the economy and accounts for almost 60% of electricity consumption in buildings. With the relatively low electricity tariff, Brunei Darussalam enjoys a relatively cheap cost for air conditioning, which may not be sustainable in the long-term. In fact, Mr Asrul Sany Haji Mohammad Ali's presentation on the new tariff shows that Brunei Darussalam's average tariff is the lowest by half of nine other ASEAN countries.

Nonetheless, Brunei Darussalam has charted a good path forward. In addition to the upgrading of old inefficiency power stations to CCGT or combined heat and power (CHP), tariff reform, and prepaid meter programs mentioned above, new demand side efforts are underway in developing appliance standards for the two largest appliance/products in the economy; air conditioners and lighting (fully discussed in Section 7 of this report).

Furthermore, Brunei Darussalam is pursuing a sustainable development funding vehicle to drive more energy efficiency into the economy. The Brunei Darussalam Energy Efficiency Fund was proposed by the Sustainable Development Capital (Asia) Limited (SDCL) and under this proposal, subsides currently paid to the utility will be shifted to the fund to pay for verified energy savings resulting from successful energy efficiency and conservation projects.

SDCL's analysis of the power sector shows that energy efficiency could eliminate six new power plants by 2035 and the corresponding dollar savings are very large (SDCL's independent analysis verifies a Mitsubishi consulting report from a few years ago which showed a very similar result). This fund is a critical piece needed to ensure that the capital is available to improve the efficiency on the supply side of the equation.

Brunei Darussalam's path forward for the electricity sector is well thought out and takes into account both supply and demand side efficiency measures. On the supply efficiency side, the government's goals are threefold:

Reduce line losses by 50%. Line losses are calculated to be only 6% at this time (this might be a hard goal to meet from both a technical and cost effective perspective).

More optimal operation of the transmission network. It should also be noted that although there was very little discussion about this in our meetings, it was mentioned that equipment maintenance will be increased to improve distribution efficiency.

Enhance grid control. Some of this would be done through smart metering and controls, while the 1.2 MW Seria Solar power plant (which is being used to study 6 types of PV cells) is also being used as a test-bed to provide the DES with experience related to connecting renewable energy technologies to the grid.

On the demand side, many new initiatives across all the sectors have been implemented or are being contemplated:

A new pricing structure was implemented as of January 2012. The new tariff for electricity consumption moved from a regressive system (in which the more electricity a consumer used, the less the consumer was charged for it on a kWh basis) to a progressive system (in which consumers have a lower price for the first 2,500 kWh used and higher prices when they use more than that first level of consumption). The latter tariff encourages efficiency and conservation, while the former tariff encourages waste of electricity.

Prepaid meters have been installed as a means to adjust consumer behaviour by making the consumer more directly aware of the link between energy use and cost.

Incentives to subsidize the cost of a variety of energy efficiency technologies are being discussed under the EE&C regulatory framework being developed by the EDPMO. These technologies include equipment, such as; energy efficient air conditioners, chillers, lighting equipment (from lamps to controls and sensors, solar hot water heaters, and smart meters).

Brunei Darussalam is developing new appliance standards for air-conditioners and lighting. The economy is also developing a labelling scheme for appliances. Upon advice of the experts, they are now looking at harmonizing the standards and labels with other economies in the region. See, Section 7 of this report for more details.

Brunei Darussalam is also developing energy building codes to improve the energy performance of buildings. They are looking at a number of code measures to accomplish this goal; reduction of solar heat gain, increase in insulation, reduction in air leakage, and temperature settings.

In the industrial sector, energy management is the target. As noted above, the government is looking at mandating energy managers at facilities.

Fuel economy standards set to European Union (EU) levels is another initiative undertaken by the government.

Awareness-raising through customer education is also recognized by both the government and the power plant operators as a key element to get their consumers to be more efficient by understanding the connection of energy use and cost.

The above measures are critical to the power sector and the government as they are committed to a more energy efficient economy that can provide Brunei Darussalam a more secure and reliable power sector in the future.

6.2 RECOMMENDATIONS

Recommendation 34: *DES should develop a roadmap to improve overall power systems efficiency.*

Older, inefficient power generation capacity should be phased out and replaced by new CCGT or cogeneration units on a pre-set schedule.

The older transmission and distribution assets should be upgraded to have SCADA or smart grid applications for better efficiency.

Recommendation 35: *DES should work closely with the Ministry of Finance to ensure that a well structured finance plan is put in place to provide the capitalization needed to finance the roadmap.*

Recommendation 36: *DES should implement ISO 50001 in all of its power generating stations.*

Recommendation 37: *Continue to implement progressively increasing tariffs over a specified long-term schedule, similar to what is currently being practiced in Japan and California.*

Daily load profile monitoring of the total power consumption and by sector in Brunei Darussalam should be conducted to enable better understanding of their characteristics that can be used as a basis for further enhancing the electricity pricing policy.

Recommendation 38: *Consider using other innovative tariffs such as "time of use (TOU) tariffs" to encourage consumers to increase their use of energy efficiency and lower overall system consumption.*

Recommendation 39: *Install smart meters for enhancing both demand side and supply side operations and programs.*

Recommendation 40: *Accelerate efforts to implement demand-side measures such as those being implemented for air conditioning units, chillers and lighting and consider Building Management Systems (BMS) for the commercial sector.*

Recommendation 41: *Consider implementing an energy efficiency (and water saving) program for drinking water and waste water treatment facilities.*

Recommendation 42: *As part of the efforts to supply electricity to the eco-tourism Temburong area, conduct a feasibility study that applies intensive energy efficiency measures integrating small-scale renewable energy supply (keeping the diesel generation facility as a back-up if needed).*

The results of this feasibility study can be compared with the proposed transmission line projects or other options.

Examples of Ecotourism and Small-Scale Renewable Energy Installations

a. A few energy efficiency handbooks targeted specifically for the hotel industry have been published, including an Energy Efficiency Handbook for Thai Hotels by the World Tourism Organization[46] and an Energy Wise Hotels Toolkit by the Melbourne City Council[47]. The United States Energy Star organization has compiled a list of resources on energy efficiency in the hospitality industry in its website[48].

b. The Mae Kam Pong 40 KW Micro-Hydro Electric Project in Thailand was constructed in 1980s by the local community with budget and technical assistance from the government[49]. The project is now operated by the village cooperative and is part of the attractions for this community-based eco-tourism village[50].

7. POLICY MEASURES – APPLIANCES AND EQUIPMENT

7.1 ACHIEVEMENTS AND CHALLENGES

Brunei Darussalam commissioned a study by the Mitsubishi Research Institute in 2011 which, among other things, determined that the economy needs to implement a standards and labelling program for appliances and equipment that would ensure that Brunei Darussalam's goal of a 45% energy intensity reduction by 2035 (using 2005 as the base year) can be achieved. The Energy Department, Prime Minister's Office (EDPMO) is responsible for the policy recommendations and legislative measures for both appliance and equipment standards as well as labelling.

Regarding legislation, EDPMO is collaborating with Brunei National Energy Research Institute (BNERI) to develop a National Energy Efficiency Standards and Labelling Regulation, which initially will be applied to air-conditioners and lighting and later will be extended to cover other appliances and products.

The objective of developing and implementing a National Standards and Labelling Regulation is to halt the importation of non-efficient electrical appliances and products (air conditioners and lighting) into the economy while educating and permitting consumers to still have choices without triggering significant increases in price.

Also, with the implementation of the National Standard and Labelling Regulation, consumers will have a better understanding of which products have better efficiency ratings and therefore, when purchased will reduce the energy consumption nationwide. A labelling scheme is regarded to be one of the most important measures to raise awareness and provide information to the public regarding the energy efficiency of products. Brunei Darussalam's recognition of the importance of labels that rate equipment and appliances is critical as a means to transform the market from inefficient equipment and products to those that are more efficient.

Standards:

The Asia Pacific Energy Research Centre's (APERC) own Policy Template[52] endorses energy efficiency standards that set a minimum level of energy performance (MEPS) that all products must meet. By developing energy efficiency standards, the economy can prevent the manufacture, import or sales of products that do not meet the standard. However, a robust and effective energy efficiency standards program must also contain a reliable program of testing at two stages; first to set the standard, and second to ensure compliance with the standard.

[52] APERC's *Appliance Efficiency Standards and Labels* policy template is quoted throughout this section. A link to the Policy template is available at http://www.ase.org/global-policy-making. An example of a report that used the policy template concept is from the first Cooperative Energy Efficiency Design for Sustainability on Standards and Labelling is located at http://aperc.ieej.or.jp/file/2010/9/26/Final_Report_CEEDS_Phase_1_20100114.pdf

Economies across the world, both developed and developing, acknowledge that energy efficiency standards (and building energy codes) have had the greatest impact on increasing energy efficiency worldwide. Plug loads (i.e. electrical appliances from refrigerators to air conditioners, televisions to lighting, and computers to charging devices, etc.) are rapidly increasing across all

For additional analytical, marketing, investment and business opportunities information, please contact
Global Investment & Business Center, USA
(202) 546-2103. Fax: (202) 546-3275. E-mail: rusric@erols.com

economies. At the same time, the buildings where these electrical products are housed account for approximately 40% of the total energy consumption worldwide. Since electrical products have much shorter lives than buildings or industrial facilities, rapid turnover of these products can lower energy use at a faster pace (compared to improvements in buildings or industry) if a strong standards setting program is in place.

Consequently, many economies have adopted appliance/product standards and have experience in the design and implementation of such standards programs. In fact, efficiency (and labelling) programs are in place in at least 19 APEC economies and more than 57 economies worldwide, and in aggregate cover more than 80 different categories of appliances and products[53]. These programs have helped transform those market economies to ones that consume less energy and increase the share of efficient appliances and products in their market.

From a manufacturer's perspective, energy efficiency standards (and labelling) programs create an incentive for them to innovate and gain market share. For the consumer, high efficiency appliances and products bring significant savings in their electricity bills. For utilities, these high efficiency products help them meet their increasing demand for electricity without the need or expense of building costly generating plants.

During our discussions in Brunei Darussalam, the question of whether imposing energy efficiency products would cause an adverse action from the World Trade Organization was raised. In fact, just the opposite is true. Trade in the global market has increasingly turned to clean energy and higher energy efficiency as a significant criterion in looking at trade patterns. Dumping inefficient products on economies that have low, lax, or no appliance/product standards is generally not tolerated under trade agreements.

As for standard setting in Brunei Darussalam, a MEPS standard does help meet the multiple objectives set forth by the EDPMO which include promoting and encouraging the use of more energy efficient appliances, ensuring that products sold in (or imported into) Brunei Darussalam meet efficiency standards set by the economy, and with a corresponding labelling program, it helps consumers to understand which products are more efficient and therefore less costly to operate.

However, even after establishing the starting point at which the MEPS standard is set, it is just as critical to set up the process by which the energy efficiency standard can be "ratcheted up" over time (as new, more efficient technologies raise the efficiency of covered products). This step is important for an economy to have a sustainable program over the long-term. Energy efficiency technologies, and the products they are used in, historically show an improvement over time. Two common methods for determining the appropriate efficiency levels over time include both an engineering analysis and a market penetration analysis. While the former looks at the technical options available and the likely cost impact, the latter is a market-based approach that looks at the products and their efficiency in the market to determine where the new higher standard should be set. These methods complement each other and a robust program will include both.

Developing the metrics and testing for each appliance or product is also a critical, and sometimes, difficult task. Collaborating with other economies can greatly assist with this effort. Harmonizing the standard levels with another economy and collaborating with that other economy can make a significant impact on reducing the time and effort when either raising energy efficiency standards for products or ensuring that products meet their stated efficiency rating. Also, this collaboration can mean huge savings for the manufacturers as well since they will have one less set of testing and reporting to carry out.

For additional analytical, marketing, investment and business opportunities information, please contact
Global Investment & Business Center, USA
(202) 546-2103. Fax: (202) 546-3275. E-mail: rusric@erols.com

Involving the major stakeholders in the development of standards is a best practice, but one that may sometimes lead into contentious battles, while other times it may lead into a consensus that can more quickly move the market to higher efficiencies. Nevertheless, a frank, open and transparent discussion with all the major stakeholders is a "must" for a viable standards program. Policy decision makers, manufacturers, retailers, importers, distributors, and end-users should all be brought together to craft the "best" standard and get the most buy-in from all of the stakeholders. This will lead to all the parties to be more willing to comply with the new standards.

Finally, as mentioned earlier, decisions must be made as to whether the standard levels should be pegged to other economies' standards so as to have a strong regional program, which gives product manufacturers and resellers the certainty and ability to have the benefits of high-volume production and sales in the region. And even after all these decisions are made, one will still encounter implementation challenges, such as how the economy handles inventories of inefficient products in the market before the standard becomes effective.

Because of the high use of cooling and lighting in Brunei Darussalam's residential and commercial sector, Brunei Darussalam has determined that the first two MEPS should be for air conditioning equipment and lighting. The charts below show that cooling consumes between 62% and 74% of building energy and lighting consumes up to 14%.

Nonetheless, there are challenges to setting appropriate levels of standards and developing ratings (labels) that provide the recognition by and information for consumers. For example, in setting appliance and equipment standards, it is critical to set the appropriate level for the desired minimum energy performance, particularly when this is being done in an economy for the first time. Prioritizing which products or equipment to do first is crucial, in order to get the maximum energy savings at the earliest time. It is recommended Brunei Darussalam choice to first select air conditioners considering the amount of energy consumed by this product and there is no prior experience in implement standards and labeling. However, the government should look at establishing a priority list of other products and a timetable as to when it would be appropriate to set energy efficiency standards for them as well.

For additional analytical, marketing, investment and business opportunities information, please contact
Global Investment & Business Center, USA
(202) 546-2103. Fax: (202) 546-3275. E-mail: rusric@erols.com

As for setting standards on air conditioners, the EDPMO has begun to look at what levels other economies have set for their air conditioning standard. This process has also provided the government with a benchmark to view where Brunei Darussalam stands with other economies. For example, looking at the chart below, it can be easily seen that Japan's standard for the common small air conditioners (which are the majority of units sold in the economy), particularly those under 3.6kW but also for under 5kW, are much higher than those sold in Brunei Darussalam.

Brunei Darussalam has also looked at a more similar economy to itself, that of Singapore which has a similar market structure and a similar technology pattern. Using Singapore's standards to benchmark the Brunei Darussalam's standards makes sense from a number of perspective; it will be less work and costly than developing its own standards, it will be expanding the market and volume of those products (and likely bringing down the cost), and it will help harmonize the standard in the region (which benefits the manufacturers as they will not have to manufacture different products with different standards in a single region). However Singapore has recently increased its MEPS, which may make it difficult for a beginner to follow up.

Lighting is the other area where Brunei Darussalam may set an efficiency standard. They have completed the preliminary analysis to determine that a ballast standard for fluorescent lighting is needed since it represents the largest of the various lighting products sold in the economy. As seen in the chart below, standards for ballasts based on the European Community's standard EC 245/2009. It has been suggested that the first standard for electronic ballasts in Brunei Darussalam should be set to the Level 1 standard. The PREE Review Team believes this to be a reasonable level and a good starting point for the new lighting/ballast standard.

Table 7-1: Standards and Ratings for Ballasts in Brunei Darussalam, based on EC 245/2009

During our discussions with the government officials two questions were raised concerning the possible phase out of magnetic ballasts and incandescent lamps. In both instances, the PREE Review Team was in favour of such a phase out as these are two of the most energy consuming products in the lighting industry. The United States, Japan and the European Union have all moved in the past few years to phase out these products. Phasing them out over time was preferred by the manufacturers who knew that the phase out of the wasteful energy products would require them to increase their manufacturing output of the more efficient products and that

For additional analytical, marketing, investment and business opportunities information, please contact
Global Investment & Business Center, USA
(202) 546-2103. Fax: (202) 546-3275. E-mail: rusric@erols.com

they could do so, given a reasonable amount of time. Because these more efficient products are now a much larger share of the market (globally), it means that Brunei Darussalam can phase out the products, but on a faster timeframe.

Overall, the government is proceeding down the proper road in developing energy efficiency standards for its two highest energy consuming products, air conditioners and lighting. Supporting this effort requires both short-term and long-term policy considerations and the resources to fund and staff those who will be responsible for ensuring that the standards setting program will remain robust and viable over the years.

Labels:

Labels are an important part of an appliance/product standard program. Labels help consumers make informed choices about which products to buy when they can compare energy cost savings, consumption, or operating costs when they are ready to purchase a product. Performance labels such as just described are important for consumer education, but an endorsement label which identify products that meet or exceed a specific energy efficiency label are also important.

One of the most widely recognized endorsement labels is that of the United States' Energy Star label – consumers recognize the Energy Star brand and know they are purchasing a product in the highest efficiency category.

Malaysia has a comparative "five star" label system that is easily recognizable and provides a rating (one star worst, 5 stars best) and good consumer information. In addition, Malaysia has a companion label to the Star Label system; an Endorsement Label from its Energy Commission[54].

Labels also pose a number of challenges. For example, just deciding on the type of label and rating scheme can be difficult. Recognition by consumers of the rating scheme (Is 5 stars the highest rating?), the need to brand the label over time, and the amount of information that can be displayed on the label are all important aspects that must be addressed.

A simple and straightforward label is generally best, but some energy (and cost) saving information can be critical to the consumer understanding the full benefit that will accrue to them if they purchase the item. An example of a label that shows both energy use on a comparative basis with other similar product models and the cost to operate the specific product can help the consumer easily determine their cost savings and make a decision as to the product they want to purchase.

Endorsement labels also pose a challenge as over time as more products meet the level set to achieve the label (say that level is the top 25% of all products but over time 50% of all products are at that level), a new higher level must be set to once more ensure the label is endorsing only the top 25% of all products in that category. Consequently, there are many points to ponder in the development of effective labels.

For the most part, EDPMO is at the early stages of label designing and the experts provided many suggestions about characteristics of labelling schemes as described above. When questioned about what types of information to include on a label, the PREE Review Team were unanimous in proposing that cost savings is a critical element to include as it is the most understandable item by the public and the one that will likely influence their decision to purchase. EPDMO acknowledged this advice and will continue the process of developing a label to complement their standard setting program.

For additional analytical, marketing, investment and business opportunities information, please contact
Global Investment & Business Center, USA
(202) 546-2103. Fax: (202) 546-3275. E-mail: rusric@erols.com

7.2 RECOMMENDATIONS

Recommendation 43: *The EDPMO and BNERI should accelerate the development of the National*

Standard and Labelling Regulation, in order to achieve a more rapid transformation of the energy

efficiency market in Brunei Darussalam.

The National Standard and Labelling Regulation should be crafted carefully to ensure that a process is developed to regularly update the standards.

Priority should be given to air-conditioner standards first considering the amount of energy consumed by this product, with lighting standards to follow.

EDPMO should also consider establishing a priority list for other products and a timetable for when it would be appropriate to set energy efficiency standards for these products as well.

Recommendation 44: *Benchmark Brunei Darussalam's standards to established international or other regional standards.*

For instance, the air conditioner standard may be set to the level of energy performance required under other regional economies level (e.g. at Singapore's coefficient of performance (COP)) while for ballasts in lighting products, the EC Level 1 standard may be the initial benchmark.

The benchmark should be updated in step with the other economies' benchmarked standards and signal the market in advance.

Recommendation 45: *Enforcement of the set standards should be a priority. Therefore, plan resources to ensure that stringency is maintained and enforcement is carried out.*

Recommendation 46: *Allow a grace period for sellers to sell out their existing inventory of inefficient products and limit their ability to import such products prior to the standards' effective date.*

Recommendation 47: *Develop a product label that is easily identifiable by consumers and uses a simple rating system.*

For example, use a five-star system, such as the rating systems used on labels in some other Asian economies. Cost savings data should be provided on the label as this is the most understandable metric for consumers and will help them make the most cost effective choice of energy efficient products.

STRATEGIC GOVERNMENT CONTACT IN BRUNEY

Prime Minister's Office
E-Mail: PRO@jpm.gov.bn
Telephone: 673 - 2 - 229988
Fax: 673 - 2 - 241717
Telex: BU2727
Address:
Prime Minister's Office
Istana Nurul Iman
Bandar Seri Begawan BA1000

Audit Department
Prime Minister's Office
Jalan Menteri Besar
Bandar Seri Begawan BB 39 10
Brunei Darussalam
Telephone: (02) 380576
Facsimile: (02) 380679
E-mail: jabaudbd@brunet.bn

Information Department
Prime Minister's Office
Berakas Old Airport
Bandar Seri Begawan
BB 3510
Brunei Darussalam.
E-mail:- pelita@brunet.bn
Fax: 673 2 381004
Tel: 673 2 380527

Narcotics Control Bureau
Prime Minister's Office
Jalan Tungku Gadong
Bandar Seri Begawan BE 2110
Tel No: 02-448877 / 422479 / 422480 / 422481
Fax No: 02-422477
E-mail: ncb@brunet.bn

One-Stop Agency
The Ministry of Industry and Primary Resources
Bandar Seri Begawan 1220
Brunei Darussalam

Telefax: (02) 244811
Telex: MIPRS BU 2111
Cable: MIPRS BRUNEI

Head Policy and Administration Division
Ministry of Industry and Primary Resources
Jalan Menteri Besar, Bandar Seri Begawan 1220
Brunei Darussalam
Tel: (02) 382822

Secretary of Public Service Commission
Old Airport
Bandar Seri Begawan BB 3510
Tel No: 02-381961
E-mail: bplspa@brunet.bn

Semaun Holdings Sdn Bhd
Unit 2.02, Block D, 2nd Floor
Yayasan Sultan Haji Hassanal Bolkiah Complex
Jalan Pretty
Bandar Seri Begawan BS8711
Brunei Darussalam
E-mail address: semaun@brunet.bn

Department of Agriculture
Ministry of Industry & Primary Resources
BB3510
Brunei Darussalam
Telephone: + 673 2 380144
Fax: + 673 2 382226
Telex: PERT BU 2456

Land Transport Department
KM 6, Jalan Gadong,
Beribi BE1110,
Brunei Darussalam.
Tel : (673-2) 451979
Fax : (673-2) 424775
Email : latis@brunet.bn

FOREIGN MISSIONS

AUSTRALIA

Australian High Commission
(His Excellency Mr. Neal Patrick Davis -

High Commissioner)
4th flr Teck Guan Plaza, Jln Sultan
Bandar Seri Begawan BS8811
Brunei Darussalam
or
P.O. Box 2990
Bandar Seri Begawan, BS8675
Brunei Darussalam
Tel: 673 2 229435/6
Fax: 673 2 221652

AUSTRIA

Austrian Consulate General
No. 5 Taman Jubli, Spg 75,
Jalan Subok,
Bandar Seri Begawan BD2717
Brunei Darussalam
or
P.O. Box 1303,
Bandar Seri Begawan, BS8672
Brunei Darussalam
Tel : 673 2 261083
Email: austroko@brunet.bn

BANGLADESH

High Commission of People's Republic of Bangladesh
(His Excellency Mr. Muhammad Mumtaz Hussain - High Commissioner)
AAR Villa, House No. 5,
Simpang 308, Jalan Lambak Kanan,
Berakas, BB1714
Brunei Darussalam
Tel: 673 2 394716
Fax: 673 2 394715

BELGIUM

Consulate of Belgium
2nd Floor, 146 Jln Pemancha
Bandar Seri Begawan BS8711
Brunei Darussalam
or
P.O.Box 65,
Bandar Seri Begawan, BS8670
Brunei Darussalam
Tel: 673 2 222298
Fax: 673 2 220895

BRITAIN

British High Commission
(His Excellency Mr. Stuart Laing - High Commissioner)
Unit 2.01, Block D of Yayasan Sultan
Hassanal Bolkiah
Bandar Seri Begawan BS8711
Brunei Darussalam
or
P.O.Box 2197
Bandar Seri Begawan, BS8674
Brunei Darussalam
Tel: 673 2 222231
Fax: 673 2 226001

CAMBODIA

Royal Embassy of Cambodia
(His Highness Prince Sisowath Phandaravong - Ambassador)
No. 8, Simpang 845
Kampong Tasek Meradun, Jalan Tutong, BF1520
Brunei Darussalam
Tel: 673 2 650046
Fax: 673 2 650646

CANADA

High Commission of Canada
(His Excellency Mr. Neil Reeder - High Commissioner)
Suite 51 - 52, Britannia House, Jalan Cator
Bandar Seri Begawan, BS8811
Brunei Darussalam
Tel: 673 2 220043
Fax: 673 2 220040

CHINA

Embassy of People's Republic of China
(His Excellency Mr. Wang Jianli - Ambassador)
No. 1, 3 & 5, Simpang 462
Kampong Sungai Hanching,
Jln Muara, BC2115
Brunei Darussalam
or
P.O.Box 121
M.P.C, Berakas BB3577
Brunei Darussalam
Tel: 673 2 339609
Fax: 673 2 339612

**For additional analytical, marketing, investment and business opportunities information, please contact
Global Investment & Business Center, USA
(202) 546-2103. Fax: (202) 546-3275. E-mail: rusric@erols.com**

DENMARK

Consulate of Denmark
Unit 6, Bangunan Hj Tahir,
Spg 103, Jln Gadong
Bandar Seri Begawan
Brunei Darussalam
or
P.O.Box 140
Bandar Seri Begawan, BS8670
Brunei Darussalam
Tel: 673 2 422050, 427525, 447559
Fax: 673 2 427526

FINLAND

Consulate of Finland
Bee Seng Shipping Company
No.7 1st Floor Sufri Complex
KM 2, Jalan Tutong
Bandar Seri Begawan, BA2111
Brunei Darussalam
or
P.O.Box 1777
Bandar Seri Begawan, BS8673
Brunei Darusslaam
Tel: 673 2 243847
Fax: 673 2 224495

FRANCE

Embassy of the Republic of France
(His Excelleny Mr. Jean Pierre Lafosse - Ambassador)
#306-310 Kompleks Jln Sultan,
3rd Floor, 51-55 Jln Sultan
Bandar Seri Begawan BS8811
Brunei Darussalam
or
P.O.Box 3027
Bandar Seri Begawan, BS8675
Brunei Darussalam
Tel: 673 2 220960 / 1
Fax: 673 2 243373

GERMANY

Embassy of the Federal Republic of Germany
(His Excellency Klaus-Peter Brandes - Ambassador)
6th flr, Wisma Raya Building
Lot 49-50, Jln Sultan
Bandar Seri Begawan, BS8811
Brunei Darussalam
or
P.O.Box 3050
Bandar Seri Begawan, BS8675
Brunei Darussalam
Tel: 673 2 225547 / 74
Fax: 673 2 225583

INDIA

High Commission of India
(His Excellency Mr. Dinesh K. Jain - High Commissioner)
Lot 14034, Spg 337,
Kampong Manggis, Jln Muara, BC3515
Brunei Darussalam
Tel: 673 2 339947 / 339751
Fax: 673 2 339783
Email: hicomind@brunet.bn

INDONESIA

Embassy of the Republic of Indonesia
(His Excellency Mr. Rahardjo Djojonegoro - Ambassador)
Lot 4498, Spg 528
Sungai Hanching Baru, Jln Muara, BC3013
Brunei Darussalam
or
P.O.Box 3013
Bandar Seri Begawan, BS8675
Brunei Darussalam
Tel: 673 2 330180 / 445
Fax: 673 2 330646

IRAN

Embassy of the Islamic Republic of Iran
No. 2, Lot 14570, Spg 13
Kampong Serusop, Jalan Berakas, BB2313
Brunei Darussalam
Tel: 673 2 330021 / 29
Fax: 673 2 331744

JAPAN

Embassy of Japan
(His Excellency Mr. Hajime Tsujimoto - Ambassador)
No 1 & 3, Jalan Jawatan Dalam

For additional analytical, marketing, investment and business opportunities information, please contact
Global Investment & Business Center, USA
(202) 546-2103. Fax: (202) 546-3275. E-mail: rusric@erols.com

Kampong Mabohai
Bandar Seri Begawan, BA1111
Brunei Darussalam
or
P.O.Box 3001
Bandar Seri Begawan, BS8675
Brunei Darussalam
Tel: 673 2 229265 / 229592, 237112 - 5
Fax: 673 2 229481

KOREA

Embassy of the Republic of Korea
(His Excellency Kim Ho-tae - Ambassador)
No.9, Lot 21652
Kg Beribi, Jln Gadong, BE1118
Brunei Darussalam
Tel: 673 2 650471 / 300, 652190
Fax: 673 2 650299

LAOS

Embassy of the Lao People's Democratic Republic
(His Excellency Mr. Ammone Singhavong - Ambassador)
Lot. No. 19824, House No. 11
Simpang 480, Jalan Kebangsaan Lama
Off Jalan Muara, BC4115
Brunei Darussalam
or
P.O.Box 2826
Bandar Seri Begawan, BS8675
Brunei Darussalam
Tel: 673 2 345666
Fax: 673 2 345888

MALAYSIA

Malaysian High Commission
(His Excellency Wan Yusof Embong - High Commissioner)
No.27 & 29, Simpang 396-39
Kampong Sungai Akar
Jalan Kebangsaan, BC4115
Brunei Darussalam
or
P.O.Box 2826
Bandar Seri Begawan, BS8675
Brunei Darussalam
Tel: 673 2 345652
Fax: 673 2 345654

MYANMAR

Embassy of the Union of Myanmar
(His Excellency U Than Tun - Ambassador)
No. 14, Lot 2185 / 46292
Simpang 212, Kampong Rimba, Gadong
BE3119
Brunei Darussalam
Tel: 673 2 450506 / 7
Fax: 673 2 451008

NETHERLANDS

Netherlands Consulate
c/o Brunei Shell Petroleum Co. Sdn Bhd
Seria KB3534
Brunei Darussalam
Tel: 673 3 372005, 373045

NEW ZEALAND

New Zealand Consulate
36A Seri Lambak Complex,
Jalan Berakas, BB1714
Brunei Darussalam
or
P.O.Box 2720
Bandar Seri Begawan, BS8675
Brunei Darusslam
Tel: 673 2 331612, 331010
Fax: 673 2 331612

NORWAY

Royal Norwegian Consulate
Unit No. 407A - 410A
4th Floor, Wisma Jaya
Jalan Pemancha
Bandar Seri Begawan, BS8811
Brunei Darussalam
Tel: 673 2 239091 / 2 / 3 / 4
Fax: 673 2 239095/6

OMAN

Embassy of the Sultanate of Oman
(His Excellency Mr. Ahmad Moh,d Masoud Al-Riyami - Ambassador)
No.35 Simpang 100,
Jalan Tungku Link
Kampong Pengkalan, Gadong BE3719
Brunei Darussalam

For additional analytical, marketing, investment and business opportunities information, please contact
Global Investment & Business Center, USA
(202) 546-2103. Fax: (202) 546-3275. E-mail: rusric@erols.com

or
P.O.Box 2875
Bandar Seri Begawan, BS8675
Brunei Darussalam
Tel: 673 2 446953 / 4 / 7 / 8
Fax: 673 2 449646

PAKISTAN

Pakistan High Commission
(His Excellency Major General (Rtd) Irshad Ullah Tarar - High Commission)
No.5 Kampong Sungai Akar
Jalan Kebangsaan, BC4115
Brunei Darussalam
Tel: 673 2 6334989, 339797
Fax: 673 2 334990

PHILIPPINES

Embassy of the Republic of Philippines
His Excellency Mr. Enrique A. Zaldivar - Ambassador)
Rm 1 & 2, 4th & 5th floor
Badiah Building, Mile 1 1/2 Jln Tutong
Brunei Darussalam, BA2111
or
P.O.Box 3025
Bandar Seri Begawan, BS8675
Brunei Darussalam
Tel: 673 2 241465 / 6
Fax: 673 2 237707

SAUDI ARABIA

Royal Embassy of Kingdom of Saudi Arabia
No. 1, Simpang 570
Kampong Salar
Jalan Muara, BU1429
Brunei Darusslam
Tel: 673 2 792821 / 2 / 3
Fax: 673 2 792826 / 7

SINGAPORE

Singapore High Commission
(His Excellency Tee Tua Ba - High Commissioner)
No. 8, Simpang, 74,
Jalan Subok, BD1717
Brunei Darussalam

or
P.O.Box 2159
Bandar Seri Begawan, BS8674
Brunei Darussalam
Tel: 673 2 227583 / 4 / 5
Fax: 673 2 220957

SWEDEN

Consulate of Sweden
Blk A, Unit 1, 2nd Floor
Abdul Razak Plaza,
Jalan Gadong,
Bandar Seri Begawan, BE3919
Brunei Darussalam
Tel: 673 2 448423, 444326
Fax: 673 2 448419

THAILAND

Royal Thai Embassy
(His Excellency Thinakorn Kanasuta - Ambassador
No. 2, Simpang 682,
Kampong Bunut, Jalan Tutong, BF1320
Brunei Darussalam
Tel: 673 2 653108 / 9
Fax: 673 2 262752

UNITED STATE OF AMERICA

Embassy of the United States of America
3rd Flr, Teck Guan Plaza,
Jalan Sultan
Bandar Seri Begawan BS8811
Brunei Darussalam
Tel: 673 2 229670
Fax: (02) 225293

VIETNAM

Embassy of the Socialist Republic of Vietnam
(His Excellency Tran Tien Vinh - Ambassador)
No. 10, Simpang 485
Kampong Sungai Hanching
Jalan Muara,BC2115
Brunei Darussalam
Tel: 673 2 343167 / 8
Fax: 673 2 343169

For additional analytical, marketing, investment and business opportunities information, please contact
Global Investment & Business Center, USA
(202) 546-2103. Fax: (202) 546-3275. E-mail: rusric@erols.com

BRUNEI'S MISSIONS IN ASEAN, CHINA, JAPAN AND KOREA

CAMBODIA
Embassy of Brunei Darussalam
No : 237, Pasteur St. 51
Sangkat Boeung Keng Kang I
Khan Chamkar Mon
Phnom Penh
Kingdom of Cambodia
Tel : (855) 23211 457 & 23211 458
Fax : (855) 23211 456
E-Mail : Brunei@bigpond.com.kh

CHINA
Embassy of Brunei Darussalam
No. 3 Villa, Qijiayuan Diplomatic Compound
Chaoyang District
Beijing 100600
People's Republic of China 1000600
Tel : 86 (10) 6532 4093 - 6
Fax : 86 (10) 6532 4097
E-Mail : bdb@public.bta.net.cn

INDONESIA
Embassy of Brunei Darussalam
Wisma GKBI
(Gabungan Koperasi Batik Indonesia)
Suite 1901, Jl. Jend. Sudirman No. 28
Jakarta 10210
Indonesia
Tel : 62 (21) 574 1437 - 39 / 574 1470 - 72
Fax : 62 (21) 574 1463

JAPAN
Embassy of Brunei Darussalam
5-2 Kitashinagawa 6-Chome
Shinagawa-ku
Tokyo 141
Japan
Tel : 81 (3) 3447 7997 / 9260
Fax : 81 (3) 344 79260

REPUBLIC OF KOREA
Embassy of Brunei Darussalam
7th Floor, Kwanghwamoon Building
211, Sejong-ro, Chongro-Ku
Seoul
Republic of Korea.
Tel : 82 (2) 399 3707 / 3708
Fax : 82 (2) 399 3709
E-Mail : kbrunei@chollian.net

LAOS
Embassy of Brunei Darussalam
No. 333 Unit 25 Ban Phonxay
Xaysettha District
Lanexang Avenue
Vientiane
Laos People's Democratic Republic
Tel : (856) 2141 6114 / 2141 4169
Fax : (856) 2141 6115
E-Mail : kbnbd@laonet.net

MALAYSIA
High Commission of Brunei Darussalam
Tingkat 8 Wisma Sin Heap Lee (SHL)
Jalan Tun Razak
50400 Kuala Lumpur
Malaysia.
Tel : 60 (3) 261 2828
Fax : 60 (3) 263 1302
E-Mail : Sjtnbdkl@tm.net.my

THE UNIION OF MYANMAR
Embassy of Brunei Darussalam
No : 51 Golden Valley
Bahan Township
Yangon
The Union of Myanmar.
Tel: 95 (1) 510 422
Fax: 95 (1) 512 854

PHILIPPINES
Embassy of Brunei Darussalam
11th Floor BPI Building
Ayala Avenue, Corner Paseo De Roxas
Makati City, Metro Manila
Philippines
Tel : 63 (2) 816 2836 - 8
Fax : 63 (2) 816 2876
E-Mail : kbnbdmnl@skynet.net

SINGAPORE
High Commission of Brunei Darussalam
325 Tanglin Road
Singapore 247955
Tel : (65) 733 9055
Fax : (65) 737 5275
E-Mail : comstbs@singnet.com.sg

THAILAND
Embassy of Brunei Darussalam
No. 132 Sukhumvit 23 Road
Watana District

Bangkok 10110
Thailand
Tel : 66 (2) 204 1476 - 9
Fax : 66 (2) 204 1486

VIETNAM
Embassy of Brunei Darussalam
No. 4 Thien Quang Street
Hai Ba Trung District
Hanoi
Vietnam
Tel : (84) 4 826 4816 / 4817 / 4818
Fax : (84) 4 822 2092
E-Mail : bruemviet@hotmail.com

FOOD AND RESTAURANTS

Brunei restaurants, including western style fast food centres, cater to a wide range of tastes and palates.
Visitors can also sample authentic local food offered at the tamu night market in the capital.
The market, along the Kianggeh river, is actually open from early morning. It takes on a special atmosphere at night when crowds throng its alleys to shop and eat at the lowest prices in town.
Tropical fruits like watermelon, papaya, mango and banana are also available.
Locals are fond of the Malay-style satay, bits of beef or chicken in a stick, cooked over low fire and dipped in a tangy peanut sauce.

Brunei's first Chinese halal restaurant is Emperor's Court, owned by Royal Brunei Catering, which caters to Cantonese and Western tastebuds.

A list of restaurants in the capital and Seria-Kuala Belait areas follows:
Bandar Seri Begawan
Aumrin Restaurant, 1 Bangunan Hasbullah, 4 Jalan Gadong
Airport Restaurant, Brunei International Airport
Coffee Tree, Unit 3, top floor ,Mabohai Shopping Complex
Emperor's Court, 1st Floor, Wisma Haji Mohd Taha, Jalan Gadong
Excellent Taste, G5 Gadong Properties Centre, Jalan Gadong
Express Fast Food, 22/23 Jalan Sultan
Ghawar Restaurant, 3 Ground Floor Bang Hasbullah 4
Jade Garden Chinese Restaurant, Riverview Inn, Km 1 Jalan Gadong
Jolibee Family Restaurant, Utama Bowling Centre, Km 11/2 Jalan Tutong
Kentucky Fried Chicken (B) Sdn Bhd, G15-G16 Plaza Athirah
Lucky Restaurant, Umi Kalthum Building, Jalan Tutong
McDonald's Restaurant, 10-12 Block H, Abdul Razak Complex, Simpang 137, Gadong
Phongmun Restaurant, Nos. 56-60, 2nd Floor Teck Guan Plaza
Pizza Hut, Block J, Unit 2 & 3 Abdul Razak Complex
Pondok Sari Wangi, 12 Blk A, Abdul Razak Complex, Jalan Gadong
Popular Restaurant, 5, Ground floor, PAP Hajjah Norain Building
QR Restaurant, Blk C, Abdul Razak Complex, Jalan Gadong
Rainbow Restaurant, 110 Jalan Batu Bersurat, Gadong
Rasa Sayang Restaurant, 607 Bangunan Guru-Guru Melayu
Rose Garden Restaurant, 8 Blk C, Abdul Razak Complex, Jalan Gadong
Season's Restaurant, Gadong Centrepoint
SD Cafe, 6-7 Bangunan Hj Othman, Simpang 105, Jalan Gadong
Seri Kamayan Restaurant, 4 & 5 Bangunan Hj Tahir ,Simpang 103, Jalan Gadong
Seri Maradum Baru, Block C6, Abdul Razak Complex
Sugar Bun Fast Food, Lot 16397 Mabohai Complex, Jalan Kebangsaan
Schezuan's Dynasty Restaurant, Gadong Centrepoint
Swensen's Ice Cream and Fine Food Restaurant, 17-18 Ground Floor Bagunan Halimatul Sa'adiah, Gadong
Tenaga Restaurant, 6 1st Floor Bangunan Hasbollah 4
The Stadium Restaurant, Stadium Negara Hassanal Bolkiah

For additional analytical, marketing, investment and business opportunities information, please contact
Global Investment & Business Center, USA
(202) 546-2103. Fax: (202) 546-3275. E-mail: rusric@erols.com

Tropicana Seafood Restaurant, Block 1 Ground Floor, Pang's Building,Muara
Kuala Belait/Seria
Belait Restaurant, Jalan Bunga Raya
Buccaneer Steak House, Lot 94 Jalan McKerron
Cottage Restaurant, 38 Jalan Pretty
Jolene Restaurant, 83,1st Jalan Bunga Raya
New China Restaurant, 39/40 3rd Floor, Ang's Building, Jalan Sultan Omar Ali, Seria
New Cheng Wah Restaurant, 14 Jalan Sultan Omar Ali, Seria
Orchid Room, B5, 1st Floor, Jalan Bunga Raya
Red Wing Restaurant, 12 Jalan Sultan Omar Ali, Seria
Tasty Cake Shop/Pretty Inn, 26 Jalan Sultan Omar Ali, Seria
Tasconi's Pizza, Simpang 19, Jalan Sungai Pandan

WHERE TO SHOP

For many travellers one of the pleasures of visiting another country is finding something of interest and value for one's self, family or friends. There are many shops in Brunei offering a wide variety of goods at competitive prices. These range from modern department stores to small market stalls where bargaining is still commonly practised.

Modern department stores are found in the major towns of Bandar Seri Begawan, Tutong, Kuala Belait and Seria. In addition to these departmental stores there is a wide variety of old-fashioned shophouses as well as more modern air-conditioned shops.

Most items ranging from the latest electronic goods and imported luxury goods to common household items and groceries can be conveniently found in these shops.

Traditional items that reflect the culture of Brunei like the brass cannon, kris and kain songket, better known as "jong sarat" are excellent souvenirs to bring home from a visit to the country. These can be purchased at the Arts and Handicrafts Centre which is located off Kota Batu, and also at the airport.

Before leaving Brunei make sure you stop by the Duty Free shops at the airport. These offer a wide range of luxury goods, garments, jewellery, writing instruments, perfumes, handicrafts, Brunei souvenirs, books and chocolates at very reasonable prices.

SHOPPING CENTRES

Hua Ho Department Store, Jln Gadong, Bandar Seri Begawan

Kota Mutiara Department Store, Bangunan Darussalam, Bandar Seri Begawan

Lai Lai Department Store, Mile 1 Jln Tutong, Bandar Seri Begawan

Millimewah Department Store (BSB), Bangunan Darussalam, Bandar Seri Begawan

Millimewah Department Store (Tutong),Tutong

Millimewah Department Store (Seria), Seria

For additional analytical, marketing, investment and business opportunities information, please contact
Global Investment & Business Center, USA
(202) 546-2103. Fax: (202) 546-3275. E-mail: rusric@erols.com

Princess Inn Department Store, Mile 1 Jln Tutong , Bandar Seri Begawan

Tiong Hin Superstore,Jln Muara, Bandar Seri Begawan

Megamart,Jln Gadong, Bandar Seri Begawan

Wisma Jaya Complex, Jln Pemancha, Bandar Seri Begawan

First Emporium & Supermarket, Mohammad Yussof Complex, Jln Kubah Makam DiRaja, Bandar Seri Begawan

Seria Plaza, Seria

Seaview Department Store, Jln Maulana, Kuala Belait

TRAVEL AGENTS

BANDAR SERI BEGAWAN

Antara Travel & Tours Sdn Bhd 02-448805/808
Anthony Tours & Travel Sdn Bhd 02-228668
Borneo Leisure Travel Sdn Bhd 02-223420
Brunei Travel Services Sdn Bhd 02-236006
Century Travel Centre Sdn Bhd 02-227296
Churiah Travel Service 02-224422
Darat Dan Laut 02-426321
Freme Travel Services Sdn Bhd 02-234277
Halim Tours & Travel Sdn Bhd 02-226688
Intan Travel & Trading Agencies 02-427340
Jasra Harrisons (B) Sdn Bhd 02-236675
JB Travel & Insurance Agencies 02-239132
JJ Tour Service (B) Sdn Bhd 02-224761
Ken Travel & Trading Sdn Bhd 02-223127
Mahasiswa Travel Service 02-243452
Oriental Travel Services 02-226464
Overseas Travel Services Sdn Bhd 02-445322
Sarawak Travel Service Sdn Bhd 02-223361
Seri Islamic Tours & Travel Sdn Bhd 02-243341
Straits Central Agencies (B) Sdn Bhd 02-229356
Sunshine Borneo Tours & Travel Sdn Bhd 02-441791
SMAS 02-234741
Travel Centre (B) Sdn Bhd 02-229601
Travel Trade Agencies Sdn Bhd 02-229601/228439
Tai Wah Travel Service Sdn Bhd 02-224015
Tenega Travel Agency Sdn Bhd 02-422974
Titian Travel & Tours Sdn Bhd 02-448742
Twelve Roofs / Perusahaan Hj. Asmakhan 02-340395
Wing On Travel & Trading Agencies 02-220536
Zizen Travel Agency Sdn Bhd 02-236991
Zura Travel Service Sdn Bhd 02-234738

KUALA BELAIT

Freme Travel Services Sdn Bhd 03-335025
Jasra Harrisons Sdn Bhd 03-335391
JJ Tour Service Sdn Bhd 03-334069
Limbang Travel Service Sdn Bhd 03-335275
Overseas Travel Service Sdn Bhd 03-222090
Southern Cross Travel Agencies Sdn Bhd 03-334642
Straits Central Agencies Sdn Bhd 03-334589
Usaha Royako Travel Agency 03-334768

SELECTED COMPANIES

- Advance Computer Supplier and Services
- AJYAD Publishing
- Akitek SAA Home Page
- Amalgamated Electronic Sdn. Bhd.
- Anthony Tours & Travel Agency
- Baharuddin & Associates Consulting Engineers
- Beseller Sdn Bhd Homepage
- BIT Computer Services
- BruDirect Business Centre
- Brunei Hotel
- Brupost
- CfBT Homepage
- Compunet Computer & Office Systems
- Dalplus Technologies, Brunei
- DN Private Investigation and Security Consultant
- DP Happy Video House
- Elite Computer Systems Sdn. Bhd.
- Fabrica Interior Furnishing Co
- Glamour Homepage
- HSBC
- HSE Engineering Sdn. Bhd.
- Indah Sejahtera Development & Services
- Insurans Islam Taib
- Interhouse Marketing Sdn. Bhd.
- International School Brunei
- IP and Company
- ISS Thomas Cowan Sdn. Bhd.
- Jerudong Park Medical Centre
- Kristal
- L & M Prestressing Sdn. Bhd.
- Megamas Training Company Sdn. Bhd.
- Mekar General Enterprise Homepage
- Micronet Computer School
- National Insurance Company Berhad
- Paotools Supplies & Services Co.
- Petar Perunding Sdn. Bhd.
- Petrel Jaya Sdn Bhd
- Phongmun Restaurant Homepage
- Poh Lee Trading Company
- Q-Carrier

- Sabli Group of Companies - Brunei Darussalam
- Scanmark Design Sdn Bhd
- SDS System (B) Sdn. Bhd.
- SEAMEO VOCTECH Homepage
- Singapore Airlines
- Sistem Komputer Alif Sdn Bhd
- SPCastro And Associates Sdn Bhd
- Sunshine Borneo Tour & Travel Sdn.Bhd.
- Survey Service Consultants
- Syabas Publishers
- Syarikat Suraya Insan
- Syarikat Intellisense Technology
- Tabung Amanah Islam Brunei
- Tang Sung Lee Sdn. Bhd.
- The Lodge Resort (In Brunei)
- Trinkets Enterprise
- Twelve Roofs / Perusahaan Hj. Asmakhan
- Unicraft Enterprises
- Utama Komunikasi

BRUNEI LEGAL SYSTEM BASICS

The British Residential system was introduced in Brunei Darussalam by virtue of the Courts Enactment of 1906. Another enactment was later introduced, known as the 1908 Enactment and had repealed the 1906 Enactment. The purpose of this second Enactment was to amend the law relating to the constitution and powers of the Civil and Criminal Courts and the law and procedures to be administered in Brunei Darussalam (hereafter called the "State").

By virtue of section 3 of the 1908 Enactment, five courts were constituted in the State for the administration of Civil and Criminal justice. There were:

(1) The Court of the Resident

(2) Courts of Magistrate of the First Class

(3) Courts of Magistrate of the Second Class

(4) Courts of Native Magistrates

(5) Courts of Kathis.

The first court would be the Court of the Resident, which had and exercised original and appellate jurisdiction in civil and criminal matters. The Officer, which presided the Court of the Resident, should either be the Resident; or the District Judge of the District Court of Labuan or any District Judge of the Colony of the Straits Settlements[1].

The Court of the Resident had jurisdiction in all suits, matters and questions of a civil nature except the power to authorize any Court in the State to dissolve or annul a marriage lawfully solemnised in the United Kingdom of Great Britain and Ireland or in any British Colony, Protectorate or Possession[2].

For additional analytical, marketing, investment and business opportunities information, please contact
Global Investment & Business Center, USA
(202) 546-2103. Fax: (202) 546-3275. E-mail: rusric@erols.com

Its appellate jurisdiction in both civil and criminal matters would be to hear and determine all appeals from the decisions of the lower Courts; and in doing so might exercise full powers or supervision and revision in respect of all proceedings in such Courts[3].

Section 8A of the 1908 Enactment stated that the Courts of Magistrates was of two kinds

i.e. Courts Magistrates of the First Class, and Courts Magistrates of the Second Class.

For the Court of Magistrate of the First Class, its criminal jurisdiction would be to try all offences for which the maximum term of imprisonment provided by law did not exceed a term of 7 years imprisonment of either description or which were punishable with fine only and for any other offence in respect of which jurisdiction was given by law; whereas

[1] Section 4 of the 1908 Enactment. [2] Section 5(i) of the 1908 Enactment. [3] Section 7 of the 1908 Enactment.

for civil jurisdiction it would hear and determine all suits when the amount in dispute or the value of the subject matter did not exceed $1,000 [4].

In addition to that, such Court had power to grant, alter, revoke and annul probates of wills and letters of administration in the estate of all persons leaving movable or immovable property in the State or the time of death having a fixed place of abode within the State where such estate does not exceed in value $2,500[5]. Such Court also had power to appoint and control guardians of infants and lunatics[6].

For its appellate jurisdiction, the Court of Magistrate of the First Class had power to hear and determine all appeals from the decisions of inferior Courts both in civil and criminal matters, and had power for revision and supervision in respect of all proceedings in such Courts[7].

For the Court of Magistrate of the Second Class, its criminal jurisdiction would be to try all offences for which the maximum term of imprisonment provided by law does not exceed 3 years imprisonment of either description or which were punishable with fine only of a sum not exceeding $100 and any offence in respect of which jurisdiction is given to the Court of a Magistrate of the Second Class.[8]

In its civil jurisdiction, the Court of Magistrate of the Second Class would hear and determine all suits when the amount in dispute or the value of the subject matter does not exceed $ 100.[9]

Unlike the Court of Magistrate of the First Class, the Court of Magistrate of the Second Class had no power to grant probate of wills or letters of administration, to appoint and control guardians of infants and lunatics, or even to hear appeals in civil or criminal matters[10].

As for the Court of a Native Magistrate, it could hear and determine all suits brought by or against Malays or other Asiatics in which the amount in dispute or the subject matter does not exceed $25 while its criminal jurisdiction would be to try and determine cases in which the maximum amount of imprisonment prescribed by law did not exceed three months[11].

And lastly, the Court of a Kathi that had such powers in all matters concerning Islamic religion, marriage and divorce as may be defined in his "Kuasa."[12].

For additional analytical, marketing, investment and business opportunities information, please contact
Global Investment & Business Center, USA
(202) 546-2103. Fax: (202) 546-3275. E-mail: rusric@erols.com

[4] Section 8B (i) of the 1908 Enactment. [5] Section 8B (ii)(a) of the 1908 Enactment. [6] Section 8B (ii)(b) of the 1908 Enactment. [7] Section 8B (iii) of the 1908 Enactment. [8] Section 8C (i) of the 1908 Enactment. [9] Section 8C (i) of the 1908 Enactment. [10] Section 8C (ii) of the 1908 Enactment. [11] Section 9 of the 1908 Enactment. [12] Section 9 of the 1908 Enactment.

Sentences that might be imposed by the various Courts:

(1) Court of the Resident – any sentence authorized by law.

(2) Courts of Magistrate of the First Class – Imprisonment for a term not exceeding two years. Fine not exceeding $1,000. Whipping not exceeding 12 strokes.

(3) Courts of Magistrate of the Second Class – Imprisonment for a term not exceeding fourteen days. Fine not exceeding $50.

(4) Courts of Native Magistrates and Kathis – Fine not exceeding $10.[13]

Apart from the five courts mentioned earlier, there was the Supreme Court. The is court or any Judge thereof would have the original jurisdiction in the case of any offence charged to had been committed within the State for which the punishment of death is authorised by law[14].

The Supreme Court had civil appellate jurisdiction for an appeal from the final decision of the Court of the Resident in any civil action or proceeding where the amount in dispute or the subject matter exceeded$1,000 except in any of the following cases where no such appeal might be made:

(1) where the judgment or order was made by the consent of parties;

(2) where the judgment or order relates to costs only;

(3) where by any Enactment for the time being in force the judgment or order of the Court of the Resident was expressly declared to be final[15].

The criminal appellate jurisdiction of the Supreme Court would be to hear appeal from any decision of the Court of the Resident in the exercise of its original jurisdiction whereby any person had been convicted and sentenced to not less than two years imprisonment or to a fine of not less than $ 500[16].To make an appeal, the appellant would lodge a petition of appeal at the Court of the Resident addressed to the Supreme Court within seven days from the date when the judgment or order was pronounced or within such further time as may be allowed by the Court of the Resident[17]. Any judgment of order of the Court of Appeal or of the Supreme Court made under this Enactment should be executed, enforced and be given effect by the Court of the Resident[18].

However, under this Enactment there was still scope for an appeal against any judgment or order of the Court of Appeal in any civil matter. This appeal might be made to His Britannic Majesty in Council (i.e. Privy Council) subject to such rules and regulations as may be prescribed by order of His Majesty in Council[19].

[13] Section 13 of the 1908 Enactment. [14] Section 14 (i) of the 1908 Enactment. [15] Section 15 (i) of the 1908 Enactment. [16] Section 16 (1) of the 1908 Enactment. [17] Section 16(2) of the 1908 Enactment. [18] Section 17 of the 1908 Enactment. [19] Section 18 of the 1908 Enactment.

For additional analytical, marketing, investment and business opportunities information, please contact
Global Investment & Business Center, USA
(202) 546-2103. Fax: (202) 546-3275. E-mail: rusric@erols.com

THE COMING OF ISLAM TO BRUNEI DARUSSALAM

Being a state where majority of the populations are Muslims, Islam has been made the official religion of Brunei Darussalam. To say that Islam has only been practiced in this country in recent years are quite incorrect as there are sources, which date the establishment of a Muslim sultanate rule. In fact, Islamic laws have always been the governing laws in Brunei Darussalam even before the coming of the British.

There are evidences which show that Islam had come to Brunei since the 10th century. However, its reception was slow probably because most of the populations during that time were still holding on to their beliefs in Hinduism. Muslims were comprised of just a small section of the population including those traders who came to Brunei[20]. And it was believed that the acceptance of the Sultans and nobles had started the spread of Islam among the community. Awang Alak Betatar, the first ruler of Brunei, embraced Islam when he married the princess of Johore [21]. He changed his name to Sultan Mohammad Shah and since then Islam slowly spread within Brunei.

Islam was quickly spread among most of the people in Brunei when Sultan Sharif Ali, the third Sultan of Brunei, ascended to the throne. Believed to be a descendant of the Prophet Muhammad (Peace Be Upon Him)[22], he was a pious person and was the one who had started to build mosque and had been the one who determined the direction of the Qiblat[23]. From then on Islam has become an important aspect in the life of people in Brunei where eventually it has become the official religion of Brunei Darussalam.

Other evidence that shows Brunei was indeed been governed by Islamic law can be seen in written and codified form. There exist two manuscripts, the first manuscript was called the "Hukum Kanun Brunei" which, contained 96 pages and is kept at the Language and Literature Bureau, whilst copy for reference can be found at the Brunei Museum reference no. A/BM/98/90[24]. While the second manuscript was known as "Undang-Undang dan Adat Brunei Lama" (Old Brunei Law and Custom). It consists of 68 pages and is now reserved in the Sarawak Museum[25].

The content of the first manuscript covered a wide range of laws including the Islamic laws of hudud and qisas. The overall content of the manuscript is in harmony with the Islamic law. For example: Clause One of the manuscript talks about relationship between people and its ruler, conditions of becoming a ruler, responsibilities of the people towards

[20] Prof. Dato Dr. Haji Mahmud Saedon A. Othman, *Ke Arah Pelaksanaan Undang-Undang Di Negara Brunei Darussalam*, Jurnal Undang-Undang Syariah Brunei Darussalam, Januari-Jun 2002 Jilid 2 Bil. 2 p.

[21] Pehin Jawatan Dalam Seri Maharaja Dato Seri Utama Dr. Haji Awang Mohd. Jamil Al-Sufri, *Tarsilah Brunei: Sejarah Awal dan Perkembangan Islam*, Jilid 1, Pusat Sejarah Brunei 2001, p. 33. [22] Ibid p. 80. [23] Ibid p. 90. [24] Prof. Dato' Dr. Hj Mahmud Saedon bin Awang Othman, *Undang-Undang Islam Dalam Kesultanan Melayu Brunei hingga Tahun 1959,* International Seminar on Brunei Malay Sultanate in Nusantara 1999, p.

its rulers; Clause Four talks about various kind of offences such as murder, stabbing, slaying, hitting, robbery, stealing and many other though no punishment for those offences were stated in this Clause; Clause Five talks about the punishment of qisas for murder and also for the murderer to be killed in return for his crime; Clause Seven talks about offence of stealing, the punishment of which would be to cut off certain part of his hand; Clause Twenty-Five talks about marriage, requirements of marriage and the words to be uttered during the marriage contract; Clause

For additional analytical, marketing, investment and business opportunities information, please contact
Global Investment & Business Center, USA
(202) 546-2103. Fax: (202) 546-3275. E-mail: rusric@erols.com

twenty-Six talks about number of witnesses in a marriage contract; Clause Thirty-One talks about the rule and conditions in sale and purchase contract; and other clauses which talks about wide ranges of laws that is in accordance with Islamic laws. [26]

The *Hukum Kanun Brunei* was written during the reign of Sultan Hassan though it was believed that it had been started even earlier than that. It was completed and enforced during the reign of Sultan Jalilul Akbar and then continued during the reign of his son, Sultan Jalilul Jabbar. With the enforcement of this law, Islamic law has been enforced and that it had became the basic law and policy of Brunei Darussalam at that time[27].

THE CONSTITUTION

The governing structure of Brunei Darussalam rests on the country's written Constitution along with the three pillars of its national philosophy, namely Malay, Islam and Monarchy.

Brunei Darussalam's written Constitution sets out its governing authorities along with their respective functions and responsibilities. Specifically, the Constitution sets out the executive authority over the affairs of Brunei Darussalam and further creates the Council of Ministers, the Religious Council, the Privy Council, the Legislative Council, the *Adat Istiadat* (Customs and Traditions) Council and the Council of Succession. The basic order, structure, functions, responsibilities and underlying principles of the governing authorities are premised on what is prescribed in the Constitution. In relation to the law making process, it sets out the procedure within Brunei Darussalam with the recent rejuvenation of the Legislative Council, which will be discussed in detail later.

The Constitution of Brunei Darussalam was originally enacted in September 1959 much to the efforts of our then Sultan, Al-Marhum Sultan Haji Omar Ali Saifuddien Sa'adul Khairi Waddien, who is also the present Sultan's late father. The enactment of the 1959 Constitution represented the country's primary stepping stone in its move towards full independence, which eventually came in 1984.

Since 1959, the Constitution has been subject to a number of important amendments, in particular in 1971, 1984 and most recently in 2004. In fact, a newly revised Constitution was published in 2004 incorporating all the amendments that have been made since its birth year of 1959.

STATUTES/LEGISLATIVE ENACTMENTS

Brunei Darussalam has in place a set of acts compiled in volumes called "Laws of Brunei." At present, there are 193 Acts in place which are in loose leaf form kept in ring binder volumes that consist of legislations that were passed prior to Independence Day and those that were enacted after it. Some of the legislations are also Acts that were extended from the United Kingdom, some dating back as early as 1958. However, some have been notably repealed, either in whole or in part to reflect updates in the development of the law. There are however some old enactments that have been merely omitted from the Laws of Brunei as authorized by His Majesty for the Attorney General to omit. Nevertheless, its omission does not mean that they do not have the force of law and hence would still be considered valid unless it is otherwise provided.[1]

There are also a number of *Government Gazettes* which consists of: i) new laws that has not been revised to become an Act;

For additional analytical, marketing, investment and business opportunities information, please contact
Global Investment & Business Center, USA
(202) 546-2103. Fax: (202) 546-3275. E-mail: rusric@erols.com

Since Brunei Darussalam at present pass their laws in accordance with article 83(3) of the Constitution, any new laws that has been approved by His Majesty will be published in *Government Gazette* form and will come into force on the date His Majesty approves of. Hence that new law will for the time being be referred to as an Order and not an Act.

The Law Revision Act is in place to govern the revision of such *Gazettes* to turn into Acts. After the 1st of January of every year, the Attorney General revises the law and publishes a revised edition of the new law to be included in the Laws of Brunei volumes. He also does this with existing law that has been amended so he will publish a new revised edition of that law incorporating all the recent amendments. [2]

The following constitutional and legislative documents are also considered part of the Laws of Brunei.[3] They are:

i) Treaty of Friendship and Co-operation between Brunei Darussalam and the

United Kingdom dated 7th January 1979;

ii) The Continental Shelf Proclamation 1954

iii) The North Borneo (Definition of Boundaries) Order in Council 1958; and

iv) The Sarawak (Definition of Boundaries) Order in Council 1958.

ISLAMIC LAWS

In Islam, the main source of law is the Holy Qur'an then followed by the tradition of the Prophets or Hadith as the second source of the Islamic Laws[4]. Other sources of law in Islam includes *Ijma'* or consensus of opinion[5], *Qiyas* (Analogical Deduction)[6], *Istihsan* or Equity in Islamic Law[7], *Maslahah Mursalah* (Consideration of Public Interest)[8], *'Urf* (Custom)[9], *Istishab* (presumption of Continuity)[10], *Saad al-Dhara'i* (Blocking the Means)[11].

Similarly, Islamic laws in Brunei Darussalam are guided mainly by the principles in the Holy Qur'an and the Prophet's tradition or Hadith as well as other sources mentioned earlier. Islam as the official religion in Brunei Darussalam is clearly stated in the Constitution of Brunei Darussalam:

[2] Section 7 of the Law Revision Act [3] Schedule to the Law Revision Act [4] Mohammad Hashim Kamali, *Principles of Islamic Jurisprudence*, Second Revised Edition, Ilmiah Publishers Sdn. Bhd., Kuala Lumpur 1998, p. 58. [5] ibid p.168. [6] ibid p.197. [7] ibid p.245. [8] ibid p.267. [9] ibid p.283. [10] ibid p.297. [11] ibid p.310.

"The official religion of Brunei Darussalam shall be the Islamic Religion: Provided that all other religions may be practiced in peace and harmony by the persons professing them.[12]"

Islamic law in Brunei is still governed under the Religious Council and Kadis Courts Act (Chapter 77), an Act which consolidates the law relating to the Religious Council and the Kadis Courts, the constitution and organization of religious authorities and the regulation of religious affairs.

Apart from this Act, there are also other legislations enforced in Brunei Darussalam to govern the conduct of Muslims in this country, these legislations are for example:

For additional analytical, marketing, investment and business opportunities information, please contact
Global Investment & Business Center, USA
(202) 546-2103. Fax: (202) 546-3275. E-mail: rusric@erols.com

i) the Syariah Courts Act (Chapter 184), an Act which make specific provisions in respect of the establishment of Syariah Courts, appointments, powers of Syar'ie Judge and jurisdiction of Syariah Courts and other matters connected with the proceedings of Syariah Courts, and for the determination and confirmation of the new moon;

ii) the Syariah Courts Evidence Order, 2001, an Order relating to the law of evidence for the Syariah Courts;

iii) the Emergency (Islamic Family Law) Order, 1999, an Order that make certain provisions relating to Islamic family law in respect of marriage, divorce, maintenance, guardianship and other matters connected with family life;

iv) the Islamic Adoption of Children Order, 2001, an Order to make certain provisions on the law of adoption of children according to Islam; and

v) the Halal Meat Act (Chapter 183) an Act which regulate the supply and importation of halal meat and related matters.

SUBSIDIARY LEGISLATION

We also have in place as part of the Laws of Brunei, a number of subsidiary legislations which include rules, regulations, orders, proclamations or other documents that has the force of law and annexed to their relevant parent Acts. Other government departments whose work is relevant to that particular legislation would usually prepare the drafts for subsidiary legislations.

The power to make subsidiary legislation is conferred under section 13 of the Interpretation and General Clauses Act (CAP. 4). Section 16 further states that the subsidiary legislation should be published in the *Government Gazette.*

CASE LAW/JUDICIAL PRECEDENT

The Supreme Court of Brunei Darussalam is largely guided by the written Constitution and the Laws of Brunei in executing their responsibility of upholding the law in Brunei Darussalam. However where there are no written laws on a particular matter, the courts would then turn to principles of law that are found in case law or judicial precedent.

[12] Article 3(1) of the Constitution of Brunei Darussalam.

Cases heard in Brunei Darussalam are compiled in annual volumes of what are called "Judgments of Brunei Darussalam." Similar to other members in the family practicing the English Legal System, Brunei Darussalam also practice the doctrine of *stare decisis,* where decisions of a higher court are binding on the lower courts. The advantages of following binding precedent include certainty, flexibility, comprehensiveness and practicality in its practice. However, it is recognized that sometimes it can be difficult for lower courts that are bound by the decision and therefore cannot alter it. For that reason also, it may create more appeals.

The courts of Brunei Darussalam would also occasionally refer to cases from Malaysia, Singapore, India and the United Kingdom, all practicing the English legal system though the decisions in those cases would not be binding but instead would only be regarded as "persuasive authority" in the courts of Brunei Darussalam.

For additional analytical, marketing, investment and business opportunities information, please contact
Global Investment & Business Center, USA
(202) 546-2103. Fax: (202) 546-3275. E-mail: rusric@erols.com

COMMON LAW OF ENGLAND

Under the Application of Laws Act, the Common Law of England and the doctrine of equity, together with the statutes of general application that are administered or in force in England, also have the force of law in Brunei Darussalam. This provision is however on the condition that the said common law, doctrine of equity and statutes of general application does not contradict the circumstances of Brunei Darussalam, its inhabitants and subject to such qualifications or local circumstances and custom may render necessary.

GOVERNMENT AND THE STATE

THE EXECUTIVE

As stated under section 4 of the Constitution, the supreme executive authority of Brunei Darussalam is vested in and shall be exercised by His Majesty the Sultan and Yang Di-Pertuan of Brunei Darussalam who is also the Prime Minister of Brunei Darussalam. Nevertheless, His Majesty the Sultan may still appoint Ministers or Deputy Ministers to exercise that executive authority whilst solely being responsible to him in the course of their duties. These appointed ministers shall also assist and advise His Majesty the Sultan in the event His Majesty discharges his executive authority.

THE LEGISLATIVE COUNCIL

Under the Constitution, any member of the Legislative Council may introduce any bill and a bill will only become law when His Majesty the Sultan has assented, signed and sealed the bill with the Seal of the State.

The Legislative Council was temporarily suspended in 1983 but was recently reestablished at its first official meeting in September 2004. During the period where the Council was inactive, laws were passed in the form of emergency orders by His Majesty in accordance with article 83(3) of the Constitution. The normal procedure of the law making process during this period would be initiated by a particular Ministry or Government Department who would either propose or prepare the draft legislation and would then pass it to the Attorney General's Chambers to give legal advice on. Where a Ministry or Governmental Department merely propose the drafting of such legislation, the Attorney General's Chambers will then prepare the draft based on substantive points the former provides. Once the draft is ready to be adopted, it will be presented to His Majesty for his approval. The draft legislation that His Majesty approves of will be passed in an **Emergency Order** form and will be published in the *Government Gazette.*

Every order made under article 83(3) however are deemed to have been validly made, to be fully effectual and to have had full force from the date on which such Proclamation or Order was declared or made and they are deemed to have been passed by the Legislative Council.[1]

The law making process by the Legislative Council is prescribed under Part VII of the Constitution. Basically, any member of the Legislative Council may

(i) introduce a new bill;
(ii) propose a motion for the Council to debate on; or

(iii) present any petition to the Council. The bill, motion or petition will then be debated on and disposed of in accordance with the Standing Orders of the Legislative Council.

For additional analytical, marketing, investment and business opportunities information, please contact
Global Investment & Business Center, USA
(202) 546-2103. Fax: (202) 546-3275. E-mail: rusric@erols.com

[1] Article 83A

Every bill that is going to be introduced needs to be published in the gazette and within 7 days of the publication of the bill in a gazette, the bill shall then be laid before the Legislative Council.[2]

There are certain matters however that are generally excluded from being discussed by the Legislative Council, unless His Majesty the Sultan approves otherwise, and these include matters relating to the issue of bank notes, the establishment of any bank association, amendment of the constitution in relation to both those matters. Matters that would also be disqualified are where the issues are inconsistent with any obligations imposed upon His Majesty under any international treaty or agreement with another power of state. Other disqualified matters include those having the effect of lowering or adversely affecting the rights, positions, discretions, powers, privileges, sovereignty or prerogatives of His Majesty, the standing or prominence of Brunei Darussalam's national philosophy that is Malay Islamic Monarchy and the finances or currency of Brunei Darussalam.[3]

All questions proposed to the Legislative Council to decide upon shall be concluded by way of majority vote taken from the members that are present and voting. Once a bill has been debated on, the Legislative Council will then make a decision whether or not to pass it. If the Council rejects it, which is called a "negative resolution", the Speaker of the Council will then have to submit a report to His Majesty the Sultan incorporating a summary of the debate and the reasons why the Council reached such a resolution. Nevertheless, His Majesty may still declare the Bill to have effect, notwithstanding the negative resolution and he may order it to have effect either as an Act in the form in which it was introduced or to include any amendments that he may think fit to include.[4]

When the Legislative Council decides to pass the Bill, such Bill will only become law if His Majesty the Sultan assents to it, signs it and thereafter seals the Bill with the official State Seal. Again, the bill might take effect as an Act either in its original form as to how it was introduced or His Majesty the Sultan may still make amendments to it as he thinks fit. Such law once assented, signed and sealed by His Majesty shall come into operation on the date on which such assent shall be given.[5]

All the laws made through the Legislative Council shall be styled as "Acts" which will always have the enacting words as follows: "Be it enacted by His Majesty the Sultan and Yang DI-Pertuan with the advice and consent of the Legislative Council as follows."[6]

His Majesty the Sultan also has reserved powers over any bills that was not or has not yet been passed by the Legislative Council if in his opinion, the passing or expedited passing of the Bill is in the interests of public order, good faith and good government. In such

[2] Article 41, the Constitution [3] Article 42 [4] Article 43 [5] Article 45 [6] Article 46

cases, he can declare that bill/motion/petition /business to have effect as if it had been passed or carried by that Council even though it has not been done so.[7]

THE JUDICIARY

THE SUPREME COURT

For additional analytical, marketing, investment and business opportunities information, please contact
Global Investment & Business Center, USA
(202) 546-2103. Fax: (202) 546-3275. E-mail: rusric@erols.com

The Supreme Court of Brunei Darussalam is the body wholly responsible for the administration of justice in civil law (as opposed to "syariah law") and strictly speaking has within its hierarchical structure, the Court of Appeal and the High Court. Within the same building of the Supreme Court, we can also find the Intermediate Courts and the Courts of Magistrates (also known as the Subordinates Courts).

The head of administration for the Judiciary Department is the Chief Registrar whereas the entire judicial system is presided over and supervised by the Chief Justice.

Introduction

The Supreme Court is governed by the Supreme Court Act[8] along with its Rules annexed to the Act. The Rules of the Supreme Court regulates the practice and procedure of the High Court and the Court of Appeal. The Supreme Court consists of the President of the Court of Appeal, the Chief Justice, the Judges and the Judicial Commissioners of the Supreme Court. The jurisdiction of the Supreme Court is over any original and appellate criminal and civil cases by the High Court and also appellate criminal and civil jurisdiction by the Court of Appeal.[9]

The judges of the High Court at present consist of the Chief Justice along with two judges who are often referred to as Justices. The Court of Appeal judges are the President and two other appellate judges.

Jurisdiction

The civil jurisdiction of the High Court consists of the original jurisdiction and authority similar to that held and exercised by the Chancery, Family and Queen's Bench Divisions of the High Court of England and shall also include any other jurisdiction, original or appellate as may be conferred upon it by any other written law.[10]

The criminal jurisdiction of the High Court consists of such jurisdiction, original or appellate, as may be conferred upon it by any written law, which includes the Penal Code, the Criminal Procedure Code or the Criminal Conduct (Recovery of Proceeds) Order. In the Criminal Procedure Code specifically,[11] the High Court will have jurisdiction over any offence that was committed wholly or partly within Brunei Darussalam, or committed on board any ship or aircraft registered in Brunei Darussalam,

[7] Article 47, The Constitution [8] CAP 5 of the Laws of Brunei [9] Section 6, Supreme Court Act [10] Section 16, Supreme Court Act [11] Section 7 of the Criminal Procedure Code

or committed on the high seas if the offence is one of piracy by the law of nations. The Court will also have jurisdiction over an offence whether or not it was committed in Brunei Darussalam if it was committed by a subject of His Majesty the Sultan or by a person who abets, or enters a conspiracy to commit, an offence of Brunei Darussalam whether or not any overt act in furtherance of such conspiracy takes place within Brunei Darussalam. The High Court may also pass any sentence authorized by law. [12]

Any civil or criminal appeals from the High Court can be brought to the Court of Appeal.

The civil jurisdiction of the Court of Appeal consists of appeals from a judgment or order of the High Court in a civil cause or matter and again, such other jurisdiction conferred upon it by any

For additional analytical, marketing, investment and business opportunities information, please contact
Global Investment & Business Center, USA
(202) 546-2103. Fax: (202) 546-3275. E-mail: rusric@erols.com

other written law. The criminal jurisdiction of the Court of Appeal consists of appeals from the High Court.[13]

Appeals

Any civil appeals made from the Court of Appeal can only be referred by His Majesty the Sultan to the Judicial Committee of Her Britannic Majesty's Privy Council. For criminal cases however, no such appeals from the Court can be further made. There can be no civil appeals made if the appeal is[14]:

(i) against an order made allowing for an extension of time for appealing against a judgment or order;
(ii) a judgment that has been expressed to be final by any law;

(iii) any order made with the consent of all parties to the case;

(iv) any order relating only to costs;
(v) made without leave of the High Court of the Court of Appeal where the amount or value of the subject matter does not exceed $10,000 or where it is from any interlocutory order of judgment.

Extended jurisdiction of the High Court

Along with the exercise of its own jurisdiction as mentioned above, the High Court also has a general supervisory and revisionary jurisdiction over the Intermediate Courts and the Magistrates' Courts. Any time during a proceeding in an Intermediate Court or a Magistrates' Court, a High Court judge can always call for and check the record of proceedings and thereafter can either transfer the matter or proceedings to the High Court of he could also give directions as to the further conduct of the proceeding by the Intermediate or Magistrates' Court. Upon the High Court calling for any record in this instance, all such proceedings in the Intermediate or Subordinate Courts shall be stayed pending further what the High Court will order later on. The High Court may also feel the need to call on any decision recorded or passed by the Intermediate or Magistrates' Courts to assess the correctness, legality or propriety of the decision recorded. If they are not satisfied with their findings, they can direct for a new trial or whatever action that is necessary to secure that substantial justice is done.[15]

[12] Section 10 of the Criminal Procedure Code [13] Section 18, 19, Supreme Court Act [14] Section 20, Supreme Court Act [15] Section 20A to 20E, Supreme Court Act

INTERMEDIATE COURTS

Introduction

The Intermediate Court is governed by the Intermediate Courts Act.[16] It is an open court to which the public generally has access to.[17] However, the same provisions with regards to power to hear proceedings in camera that was are mentioned below for Magistrates Court likewise applies to the Intermediate Courts. The Intermediate Court is presided over by a Judge who sits alone.[18] There are also registrars and deputy registrar who shall also be ex-officio commissioners for oaths and notaries public.[19]

Jurisdiction

The Intermediate Court's criminal jurisdiction[20] runs concurrently with the High Court. Hence, it has all the jurisdiction, powers, duties and authority as are vested, conferred and imposed on the High Court in the exercise of its **original** criminal jurisdiction.

The Court however does not have jurisdiction in respect of any offence that is punishable with death or with imprisonment for life. Nor does it have jurisdiction in respect of any offence that imposes a period of imprisonment that is longer than 20 years. If it so happens that after the trial ends and a conviction is secured, and it appears to the Court that the imprisonment imposed should be longer than 20 years or should carry a more serious penalty, then the Intermediate Court may commit the case to the High Court for sentencing.

Where the High Court and the Intermediate Court has concurrent jurisdiction in respect of any prosecution or proceeding, the Public Prosecutor or any person expressly authorized by him in writing, can direct in which those courts the proceeding should be instituted in.

The Intermediate Court exercises its original civil jurisdiction[21] in every action where the amount claimed or the value of the subject matter in dispute exceeds $15, 000 but does not exceed $100,000 or any higher sum that the Chief Justice may further prescribe. Similarly to the provisions for the Magistrate Court, to obtain this jurisdiction, one has to further prove that the cause of action arose in Brunei Darussalam or the defendant at the time the proceedings were instituted has some form of connection with Brunei Darussalam, be it being a resident or carrying on a business etc, or the facts of the case the proceedings are based on must be alleged to have occurred in Brunei Darussalam.

[16] CAP 162 of the Laws of Brunei [17] Section 7, Intermediate Courts Act [18] Section 10, Intermediate Courts Act [19] Section 11, Intermediate Courts Act [20] See Part IV of the Intermediate Courts Act [21] See Part V of the Intermediate Courts Act

The Court does not have civil jurisdiction over the recovery of immovable property or where there is a dispute as to a title registered under the Land Code, over the interpretation of a trust instrument, the grant or revocation of probate, over the interpretation of a will, over a declaratory decree, over the legitimacy of any person, over the guardianship or custody of a minor and over the validity or dissolution of any marriage.

In an action concerning immovable property that commenced in the Intermediate Court, a defendant may within one month apply to the High Court for the action to be transferred to the High Court if he feels that there is a dispute as to a title registered under the Land code. If a High Court judge is satisfied, he may order the action to be transferred to the High Court.

Also, not taking into account that the amount claimed should not be more than $100,000, an Intermediate Court has jurisdiction over any action for the recovery of immovable property with or without a claim for rent or profits if there is no dispute as to title registered under the Land Code.

Any judgement of an Intermediate Court should be regarded by the Parties as final and conclusive between themselves.

The Intermediate Court also has jurisdiction to grant probate and letters of administration in respect of the estate within Brunei Darussalam of a deceased person and the estate in respect of which the grant is applied for but it must be exclusive of what the deceased possessed of and over what the applicant is entitled to as a trustee and not a beneficiary, and without deducting anything on the account of debts due or owing, the amount claimed must not exceeds $250,000.

For additional analytical, marketing, investment and business opportunities information, please contact
Global Investment & Business Center, USA
(202) 546-2103. Fax: (202) 546-3275. E-mail: rusric@erols.com

When a plaintiff has a cause of action for more than $100,000, which the Intermediate Court does not have jurisdiction over, it is possible for him to abandon the excess amount in order to bring it within the jurisdiction of the Intermediate Court. However he will not be able to recover any of the excess amounts that he abandoned. Nevertheless, if the amount is more than $100,000, the Intermediate Court can still have jurisdiction when and if the parties concerned agree by a signed memorandum filed in the Intermediate Court that it shall have jurisdiction, even though the amount claimed exceeds $100,000.

In an Intermediate Court proceeding, if the counterclaim or defence of any defendant involves a matter beyond the Intermediate Court's jurisdiction, any party may apply to the High Court within one month of being served the counterclaim, for an order that the whole proceedings, or just proceedings on the counterclaim defence to be transferred to the High Court.

Appeals

Civil appeals goes straight to the Court of Appeal as if it was an appeal from the High Court. However there will be no right of appeal entertained if the parties to the action have agreed in writing that the judgment of the court shall be final and conclusive between them.[22]

Criminal appeals also go to the Court of Appeal. The Court of Appeal can also review any sentencing that has been passed by the Intermediate Court on any person or provide an opinion on a point of law that has been referred to it.[23] The practice and procedure as contained in the Supreme Court Rules for the High Court and the Court of Appeal shall also apply to the Intermediate Court.

MAGISTRATES' COURT

Introduction

The Magistrate Courts are governed by the Subordinate Courts Act[24], in terms of its civil jurisdiction and by the Criminal Procedure Code[25] in the exercise of its criminal jurisdiction. There is also in place a set of Subordinate Courts Rules regulating and prescribing the procedure (including methods for pleading) and the practice in the Magistrate Courts in the exercise of its civil jurisdiction. These Rules of Court extends to all matters of procedures, practice relating to or concerning the effect or operation in law of any procedure or practice, enforcement of judgments or orders, in any case within the cognizance of the Magistrate Court.

All magistrate courts are deemed to be open and allow public access, however there are some instances when a Court may still direct to have the whole proceedings or only in part to be in camera sitting only[26]. In particular, where references are made, whether orally or in writing, directly to any act, decision, grant, revocation, suspension, refusal, omission, authority or discretion by His Majesty the Sultan or if there are cases that intends to refer to any issue that may directly or indirectly concerns the inviolability, sanctity or interests of the position, dignity, standing, honour, eminence or sovereignty of His Majesty the Sultan, then the Magistrate Court shall hold such proceedings in camera, so long as His Majesty the Sultan has not himself issued a direction that such proceedings need not be heard in camera.

Jurisdiction

The Magistrate Court exercises its civil jurisdiction[27] over every civil proceeding where the amount claimed or the value of the subject matter in dispute does not exceed B$30,000.

For additional analytical, marketing, investment and business opportunities information, please contact
Global Investment & Business Center, USA
(202) 546-2103. Fax: (202) 546-3275. E-mail: rusric@erols.com

However, if the matter is heard before the Chief Magistrate, Chief Registrar, Deputy Chief Registrar, Senior Magistrate or the Senior Registrar this prescribed limit would be B$50,000.

[22] Section 26, Intermediate Courts Act [23] Section 27, Intermediate Courts Act [24] CAP 6 of the Laws of Brunei [25] CAP 7 of the Laws of Brunei [26] Section 7, Subordinate Courts Act [27] See Section 17 of the Subordinate Courts Act

For the court to have jurisdiction of the case, the cause of action need to have arose in Brunei Darussalam, the defendant at the time the proceedings were instituted has some form of connection with Brunei Darussalam, be it being a resident or carrying on a business etc, and the facts of the case the proceedings are based on must be alleged to have occurred in Brunei Darussalam.

Furthermore, a Magistrate Court also has jurisdiction in any proceedings for the recovery of immovable property where the rent payable in respect of such property does not exceed $500 per month. This excludes cases where there is a genuine dispute as to title registered under the Land Code.

A Magistrate Court does not have any civil jurisdiction over acts done by the order of His Majesty the Sultan, over the recovery of immovable property where there is a genuine dispute as to the title registered under the Land Code, over cases involving specific performance and rescission of contracts, over the cancellation or rectification of instruments, over the interpretation of trust instruments and the enforcement of administration of trusts, the grant of probate or letters of administration in respect of a deceased person, over the interpretation of wills, administration of estate of any deceased person and lastly it does not have civil jurisdiction over declaratory decrees.

The Magistrate's court criminal jurisdiction[28] is similar to the High Court's criminal jurisdiction as mentioned above. Namely, the court will have jurisdiction over any offence that was committed wholly or partly within Brunei Darussalam, or committed on board any ship or aircraft registered in Brunei Darussalam, or committed on the high seas if the offence is one of piracy by the law of nations. The Court will also have jurisdiction over an offence whether or not it was committed in Brunei Darussalam if it was committed by a subject of His Majesty the Sultan or by a person who abets, or enters a conspiracy to commit, an offence of Brunei Darussalam whether or not any overt act in furtherance of such conspiracy takes place within Brunei Darussalam. Furthermore, the types of offences the magistrate court may try are any offence that is shown in the eighth column of the First Schedule of the Criminal Procedure Code to be so triable. However, if the offence it is given the power to try carries a maximum punishment the court has no power to award, it shall then commit the defendant for trial by the High Court if it holds the opinion that the punishment it has power to award is inadequate.

The criminal jurisdiction of magistrates conferred by the Criminal Procedure Code include hearing, trying, determining and disposing of summarily prosecutions for offences cognized by such magistrate and inquiring into offences committed with a view to committal for trial by the High Court. Magistrates also have the power and authority to inquire into complaints of offences, summon and examine relevant witnesses, summon and issue warrants for the apprehension of criminals and offenders, and deal with them according to law, issue search warrants, hold inquests and do all other matters and things which a magistrate is empowered to do by this Code or any other Act.

[28] See section 7 of the Criminal Procedure Code

For additional analytical, marketing, investment and business opportunities information, please contact
Global Investment & Business Center, USA
(202) 546-2103. Fax: (202) 546-3275. E-mail: rusric@erols.com

Appeals

Any appeal in a civil matter in the Magistrate Court goes to the High Court.[29] Such appeals that has right to do so are cases where a Magistrate Court has given a final judgment in any proceedings for the recovery of immovable property or in any proceedings where the amount in dispute exceeds $500. Leave for appeal is needed from a judge with respect of an interlocutory order, from a final judgment of a Magistrate Court where the amount claimed or the value of the subject matter in dispute does not exceed $500. Leave from the judge is also required from an order relating to costs and also for any orders that were made by consent of the parties.

It is important for the appellant to keep in mind that he must also fulfill all other conditions of appeal imposed in accordance with the Rules of Court of the Supreme Court Act.

In a criminal matter, if a defendant, the complainant or the Public Prosecutor is not satisfied with any judgment, sentence or order given by the magistrate, he may appeal to the High Court against such judgment, sentence or order for any error in law or in fact, or on the ground that the sentence is either to extensive or too inadequate.

A Magistrate Court can also, at any time before or during any civil proceeding, request a legal opinion from the High Court if it desires to do so. Either the Magistrate initiates the request or it can also be made on the application of any of the parties. They shall forward a statement of the facts of the case and specify the exact points on which legal opinion is being sought. The High Court will then make a declaration or order in response to the query as it thinks fit.[30]

APPOINTMENT OF JUDGES, REGISTRARS AND OTHER RELEVANT PERSONS WITHIN THE SUPREME COURTS, INTERMEDIATE COURTS AND SUBORDINATE COURTS

The High Court and Court of Appeal judges are appointed by His Majesty the Sultan by instrument under his sign manual and the State Seal.[31] To become a judge of the Supreme Court, one has to be or has been a judge of a Court having unlimited jurisdiction over civil and criminal matters in some part of the Commonwealth or a Court having jurisdiction in appeals from any such Court. He must also have been entitled to practice as an advocate in such a court for a period of not less than 7 years. The judges of the Supreme Court hold their positions until the age of 65 or at a later time where His Majesty may approve of.

His Majesty may also from time to time appoint someone who satisfies the same conditions as mentioned above for the Supreme Court judges to be a Judicial Commissioner of the Supreme Court.[32] The Judicial Commissioner has the power to act as a Judge of the Supreme Court and all things done by him in accordance with the terms

[29] Section 17, Subordinate Courts Act [30] Section 22, Subordinate Courts Act [31] Section 7, Supreme Court Act [32] Section 11, Supreme Court Act

of this appointment will be deemed to have the same validity and effect as if it has been done by a judge.

An Intermediate Court judge is also appointed by His Majesty. To qualify for appointment, he must have been entitled to practice in a court having unlimited jurisdiction in civil and criminal matters in Brunei Darussalam or some part of the Commonwealth for not less then 5 years.[33]

For additional analytical, marketing, investment and business opportunities information, please contact
Global Investment & Business Center, USA
(202) 546-2103. Fax: (202) 546-3275. E-mail: rusric@erols.com

Finally, magistrates are also appointed by His Majesty, in particular a Chief Magistrate who shall have seniority over all other Magistrates and Coroners. His Majesty can also appoint any fit and proper person to be a Coroner who shall have the same power to act as a Magistrate for the purpose of discharging the functions of a Magistrate. Hence, their actions shall have the same validity and effect as if they had been done by a Magistrate.[34]

SYARIAH COURT

The Syariah Courts in Brunei Darussalam consist of the Syariah Subordinate Courts, the Syariah High Court and the Syariah Appeal Court. These courts will have such jurisdiction, powers, duties and authority as are conferred and imposed by the Syariah Courts Act (Chapter 184) as well as by any other written law.[35]

For appointment of Judges in the Syariah Courts, Part II of this Act, among others, talks about the appointment of Chief Syar'ie Judge, the Syariah Appeal Court Judges, Syariah High court Judges and Syariah Subordinate Courts Judges.

Section 8(1) of this Act, stated that His Majesty the Sultan and Yang Di-Pertuan may, on the advice of the President of the Majlis Ugama Islam and after consultation with the Majlis, appoint a Chief Syar'ie Judge.[36] To be qualified as a Chief Syar'ie Judge, a person must be a citizen of Brunei Darussalam; and he has served as either a Judge of a Syariah Court, or Kadi, or in both capacities, for a cumulative period of not less than 7 years prior to his appointment or that he is a person learned in *Hukum Syara*'[37].

For Syariah Appeal Court Judges, section 9(1) of this Act, stated that His Majesty the Sultan and Yang Di-Pertuan may, on the advice of the President of the Majlis and after consultation with the Majlis, appoint and re-appoint not more than 5 Muslims to form a standing panel of Judges, for a period of not exceeding 3 years. For each proceeding in the Syariah Appeal Court, the Chief Syar'ie Judge shall elect 2 of them to constitute a quorum of Judges. Again, a person qualified to be appointed as one of the Judges in the Syariah Appeal Court must be a citizen of Brunei Darussalam and he has served as either a Judge of a Syariah Court, or Kadi, or in both capacities, for a cumulative period of not

[33] Section 10, Intermediate Courts Act [34] Section 9-11, Subordinate Courts Act [35] Section 6(1) of the Syariah Courts Act (Chapter 184). [36] Section 8(1) of the Syariah Courts Act (Chapter 184). [37] Section 8(2) of the Syariah Courts Act (Chapter 184).

less than 7 years prior to his appointment, or that he is a person learned in *Hukum Syara*'[38].

Section 10(1) of this Act provides for appointment of Syariah High court Judges whereby His Majesty the Sultan and Yang Di-Pertuan may, on the advice of the President of the Majlis and after consultation with the Majlis, appoint Judges of the Syariah High Court. To be qualified as one, a person must be a citizen of Brunei Darussalam; and has, for a cumulative of not less than 7 years prior to his appointment, served as either a Judge of a Syariah Subordinate Court, or Kadi, or registrar, or Syar'ie Prosecutor, or in more than one of such capacities; or that he is a person learned in Hukum Syara'[39].

And for appointment of Syariah Subordinate Courts Judges, section 11 of this Act provides that His Majesty the Sultan and Yang Di-Pertuan may, on the advice of the President of the Majlis and after consultation with the Majlis, appoint Judges of the Syariah Subordinate Courts.

For additional analytical, marketing, investment and business opportunities information, please contact
Global Investment & Business Center, USA
(202) 546-2103. Fax: (202) 546-3275. E-mail: rusric@erols.com

Under this Act, the Chief Syar'ie Judge and Syariah High Court Judges shall hold office until the age of 65 years or until such later time as may be approved by His Majesty the Sultan and Yang Di-Pertuan[40]. However, any Syar'ie Judges including the Chief Syar'ie Judge, may at any time resign from his office by sending to His Majesty the Sultan and Yang Di-Pertuan a letter of resignation under his hand, through the Majlis or the Chief Syar'ie Judge, but he may not be removed from his office or his service terminated except in accordance with the provisions of subsections (3), (4) and (5) of section 12(1) of this Act.

As mentioned earlier, Syariah Courts in Brunei Darussalam consists of Syariah Subordinate Courts, the Syariah High Court and the Syariah Appeal Court each with its own jurisdictions.

The Syariah High Court has both criminal and civil jurisdiction. In its criminal jurisdiction it shall try any offence punishable under any written law which provides for syariah criminal offences, under any written law relating to Islamic family law or under any other written law which confers on it jurisdiction to try any offence, and may impose any punishment provided therein[41].

In its civil jurisdiction, the Syariah High Court shall hear and determine all actions and proceedings relating to –

(i) betrothal, marriage (including *ta'at balik*), divorce, *khulu'*, *fasakh*, *cerai ta'liq*, determination of turns, *li'an*, *illa* or any matrimonial matter;
(ii) any disposition of or claim to any property arising out of any matter set out in the above paragraph.

[38] Section 9(2) of the Syariah Courts Act (Chapter 184). [39] Section 10(2) of the Syariah Courts Act (Chapter 184). [40] Section 12(1) of the Syariah Courts Act (Chapter 184). [41] Section 15*(a)* of the Syariah Courts Act (Chapter 184).

(iii) maintenance of dependants, legitimacy (*ithbatun nasab*) or guardianship or custody (*hadanah*) of infants;

(iv) division of or claims to *harta sepencarian*;
(v) wills or gifts during *maradal-maut* of a deceased Muslim;
(vi) gift *inter vivos* (*hibah*), or settlement (*sulh*) made without adequate monetary consideration or value by Muslim;

(vii) *waqaf* or *nazar*;

(viii) division of and inheritance of property, testate or intestate;

(ix) determination or persons entitled to part of the estate of a deceased Muslim or part of the property which such persons are respectively entitled to; or
(x) other matters in respect of which jurisdiction is conferred by any written law.[42]

For Syariah Subordinate Courts, their criminal jurisdiction are to try offence punishable under any written law which provides for syariah criminal offences, prescribing offences where the maximum punishment provided for does not exceed $10,000 or imprisonment for a period not exceeding 7 years or both and may impose any punishment provided therefor[43].

In their civil jurisdiction, the Syariah Subordinate Courts shall hear and determine all actions and proceedings which the Syariah High Court is empowered to hear and determine, where the

For additional analytical, marketing, investment and business opportunities information, please contact
Global Investment & Business Center, USA
(202) 546-2103. Fax: (202) 546-3275. E-mail: rusric@erols.com

amount or value of the subject-matter in dispute does not exceed $500,000 or is not capable of estimation in terms of money[44]. This jurisdiction may, form time to time, be increased by His Majesty the Sultan and Yang Di-Pertuan on the recommendation of the Chief Syar'ie Judge, by notifying it in the *Gazette*[45].

Jurisdiction of the Syariah Appeal Court shall be to hear and determine any appeal against any decision made by the Syariah High Court in the exercise of its original jurisdiction[46]. Whenever an appeal against a decision of the Syariah Subordinate Court has been determined by the Syariah High Court, the Syariah Appeal Court may, on application by any party, grant leave for any question of law in the public interest which has arisen in the course of the appeal, and where the decision of the Syariah High Court has affected the determination of the appeal, to be referred to the Syariah Appeal Court for its decision. Whenever leave is granted by the Syariah Appeal Court, it shall hear and determine the questions allowed to be referred for its decision and make any order which the Syariah High Court might have made, and as it thinks just for the disposal of the appeal.

[42] Section 15*(b)* –do-. [43] Section 16(1)*(a)* of the Syariah Courts Act (Chapter 184). [44] Section 16(1)*(b)* Ibid. [45] Section 16(2) Ibid. [46] Section 20(1) Ibid.

Apart from having its original jurisdiction, the Syariah High Court shall have supervisory and revisionary jurisdiction over all Syariah Subordinate Courts[47]. Similarly, the Syariah Appeal Court shall have that same power over the Syariah High Court[48].

OTHER RELEVANT LEGAL DEPARTMENTS

The Attorney General's Chambers

The Attorney General is the principal legal adviser to the Government of His Majesty the Sultan and shall advise on all legal matters connected with the affairs of Brunei Darussalam or by the Government of Brunei Darussalam.[49] He is assisted by the Solicitor General and counsels, in advising the Government and representing the Government in civil and criminal cases. The Attorney General is also responsible for the drafting of legislation. In carrying out the task of legislative drafting, the Attorney General's Chambers work closely with other Government Ministries and Departments.

The Attorney General is vested with the power under the Constitution to institute, proceed and discontinue once instituted, any criminal proceedings. All criminal prosecutions are instituted in the name of the Public Prosecutor. In carrying out this duty, the Attorney General is not subject to the direction or control of any other person or authority. He is assisted by Deputy Public Prosecutors in the conduct of criminal trials held in the Supreme Court and the Subordinate Courts.

The Attorney General basically has the exercisable power to institute, conduct or discontinue, at his discretion, any proceedings of an offence other than proceedings before a Syariah Court or a Court Martial, subject to the provisions of any other written law.

In addition, the Public Prosecutor and his Deputies also advise, and direct prosecution undertaken by the police and other law enforcement departments including rendering advice in their investigations.

Apart from carrying out the above duties, the Attorney General's Chambers also provides services to the public by maintaining the following registries; Companies, Business names, Trade Marks, Industrial designs, Inventions, Power of Attorney, Marriages, Bills of Sales.

There are five legal divisions in the Attorney-General's Chambers: Civil Division, Criminal Justice Division, International Law Division, Legislative Drafting Division and the Registry Division.

Syariah department

In 1980, a Committee of Harmonizing Laws In Accordance With Islam[50], was formed. To increase this effort, a Legal Unit[51] chaired by the Chief Kadi was established in 1988 by the Ministry of Religious Affairs its task mainly to replace the earlier committee. In 1993, a Committee for the establishment of Syariah Supreme Court known as the Action Committee Towards the Establishment of Syariah Supreme Court[52] was formed. Another committee known as the Islamic Family Law Legislative Committee[53] was later established in 1995, its tasks are to study, legislate and prepare Islamic family laws as well as other laws governed by the Kadis Court. This Legal Unit, in 1997, was eventually alleviated to its present position as a separate department in the Ministry of Religious Affairs now known as the Islamic Legal Unit.[54]

Among the duties of this Unit are to study, examine and do research on provisions in the Laws of Brunei now enforced to see whether or not there is any conflict with *Hukum Syara'*; prepare proposed draft amendment for any legal provision that conflict with *Hukum Syara'* and prepare draft legislation in accordance with *Hukum Syara'* if there is no such legislation available yet. This Unit is also appointed secretariat for several committees that had been mentioned above. Apart from that, this Unit also gives advice concerning Islamic laws to the Syariah Courts, the Faith Control Unit (Unit Kawalan Akidah), the Prosecution Section, the Investigation Section, the Family Counseling Section, the Attorney General's Chambers as well as other government departments and private firms.[55]

LEGAL PROCEDURE

CRIMINAL PROSECUTION

As stated in the Criminal Procedure Code, the general direction and control over criminal prosecutions and proceedings in Brunei Darussalam is under the responsibility of the Attorney General who is also the Public Prosecutor. His Majesty may also from time to time appoint Deputy Public Prosecutors who will be under the general control and direction of the Public Prosecutor. Deputy Public Prosecutors are conferred the powers under the Criminal Procedure Code as are delegated to them by the Public Prosecutor.

The Public Prosecutor may also by notification in the *Government Gazette* delegate all or any of his powers vested to him under the Criminal Procedure Code to any Deputy Public Prosecutor. Thus the exercise of these powers by the Deputy Public Prosecutor would be treated as if they had been exercised by the Public Prosecutor so long as Public Prosecutor does not revoke the delegation.

The Criminal Procedure Code also specifically states that every criminal prosecution and every inquiry can also be conducted by some other person expressly authorized in writing by the Public Prosecutor or His Majesty the Sultan. In those cases, a police officer or an officer of a Government Department in relation to minor cases and cases that is relevant to that particular Government Department, such as the Customs Department, the Immigration Department, the

For additional analytical, marketing, investment and business opportunities information, please contact
Global Investment & Business Center, USA
(202) 546-2103. Fax: (202) 546-3275. E-mail: rusric@erols.com

Narcotics Control Bureau and the Anti-Corruptions Bureau who do have their own prosecuting officers also conduct criminal prosecution for their relevant cases.

CRIMINAL PROCEDURE

INVESTIGATIONS

The Police are given powers to search a property and in doing so they are required to prepare a list of the things that have been seized and this document is to be signed by the officer in charge of the search and seizure. The owner of the property being searched must be present at the time the search is conducted. [1]

The police officer during the investigation stage can also take a written statement from a witness or a suspect and the person being interviewed is required to answer all questions posed to him in relation to the case being investigated on. The police officer is required to repeat the statement back to the person being questioned and he must thereafter sign the statement. [2] All statements made can be used as evidence if the person questioned becomes a witness during proceedings thereafter.[3]

[1] Section 69 of the Criminal Procedure Code [2] Section 116 of the Criminal Procedure Code [3] Section 117 of the Criminal Procedure Code

When interviewing a potential defendant, the police officer is always required to read out the defendant's rights to him after the charge is explained to him. The Courts only accept voluntarily made statements whether or not the contents of the statement are true. There is no right of silence in Brunei Darussalam as the Courts may as a consequence treat silence as a detrimental factor for the defendant.

Once a suspect is arrested, he shall be placed in remand or released on bail. If the remand is ordered by the Magistrate, the defendant cannot be remanded for more than 15 days. On the other hand, if it was ordered by the High Court, there is no time limit.[4]

PRE-TRIAL PROCEDURE

With the exception of some offences that would need the prior sanction of the Public Prosecutor or the official complaint of a concerned public servant, a Judge or magistrate may take cognizance of an offence upon receiving a complaint launched by a complainant[5], upon his own knowledge or suspicion that an such offence has been committed or when any person who is in custody without process, has been brought before him for committing an offence that the Judge or magistrate has jurisdiction to inquire into or try.[6]

Once the Judge or magistrate takes cognizance of the offence and is satisfied that there is sufficient ground for proceeding, he will either issue a summons for the accused to attend court or if it is in relation to an offence that requires a warrant to be issued first, he would then issue the warrant in the first instance and also issue a summons that specifies the accused to appear at a certain time before him or some other Judge or magistrate having jurisdiction over the case. [7]

Preliminary Inquiries

Preliminary inquiries are always held for offences against the State, murder or any offence which carries a death penalty. [8]

For additional analytical, marketing, investment and business opportunities information, please contact
Global Investment & Business Center, USA
(202) 546-2103. Fax: (202) 546-3275. E-mail: rusric@erols.com

Preliminary Inquiries are generally held for a magistrate to determine whether there is sufficient evidence to commit the case for trial in the High Court (filteration). Other cases like trafficking of drugs and rape cases go straight to the High Court without any preliminary inquiries. All other cases are generally tried summarily in the Magistrate Court.

At a preliminary inquiry, the Prosecutor will present its case and set out all the evidence, including examining witnesses, in support of its case to the Magistrate. The defendant is allowed to cross examine the witnesses who can then also be re-examined by the Prosecutor. If the magistrate, after hearing all the evidence, feels that there are insufficient grounds for committing the accused, he could either discharge him or he can

[4] Section 223 of the Criminal Procedure Code [5] Section 133 of the Criminal Procedure Code [6] Section 131 of the Criminal Procedure Code [7] Section 136 of the Criminal Procedure Code [8] Section 138 of the Criminal Procedure Code

still order that the defendant be tried before himself or before some other magistrate. In the latter case, he will consequently frame a charge and call upon the defendant to plead to those charges. [9] However if the magistrate finds that there are sufficient grounds for committing him for trial, he shall then commit the accused for trial before the High Court.[10]

If the accused is committed to trial to High Court, the magistrate will give the accused the opportunity to give a list of witnesses he wishes to be summoned to give evidence for his trial. The final list of witnesses shall be included in the record of the magistrate.[11]

Once the accused has been committed for trial, the committing magistrate shall then send the original record and all the relevant documents, weapons (if any) or any other thing which is to be produced in evidence to the Court the accused is committed to. A list of all the exhibits is also forwarded with the record. The record will specifically contain the following information[12]:

i) the serial number of the case;

ii) the date of the commission of the offence;

iii) the date of the complaint, if any;

iv) the name, age, sex, residence, if known, and nationality (or race) of the accused;

v) the offence complained of and the offence proved, and the value of the

property, if any, in respect of which the offence has been committed;

vi) the date of the summons or warrant and of the return day of the summons, if any, or on which the accused was first arrested;

vii) the date on which the accused first appeared or was brought before a magistrate;

viii) the name and title of the officer or other person conducting the prosecution;

ix) the date of making each adjournment or postponement, if any, and the date to

For additional analytical, marketing, investment and business opportunities information, please contact
Global Investment & Business Center, USA
(202) 546-2103. Fax: (202) 546-3275. E-mail: rusric@erols.com

which such adjournment or postponement was made and the grounds for making the same;

x) the date on which the proceedings terminated;

xi) the order made;

xii) the depositions;

xiii) the statement, if any, of the accused;

xiv) the charge; and

xv) the list of witnesses as provided by the accused.

The law also allows for committal without the consideration of evidence. This method is referred to as paper committal and is done through the submission of written statements only. [13] Hence a written statement can be substituted for oral evidence and it would have

[9] Section 141 of the Criminal Procedure Code [10] Section 144 of the Criminal Procedure Code [11] Section 145 of the Criminal Procedure Code [12] Section 147 of the Criminal Procedure Code [13] Section 151A and 151B of the Criminal Procedure Code

a similar effect to be admissible under the Evidence Act. It must however satisfy the following conditions:

a) the statement must be signed by the person who made it;

b) the statement must contain a declaration by that person that the information he has written is true to the best of this knowledge and belief;

c) a copy of the statement must be given to each of the other parties to the proceedings not less then 7 days before the statement is tendered in evidence;

d) none of the other parties objects to the statement being tendered in evidence.

Bail applications[14]

The defendant or his counsel may also apply for bail (whilst investigations are still being carried out) before a magistrate, High Court Judge or Intermediate Court Judge, depending on the seriousness of the case. In deciding to grant that application, the magistrate will consider two opposing factors. [15] On one hand, the Court must remember that the accused is innocent only until proved otherwise. However, the Court shall also take into consideration that the interests of justice will be perverted if the accused absconds or tampers with the witnesses.

At present, all magistrates have the power to grant bail for all type of cases by virtue of their appointments as Registrars of the Supreme Court. However, in practice, bail applications in serious cases that are triable in the High Court or Intermediate Court will be remitted to either court for such applications to be heard. These particular points will be taken into account on deciding whether or not the defendant should be released on bail:

For additional analytical, marketing, investment and business opportunities information, please contact
Global Investment & Business Center, USA
(202) 546-2103. Fax: (202) 546-3275. E-mail: rusric@erols.com

i) Is the offence bailable or non bailable under Schedule 1 of the Criminal

Procedure Code? However, the Court still has discretion to grant bail for non-bailable offences;

ii) The nature and gravity of the offence;

iii) The number of charges;

iv) The likelihood of the accused absconding;

v) The previous record of the accused;

vi) Strength of evidence; and

vii) Other relevant factors like the age and health of the accused.

The usual conditions attached to bail are cash bail, the duty to report to the nearest police station at a prescribed number of times a week, the assurance that the accused will not tamper with witnesses and to not approach certain places, to surrender his passport and other travel documents and to remain indoors between certain hours.

Pre-Trial Review

Sometimes, a pre-trial review is also held by the High Court Judge prior to the trial. There is no legislative requirement for this and hence is not mandatory but in practice is usually held for High Court and Intermediate Court cases where the Judge will go

[14] Sections 346-353 of the Criminal Procedure Code [15] Public Prosecutor V Haji Sadikin (2000) JCBD Vol. 1 349

through the relevant documents such as the list of witnesses, list of exhibits and agreed facts (if any) with both the prosecution and the defence.

Withdrawal of Charges

At any time before a judgment is entered, charges against the defendant and all evidence against him may be discharged. If the discharge is one not amounting to an acquittal, this would mean that prosecution can be made at another time based on the same factors. [16] The power to withdraw a charge only lies with the prosecution. The person who reported the offence and initiated the prosecution cannot withdraw his claim once a police report or a statement has been prepared.

TRIAL PROCEDURE

Chapter XIX of the Criminal Procedure Code governs the procedure for trials in Brunei Darussalam.

When the defendant first appears before the Court, the charge containing the particulars to the offence or offences he is accused of shall be read out and explained to him and he shall then be asked to enter his plea, guilty or not guilty. If the accused pleads guilty, the plea will be recorded

For additional analytical, marketing, investment and business opportunities information, please contact
Global Investment & Business Center, USA
(202) 546-2103. Fax: (202) 546-3275. E-mail: rusric@erols.com

and he may be convicted thereon. However, the Judge would first need to hear the complainant and other evidence first as it considers necessary and he would also make sure the defendant truly understands the nature and consequences of his plea and intends to admit, without qualification, the offence or offences alleged against him.

Where the defendant pleads not guilty, a trial will be held ad witnesses would be called to give evidence. At the start of the trial, the prosecution will first open the case by stating briefly the nature of the offence charged and disclosing the evidence, including the appearance of witnesses, by which he proposed to prove guilt of the defendant. The burden of proof lies with the prosecution beyond reasonable doubt. If the defendant is not represented by counsel, (there is no legal aid in Brunei Darussalam with the exception of cases carrying a death penalty where the defendant will be provided a defence counsel) the Court will assist the defendant in the cross examination of witnesses.

At the close of the prosecution's case, the Court will lay down the choices for the defendant, either to given his own evidence or maintain his silence. Usually, if they choose to keep silent, and where the evidence against him is strong, a conviction will be given. However, if he decides to give his own evidence, he will then in turn open his case by stating the facts or law on which he intends to rely and make whatever comments in response to the evidence put forward by the prosecution. Before summing up his case, he would then be called upon to enter his defence and then produce his own evidence which may include witnesses that are examined on his behalf. The prosecution will then have the right of reply on the whole case.[17]

[16] Section 186 of the Criminal Procedure Code [17] Section 184 of the Criminal Procedure Code

At the end of the trial, if the Court finds the defendant not guilty, the Court shall record an order of acquittal. If the Court finds otherwise or if the defendant entered a plea of guilty, the Court shall pass sentence in accordance with the law. [18]

Sentencing

The types of sentences in Brunei Darussalam are: i) Death Penalty: The most serious punishment in Brunei Darussalam is the death penalty. In sentencing hearings dealing with the death penalty, there must be 2 judges present and both these judges must agree with the sentencing decision. Death penalties are not imposed on pregnant women who would get life imprisonment instead.

ii) Life imprisonment: The defendant will be imprisonment for as long as he shall live.

iii) Whipping: There is also whipping in Brunei Darussalam, usually a maximum of 24 whips for an adult and a maximum of 18 whips for a defendant below the age of 18.[19] Women, men above 50 years old and those that are imposed the death penalty are exempted from whipping.[20]

iv) Fines: Fines are imposed according to the relevant written law. If that does not exist, the court will decide on the appropriate amount.

v) Pay compensation: On top of the above punishments, the Court can order the defendant to pay compensation if it is satisfied that the defendant can afford to pay such amount imposed. He will be imposed imprisonment or further imprisonment on default of payment. [21]

POST-TRIAL PROCEDURE (APPEALS)

If an appeal is made from the Magistrates Court, the appeal will be heard by the High Court. Any party can make an appeal against a judgment or sentence, be it the prosecution or the defendant. Appeals made from the High Court are heard by the Court of Appeal and these are governed by the Criminal Procedure Code (Criminal Appeal Rules) 2002. A person shall commence his appeal by sending a notice of appeal to the Registrar within 14 days of the judgment or sentence made. He can at any time abandon his appeal after serving his notice of appeal by giving notice of abandonment to the Registrar. His appeal should then be dismissed.

CIVIL PROCEDURE

Civil proceedings are usually private matters between parties that relates to breach of contracts or for compensation. The civil procedure in Brunei Darussalam is governed by the Supreme Court Rules for the High Court and the Magistrates' Court Rules (Civil

[18] Section 181 of the Criminal Procedure Code [19] Section 257 of the Criminal Procedure Code [20] Section 258 of the Criminal Procedure Code [21] Section 382 of the Criminal Procedure Code

Procedure and Civil Appeals Procedure) for the Magistrate Courts. These rules mainly prescribe regulations for types of action, procedure, process, addresses and forms.

Procedure in the Magistrate Court

INTRODUCTION

Civil proceedings in the Magistrate Court would include a civil action, an order for payment of any sum or money or an order for doing or abstaining from doing any act or thing not enforceable through a mere fine or by imprisonment. All civil proceedings heard by the Magistrate Court are dealt with summarily.[22]

PRE-HEARING PROCEDURE

A person who wishes to institute civil proceedings in the Magistrate Court would need to register a written statement to the Clerk of the Court to be included in the Civil Cause Book. This written statement is often referred to as the "plaint" and it shall state the names and last known place of residence of the parties and also include a statement on the substance of the action intended to be brought. Upon doing so, he is also required to pay a prescribed fee to the Court. The magistrate has discretion to refuse the plaint if it appears that there is no cause of action. They would naturally refuse the plaint if the matter is outside their jurisdiction. Any person dissatisfied with the magistrate's decision in refusing his plaint is allowed to appeal against that decision as if it was an order of the magistrate.[23]

Once the magistrate registers the plaint, it shall next issue a summons for the defendant requiring him to attend before him at a certain time but normally not more than 7 days after the summons have been served on him. The defendant will also be required to file his written statement of defence in answer to the plaint against him.[24] However, if he decides to admit the claim wholly or partially, he can then sign a statement admitting the amount of the claim or part of the amount of the claim entered against him. If this is the case, the Clerk of the Court shall send a notice regarding this admission to the plaintiff who is then required to prove the aforesaid claim. The magistrate shall then upon proof of the signature of the party enter judgment for the admitted claim.[25]

For additional analytical, marketing, investment and business opportunities information, please contact
Global Investment & Business Center, USA
(202) 546-2103. Fax: (202) 546-3275. E-mail: rusric@erols.com

The defendant will then pay into Court the sum of money in full satisfaction of the claim against him together with the costs incurred by the plaintiff up to the time of such payment and this payment should then be notified to the plaintiff. This payment shall then be paid out to the plaintiff without further delay.[26]

A plaintiff may also apply for the magistrate to make a judgment when no defence or counterclaim has been filed. Once satisfied that the plaint was served on the defendant and yet he did not appear in Court, the Court can then enter judgment for the plaintiff

[22] Rule 3 of the Magistrates' Court (Civil Procedure) Rules 2001 [23] Rule 13 of the Magistrates' Court (Civil Procedure) Rules 2001 [24] Rule 14 of the Magistrates' Court (Civil Procedure) Rules 2001 [25] Rule 38 of the Magistrates' Court (Civil Procedure) Rules 2001 [26] Rule 40 of the Magistrates' Court (Civil Procedure) Rules 2001

with costs. If the defendant manages to file a defence or counterclaim before judgment bas been entered, then a judgment in default cannot be made by the Court.[27]

PROCEDURE AT HEARING[28]

All hearings in the Magistrate Court are heard in public but the magistrate may still decide to hear the matter in the presence of the parties only. The persons permitted to address the Court in a civil proceeding are any party to the proceedings, any advocate and solicitor qualified and admitted under the Legal Profession Act and also any person permitted by the magistrate if he is satisfied that that person is not appearing for fee or reward.

If both the plaintiff and defendant are present at the hearing, the plaint would first be read out to the defendant who will then be required to make his defence. On hearing his defence, the magistrate shall then proceed with the case. During the hearing, the magistrate shall take into consideration any question of law raised, legal submissions made and the substance of the oral evidence given. The party on whom the burden of proof lies shall commence the case before the magistrate. Once he has closed his case, his opponent may adduce his own evidence. If he does not choose to do so, the initiating party shall address the magistrate for the second time and will sum up his evidence. The opponent is then given his right to reply. When the initiating party has concluded his case, the opponent can decide to call his own witnesses and he is free to open his own case, calls his own witnesses and in the end sums up not only on his own evidence but also on his own case. The initiating party will in turn have the right to reply to his opponent. [29]

On the conclusion of the hearing, the magistrate can deliver judgment either at the same or at a subsequent sitting. A certified copy of the judgment can also be delivered to the parties upon payment of a prescribed fee to the court.

However, in the case where only the defendant appears in court either on the day of the hearing or at any continuation the case, the claim or case shall be struck out by the magistrate but excluding any counter-claims that may have been made by the defendant against the plaintiff. But if the defendant admits to the cause of action, the magistrate may then proceed to give judgment, with or without costs, as if the plaintiff were present. Where there has been a counter claim, the magistrate, if satisfied that the counter claim has been served on the plaintiff, may proceed to hear the defendant's case and may give judgment on the evidence adduced by the defendant or may postpone the hearing on the counter claim. Such postponement will be notified to the plaintiff. The magistrate may also award costs to the defendant when the plaintiff fails to appear.

For additional analytical, marketing, investment and business opportunities information, please contact
Global Investment & Business Center, USA
(202) 546-2103. Fax: (202) 546-3275. E-mail: rusric@erols.com

Where the defendant is the party that has failed to appear in court, the magistrate once satisfied with the proof of service on the defendant and that the defendant lacks sufficient excuse for his non attendance, can determine the case and enter judgment. That judgment

[27] Rule 41 of the Magistrates' Court (Civil Procedure) Rules 2001 [28] Part VIII of the Magistrates' Court (Civil Procedure) Rules 2001 [29] Rule 61 of the Magistrates' Court (Civil Procedure) Rules 2001

shall be as valid as if both parties had appeared before him. Otherwise, the magistrate can still adjourn the hearing to a convenient date to allow more time for the defendant.

APPEALS

Any civil appeals are governed by the Magistrates' Courts (Civil Appeal) Rules 2001. Every notice of appeal will be lodged in the magistrates court within a month of the decision appealed from was made and shall be served on all other parties affected by the appeal.[30]

The contents of the notice of appeal should include the reference number of the proceedings, names of parties, date of decision appealed, grounds of appeal and be accompanied by a certified copy of the decision appealed against.[31]

Appeals shall be heard by one Judge of the High Court who may reserve for the consideration of the Court of Appeal ay question of law which may arise on the hearing of such an appeal.[32]

The Registrar will notify the parties the date and time of the appeal hearing. If the appellant fails to appear at the appeal hearing, the case shall then be struck out and the decision shall be affirmed. If the respondent appeared at that appeal where the appellant failed to do so, the appellant shall be ordered to pay the costs of the appeal. But if the respondent did not appear, the High Court will need to consequently decide on the costs of the appeal. [33]

However if the appellant appears and whether or not the respondent appears, the High Court shall proceed with the hearing and determination of the case and shall thereafter give judgment according to the merits of the case. During the hearing, the appellant is not allowed to argue on any other points that are separate from the reasons for appeal and those set forth in his notice of appeal. But the Judge may allow amendments to the notice of appeal if he feels that there are actually other grounds than was not mentioned that should be included and also if he feels that the statement of grounds of appeal is defective.[34]

Once the Judge decides on the appeal, the High Court shall certify the judgment made and notify it to the magistrates' court. The magistrates' court will then act upon the judgment either by making such orders that are necessary and amending its own records in accordance with the judgment. The magistrate shall then have the same jurisdiction and power to enforce the High Court's judgment as if he himself made it.

[30] Rule 4 of the Magistrates' Court (Civil Appeals Procedure) Rules 2001

[31] Rule 5 of the Magistrates' Court (Civil Appeals Procedure) Rules 2001 [32] Rule 11 of the Magistrates' Court (Civil Appeals Procedure) Rules 2001 [33] Rule 12 and 13 of the Magistrates' Court (Civil Appeals Procedure) Rules 2001 [34] Rule 15 of the Magistrates' Court (Civil Appeals Procedure) Rules 2001

For additional analytical, marketing, investment and business opportunities information, please contact
Global Investment & Business Center, USA
(202) 546-2103. Fax: (202) 546-3275. E-mail: rusric@erols.com

PROCEDURE IN THE HIGH COURT

INTRODUCTION

High Court Proceedings are initiated by writ, originating summons, originating motion or petition.[35]

There are certain proceedings that **must** be initiated by a writ and these are those relating to claims for relief or remedy for any tort (other than trespass to land), relating to an allegation of fraud, claims for damages for breach of duty (whether duty exists by virtue of a contract or of a provision made by any written law), claims for breach of promise of marriage and also relating to infringement of a patent.

Any applications that are made to a High Court Judge under any written law must be initiated by originating summons. There are also some proceedings that may be begun either by writ or by originating summons where the plaintiff can choose which is more appropriate for him. Such proceedings include those where the sole or principal question at issue is the construction of any written law, of any instrument made under any written law or of any deed, will contract or other document and also where there is unlikely to be any substantial dispute of fact in those proceedings.

PRE-HEARING PROCEDURE

Writ of Summons

All writs prior to them being issued must be indorsed with a statement of the nature of the claim made or the relief or remedy required in the action begun or a statement of the amount claimed in respect of a debt demand. It should also state that further proceedings will be stayed if the defendant pays the amount claimed to the plaintiff or the Court within a certain time limit. The Plaintiff upon presenting a writ for sealing and to be served must leave with the Registrar the original writ along with as many copies of it to be served on the defendant or defendants. The Registrar shall then assign a serial number to the writ and shall sign, seal and date the writ which shall deem the writ to be issued.[36]

Originating Summons

An originating summons must include the questions the plaintiff seeks the determination or direction of the High Court or a concise statement of the relief or remedy claimed in the proceedings with sufficient particulars to identify the cause or causes of action in respect of that claim. Similar to the process in writ of summons, the Registrar will assign a serial number to the originating summons and it will be signed, sealed and dated and thereupon issued.[37]

Originating Motion and Petition No originating motion can be made *ex parte* and without previous notice to the affected parties. However if the Court is satisfied that there will be a delay in proceedings, it may make an order *ex parte* on terms such as costs or otherwise. (Any affected party may apply to the Court to set that order aside). The notice of a motion must include a concise statement of the nature of the claim made or the relief or remedy required. The plaintiff can serve a notice of motion on the defendant together with the writ of summons or originating summons or at any time after service of such writ or summons whether or not the defendant has entered on appearance in the action.[38]

For additional analytical, marketing, investment and business opportunities information, please contact
Global Investment & Business Center, USA
(202) 546-2103. Fax: (202) 546-3275. E-mail: rusric@erols.com

Petitions must also include a concise statement on the nature of the claim sought and the names of the persons the petition should be served with. The petition should be served on the defendant not less than 7 days before the day the Registrar has fixed to be the day and time for the hearing of the petition.[39]

Similar to writ of summons and originating summons, originating motion and petitions shall also be assigned by the Registrar a serial number and be signed, sealed and dated before it is deemed to be issued.

Service of Process[40]

All writs, originating summons to which an appearance by the defendant is required, an originating summons, notices of originating motion and petitions must be served personally on each defendant.

A plaintiff must serve a statement of claim to the defendant either when the writ or notice of writ is served on the defendant or at any time after the service of the writ or notice of writ but it must be before the expiration of 14 days after the defendant enters an appearance. Thereafter, the defendant who has entered an appearance and intends to defend himself must serve a defence on the plaintiff not more than 14 days either after the time that has been limited for him to appear or after the statement of claim is served on him, whichever is the later. Next, the plaintiff who has been served the defence must serve a reply back to the defendant. If the plaintiff was also served a counter claim from the defendant and he intends to defend it, should also serve a defence on the defendant along with the reply. In each of the pleadings served, they must contain a statement setting out summarily the material facts on which the party pleading relies for his claim or defence.[41] In particular, he must plead specifically what his claim is in relation to, for instance, performance, release, statutes of limitation, fraud or any fact showing illegality and stat that the opposite party cannot claim or defend on it. This information must always be included to avoid taking the opposite party by surprise.

It is possible for the plaintiff or the defendant to apply to the Court by summons for an order that the action be tried without pleadings or further pleadings. If the Court is satisfied that the issues in dispute can be defined without pleadings or further pleadings, then it shall direct the parties to prepare a statement of the issues in dispute or if the parties are unable to agree on such a statement, the Court may settle the statement itself.

[38] Order 8 of the Supreme Court Rules [39] Order 9 of the Supreme Court Rules [40] Order 10 of the Supreme Court Rules [41] Rule 6, Order 8 of the Supreme Court Rules

Cases involving libel, slander, breach of promise of marriage and allegations of fraud does not apply in this type of action.

Where the plaintiff fails to serve a statement of claim on the defendant, the defendant may, after the expiration of the period for him to appear apply for the Court to dismiss the action.[42] If the claim relates to a liquidated demand and if the defendant fails to serve a defence, then the plaintiff may enter a final judgment against the defendant for a sum not exceeding what is claimed in the writ and also for costs.

Entering of appearance

For additional analytical, marketing, investment and business opportunities information, please contact
Global Investment & Business Center, USA
(202) 546-2103. Fax: (202) 546-3275. E-mail: rusric@erols.com

A defendant to an action that was begun by writ may appear in the action and defend the claim either by a solicitor or by himself. Where the defendant is a body corporate, they may not enter an appearance at the action and can only be defended by a solicitor. Entering an appearance entails completing the requisite documents, namely a memorandum of appearance and sending it along with a copy of it to the Registry.[43] A memorandum of appearance basically requests the Registry to enter an appearance for the defendant or defendants specified in the memorandum. It must specify the address of the defendant's place of residence or the business address if his solicitor.

Where the defendant fails to enter an appearance, the plaintiff may after the time limited for appearing has expired, enter final judgment against that defendant for a sum not exceeding the amount claimed by the writ and for costs and proceed with the action against other defendants, if there are any.[44] He may enter an interlocutory judgment in the case of claims for unliquidated damages.

Preparing for trial[45]

A cause or matter may be tried before a Judge or the Registrar of the Supreme Court. Notice of trial may be given by the plaintiff or the other party at any time after a reply has been delivered or after the time for delivery of a reply has expired. At least 14 days before the date for trial has been fixed, the defendant shall identify to the plaintiff those documents that are central to his case that he wishes to be included in the trial bundle. At least 2 days before the trial, the plaintiff shall have 2 bundles consisting of one copy of the following documents: a) witness statements that have been exchanged including expert's reports; b) the defendant's documents that he wishes to be included in the bundle; and c) a note agreed by the parties giving a summary of the issues involved, a summary of the propositions of law, the list of authorities to be cited and a chronology of relevant events.

A pre-trial conference may also be held at any time after the commencement of proceedings, and the Court may direct the parties to attend such a conference to discuss matters relating to the action.[46] Points to consider at this pre-trial conference would

[42] Rule 1, Order 19 [43] Rule 1, Order 12 [44] Order 13 [45] Order 34 [46] Order 34A

include any possibility of settlement, the need for the parties to furnish the Court with further information as the Court would require and the Court can also give directions as it appears necessary or desirable for securing a just, expeditious and economic disposal of the action. The parties can agree to settle at any time during the pre-trial conference on all or some of the matters in dispute. The Court can then enter judgment and make an order to give effect to that settlement.

PROCEDURE AT HEARING

At the trial, the Judge will first give directions as to which party may begin the proceedings and prescribe the orders of speeches at the trial. If the defendant decides not to adduce any evidence, the plaintiff may at the close of his case make a second speech closing his case and thereafter the defendant shall make a speech in closing his case. If the defendant does decide to adduce evidence, ha may do so at the closing of the plaintiff's case. At the close of the defendant's case, the plaintiff may make a speech in reply. Rules on evidence are prescribed under Order 38 of the rules.

Where a judgment has been given for damages and there is no provision made by the judgment in how damages are to be assessed, then the damages shall be assessed by the Registrar.[47] The Court may also make an award of provisional damages if the plaintiff has made a claim for one.[48]

Every judgment after a hearing is delivered in open Court or in Chambers, either on the conclusion of the hearing or on a subsequent day of which such notice shall be given to the parties.[49] A Judge can also give judgment and his reasons, in writing at a later date by sending a copy of it to all parties to the proceedings. In this case, the original copy of the written judgment must be signed and filed. The proper officer of the Registrar must enter into the cause book a minute of every judgment or order given by the Court.

In the enforcement of a judgment for the payment of money (and not one for the payment of money into Court), it can be enforced through writ of seizure or sale, garnishee proceedings, charging orders, appointment of a receiver, and an order of committal.[50]

To avoid hearing

Payment into and out of court[51]

In any action for a debt or damages, any defendant may pay into Court a sum of money as the plaintiff claims. Within 14 days of the payment, the plaintiff may accept the money in satisfaction of that cause of action by giving such notice to the defendant.

Offer to settle[52]

Parties to any proceeding may also serve on any other person an offer to settle any one or more of the claim in the proceedings. These can be made at any time before the Court disposes of the matter.

Summary Judgment[53]

A plaintiff can apply to the Court for a summary judgment against the defendant on the ground that that defendant has no defence to the claim included in the writ. Claims relating to libel, slander, malicious prosecution, false imprisonment, seduction or breach of promise of marriage are excluded from this application.

Application for summary judgments must be made by summons supported by an affidavit verifying the facts on which the claim, or the part of the claim, to which the application relates to is based on and it should also state the plaintiff's belief that there is no defence to that claim or no defence except as to the amount of any damages. Thereafter, the Court may dismiss the plaintiff's application especially where the defendant had satisfied the Court that there is still an issue or question in dispute which ought for some reason to be tried. On the other hand, the Court may also give such judgment for the plaintiff against the defendant on that claim.

APPEALS

Any appeal from a decision of a Registrar shall lie to a Judge in Chambers.[54] The appeal shall be brought by serving a notice on every other party to the proceedings to attend an appeal hearing before a Judge on a day specified in the notice. Appeals from a Judge shall lie to the Court of Appeal.

For additional analytical, marketing, investment and business opportunities information, please contact
Global Investment & Business Center, USA
(202) 546-2103. Fax: (202) 546-3275. E-mail: rusric@erols.com

An appeal to the Court of Appeal shall be by way of rehearing and must be brought by a notice of appeal. Every notice of appeal must be filed and served within one month from the date when such order was pronounced (in the case of an appeal from a Judge in Chambers), from the date of refusal (in the case of an appeal against the refusal of an application), and in all other cases, from the date on which the judgment or order appealed against was pronounced.

RECIPROCAL ENFORCEMENT OF FOREIGN JUDGMENTS AND FOREIGN MAINTENANCE ORDERS

Brunei Darussalam also has in force a Maintenance Orders Reciprocal Enforcement Act[55] and a Reciprocal Enforcement of Foreign Judgments Act.[56] The Maintenance Orders Act basically provides for the enforcement in Brunei Darussalam any maintenance orders made in reciprocating countries listed in the Schedule and also for maintenance order made in Brunei Darussalam to be enforced in the listed reciprocating countries. To date, the reciprocating countries are Malaysia, Singapore, Australia and Hong Kong Special

[52] Order 23 [53] Order 14 [54] Order 56 [55] CAP 175 of the Laws of Brunei [56] CAP 176 of the Laws of Brunei

Administrative Region of the People's Republic of China. Maintenance orders are those that provide for the periodical payment of money towards the maintenance of any persons the person paying is liable to maintain.

The Foreign Judgments Act makes provision for the enforcement in Brunei Darussalam any judgments given in foreign countries listed in the Schedule who will in turn also enforce judgments given in Brunei Darussalam. Judgment in this case means a judgment or order given or made by a court in any civil proceedings, judgment in any criminal proceedings for the payment of a sum of money in respect of compensation or damages to an injured party and an award in proceedings on arbitration.[57] The countries listed for the purposes of this Act as at now are only Malaysia and Singapore, through their respective High Courts.

LEGAL PROCEDURE IN THE SYARIAH COURTS

With regards to procedure in general, the Syariah Courts Act (Chapter 184) has stated that every Syariah Court in Brunei Darussalam shall have and use where necessary a seal of such form and format as may be approved by the Majlis[58]. The language that shall be used in the Syariah Courts shall be the Malay language though it may allow the use of any other language in the interest of justice[59]. However, the courts may choose for all documents or records of proceedings to be written in jawi or rumi script[60].

PROCEDURE IN CRIMINAL PROCEEDINGS

In pre-trial procedure, section 69(1) of the Religious Council and Kadis Courts Act (Chapter 77) has laid down some guidelines concerning charge. A charge shall be framed by the prosecutor or by the Court and which shall contain sufficient particulars of the offence alleged. However in practice, during the initial stage of the case, the prosecutor would normally frame the charge, whereas at the closing of the prosecution's case, it would be up to the Court (at the stage of a prima facie) to frame or amend a charge if it thinks it is not appropriate with the charge by the prosecution based on the evidence given in Court[61].

For additional analytical, marketing, investment and business opportunities information, please contact
Global Investment & Business Center, USA
(202) 546-2103. Fax: (202) 546-3275. E-mail: rusric@erols.com

For procedure during trial, section 70 of the Religious Council and Kadis Court (Chapter 77) has outlined procedure for hearing. Section 70(1) of this Act says that any necessary sanction to prosecute shall be proved. This is in accordance with section 62 which mentioned that for any offence under section 182, 183, 185, 186, 187 or 190, no prosecution shall be instituted except by resolution of the Majlis Ugama Islam sanctioning such prosecution.

[57] Section 2 of the Reciprocal Enforcement of Foreign Judgments Act [58] Section 7(1) of the Syariah Courts Act (Chapter 184). [59] Section 7(2)(a) Ibid. [60] Section 7(2)(b) Ibid. [61] Haji Sawas Haji Jebat, *Prosedur Perbicaraan Di Mahkamah Kadi*, Jurnal Undang-Undang Syariah Brunei Darussalam, Januari-Jun 2002 Jilid 2 Bil.2, p.35.

Section 70(2) of the Act also stated that the accused shall be charged and if he pleads guilty he may be sentenced on such plea. Though it seems too simple, in practice however, the plea will only be accepted if it is made without any qualification and that the accused understood the charge made against him as well as consequences of the charge. In addition to that, section 175(1) of the Criminal Procedure Code (Chapter 7) is also practiced whereby a charge containing the particulars of the offence of which he is accused shall be framed and explained to him, and he shall be asked whether he is guilty of the offence charged or claims to be tried. And the court before recording the plea may hear the complainant and such other evidence as it considers necessary and shall ascertain that the accused understands the nature and consequences of his plea and intends to admit, without qualification, the offence alleged against him[62].

If an accused claims trial or refuses to plead, the prosecutor shall outline the facts to be proved and the relevant law and shall then call his witnesses[63]. As laid down in section 70(4), each witness shall be examined by the party calling him[64] and this shall be called his examination-in-chief[65]; be cross-examined thereafter by the party opposing him, which shall be called his cross-examination[66] and, such cross-examination may be directed to credibility[67]. Each witness may thereafter be re-examined on matters arising out of cross-examination by the party calling him[68], and such examination shall be called his re-examination[69]. Each witness have put to him at any time any question by the Court[70] and may have any further questions put to him or be recalled at any time, by leave of the Court[71]. For particulars on examination of witnesses and in ensuring the truth of syahadah syahid reference shall be made to the Syariah Courts Evidence Order, 2001[72].

After hearing the witnesses for the prosecution the Court shall either dismiss the case or call on the accused for his defence[73]. This section is to be read together with section 177(1) of the Criminal Procedure Code (Chapter 7):

"If upon taking all evidence referred to in section 176 and making such examination (if any) of the accused under section 220 as the Court considers necessary it finds that no case against the accused has been made out which, if unrebutted, would warrant his conviction, the Court may, subject to the provisions of section 186, record an order of acquittal.

If called on for his defence, the accused may address the Court and may then either give evidence or make a statement without being sworn or affirmed, in which case he shall not

[62] Section 175(2) of the Criminal Procedure Code (Chapter 7). [63] Section 70(3) of the Religious Council and Kadis Courts Act (Chapter 77). [64] Section 70(4)*(a)* Ibid. [65] Section 120(1) of the Syariah Courts Evidence Order, 2001(S 63/2001). [66] Section 120(2) Ibid. [67] Section 70(4)*(b)* of the Religious Council and Kadis Courts Act (Chapter 77). [68] Section 70(4)*(c)* Ibid. [69] Section 120(3) of the Syariah Courts Evidence Order, 2001(S 63/2001). [70] Section 70(4)*(d)* of the Religious Council and Kadis Courts Act (Chapter 77). [71] Section 70(4)*(e)* Ibid. [72] Chapters IX and

For additional analytical, marketing, investment and business opportunities information, please contact
Global Investment & Business Center, USA
(202) 546-2103. Fax: (202) 546-3275. E-mail: rusric@erols.com

IV respectively, (S 63/2001) [73] Section 70(5) of the Religious Council and Kadis Courts Act (Chapter 77).

be liable to be cross-examined, or may stand silent provided that if the accused gives evidence, he may be cross-examined, but not as to character or as to other offences not charged[74].

In doing so the accused may then call his witnesses[75]. He may sum up his case[76], and the prosecutor may reply generally[77]. As in any other Court, the Syariah Court, after considering the case shall then either convict or acquit the accused[78]. If the accused is convicted, the court may be informed of previous offences and shall have regard to any plea of leniency[79]. The Court shall then pass sentence according to law[80].

One important section in the Religious Council and Kadis Courts Act (Chapter 77) relating to criminal procedure is section 78 where it says that in matters of practice and procedure not expressly provided for in this Act or any rules made thereunder, the Court shall have regard to the avoidance of injustice and the convenient dispatch of business and may in criminal proceedings have regard to the practice and procedure obtaining in the civil courts.

PROCEDURE IN CIVIL PROCEEDINGS

For civil proceedings, provisions used are as mentioned in the Religious Council and Kadis Courts Act (Chapter 77) in section 80 until section 93; section 95 and section 96. In practice, the Emergency (Islamic Family Law) Order, 1999 (S 12/2000) as well as relevant provisions being used in the civil courts are also applied. This is to ensure that justice is served especially for those matters not provided for in the Act or any rules thereunder. Section 96 of the Religious Council and Kadis Courts (Chapter 77) states that:

"In matters of practice and procedure, not expressly provided for in this Act or any rules made thereunder, the Court may adopt such procedure as may seem proper for the avoidance of injustice and the disposal of the matters in issue between the parties, and may in particular, but without prejudice to the generality of the foregoing, adopt the practice and procedure for the time being in force in the Magistrates' Courts in civil proceedings."

THE LEGAL PROFESSION

LEGAL QUALIFICATIONS

A person that would qualify for admission to practise as an advocate and solicitor in Brunei Darussalam must possess one of the following requirements[1]:

i) He is a barrister-at- law of England, Northern Ireland or he must be a member of the Faculty of Advocates of Scotland; or

ii) He is a solicitor in England, Northern Ireland or a Writer to the Signet, law agent or solicitor in Scotland; or

iii) He has been in active practice as an advocate and solicitor in Singapore or in any part of Malaysia; or

iv) He possesses the Certificate of Legal Practice issued by the Qualifying Board pursuant to section 5 of the Legal Profession Act 1976 of Malaysia; or

v) He possesses a degree in law conferred by the Universiti Islam Antarabangsa in Malaysia.

Furthermore, he must also be either a Brunei national or a person to whom a residence permit has been granted under regulations made under the Immigration Act.[2] If a person is not a Brunei national or no residence permit has been granted to him, he can only apply for admission if (along with having the academic requirements mentioned above) he has been in active practice in any part of the United Kingdom, Singapore, Malaysia, or in any other country or territory of the Commonwealth designated by the Attorney General for at least 7 years immediately preceding his application.

Admission is at the Chief Justice's discretion and he shall further take into consideration the following criteria[3]:

i) if the applicant has attained the age of 21 years;

ii) if he is of good character;

iii) if he has served satisfactorily his required period of pupilage as prescribed by the Pupillage Rules. [4]

[1] Section 3(1), Legal Profession Act (CAP 132)/Alternative Qualifications Rules 1999 [2] See Part III, Immigration Act (CAP 17) [3] Section 4, Legal Profession Act [4] Under the Pupillage Rules 2000, a pupil shall serve a period of pupilage with a qualified person who has been practicing for not less then 7 years for a period of 9 months. A qualified person can be exempted by the Chief Justice from any part of his pupilage (not more than 6 months) looking at special circumstances, if he has been a pupil of a master who is a barrister at law in England and Northern Ireland or a member of the Faculty of Advocates of Scotland or of an advocate and solicitor in Singapore or Malaysia practicing for not less than 7 years. He can also be exempted if the is or has been a solicitor in England and Northern Ireland, or a Writer of the Signet, law agent or solicitor in Scotland or he has been engaged in legal practice for not less than 6 months in any Commonwealth country or territory.

PRACTITIONERS

All advocates and solicitors that have been admitted to practise have the exclusive right to appeal and plead in all the courts of justice in Brunei Darussalam.[5]

The application process

All application for admission to become an advocate and solicitor shall be made by petition to the Chief Justice and shall be verified by affidavit.[6] The petitioner shall first file his petition at the Chief Registrar's office, accompanied by a notice intimating that he has applied. A notice shall be posted at the Supreme Court for one month before the petitioner is heard to be admitted.

A month before the petitioner is heard, he shall file an affidavit exhibiting documentary evidence which he states that he is qualified, if he has been practising law outside Brunei, evidence that there has been no disciplinary proceedings pending or contemplated against him and that his professional conduct was not under investigation. He would also need to show 2 recent certificates as to his good character and a certificate of diligence from each Master with whom he

For additional analytical, marketing, investment and business opportunities information, please contact
Global Investment & Business Center, USA
(202) 546-2103. Fax: (202) 546-3275. E-mail: rusric@erols.com

served his pupilage. The court may also request for other information or evidence as it may require.

These documents would then be filed by the Chief Registrar and within 5 days after, they shall be served on the Attorney General and upon any other relevant persons.[7]

After the application is heard and once the petitioner is admitted, his name would be entered into the roll. The Chief Registrar keeps a roll of advocates and solicitors' names with the dates of their respective admission. The name with the date of admission of every person admitted shall be entered upon the roll in order of admission.

Every advocate and solicitor is responsible for deliver to the Chief Registrar an application for a Practising Certificate every year before he does any act in the capacity of an advocate and solicitor[8]. The application shall be accompanied by a declaration in writing by the applicant stating his full name, the name under which he practices or the name of the advocate and solicitor or the firm of advocates and solicitors employing him at which he practice in Brunei Darussalam.

If he is not a Brunei Darussalam national or does not have a residence permit, he must also state that during the period in respect of which his immediately preceding practising certificate was issued, he had been in active practice in Brunei Darussalam for at least 3 months in aggregate if it was his first Practising Certificate or at least 9 months in the aggregate in any other case. All applicants are also required to pay a prescribed fee to obtain the Practising Certificate.

[5] Section 17, Legal Profession Act [6] Section 4, Legal Profession Act [7] Section 6, Legal Profession Act [8] See Part III, Legal Profession Act

Once the Chief Registrar is certain that the applicant's name is on the roll, and is satisfied with all the accompanying documents the applicant has provided, he shall issue to the applicant the practising certificate which will authorize him to practise an as advocate and solicitor in Brunei Darussalam. Every Practising Certificate shall be signed by the Chief Registrar and shall have effect from the beginning of the day of which it bears the date and shall expire at the end of the next 31st December. The Practising Certificate can however also expire once the name of the advocate and solicitor is struck off the roll or where he is adjudicated as bankrupt. In such a case, his Practising Certificate will be suspended until the Chief Justice consents to it being reinstated.

Ad- hoc admission

A judge has the discretion to admit into practice for the purpose of one case only any person who is not an ordinary resident of Brunei Darussalam but intends to come to Brunei Darussalam to appear in a case on the instructions of an Advocate and Solicitor.[9] In such cases, he must be Her Britannic Majesty's Patent as Queen's Counsel and also must possess such special skill and qualifications for the purpose of the case whether or not such special skill and qualifications are available in Brunei Darussalam.

A judge can also admit at his discretion for similar purposes, a person who is entitled to practise before the High Court in Malaysia, Singapore or Hong Kong or in any other Commonwealth country the Chief Justice may specify providing that he has not been admitted under this circumstance in respect of more than two other cases in the current calendar year.

Any person applying to be admitted on an ad hoc basis shall do so by originating motion verified by an affidavit stating the names of the parties and the brief particulars of the case he intends to

For additional analytical, marketing, investment and business opportunities information, please contact
Global Investment & Business Center, USA
(202) 546-2103. Fax: (202) 546-3275. E-mail: rusric@erols.com

appear in. The originating motion and the affidavit shall be served on the Attorney General and to the other parties to the case. The Judge prior to deciding to admit or not would usually first seek the views of each of the persons served with the application (originating motion).

The Chief Registrar shall then issue to any person admitted on an ad hoc basis a certificate to practise which would specify the case the person is to appear in. This person is deemed to be a person whose name is on the roll and to whom a practising certificate has been given to. However, his name would not be entered in the roll of names but will enter into a separate roll for such persons who are admitted on an ad-hoc basis.

Provisional admission

Advocates and solicitors can also be admitted provisionally prior to their application being heard.[10] The Chief Justice may after the petitioner has served his petition, verifying affidavit and accompanying exhibits, provisionally admit him to practise as an advocate and solicitor subject to any conditions that the Chief Justice may impose.

[9] Section 7, Legal Profession Act [10] Section 8, Legal Profession Act

Upon receiving payment of the prescribed fee, the Chief Justice will issue to every person admitted provisionally a provisional licenec to practise specifying in it any terms and conditions he has imposed. Such persons shall be entitled to practise as an advocate and solicitor as if their names were on the roll and as if a practising certificate has been issued to them. However, the Chief Justice has the discretion to revoke a provisional licence at any time. Otherwise, a provisional licence expires on the date of the final determination of admission or when a petition has been withdrawn for such person. Similar to ad-hoc cases, provisional persons' names shall be kept on a separate roll.

Other qualified practitioners

A person employed in his professional capacity as an advocate and solicitor with the Government or an approved legal department of a company incorporated in Brunei Darussalam under the Companies Act which has been designated by the Attorney General can also qualify to be practising in Brunei Darussalam providing he pays for the prescribed fee to a practising certificate.[11]

Furthermore, any person who holds the office of Attorney General, Solicitor General or Deputy Public Prosecutor also shares the rights of a qualified advocate and solicitor for as long as they continue to hold such office.[12]

To qualify to use the title of "consultant", one needs to have been either an advocate or solicitor in continuous practice for a period of not less than 10 years.[13]

Hearing and the right of appeal

All petitions and originating motions are held in open court.[14] Any appeals from any judgment or court order on any petition or originating motion lie to the Court of Appeal. The appeal can either be initiated by the petitioner himself or it could be initiated by the Attorney General or any other person that has been served with the petition or originating motion.

Miscellaneous

For additional analytical, marketing, investment and business opportunities information, please contact
Global Investment & Business Center, USA
(202) 546-2103. Fax: (202) 546-3275. E-mail: rusric@erols.com

If the Chief Justice holds the opinion that the number of advocates practising in Brunei Darussalam is sufficient to serve the community, he shall make such a declaration to that effect in the *Government Gazette*[15]. During the period after the Declaration was made and before it is revoked, no person other than a national of Brunei shall be entitled to be admitted as an advocate or even issued a provisional licence to. His Majesty in Council can also direct at 6 months after the Declaration was made, that the name of any advocate who at that time is not an ordinary resident of Brunei Darussalam to be deleted.

It is an offence for an person who is not considered a qualified person to practise law in Brunei Darussalam, to act as an advocate and solicitor and upon conviction shall be liable

[11] Section 18, Legal Profession Act [12] Section 17(2), Legal Profession Act [13] Section 28A, Legal Profession Act [14] Section 9, Legal Profession Act [15] Section 12, Legal Profession Act

to a fine of $1,000 and to imprisonment for a term of 6 months. However, if they commit such acts which includes preparing a document involving a grant of probate or letters of administration or he acts on behalf of claimant that alleges to have a legal claim and as a result writes, publishes or sends a letter or notice threatening legal proceedings etc shall only be guilty of an offence if he can prove that the act was not done for or in expectation of any fee, gain or reward.[16]

THE LAW SOCIETY

The Law Society of Brunei Darussalam was established in 2003 in accordance with the Legal Profession (Law Society of Brunei Darussalam) Order of 2003, which is a subsidiary legislation to the Legal Profession Act.

Amongst its objectives are to maintain and improve the standards of professional conduct and learning within the legal profession, to facilitate the acquisition of legal knowledge by members of the legal profession, to assist the Government and the Courts in all matters relating to the law and to establish a library housing law books and reports to help facilitate knowledge building among the profession.[17]

Membership

The Law Society consists of all advocates and solicitors who possess a valid practising certificate and they will remain as members for as long as they hold one. The society also admit as members non-practitioners and these are advocates and solicitors who does not have a valid practising certificate but non-practitioner members are not eligible to vote and they themselves cannot be elected to the Council. Honorary members are also occasionally admitted as members to the Society as they think fit and this membership could be either for life or for such a period the Council thinks appropriate.[18]

As mentioned briefly, only practitioner members are eligible to attend and vote at any general meeting of the Society but only practitioner members who are Brunei Darussalam nationals are eligible to be elected to the Council. A practitioner member can also by resolution exclude all other members from a general meeting of the society.[19]

Any member of the society other than an honorary member may, after being given a reasonable opportunity to answer all allegations made against him, be expelled from membership or be deprived from any of the rights and privileges of the membership. A practitioner member however cannot be expelled so long as he has in force a practising certificate.[20]

For additional analytical, marketing, investment and business opportunities information, please contact
Global Investment & Business Center, USA
(202) 546-2103. Fax: (202) 546-3275. E-mail: rusric@erols.com

[16] Section 19, Legal Profession Act [17] See Section 4, Law Society Order [18] Sections 5-8, Law Society Order [19] Section 9, Law Society Order [20] Section 10, Law Society Order

The Council

The Council of the Society is responsible for the proper management of the Society's affairs and also for the proper performance of its purposes and powers. The Council consists of statutory members and elected members.[21]

Statutory members are automatic members to the Council each time it is constituted. They comprise of the immediate past President of the Society, advocates and solicitors nominated by the Attorney General and advocates and solicitors appointed by the Council as soon as practicable after it is constituted. Elected members are members that need to be elected by the Society and they comprise of 4 practising members who have been in practice for not less than 10 years and who were elected by practicing members who have been in practice for more than 10 years, 3 practising members who have been in practice not less than 7 years and who were elected by practising members who have been in practice not less than 7 years and 3 practising members who have been in practice for not less than 5 years and who were elected by practising members who have been in practice for not less than 5 years. Every elected member holds office in the Council for two years.

It is compulsory for all members of the Society to vote.[22] If they fail to do so, they will be disqualified from applying for a practicing certificate unless they can satisfy the Chief Registrar with a reasonable excuse for not voting. He has to prove either he was not in Brunei Darussalam at the time of the election or he has a good and sufficient reason for not voting. To avoid disqualification, he can also pay a penalty of $500 which will go into the Compensation Fund.

Elections are held bi-annually in the month of September [23] and usually take place within 21 days after the annual General Meeting of the Society. Every Council constituted after an election shall take office on the next 1st January after the election and shall hold office for 2 years until the 31st December of the following year. The officers of Council are comprised of the President, Vice President, Secretary and Treasurer.[24]

Powers of the Council

The Council is mainly responsible for the management of the Society and its funds. Amongst its other powers include[25], making rules that are not already expressed by the Chief Justice, answering questions affecting the practice and etiquette of the profession, take cognizance of anything affecting the Society or the professional conduct of its members and to bring before any General Meeting, any material to the Society that would be in the profession's interests and make recommendations in relation to it. The Council may also propose legislation or report on any current legislation that has been submitted to them, create prizes and opportunity for scholarships for law students, communicate with other similar bodies and members of the profession in other places or countries to

[21] Section 13, Law Society Order [22] Section 16, Law Society Order [23] Section 17(1), Law Society) Order [24] Section 22(1) of the LP (Law Society) Order 2003 [25] Section 25, Law Society Order 2003

enable exchange of information that may be beneficial to the members of the Society. The full list of powers can be found under section 27 of the Law Society Order.

For additional analytical, marketing, investment and business opportunities information, please contact
Global Investment & Business Center, USA
(202) 546-2103. Fax: (202) 546-3275. E-mail: rusric@erols.com

LEGAL QUALIFICATIONS FOR SYARIAH LAWYERS

Section 25 of the Syariah Courts Act (Chapter 184) has specified who may be appointed as Syar'ie Prosecutor. His Majesty the Sultan and Yang Di-Pertuan may, on the advice of the President of the Majlis Ugama Islam and after consultation with the Majlis, appoint a person who is qualified to become Syariah High Court Judge, to be the Chief Syar'ie Prosecutor[26]. The Chief Syar'ie Prosecutor shall have powers exercisable at his discretion to commence and carry out any proceedings for an offence before a Syariah Court[27]; and he shall not be subject to the direction or control of any other person or authority[28].

His Majesty the Sultan and Yang Di-Pertuan may, on the advice of the President of the Majlis and after consultation with the Chief Syar'ie Prosecutor, appoint a fit and suitable persons from members of the public service to be Syar'ie Prosecutors who shall act under the supervision and direction of the Chief Syar'ie Prosecutor and may exercise all or any right and power vested in or exercisable by the Chief Syar'ie Prosecutor himself[29].

Whereas for Syar'ie Lawyers, section 27(1) of the Syariah Courts Act (Chapter 184) says that the Chief Syar'ie Judge may, on payment of the prescribed fee, admit a person who possesses sufficient knowledge about *Hukum Syara'* and suitable to become a Syar'ie Lawyer to represent the parties in any proceedings before any Syariah Court. Subsection

(2) of section 27 also states that no person other than a Syar'ie Lawyer shall have the right to appear as a *bil-khusumah* representative in any Syariah Court on behalf of any party to any proceeding before it.

Section 28 of the Syariah Courts Act (Chapter 184), the Chief Syar'ie Judge may, with the approval of His Majesty the Sultan and Yang Di-Pertuan, make Rules of Court to provide for the procedure, qualifications and fees for admission of Syar'ie Lawyers as well as regulate, control and supervise the conduct of Syar'ie Lawyers. By virtue of that section, the Syariah Courts (Syar'ie Lawyers) Rules, 2002 has been enacted which commences on the same date as the Syariah Courts Act (Chapter 184). Part II of this Rules talks about the Establishment of Syar'ie Lawyers Committee, Part III talks about Syar'ie Lawyers, Part IV on discipline, Part V on miscellaneous provisions; whereas fees and forms under this Rules can be found in the First and Second Schedule respectively.

Rule 9 talks about admission of Syar'ie Lawyers, which shall be made by the Chief Syar'ie Judge. Rule 10 stated that a person may be admitted to be Syar'ie Lawyers if he –

(a) (i) is a Muslim and has passed the final examination which leads to a bachelor's degree in Syariah from any university or any Islamic

[26] Section 25(1) of the Syariah Courts Act (Chapter 184). [27] Section 25(2) Ibid. [28] Section 25(3) Ibid. [29] Section 25(4) Ibid.

educational institution recognized by the Government of Brunei Darussalam;

(ii) is a Muslim advocate or solicitor enrolled under the Legal Profession Act (Chapter 132) who has passed the Syar'ie Lawyer Certificate examination;

(iii) has served as a Syar'ie Judge, Kadi or Syar'ie Prosecutor for a period of not less than 3 years; or

For additional analytical, marketing, investment and business opportunities information, please contact
Global Investment & Business Center, USA
(202) 546-2103. Fax: (202) 546-3275. E-mail: rusric@erols.com

(iv) is a Muslim who has received professional training in Islamic judicial matters which is recognized by the Government of Brunei Darussalam or who specializes in *Hukum Syara'*;

(b) has attained the age of 21 years;
(c) is of good behavior and –
(i) has never been convicted in Brunei Darussalam or in any other place of any criminal offence which makes him unfit to become a Syar'ie Lawyer;
(ii) has never been adjudged a bankrupt; and

(iii) has never been disbarred, struck off or suspended in his capacity as a legal practitioner by whatever name called in any other country.

LEGAL EDUCATION

Presently, there is no law faculty at the University of Brunei Darussalam. Most of the lawyers practicing in Brunei are either qualified in England or Malaysia.

As stated earlier in Rule 10 of the Syariah Courts (Syar'ie Lawyers) Rules, 2002, a person may be admitted as Syar'ie Lawyers if he fulfills all the necessary requirements. Therefore, in its effort to produce qualified Islamic lawyers and legal practitioners in the Syariah Court, the University of Brunei Darussalam has offered a course in Diploma In Islamic Law and Legal Practice[30], which started its first session in 2000/2001. This course stresses upon the practical aspect especially in practicality, legal administration and their executions.

Objectives of this course are, among others, to give wider opportunity for law degree holders and legal practitioners in Brunei Darussalam, in Syariah or Civil to undertake a formal program in Islamic law; to give more exposure to law graduates in Islamic law and Administration; to produce qualified Islamic lawyers; and to minimizing government expenditure on sending students abroad by providing the course locally.

Subjects offered in the program includes the Islamic Legal System, Islamic Family Law, Syariah Political Science, Islamic Judiciary and Practice, Brunei Legal System, Islamic Law and Evidence, Islamic Criminal law, Islamic Law of Contract and Trade, Procedures in Criminal and Civil and Commercial Law.

BASIC TITLES ON BRUNEI[10]

IMPORTANT!
All publications are updated annually!
Please contact IBP, Inc. at ibpusa3@gmail.com for the latest ISBNs and additional information

Title
Brunei A "Spy" Guide - Strategic Information and Developments
Brunei A "Spy" Guide - Strategic Information and Developments
Brunei Air Force Handbook
Brunei Air Force Handbook
Brunei Business and Investment Opportunities Yearbook

[10] Titles are updated annually. Please contact Intl Business Publications, Inc. at ibpusa3gmail.com for the latest ISBN numbers and additional information.

Title
Brunei Business and Investment Opportunities Yearbook
Brunei Business and Investment Opportunities Yearbook Volume 1 Strategic Information and Opportunities
Brunei Business and Investment Opportunities Yearbook Volume 2 Leading Export-Import, Business, Investment Opportunities and Projects
Brunei Business Intelligence Report - Practical Information, Opportunities, Contacts
Brunei Business Intelligence Report - Practical Information, Opportunities, Contacts
Brunei Business Law Handbook - Strategic Information and Basic Laws
Brunei Business Law Handbook - Strategic Information and Basic Laws
Brunei Business Law Handbook - Strategic Information and Basic Laws
Brunei Business Law Handbook - Strategic Information and Basic Laws
Brunei Company Laws and Regulations Handbook
Brunei Constitution and Citizenship Laws Handbook - Strategic Information and Basic Laws
Brunei Country Study Guide - Strategic Information and Developments
Brunei Country Study Guide - Strategic Information and Developments
Brunei Country Study Guide - Strategic Information and Developments Volume 1 Strategic Information and Developments
Brunei Customs, Trade Regulations and Procedures Handbook
Brunei Customs, Trade Regulations and Procedures Handbook
Brunei Diplomatic Handbook - Strategic Information and Developments
Brunei Diplomatic Handbook - Strategic Information and Developments
Brunei Ecology & Nature Protection Handbook
Brunei Ecology & Nature Protection Handbook
Brunei Ecology & Nature Protection Laws and Regulation Handbook
Brunei Energy Policy, Laws and Regulation Handbook
Brunei Energy Policy, Laws and Regulations Handbook
Brunei Energy Policy, Laws and Regulations Handbook
Brunei Export-Import Trade and Business Directory
Brunei Export-Import Trade and Business Directory
Brunei Foreign Policy and Government Guide
Brunei Foreign Policy and Government Guide
Brunei Immigration Laws and Regulations Handbook - Strategic Information and Basic Laws
Brunei Industrial and Business Directory
Brunei Industrial and Business Directory
Brunei Investment and Business Guide - Strategic and Practical Information
Brunei Investment and Business Guide - Strategic and Practical Information
Brunei Investment and Business Guide - Strategic and Practical Information
Brunei Investment and Business Guide - Strategic and Practical Information
Brunei Investment and Business Guide Volume 2 Business, Investment Opportunities and Incentives
Brunei Investment and Trade Laws and Regulations Handbook
Brunei Labor Laws and Regulations Handbook - Strategic Information and Basic Laws
Brunei Land Ownership and Agriculture Laws Handbook
Brunei Mineral & Mining Sector Investment and Business Guide - Strategic and Practical

Title
Information
Brunei Mineral & Mining Sector Investment and Business Guide - Strategic and Practical Information
Brunei Mining Laws and Regulations Handbook
Brunei Oil & Gas Sector Business & Investment Opportunities Yearbook
Brunei Oil & Gas Sector Business & Investment Opportunities Yearbook
Brunei Oil and Gas Exploration Laws and Regulation Handbook
Brunei Recent Economic and Political Developments Yearbook
Brunei Recent Economic and Political Developments Yearbook
Brunei Recent Economic and Political Developments Yearbook
Brunei Starting Business (Incorporating) in....Guide
Brunei Sultan Haji Hassanal Bolkiah Mu'izzaddin Waddaulah Handbook
Brunei Sultan Haji Hassanal Bolkiah Waddaulah Handbook Economic and Foreign Policy Handbook
Brunei Tax Guide Volume 1 Business Taxation
Brunei Tax Guide Volume 2 Personal Taxation
Brunei Taxation Laws and Regulations Handbook
Brunei Telecommunication Industry Business Opportunities Handbook
Brunei Telecommunication Industry Business Opportunities Handbook
Brunei: How to Invest, Start and Run Profitable Business in Brunei Guide - Practical Information, Opportunities, Contacts

BASIC LAWS AND REGULATIONS AFFECTING BUSINESS AND TRADE

COUTRY	LAW TITLE
Brunei	Admiralty Jurisdiction Act
Brunei	Advocates and Solicitors (Practice and Etiquette) Rules
Brunei	Advocates and Solicitors Rules
Brunei	Agricultural Pests and Noxious Plants
Brunei	Air Navigation Act
Brunei	Airport Passenger Service Charge Act
Brunei	Anti Terrorism (Financial and other Measure) Act
Brunei	Antiquities and Treasure Trove Act
Brunei	Application of Laws
Brunei	Arbitration Act
Brunei	Arms and Explosive Act
Brunei	Arms and Explosives Rules
Brunei	Asian Development Bank Act 2009
Brunei	Audit Act
Brunei	Banishment Act
Brunei	Banker's Book Act
Brunei	Banking Act
Brunei	Bankruptcy Act

Brunei	Bill of Sale Act
Brunei	Bills of Exchange Act
Brunei	Biological Weapons Act
Brunei	Bishop of Borneo Act
Brunei	Bretton Woods Agreement Act
Brunei	Broadcasting Act
Brunei	Brunei Board of Examination Act Brunei Economic Development Board Act
Brunei	Brunei Fishery Limits Act
Brunei	Brunei Investment Agency Act
Brunei	Brunei Malay Silversmiths Guild (Incorporation) Act
Brunei	Brunei National Archives Act
Brunei	Brunei Nationality Act
Brunei	Brunei Nationality Act Designation of Areas under Regulation 9
Brunei	Buffaloes Act
Brunei	Burial Grounds Act
Brunei	Business Name Act
Brunei	Censorship of Films and Public Entertainments Act
Brunei	Census Act
Brunei	Chinese Marriage Act
Brunei	Coin (Import and Export) Act
Brunei	Commission of Inquiry Act
Brunei	Commissioner for Oaths Act
Brunei	Common Gaming Houses Act
Brunei	Companies Act
Brunei	Computer Misuse Act
Brunei	Computer Misuse Order
Brunei	Constitution of Brunei
Brunei	Consular Relations Act
Brunei	Contract Act
Brunei	Cooperative Societies Act
Brunei	Criminal Appeal Rules
Brunei	Criminal Law Act
Brunei	Criminal Procedure Code
Brunei	Criminals Registration Act 2009
Brunei	Currency Act
Brunei	Customs Act
Brunei	Debtors Act
Brunei	Defamation Act
Brunei	Description of Land Act
Brunei	Diplomatic Privilege Act
Brunei	Disaffected and Dangerous Persons Act
Brunei	Dissolution of Marriage Act
Brunei	Dogs Act
Brunei	Education (Non-Government Schools) Act
Brunei	Election Offences Act

For additional analytical, marketing, investment and business opportunities information, please contact
Global Investment & Business Center, USA
(202) 546-2103. Fax: (202) 546-3275. E-mail: rusric@erols.com

Brunei	Electricity Act
Brunei	Electronic Transaction Order
Brunei	Electronic Transactions Act
Brunei	Emblems and Names Act
Brunei	Emergency Regulations Act
Brunei	Employment Information Act
Brunei	Evidence Act
Brunei	Exchange Control Act
Brunei	Excise Act
Brunei	Extradition (Malaysia and Singapore) Act
Brunei	Extradition Act
Brunei	Fatal Accident and Personal Injuries Act
Brunei	Finance Companies Act
Brunei	Fire Service Act
Brunei	Fisheries Act
Brunei	Forest Act 2002
Brunei	Geneva and Red Cross Act
Brunei	Guardianship of Infants
Brunei	Immigration Act
Brunei	Income tax Act
Brunei	Intermediate Courts
Brunei	Internal Security Act
Brunei	Internationally Protected Persons Act
Brunei	Interpretation and General Clauses Act
Brunei	Intoxicating Substances Act
Brunei	Inventions Act
Brunei	Investments Incentives Act
Brunei	Islamic Banking Act
Brunei	Kidnapping Act
Brunei	Labor Act
Brunei	Land Acquisition Act
Brunei	Land Code Act
Brunei	Law Reform (Contributory Negligence) Act
Brunei	Law Revision Act
Brunei	Legal Profession (Practicing Certificate) Rules
Brunei	Legal Profession Act
Brunei	Licensed Land Surveyors Act
Brunei	Limitation Act
Brunei	Local Newspaper Act Official Secrets Act
Brunei	Marriage Act
Brunei	Married Women Act
Brunei	Medical Practitioners Dentists Act
Brunei	Merchandise Marks Act
Brunei	Mining Act
Brunei	Minor Offences Act

For additional analytical, marketing, investment and business opportunities information, please contact
Global Investment & Business Center, USA
(202) 546-2103. Fax: (202) 546-3275. E-mail: rusric@erols.com

Brunei	Miscellaneous Licenses Act
Brunei	Misuse of Drugs Act
Brunei	Money-Changing and Remittance Businesses Act
Brunei	Moneylenders Act
Brunei	Monopolies Act
Brunei	Municipal Board Act
Brunei	National Bank of Brunei Act
Brunei	National Registration Regulations
Brunei	Nationality Registration Act
Brunei	Oaths and Affirmations
Brunei	Old Age and Disability Pensions Act
Brunei	Passport Act
Brunei	Pawnbrokers Act
Brunei	Penal Code
Brunei	Pensions Act
Brunei	Petroleum (Pipe-Lines) Act
Brunei	Petroleum Mining Act
Brunei	Poisons Act
Brunei	Post Office Act
Brunei	Powers of Attorney Act
Brunei	Preservation of Books Act
Brunei	Prevention of Corruption Act
Brunei	Price Control Act
Brunei	Prisons Act
Brunei	Probate and Administration Act
Brunei	Public Entertainment Act
Brunei	Public Health (Food)
Brunei	Public Officers (liability) Act
Brunei	Public Order Act
Brunei	Public Service Commission Act
Brunei	Quarantine and Prevention of Disease Act
Brunei	Reciprocal Enforcement of Foreign Judgments
Brunei	Registration of Adoptions Act
Brunei	Registration of Guests Act
Brunei	Registration of Marriages Act
Brunei	Religious Council and Kadis Court Act
Brunei	Road Traffic Act
Brunei	Royal Brunei Police Force Act
Brunei	Rubber Dealers Act
Brunei	Sale of Goods Act
Brunei	Second-Hand Dealers Act
Brunei	Security Agencies Act
Brunei	Sedition Act
Brunei	Societies Act
Brunei	Specific relief Act

For additional analytical, marketing, investment and business opportunities information, please contact
Global Investment & Business Center, USA
(202) 546-2103. Fax: (202) 546-3275. E-mail: rusric@erols.com

Brunei	Stamp Act
Brunei	Statistics Act
Brunei	Statutory Declarations Act
Brunei	Subordinate Courts Act
Brunei	Subscriptions Control Act
Brunei	Summonses and Warrants (Special Provision) Act
Brunei	Supreme Court (Appeals to Privy Council) Act
Brunei	Supreme Court Act
Brunei	Syariah Courts
Brunei	Telecommunications Act
Brunei	Territorial Waters of Brunei Act
Brunei	Tokyo Convention
Brunei	Trade Disputes Act
Brunei	Trade Marks Act
Brunei	Trade Union Act
Brunei	Transfer of the Functions of the Minister of Law Act
Brunei	Travel Agents Act
Brunei	Trespass on Royal Property Act
Brunei	Undesirable Publications Act
Brunei	Unfair Contact Terms Act
Brunei	University Brunei Darussalam Act
Brunei	Unlawful Carnal Knowledge Act
Brunei	Vicar Apostolic of Kuching Act
Brunei	Water Supply Act
Brunei	Weights and Measure Act
Brunei	Wild Life Protection Act
Brunei	Wills Act
Brunei	Women and Girls Protection Act
Brunei	Workmen's Compensation Act
Brunei	Workmen's Unemployment Indemnity Act

WORLD OIL & GAS SECTOR BUSINESS, INVESTMENT OPPORTUNITIES LIBRARY

Price: $199.95 Each

Title
Global Oil & Gas Sector Business & Investment Opportunities Yearbook
Algeria Oil & Gas Sector Business & Investment Opportunities Yearbook
Angola Oil & Gas Sector Business & Investment Opportunities Yearbook
Australia Oil & Gas Sector Business & Investment Opportunities Yearbook
Azerbaijan Oil & Gas Sector Business & Investment Opportunities Yearbook
Bahrain Oil & Gas Sector Business & Investment Opportunities Yearbook
Bangladesh Oil & Gas Sector Business & Investment Opportunities Yearbook
Benin Oil & Gas Sector Business & Investment Opportunities Yearbook
Brazil Oil & Gas Sector Business & Investment Opportunities Yearbook
Brunei Oil & Gas Sector Business & Investment Opportunities Yearbook
Cameroon Oil & Gas Sector Business & Investment Opportunities Yearbook
Canada Oil & Gas Sector Business & Investment Opportunities Yearbook
China Oil & Gas Sector Business & Investment Opportunities Yearbook
Colombia Oil & Gas Sector Oil & Gas Sector Business & Investment Opportunities Yearbook
Congo Oil & Gas Sector Business & Investment Opportunities Yearbook
Congo, Dem. Republic Oil & Gas Sector Business & Investment Opportunities Yearbook
Cote d'Ivoire Oil & Gas Sector Business & Investment Opportunities Yearbook
Dubai Oil & Gas Sector Business & Investment Opportunities Yearbook
Ecuador Oil & Gas Sector Business & Investment Opportunities Yearbook
Egypt Oil & Gas Sector Business & Investment Opportunities Yearbook
Equatorial Guinea Oil & Gas Sector Business & Investment Opportunities Yearbook
Gabon Oil & Gas Sector Business & Investment Opportunities Yearbook
India Oil & Gas Sector Business & Investment Opportunities Yearbook
Indonesia Oil & Gas Sector Business & Investment Opportunities Yearbook
Iran Oil & Gas Sector Business & Investment Opportunities Yearbook
Iraq Oil & Gas Sector Business & Investment Opportunities Yearbook
Kazakhstan Oil & Gas Sector Business & Investment Opportunities Yearbook

For additional analytical, business and investment opportunities information, please contact Global Investment & Business Center, USA at (202) 546-2103. Fax: (202) 546-3275. E-mail: rusric@erols.com

Title
Kuwait Oil & Gas Sector Business & Investment Opportunities Yearbook
Libya Oil & Gas Sector Business & Investment Opportunities Yearbook
Malaysia Oil & Gas Sector Business & Investment Opportunities Yearbook
Mexico Oil & Gas Sector Business & Investment Opportunities Yearbook
Morocco Oil & Gas Sector Business & Investment Opportunities Yearbook
Namibia Oil & Gas Sector Business & Investment Opportunities Yearbook
New Zealand Oil & Gas Sector Business & Investment Opportunities Yearbook
Nigeria Oil & Gas Sector Business & Investment Opportunities Yearbook
Norway Oil & Gas Sector Business & Investment Opportunities Yearbook
Oman Oil & Gas Sector Business & Investment Opportunities Yearbook
Pakistan Oil & Gas Sector Business & Investment Opportunities Yearbook
Papua New Guinea Oil & Gas Sector Business & Investment Opportunities Yearbook
Papua New Guinea Oil & Gas Sector Oil & Gas Sector Business & Investment Opportunities Yearbook
Peru Oil & Gas Sector Business & Investment Opportunities Yearbook
Philippines Oil & Gas Sector Business & Investment Opportunities Yearbook
Qatar Oil & Gas Sector Business & Investment Opportunities Yearbook
Sri Lanka Oil & Gas Sector Business & Investment Opportunities Yearbook
Romania Oil & Gas Sector Business & Investment Opportunities Yearbook
Russia Oil & Gas Sector Business & Investment Opportunities Yearbook
Saudi Arabia Oil & Gas Sector Business & Investment Opportunities Yearbook
Sudan Oil & Gas Sector Business & Investment Opportunities Yearbook
Suriname Oil & Gas Sector Business & Investment Opportunities Yearbook
Syria Oil & Gas Sector Business & Investment Opportunities Yearbook
Trinidad and Tobago Oil & Gas Sector Oil & Gas Sector Business & Investment Opportunities Yearbook
Tunisia Oil & Gas Sector Business & Investment Opportunities Yearbook
Turkey Oil & Gas Sector Business & Investment Opportunities Yearbook
Turkmenistan Oil & Gas Sector Business & Investment Opportunities Yearbook
Ukraine Oil & Gas Sector Oil & Gas Sector Business & Investment Opportunities Yearbook
United Arab Emirates Oil & Gas Sector Business & Investment Opportunities Yearbook
United Kingdom Oil & Gas Sector Business & Investment Opportunities Yearbook
United Kingdom Oil & Gas Sector Oil & Gas Sector Business & Investment Opportunities Yearbook
United States Oil & Gas Sector Business & Investment Opportunities Yearbook
Venezuela Oil & Gas Sector Business & Investment Opportunities Yearbook
Vietnam Investment Pojects and Joint Ventures Hnadbook
Vietnam Oil & Gas Sector Business & Investment Opportunities Yearbook
Yemen Oil & Gas Sector Business & Investment Opportunities Yearbook

www.ingramcontent.com/pod-product-compliance
Lightning Source LLC
LaVergne TN
LVHW080039210926
848481LV00011B/3237
* 9 7 8 1 4 3 3 0 7 8 5 9 0 *